English G

Band A4

für das 8. Schuljahr
an Gymnasien
in Bayern

Cornelsen

English G

Band A4 für das 8. Schuljahr an Gymnasien in Bayern

Im Auftrage des Verlages herausgegeben und erarbeitet von

Prof. Hellmut Schwarz, Mannheim · Carl Taylor M.A., Maidencombe, Devon · Prof. Franz Vettel, Heppenheim

unter Mitarbeit von

David W. Bygott, Oxford · StD Erich Fleischhack, Ebern/Unterfranken · StD Udo J. Hennig, Neuwied

in Zusammenarbeit mit der Fremdsprachenredaktion

Michael R. Ferguson (Projektleitung), Dr. Michael Steppat, Hartmut Tschepe; John Stevens (Redaktionsdienst Context, Bad Münstereifel)
Assistenz: Jenny Dames, Rachel Hiley

Beratende Mitwirkung

StD Burkhard Dammann, Nürnberg · John Eastwood M.A., Street, Somerset · OStR Gerhard Finster, Dillingen · StRin Susanne Schroeder-Thürauf, Erlangen

Grafik

Robert Broomfield, Tunbridge Wells
sowie Gabriele Heinisch, Berlin

Gestaltung und technische Umsetzung

Peter Richter und Bernd Lenzner

Titelfoto: Mayflower II (courtesy of Plimoth Plantation Inc., Plymouth, MA, USA)

Begleitender Tonträger zu diesem Band:

1 Cassette für Schüler und Lehrer mit allen Haupttexten und längeren Texten aus A-Teilen der Units, Hörverstehenstexten und den fünf Liedern. Ca. 90 Minuten.
Bestell-Nr. 71480

Ergänzendes Grammatikheft zu den Bänden 3/4: Bestell-Nr. 71448

Begleitende Software zu diesem Band:

English Coach Vokabeltrainer, Diskette zu Band A4 Bayern. Bestell-Nr. 914488 (PC 3,5")

1. Auflage ✔ Druck 6 5 4 3 Jahr 02 01 2000 99

Alle Drucke dieser Auflage können im Unterricht nebeneinander verwendet werden.

Druck: Cornelsen Druck, Berlin

ISBN 3-464-071413

Bestellnummer 71413

gedruckt auf säurefreiem Papier, umweltschonend hergestellt aus chlorfrei gebleichten Faserstoffen

Contents

○ = wahlfrei

The United States of America

- When people use the word "America", what do they mean: a continent, or a country?
- When people think of the USA, they often think of the American flag (the "Stars and Stripes") and the Statue of Liberty.
  What about you? What can you remember about the USA from Books 1-3?
- Choose two or three famous Americans or places in the USA and tell the class what you know about them. Write down a few notes first.

Unit 1

The USA

	United States of America	Federal Republic of Germany
Area (in sq. km)	9.3 million	357,000
Population	c. 250 million	c. 80 million
Cities with over 1 million people	6	3

1 The United States is a huge country. It consists of 50 states. The state of Texas alone is much bigger than France. Montana is about the same size as Germany, but has a population of less than 900,000. Alaska – the largest state – is almost as big as Britain, France, Germany and Spain together!
From the border with Canada in the north to the border with Mexico in the south, it is 2,500 kilometers. From the Atlantic Ocean in the east to the Pacific Ocean in the west, it is 4,500 kilometers – that is about the distance from Frankfurt to Teheran.
A train takes 45 hours to cross the country, while a plane can fly from coast to coast in just 5 hours. But if you want to make the trip by car, it will take you about a week.

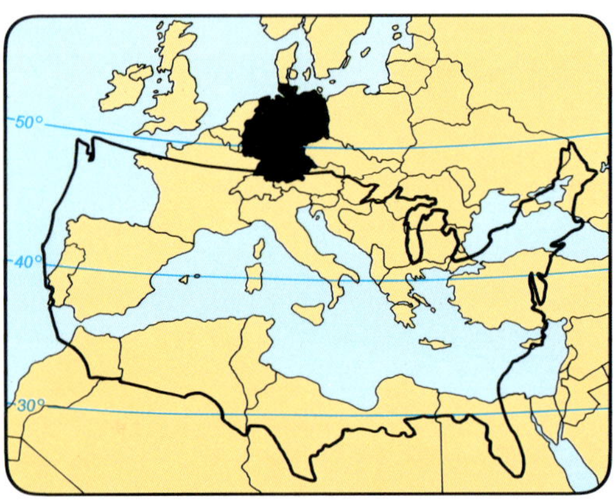

Did you realize that Florida is as far south as Egypt? What else do you find surprising/interesting when you look at this map?

2 Did you know that New York time is six hours behind German time? When it is six in the evening here, it is lunch time in New York. And within the United States there are a number of different time zones. The West Coast, for example, is three hours behind the East Coast.

- Look at the map and compare the times in different places.
  When it's 8 am in Denver, it's … in Washington, D.C. (= District of Columbia).
  When it's … in New York, it's …
- Imagine you work in an office and want to phone people in Atlanta, St Louis, Dallas, Denver and San Francisco. When must you phone if you want to talk to them at 10 am local time?

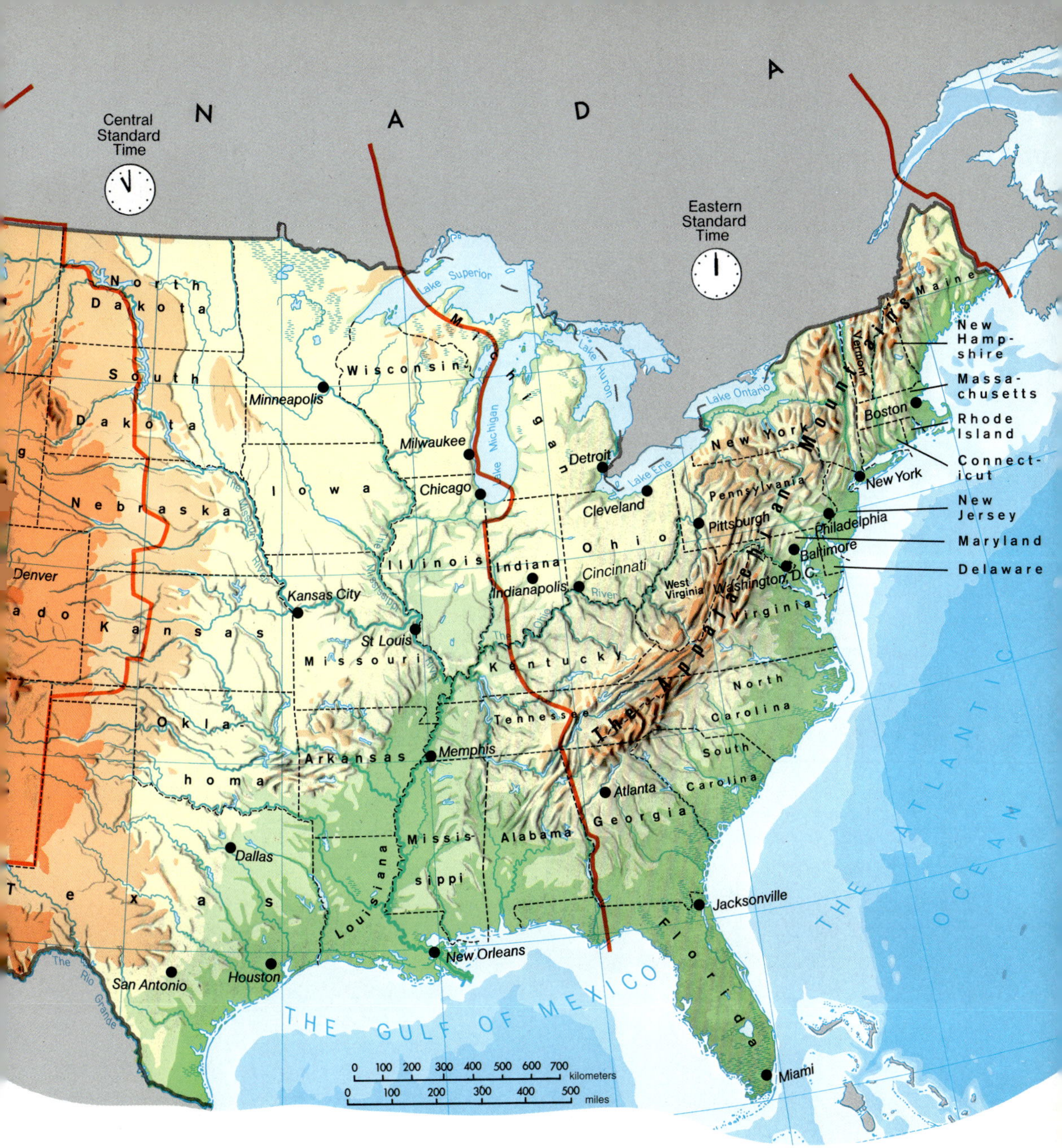

3 The USA is such a big country that you get every kind of weather and every kind of countryside – huge, snow-covered mountains, green valleys and forests, hot dry deserts. In California people say the summer is ten months long, in Alaska the winter can last more than half the year. When there is snow on the ground in New York, it is warm and sunny in Florida. The hottest place is Death Valley in California. In one summer the temperature there didn't fall below 49 °C for 43 days. The wettest place is a mountain in Hawaii, where it rains on 350 days a year. And if you like skiing, the United States has the deepest snow in the world. In one year over 31 meters fell on Mount Rainier in the state of Washington.

Collect all the information from these two pages which you think is interesting. Then write a short text.
Try and find pictures that show different kinds of countryside in the USA.

Hi!

Here are some teenagers you'll meet in the book.

My name is Maureen Donovan. I'm 14 years old. My brother Scott is 13. My ancestors left Ireland to come to the USA in 1846. People in Ireland were very poor in those days. During that time thousands of Irish died from poverty and hunger. I live in New York City, or the "Big Apple" as many Americans call it. But I'll tell you more about New York soon.

Hi! I'm Marvin Mitchell. I'm 15 and I live with my dad in Detroit. I'm an African American. My family has lived in America for over two hundred years – that's longer than most white or immigrant families. My ancestors came here from Africa, but they didn't come willingly. They were brought here as slaves.

My name is Debbie Thomas. Debbie is short for Deborah, by the way. I live with my parents and brother Kenny on a farm near Tonganoxie – a very small town in Kansas. My mother's parents came to the United States from Germany in 1937, before the Second World War. They were Jews, you see. They came to America to find political and religious freedom, because they had been persecuted in Nazi Germany. Later they and Mom left New York and moved to Kansas. They opened a grocery store in Tonganoxie, and that's where Mom met Dad. He's a farmer. His family came from Wales. My cousin Megan from Wales is going to visit me soon. I'm really looking forward to it. We've never met before.

= Text auf Cassette

Hello. My name is Megan Thomas. I'm Debbie's cousin. I'm going to visit her in September – for the first time! Isn't that great?
I'm from Swansea, a city in South Wales – not far from the capital, Cardiff.
Mum is a nurse at a large hospital. Dad is an engineer, but he's been unemployed for two years now. I'm still at school, of course.

Tenby Harbour, South Wales

My name is Lan Chi. My parents came to the USA from Vietnam to escape from the war there, and I was born in New York. I am an Asian American.
My family and I live in a poor part of Brooklyn. I have a brother, Binh. He's two years younger than me.
Both of my parents work very hard and I work hard at school. My best subject is art.

Brooklyn Bridge, New York

Unit 1 Exercises

Who is bigger, Mrs Bigger or her baby?
– Her baby, because it's a little Bigger.

Revision: Comparisons of adjectives and adverbs (Ex 1, 2)

Remember: America is bigger than Europe.
Is New York the most interesting city in the USA?
Montana is as big as Germany.
In the USA you often have to drive more slowly than in Germany.

1 Find the 'fourth man'

1. good – best bad – ?	3. hard – harder bad – ?	5. best – good least – ?	7. more carefully – carefully better – ?
2. most – least more – ?	4. near – nearer far – ?	6. furthest – far most – ?/?	8. politely – most politely fast – ?

2 The USA – a country of people's dreams

I don't really think Goethe was right. But today some people still believe that Americans have a better life than people in the rest of the world. What's your opinion?

a I think / don't think …
1. … Americans make … cars in the world. (large)
2. … American cars are … German cars. (comfortable)
3. … Americans drive … Germans. (slowly)
4. … Americans go on vacation … other people. (regularly)
5. … American food tastes … German food. (good)
6. … Americans are … sports … Germans. (interested in)

b *What else do people think about when they compare the USA with Germany, for example?*

c *Choose one or two such statements about the USA. Write down what you think of them.*

Revision: Verbs with two objects

Remember: When a verb has two objects, the usual order is I + D (indirect object + direct object).
Example: Richard sent his aunt a postcard.
However, if the indirect object is quite long, or if the direct object is *it* or *them*, the order is usually D + *to/for* + I (direct object + *to/for* + indirect object).
Example: Richard sent a postcard to his aunt in Regensburg.
He sent it to his aunt.

3 A US factory in Europe *Use the objects correctly in the following sentences.*

One of Debbie's aunts works for a US electronics firm that wants to build a factory in Europe. The factory might be built near Swansea in Wales, or perhaps in Scotland, because the Scottish Development Agency (SDA) has some suitable land. It has offered (1. the firm / it) quite cheaply. The SDA offers (2. electronics firms from all over the world / land) and so far it has sold (3. them / lots of land). The firms that have already moved to Scotland give (4. about 40,000 people / work) and now eight Scottish universities teach (5. their students / computer science). They see how important it is to teach (6. them / this subject). But Debbie's cousin, Megan, hopes that the US firm will build in Swansea, because she hopes they will give (7. her father / a job).

Revision: The passive (Ex 4-7)

Remember: All verbs that take a direct object ("transitive verbs") have a passive form.
It consists of a form of *be* + past participle *(+ by ...)*.
Example: Megan will be met at the airport (by her relatives).
When verbs that take two objects (e.g. *give, send, tell*) are used in the passive, it is usually the indirect object that is used as the subject.
Example: Megan has been sent a book about Kansas.
When a verb + preposition is used in the passive, the preposition stays after the verb.
Example: When we go on vacation, our dog is looked after by our neighbors.

4 Can you believe it? *Make sentences in the passive about the following American records.*

a

Examples: 1. Can you imagine that 96 hot dogs were eaten in six minutes by just one person? 2. It's hard to believe that . . .

1. 96 hot dogs – eat – six minutes – just one person
2. bottle of French wine – buy – $210,000 – 1985
3. $8 million – pay – used car – 1986
4. 1984 – postcard – sell – $4,400
5. at Easter 1985 – over 100,000 eggs – hide – park in Georgia
6. 64-year-old message in a bottle – find – one of the Great Lakes
7. 1986 – 40,000-kilo cake – make – 32 hours – Franz Eichenauer – Austin, Texas / then – cut – Prince of Wales

b *Do you know any other strange things that have been done by people or perhaps even animals? (There may be some books of records in your school or town library.)*

5 The Olympic Games *Make the questions and then try to answer them. You will need to use different tenses in the passive.*

1. Where / the first Olympic Games / hold?
2. Where / the Olympic Games / hold / in the year 2000?
3. How many modern Olympic Games / hold / so far?
4. How often / the Olympic Games / hold?
5. When / the last Olympic Games / hold / in Germany?

6 Heard in different places *Make sentences in the simple past active or passive.*

1. How – be – yesterday's English lesson?
   – OK. We – tell something about famous US writers and then we – give a test
2. I hear that some engineers from Munich – be – in town yesterday
   – Yes, they – show the new machines in my father's factory
3. you – go to – Lan's party last week?
   – No, I – not invite – so I – go to – movies
4. What – you – give – your birthday, Megan?
   – Well, I – get a camera – my parents – and I – send a CD – my cousin in Kansas
5. Why – Debbie – cry – way home on Friday?
   – She – leave at the café – her boyfriend

Which word is always pronounced wrongly?
– The one that's written "w-r-o-n-g-l-y".

What doesn't ask questions, but has to be answered?

7 Verbs with prepositions *For each question on the left, choose a suitable answer from the box and complete it with a passive form. Be careful with the tenses.*

1. Why is little Billy crying?
2. What about your cats when you go away?
3. Who is the taxi for?
4. How much did your vacation cost?
5. What happened to José after he left school?
6. Who do you think shot President Kennedy?
7. Have you got your passport with you?
8. Why did those passengers look so unhappy?

a) They (look after) by one of the neighbors.
b) Because of the way they (speak to).
c) No idea. He (not hear of) since then.
d) No idea. I didn't know one (phone for).
e) He (laugh at) by two girls on the bus home.
f) I'm not sure. It (pay for) by my parents.
g) That (argue about) since 1963.
h) Why? Do you think I might (ask for) it?

Example: 1e) Why is little Billy crying? – He was laughed at by two girls on the bus home.

Revision: Present perfect simple/progressive with "since" and "for" (Ex 8, 9)

Remember: When we want to show how long something has continued, we use the present perfect with ***since*** **+ point of time** (e.g. *since 1985, since then*) or ***for*** **+ period of time** (e.g. *for an hour, for two years*). We use the present perfect progressive for an activity that has continued over a period of time up to, or almost up to now.

8a What can you say about these people? *Practice using the present perfect progressive.*

Examples: Well, Maureen has been playing the guitar for two years. And Marvin has been ...

b *Make short dialogs with a partner.*

Example: How long have you been playing the guitar, Maureen? – Oh, I've been playing (the guitar) for two years now, I think.

c *What things do you/your friends do at school and in your free time? How long have you been doing them?*

9 In English, please *Practice using the present perfect simple and progressive. But remember: state verbs (e.g. "know", "be") can't be used in the progressive form.*

1. Debbie kennt ihren Freund Tommy seit etwa fünf Monaten. 2. Debbie sitzt seit einer Stunde an ihrem Fenster. 3. Warum lernt Maureen seit ein paar Wochen Spanisch? 4. Die Donovans versuchen seit letztem Januar eine Ferienwohnung in Florida zu finden. 5. Sind deine Eltern seit über 20 Jahren nicht [mehr] in Vietnam gewesen, Lan? 6. Lan malt seit einiger Zeit wirklich interessante Bilder. 7. Seit wann haben die Mitchells diese Wohnung?

Revision: Past perfect simple and past perfect progressive (Ex 10, 11)

Remember: We use the past perfect for an action or a situation before a time in the past. To show that an action was still continuing up to that time, we use the past perfect progressive; but state verbs cannot be used in the progressive form.

10 America and Germany

a **The name "America"** *Complete the text with the correct simple past and past perfect forms of the verbs.*

Martin Waldseemüller (be) a German who (live) from about 1470 to 1520. He (be) a kind of teacher, but he also (make) maps. In 1507 he (use) the name "America" on one of his maps for what is today South America. Later "America" (become) the name for the "New World" which Columbus (find). Waldseemüller (use) the name of a famous Italian, Amerigo Vespucci, who (take) part in three trips to the New World before 1504.

b **The first Germans in America** *Write a short text.*

Franz Daniel Pastorius – 1651-1720 / 1683 – able to take first group of Germans to America / group – consist of 13 families – come from – Krefeld area / after – be on their ship for 75 days – arrive in America / have a hard life in Germany – not really be free / now – be allowed to be free in the New World / name of their new home – Germantown / these Germans – be in America for five years – when speak out against people – who have slaves / they – some of the first people in America – speak publicly against slave-owners

11 Why ...? *Ask each other questions. Answer in the past perfect simple or progressive.*

Examples:
Why did Maureen want to go to Florida? – Because she had heard so much about Disney World.
Why did Megan know so much US history? – Because she had been studying it for some time.

These pictures will help with the answers.

1. Why did the Donovans want to visit Florida? 2. Why did Megan look happy when a letter from Debbie arrived? 3. Why did Debbie's friend Tommy know a lot about Megan? 4. Why did Marvin know so much about the situation of African Americans in the 1950s? 5. Why did Lan and her brother want to see the film? 6. Why did Kenny's face look so red?

Revision: Indirect or reported speech (Ex 12-14)

Remember:

a When we report what somebody has said, thought or written, we often have to change pronouns and adverbials, e.g. *I → he, yesterday → the day before.*

b If the verb that introduces the indirect speech is in the past tense (e.g. *said, thought, knew, asked*), there is often a tense change ("backshift of tenses"), e.g. *is → was*. But if it is in the present tense (e.g. *says, thinks*), the tense in indirect speech is not changed (i.e. there is no backshift).

Direct speech		Indirect speech
Marvin: "**I've** never **been** to Denver."	→	Marvin said (that) he **had** never **been** to Denver.
Kenny: "We **can win** and we **will**."	→	Kenny thought (that) they **could win** and they **would**.
Maureen: "**Do** we **go** by bus?"	→	Maureen asked if they **went** by bus.
Megan: "My new camera **is** great!"	→	Megan said/thought (that) her new camera **was** great.
	→	Megan says/thinks (that) her new camera **is** great.

The simple past (e.g. *met* in *"I met Tommy."*) is not always changed in indirect speech. You can hear, for example, *Kenny said he'd met Tommy*, or *Kenny said he met Tommy*.

c The tense needn't be changed if the statement is generally true (e.g. *The earth moves around the sun*) or if it is still true when it is reported.

Debbie: "We never **see** snow here."	→	Debbie said (that) they never **see** snow there.
Lan: "My brother **is** twelve."	→	Lan said (that) her brother **is** twelve.

d Verbs in the past perfect and the following modal verbs – *must, needn't, would, might, should, ought to* and *could* (= „könnte") – are not changed.

Debbie: "**I'd had** enough."	→	Debbie knew (that) she **had had** enough.
Maureen: "**Would** you help?"	→	Maureen asked if/whether we **would** help.

e Imperatives are reported with verbs like *tell, ask, advise* (= „raten") or *suggest*.

Dad: "**Don't stay** long."	→	Dad **told me not to stay** long.
Mom: "**Why don't we leave** early?"	→	Mom **suggested** (that) **we (should) leave** early.
		Mom **suggested leaving** early.

f Often, people don't (or can't) report everything exactly as it was said. They just give the most important points.

Kenny: "I'll win, I think. Probably."	→	Kenny thought (that) **he would win**.
Kenny: "I can't say how nervous I am."	→	Kenny said (that) **he was nervous**.

"That was funny when he said he'd get his big brother."

Some verbs that can introduce indirect speech:

add, advise, agree, answer, ask, be sorry, be sure, complain, explain, feel, hope, know, promise, remember, say, suggest, tell sb., think, want to know, wonder

12 The weather in different cities *Make short dialogs. Use indirect speech.*

a Mrs Long's three sisters and three brothers all live in different US cities. Mrs Long has called all six of them. She is telling her husband about this.

Mrs Long: I've just been on the phone with Kim.
Mr Long: Oh? And what's the weather like in Phoenix today?
Mrs Long: Kim says the sun is shining and it's very … . *Go on.*

b Later Mrs Long spoke with one of her friends.

Mrs Long: I called Kim this morning.
Mrs Lee: Your sister in Phoenix? And did she say what the weather was like?
Mrs Long: Yes, she said the sun was shining and it was very … . *Go on.*

	sun	rain	snow	hot	cold
Kim, Phoenix	✓			++	
Mike, Dallas	✓			+	
Ann, New York		✓			+
Steve, Detroit	✓		✓		++
Suzie, Miami		✓		+	
Chip, Denver			✓		++

13 What did the neighbor ask?

a When people in Megan's neighborhood heard that she was going to the USA, they were very interested. One old man who had never been out of Wales asked a lot of questions. Megan told Debbie about this in a letter.
Example:
1. One old man wanted to know where Kansas was and if it was far.
2. He asked me if …

Go on.

The old man's exact words to Megan:
1. Where is Kansas? Is it far?
2. Do you need a passport?
3. Have you been there before?
4. How long are you staying?
5. When are you going?
6. I'm sure it'll be very interesting.
7. Could you send me a postcard?
8. Has Debbie ever been to Swansea?
9. Take some photos with you and show her how nice it is here.
10. Bring her to see me if she comes.

b *What do you think Megan told the old neighbor?*
She probably/perhaps said that …

14 What did they say?

Look at the sentences on the right.
What was really said in direct speech?
Can you see more than one possible answer?
Be careful with the tenses and the pronouns.
Example:
1. "Why don't you call me, Tommy?"
"You should call me, Tommy."
"Perhaps you could call me, Tommy."

1. Debbie suggested to her friend Tommy that he should call her. 2. Lan asked if I could help her. 3. My mother suggested that I spend more time on my homework. 4. Megan said she'd send me a postcard. 5. Debbie invited us all to her birthday party. 6. Tommy said he'd be outside our house at six o'clock. 7. Marvin asked his father why he'd laughed. 8. They asked us our opinion of their town.

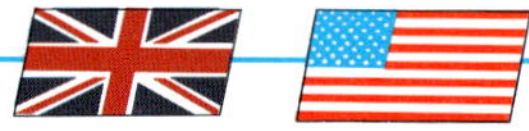

BRITISH ENGLISH (BE) – AMERICAN ENGLISH (AE)

American English is different from British English in accent and pronunciation, and also in some vocabulary items and the way some words are spelt.
But although there are these differences, speakers of AE and BE don't normally find it difficult to understand each other. The vocabulary of teenagers who are interested in rock music, films or computers, for example, is often very similar on both sides of the Atlantic.

AMERICAN ENGLISH PRONUNCIATION

Here are some examples of differences in pronunciation between AE and BE:

ɑː	ask, dance, last	æ
juː	new, Tuesday, stupid	uː
ɒ	bottle, hot, everybody	ɑː
ɪə, ɔː, ɜː, ɑː	here, more, shirt, farm	ɪər, ɔːr, ɜːr, ɑːr
t	city, better	d

Listen to the cassette, then pronounce each of these words the British way and after that the American way. This will help you to "feel" the differences between AE and BE.

AMERICAN ENGLISH SPELLING

Here are some words you already know, but here they are spelt the American way.

favorite color traveled center program catalog neighbor mom
theater dialog traveler harbor kilometer wagon pajamas favor

What is the British English spelling? Write the words down in your vocabulary book and arrange them like this:

AE '-or'	BE '-our'	AE '-er'	BE '-re'	others: AE	BE
...	...	...	...	...	...

AMERICAN ENGLISH VOCABULARY

On some ***Focus on WORDS*** pages and in the vocabulary (p. 138, p. 151) you will find short lists of words that are different in AE and BE.

In this English course we have normally used BE so far. However, in this book we use AE in units that are about the USA. So in these units we use AE vocabulary, and the speakers on the cassette speak with an American accent. AE spelling is also used.

New York New York

New York – the city that never sleeps, where life moves faster than anywhere else in the USA. A hectic city full of noise, people and traffic.

New York – the city that offers you the best of everything, whether excellent theater, music, food or sports – as long as you can afford it.

New York – the gateway to freedom, for a long time the port through which millions of immigrants from Europe entered the USA.

New York – a city with so many problems – crime, poverty, homeless people, dirty streets and subways – that nobody knows where to start.

New York – "not a city in America, an island in the middle of the world".

Not just Manhattan

New York City, the largest city in the USA, lies at the mouth of a river. So, if New Yorkers want to get from one side of their city to the other, they have to use its many tunnels, bridges or ferries. Most tourists visit only one borough, Manhattan, because that is where almost all the famous sights are. But there are five boroughs altogether, and four of them have a population of at least 1 million.

Can you answer the following questions?

1. New York City lies at the mouth of which river?
2. Is New York City the capital of the USA?
3. Is its population over 7, over 9 or over 11 million?
4. What are the names of the five New York boroughs?
5. What famous New York sights can you name?

Brooklyn – a New York borough

With a population of 2.3 million, Brooklyn is the largest of the New York boroughs. Although it is only a borough, Brooklyn is in fact bigger than most cities in the United States. Only three cities are larger – and it is also larger than Munich.
Brooklyn is the most independent borough. It has its own harbor, its own beaches and some of New York's finest buildings and parks. It even has its own dialect. And the famous Brooklyn Bridge is one of the most beautiful and oldest suspension bridges in the world. It was opened in 1883.

Brooklyn Bridge and the skyscrapers of Manhattan ▷

Pat, Kate, Maureen and Scott Donovan

Brooklyn is where Maureen Donovan and her family live. Like other New York boroughs, Brooklyn has many "ethnic neighborhoods", that is areas where people of the same national origin live together. And in New York one can find almost every nationality in the world. More "Irish" live here than in Dublin, more Jews than in Tel Aviv, more "Germans" than in Frankfurt/Main and more "Italians" than in Venice.

- What five facts about New York do you find most interesting?
  Write them down and compare with a partner.
- Imagine you are Maureen. Write a short text about Brooklyn for a visitor who has never been there before.

Focus on GRAMMAR: **Der bestimmte Artikel** (The definite article)

a What is it like to live in a city like New York? Many people live there because it is so exciting. But they also complain about different things. **Noise** is a problem, for example. **The noise** of cars, buses and planes can make people ill. **Pollution** is another problem – not only in New York. Fresh **water** is important. But **the water** of many rivers today is polluted. We can see and smell **the pollution** of our environment everywhere. **People** and **animals** cannot live healthily in a polluted environment.

b **Pollution** is a problem all over the world.
Die Umweltverschmutzung …
Life in big cities is not always fun.
Das Leben …
Noise can make drivers nervous.
Lärm …
Rivers are often polluted by **oil**.
In New York **people** seem to be in a hurry.

OHNE bestimmten Artikel stehen
- abstrakte Nomen wie *pollution, life, noise, poverty, history, unemployment, immigration, love* usw. und
- Stoffnamen wie *water, oil, sand* usw. sowie
- zählbare Nomen im Plural wie *people* (= die Menschen, die Leute), *animals, cars, books* usw.,

wenn sie ganz allgemein gebraucht werden.

The pollution of the Hudson is an example of this.
Die Verschmutzung des Hudson …
The life of a bus driver is not always easy.
Das Leben eines Busfahrers …
The noise that came from the street was terrible.
Der Lärm, der von der Straße kam, …
The oil that pollutes the harbor comes from ships.
The people I met there were very friendly.

MIT bestimmtem Artikel stehen abstrakte Nomen und Stoffnamen sowie zählbare Nomen im Plural, wenn sie näher bestimmt sind, z. B.
- durch eine *of*-phrase oder
- durch einen Relativsatz.

→ Ex 1-3

c Poor **Maureen** was ill last week.
Die arme Maureen …
Central Park is on Fifth Avenue.
Broadway is famous for its theaters.
Let's meet in **Times Square**.
Do you know where **Lincoln Center** is?

OHNE bestimmten Artikel stehen Personennamen und die meisten Namen von Straßen und Plätzen.

The Donovans live in Brooklyn.
The Bronx is one of New York's five boroughs.
The Statue of Liberty is in New York harbor.
The Empire State Building is New York's most famous building, but it is not as high as **the World Trade Center**.

MIT bestimmtem Artikel stehen Familiennamen im Plural sowie einige geographische Namen.

Manche Gebäudenamen werden ohne Artikel (z. B. *Lincoln Center*), manche mit Artikel (z. B. *the World Trade Center*) verwendet. (→ Vocabulary pp. 134/135 "Manhattan")

→ Ex 4

d The smuggler went to **prison** for three years.
Are you going to **church** on Sunday?
Maureen goes to **school** by bus.

Eine Reihe von Gebäudenamen wird ohne Artikel verwendet, wenn wir an ihren Verwendungszweck denken: *go to prison* (um eine Strafe zu verbüßen), *go to church* (zum Gottesdienst), *go to school* (als Schüler zum Unterricht), im BE auch *go to hospital* (als Patient), im AE aber *go to the hospital.*

A friend went to **the prison** to visit him.
Tourists often take pictures of **the church**.
The bus stops in front of **the school**.

Diese Gebäudenamen werden mit dem Artikel verwendet, wenn nur an den Ort oder an das Bauwerk gedacht wird.

2A

The rock concert

Maureen Donovan had often visited Manhattan with her parents, of course, but she had never been there without them before. So she was very excited when the chance came one day.

On the school bus my best friend, Sally, showed me two tickets for a rock concert in Manhattan. She'd been given them by her cousin, and I almost died when she said: "Do you want to come with me?" "YES! YES!" I shouted. Inside, I thought: What will my parents say? All day at school I thought about how to ask them.
When I got home, I said, "Sally has two tickets for the Bruce Springfield concert in Manhattan this weekend. I don't imagine I can go with her, can I?" Mom laughed. "You certainly can't. Do you know how old you are?" "But Mom, please. Sally's cousin Jody lives there and we can spend the night at her apartment. She's thirty, so you won't have to worry. I'll call you after the concert and tell you how it was, I promise." Mom looked at me hard, then said,"OK. I don't mind." But she suggested that I ask Dad, too. "Great!" I said and started my homework. I thought: "It'll be just fantastic if Dad says the same."
But when he came in, my heart sank. He looked angry. He works in Manhattan, so he has quite a trip every day. Mom's office is in Brooklyn, so she gets home earlier. Dad threw himself on the sofa and said, "I hate those subways! First an empty train goes past and doesn't stop, so you wait until another one comes. Then it's so full you have to fight to get in." "Pat," Mom said, "Maureen wants to ask you something." Dad sat down. "Can't it wait till after dinner?"
During the meal Dad talked with my brother, Scott, about basketball. Scott is already nearly 6 foot tall and he's only 13. He wants to play in the junior team this year. I waited until they had finished. Then I told Dad everything. And can you imagine? He just smiled and said, "OK. But be careful. Don't talk to strangers on the subway at night and don't get in a train if it's empty. Somebody might try to rob you. A lot of criminals carry weapons." I said, "OK, Dad. Thanks." Then I ran to tell Sally.

The New York subway runs 24 hours a day.

The concert was Friday night, and we were so excited as we rode into Manhattan – our first trip there alone. Our train wasn't too crowded, but at one station a gang of teenagers got in. We were a bit nervous. I remembered what Dad had said and we sat still. But they only played music and laughed a lot.
We got off at Spring Street. From there it was a five-minute walk to Jody's apartment in Greenwich Village. As it was six, Jody suggested that we eat in Chinatown, so we wouldn't be late for the concert. She took us to a small restaurant where everybody, it seemed, was Chinese. Jody said that some of them might spend their whole lives in this country and never leave Chinatown. I could understand that. I also feel safer in areas that I know well.
After the meal we caught a cab to Madison Square Garden. There were already hundreds of fans outside when we arrived. The doors were finally opened at eight. I almost died when everyone tried to get in. We fought through the crowd and got great seats at the front with a fantastic view of Bruce and the band. When he appeared, we all shouted and screamed. Then he sang all my favorite songs. It was so wonderful.

The next day we had an early breakfast and went for a walk around the Village. With its quieter streets and smaller houses, it was very peaceful. In Washington Square we listened to a group of street musicians. Then, as the weather was so nice, we went to Central Park. It was a different world. All around us the big city with the traffic and skyscrapers, and here in Central Park people were jogging, fishing or just lying on the grass. We had a wonderful time. In the afternoon we walked by the famous stores along Fifth Avenue, then we went back to Brooklyn. When we got off the subway, both of us thought the same thing: How soon can we do this again?

Central Park is the only big park in Manhattan. It is 4 kilometers long.

Working with the text

a The text names a lot of famous places in New York. Find out where all these places are. Follow Maureen's route through Manhattan. (The map on page 29 will help you.)

b Make two groups and ask each other questions about the Donovans.

2a Write about the Donovan family.

1. Donovans – Brooklyn / biggest – boroughs / about 2.3 million / fourth largest city – USA
2. Mrs Donovan – office – Brooklyn / Maureen – ask her first – she – home earlier – husband / at first – just laugh / then – tell her – Sally's cousin / after that – say, "OK."
3. Mr Donovan – Manhattan / that means – subway / hate – subway / trains – crowded / not always stop *Go on.*

b A week after the concert Maureen wrote to her cousin Patsy. Please finish her letter. Tell Patsy how you felt when you heard about the concert, wanted to talk to your parents, etc.

Dear Patsy,
You'll never believe what I did last week. I saw ...

Go on.

3 Say it in English: *Expressing opinions, agreeing and disagreeing*

Expressing your opinion:
I think / believe / feel ...
In my opinion ...
I'm sure ...

Agreeing with someone:
I'm sure / I think you're right.
I agree.
I love/hate big cities. – So do I. / I do, too.
I don't like Elvis. – Neither do I. / Nor do I.
I can go. – So can I. I can't go. – Nor can I.

Explaining and giving reasons:
Let me explain ...
Well, you see, ... / That's why ...
First, ...; second, ...; and then ...; finally ...

Disagreeing with someone:
I'm not sure / I don't think you can say that.
Sorry, I can't agree (with you).
I love/hate big cities. – I don't.
I don't like Elvis. – I do.
I can go. – I can't. I can't go. – I can.

a What is it like to live in New York for Maureen and for her father?

1. *Maureen:* I think – fantastic / first – largest city – USA – get the best of everything / second, – different nationalities / interesting people / exciting places – Chinatown / finally – Statue of Liberty – other famous sights / sometimes – visit them – parents / not too far – subway
2. *Mr Donovan:* I don't agree – Maureen / of course, – exciting – live here / interesting people – places / but – explain my situation / work – Manhattan / subway – every day / crowded / home – tired / sometimes – angry / in my opinion – like all big cities / noisy – crowded – unhealthy / if – work there – no time to enjoy yourself

b *Note-making practice:* Work with a partner or in a group. Make two lists, one with advantages and one with disadvantages of life in a big city. You can also make a poster to express your opinion.
Writing practice: Write an essay of about 20 lines in which you explain *your* opinion.
Discussion practice: Choose two speakers; one *for* and one *against* big cities. They read their essays to the class. Then everyone can discuss the essays and add their own opinions.

Focus on GRAMMAR: Der unbestimmte Artikel (The indefinite article)

New York … a city of dreams?

David Dinkins

It has been said that New York is a city where dreams can come true. Perhaps David Dinkins is an example. He is **an African American**, the son of a hairdresser. He grew up in one of the city's poorer areas, in Harlem. Who could guess that in 1989 he would make history and become the first black Mayor of New York City?

With its harbor and its Statue of Liberty, New York is famous **as a magnet** for people from all over the world. But, of course, people move here from other parts of the USA, too.

Barbara McClintock (1902-92) was **an American** who was born in Hartford, Connecticut, and went to school in Brooklyn. Even **as a girl**, she wanted to become **a scientist**. Her mother knew this would be hard for her, **as a woman**, but Barbara went to university when she was 17 and tried. She became **a pioneer** in genetics and in 1983 she won the Nobel Prize.

Barbara McClintock

Irving Berlin

Israel Baline (1888-1989) grew up in New York's Lower East Side, the southeastern part of Manhattan. His family had come from Siberia when he was four. They were already poor – then Izzy's father, Moses, died. So the boy had to leave school and find work. He was eight. Izzy had sung in his local synagogue – now he sang songs in the street. Later he got a job **as a waiter** in a club in Chinatown, where he also sang and played the piano. He wrote songs, too, under the name of Irving Berlin, and these became very popular. His first big hit, *Alexander's Ragtime Band*, sold a million records in only three weeks. By 1912 he was earning $100,000 **a year**.

He wrote 1,000 songs, including songs for Broadway shows and Hollywood films, and his most famous song, *I'm dreaming of a white Christmas*. This has sold over 600 million copies so far. When another songwriter, Jerome Kern, was asked about Berlin's place in American music, he said: "Irving Berlin *is* American music."

Barbara McClintock was **an American**.
… war Amerikanerin.

She wanted to become **a scientist**.
… Naturwissenschaftlerin werden.

Even **as a girl**, she wanted to be a scientist.
Schon als Mädchen …

By 1912 Berlin was earning $100,000 **a year**.
… $100.000 pro/im Jahr.

Anders als im Deutschen steht der unbestimmte Artikel *a/an*
- vor Nationalitätsbezeichnungen,
- vor Berufsangaben,
- nach *as* (= als),
- in der Bedeutung „pro" vor Zeit-, Maß- und Mengenangaben.

→ Ex 6-8

Focus on WORDS: Traffic, traveling and +public transportation

The quickest way to travel in Manhattan is often by bike. But people who travel a long way to work every day drive their own cars or use public transportation: trains, buses, etc. Today many people share their cars and travel to work together in car pools. This way they save +gas and there are fewer +traffic jams. But it is often difficult for car owners to find somewhere where they can park, and it is quite possible that their car might be stolen by car +thieves. Each year in New York, over 80,000 +vehicles are stolen. Many firms now use bike +messengers if they want to send something very quickly to another part of Manhattan. A bike messenger is twice as fast as a taxi. But the job is dangerous. In one year 37 bike messengers were killed in traffic accidents.

1 Collecting words: Find all the "travel words and phrases" in the text and put them in one of the following four groups. Then collect *more* for each group. The pictures will help you, but first try to do it without them.

a **Vehicles and parts of vehicles**

car (1), +truck (3), +motorcycle (6), …
+engine, +horn (11), +seatbelt (13), …

b **What do drivers or passengers do?**

They start the engine, put on their seatbelts, …
They catch/+miss the train/bus/…, change trains, …

c **How and when do people travel?**

They go by car, take a taxi, …
They use public transportation, e.g. buses/…
When they go on vacation, …

d **"A mixed bag"**

airport, road, +intersection (16), traffic jam, +pedestrian crossing (17), traffic lights (18), +sidewalk (19), fare, route, speed, mph, ...

gas	petrol
truck	lorry/truck
intersection	crossroads
sidewalk	pavement

2 Arranging words: Arrange the words and phrases you have collected in different ways. Look at page 24 and see how Birgit has arranged her words.

3 Words in use

a Here are five vehicles: *a train, a taxi, a truck, an ambulance, a helicopter.* Which is the most important vehicle in your opinion? Say why the others are less important.

b Make suggestions how public transportation in your city or town could be improved.

+ new words

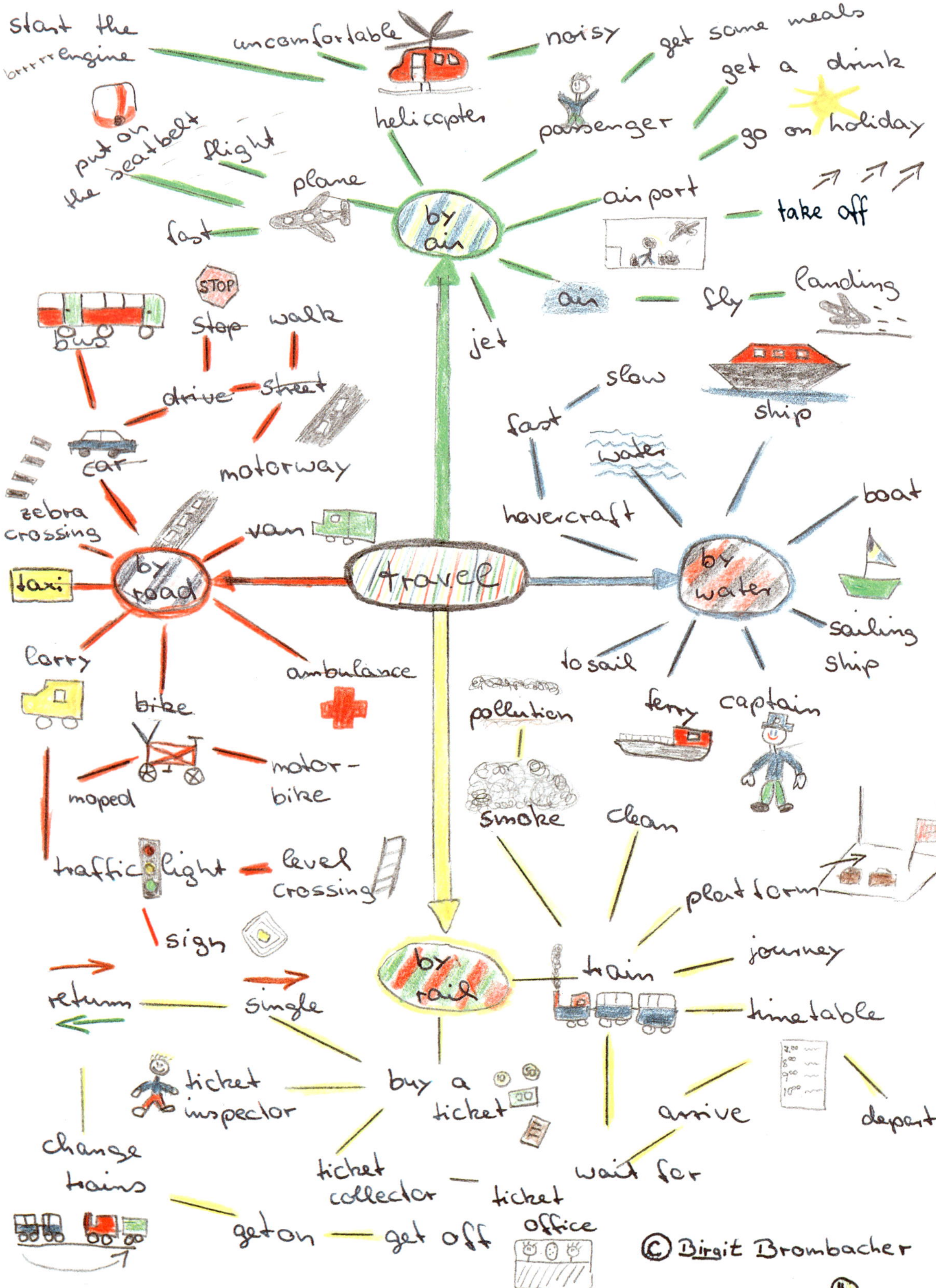
travel
by air
helicopter
uncomfortable
noisy
start the engine
brrrrr
put on the seatbelt
flight
plane
fast
passenger
get some meals
get a drink
go on holiday
airport
take off
jet
air
fly
landing
by road
STOP
stop
walk
bus
drive
street
car
motorway
zebra crossing
van
taxi
lorry
bike
ambulance
moped
motor-bike
traffic light
level crossing
sign
by water
ship
slow
fast
water
hovercraft
boat
sailing ship
to sail
ferry
captain
pollution
smoke
clean
by rail
platform
train
journey
timetable
return
single
ticket inspector
buy a ticket
arrive
depart
change trains
ticket collector
ticket office
wait for
get on
get off
© Birgit Brombacher

1 Definite article or no definite article?

1. Everybody has heard about (poverty) that is often found in big cities. But it's hard to imagine (poverty) of people in some New York neighborhoods.
2. Marvin is interested in (history). He has just been to the library to borrow some books about (history) of African Americans.
3. I can't understand why (people) choose to live in big cities. (families) I know all prefer small towns to big cities.
4. (technology) hasn't really helped everybody. (computers), for example, are one reason for (unemployment) we have now.

American ants are much smaller than the ants you find in Africa and India. Why? – Well, in Africa and India they have eleph-ants. (ants = Ameisen)

5. Although (immigrants) have always been important in (American history), the US government tried to stop (immigration) of people from some parts of Europe in the early 20th century.

2 The strangest things can happen in dreams . . .

a Just imagine. Professor Loony says that dogs can speak. – Well, perhaps the dogs he sees in his dreams can speak. But that's silly, of course. Dogs can't speak.

Make similar short dialogs in which you use nouns with and without an article:
people – walk on their heads / rocks – not sink in water / music – make you ill / rain – sometimes – be dry / kangaroos – fly

b *Make a few more short dialogs about some strange things you can think of.*

3 Graffiti – in English, please *Do you need the definite article?*

a

b *Make up similar sentences.*

c *What do you think of graffiti? Talk about your opinions in class. Then choose one sentence from* **a** *or one of your own sentences and write a short essay in which you express your opinion.*

4 Places and sights

1. *Read pages 17 to 20 and collect all the names of places and sights. Put them in two groups: one with the definite article, one without the definite article.* 2. *Then try to remember some place names and sights in London that you read about in Book 3 and add each of them to the right group.* 3. *Which of these places and/or sights would you like to see or visit?*

5 A discussion *Try to use the phrases on p. 21.*

Imagine your class wants to go on a four-day school trip. The students have different opinions about the money everybody should take. Make notes and then discuss the following opinions:

Opinion A: Everybody should be allowed to take as much as they want to take.
Opinion B: Students shouldn't be allowed to take more than 30 marks.
Opinion C: Everybody should take 20 marks.

6 Complete the sentences. *Use the indefinite article and one of the following nouns.*

hour day cup pound year month bottle

1. I usually get my wages twice … .
2. Susan has to work eight hours … .
3. We paid $8 … for that wine.
4. Bananas aren't more than 80¢ … .
5. I get 30 days vacation … .
6. Coffee is 60¢ … in here.
7. Never drive faster than 30 miles … in a town.

7 Children's dreams *Say what these children wanted to be when they were younger and what they want to become now.*

a 1. Scott

2. Maureen

3. Marvin

4. Debbie

5. Lan

Example: When Scott was younger, he wanted to be a waiter. But now he's 13 and he wants to become an ambulance man.

b *Can you still remember what you wanted to be when you were younger? And what do you want to become now?*

8 In English, please:

1. David Dinkins Vater war Friseur, aber David selber wurde nicht Friseur.
2. Barbara McClintock war Schülerin an der Erasmus-Hall-High-School in Brooklyn. Obwohl es für sie als Frau nicht immer leicht war, arbeitete sie 40 Jahre lang als Naturwissenschaftlerin in Washington.
3. Moses Baline kam nach New York, weil er als Jude in Sibirien verfolgt worden war.
4. Als Junge wurde Izzy Baline oft in den East River geworfen. Als Erwachsener wurde er sehr erfolgreich. Als er heiratete, verdiente er $100.000 im Jahr.

9 Revision: "each other" or a -self pronoun?

1. After a test I've often asked … why I made such silly mistakes. 2. Some children in our class have to cook lunch for … because both their parents go to work. 3. Yesterday Vera and Chris helped … with their homework. 4. Did you buy this book for … or for your sister? 5. Andy and Nico usually lend … their new CDs. 6. Tim and Anne really enjoyed … in our last music lesson.

"Our sandwiches speak for themselves."

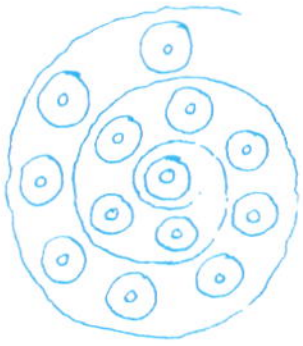

What's this?
– Thirteen Mexicans who are following each other up a hill.

10 Revision: Check your tenses (simple present, present progressive, present perfect, simple past, will-future)

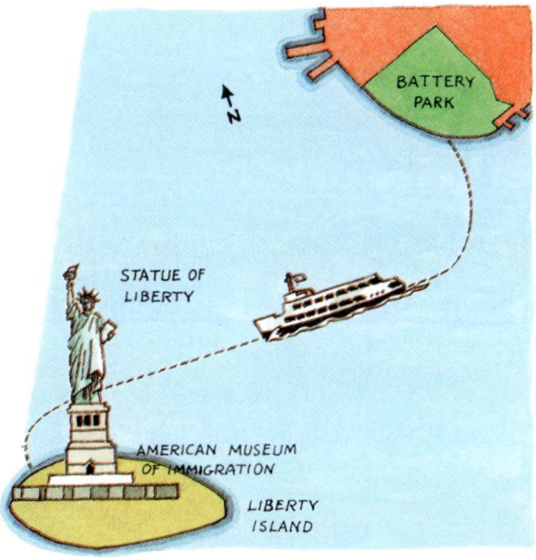

Maureen:
Mom, last Easter vacation you (promise) to take me to the Museum of Immigration. Now it (be) October and we (not be) there yet.

Mrs Donovan:
– Well, as grandpa (not come) next weekend, I (can) take you there on Saturday.

Oh, great, Mom. You see, we (talk) about immigration in our history class at the moment. Maybe I (be able to) get more information there on Saturday.

– There (be) a ferry from Battery Park to Liberty Island, I think. (you/know) anything about it?

Yes, it (leave) Battery Park every hour.

– Fine, we (ask) Dad and Scott tonight. Maybe they (come) with us.

11 The Roeblings *Write a short text with the help of these words.*

1831 – Johann August Roebling leave – Mühlhausen in Thüringen / 25 years old / want to be – farmer – USA / but – not successful / so – go back – old job / start to build bridges / today – be best remembered – Brooklyn Bridge, – first bridge – East River / be started – 1869 / that year J.A. Roebling die – in an accident / work be continued – son, Washington A. Roebling / bridge be finished – 1883 – although W.A. Roebling become very ill / while – ill, – wife Emily help – him a lot with his work / photo next to this exercise show – Americans not only remember – J.A. Roebling and W.A. Roebling / W.A. Roebling's wife Emily also be remembered – many Americans

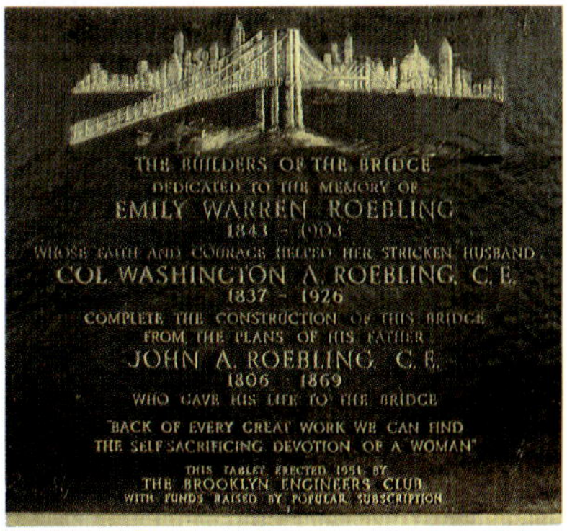

°12 Listening comprehension: A visit to the "Lady" *Listen to the cassette, then answer these questions.*

1. Who is the "Lady"? 2. Why is she so famous? 3. How do the Swytzers get to Liberty Island? 4. Why did lots of immigrants translate their names into English? 5. What do the children do on Liberty Island? 6. Why don't their parents go with them?

° = wahlfrei

13 WORDS WORDS WORDS

a New words and old words in combinations

(to) agree	criminal	(to) fight	(to) hurt	neighbor	(to) protect	(to) suggest
(to) attack	crowd	free	independent	neighborhood	right	suggestion
beautiful	danger	freedom	(to) kill	peace	safe	thief
(to) break	dangerous	(to) hit	law	peaceful	(to) save	(to) throw
careful	(to) destroy	home	(to) miss	police	(to) steal	war
(to) catch	(to) disagree	homeless	music	pollution	strange	weapon
crime	(to) escape	hospital	musician	prison	stranger	wrong

You have met the underlined words in this Unit. Here are some suggestions how to put new and old words together in combinations. Can you think of any others yourself?

1. dangerous – danger	2. right or wrong	3. beautiful	4. strange – stranger
free – ?	agree or ?	careful	crime – ?
peaceful – ?	war or ?	?	steal – ?
suggest – ?	catch or ?		music – ?

5. If you have no home, you are … . – I like the neighbors in our … . – A weapon can … or even … people. – The police keep law and order. They … . – Criminals/Thieves … .

b Trouble spot: "gehen" = "go, walk, run, leave; be; work" Translate the following sentences.

1. John geht noch zur Schule. 2. Wo gehst du denn hin? 3. Du kannst den 33er-Bus nehmen oder zu Fuß gehen. 4. Wann geht der nächste Bus zum Flughafen? 5. Zwischen 22 Uhr und 5 Uhr gehen keine Busse. 6. Die Klingel geht (= funktioniert) nicht. 7. Wie geht's deinem Bruder? Geht's ihm wieder gut? 8. Deine Uhr geht falsch. 9. Wenn ich jetzt nicht gehe, verpass ich meinen Zug. 10. Mach dir keine Sorgen! Mir geht's gut.

c WORD BUILDER'S CORNER **Abstract nouns that end in "-ness"**

You can often add **-ness** to an adjective to make an abstract noun.

	English:	**-ness**	German: **-heit**	**-keit**	**others**
Examples:	ill + **-ness**	= ill**ness**	Krank**heit**		
	lonely + **-ness**	= loneliness		Einsam**keit**	
	nervous + **-ness**	= nervous**ness**			Nervosität

1. Here are some more adjectives like this. Add them to the list.

clever fit friendly happy
polite sick silly impolite weak
ugly unfair unfriendly

2. Now change the adjectives in the following sentences into "-ness nouns". You will have to change other parts of the sentence or the word order, too.

Example: How do you explain the fact that he was so silly?
How do you explain his silliness?

1. Kate is seriously ill. 2. I can understand that he is bitter. 3. It always helps to be polite. 4. You didn't pass the exam because you were too lazy. 5. It is important for a disc jockey to be lively. 6. I don't know the reason why he is so sad.

○ *Getting along in the USA: In Manhattan*

In Manhattan most streets and avenues have numbers and not names. The streets go from west to east, the avenues from north to south. Fifth Avenue divides Manhattan into the West Side and the East Side.

Imagine you are staying in New York – in a hotel on East 42nd Street. Make a list of the sights you want to see and then plan your tour of Manhattan. Say how you are going to get to the sights. Here are some of the places you might visit:

The Empire State Building, Wall Street, Lincoln Center, Fifth Avenue, Broadway, Central Park, the Statue of Liberty, the World Trade Center, the United Nations, Grand Central Terminal/Station, Times Square, Madison Square Garden, Rockefeller Center.

Statue of Liberty ↓

INFO BOX

New York has an excellent system of buses and subways. When you travel by bus, you have to pay when you get in. And always have the correct fare. Drivers do not carry any change because they are afraid somebody might rob them. On the subway you have to buy special tokens. They look like coins and you need one when you enter the subway. The best way to travel at night is by taxi. However, in New York taxi drivers expect a good tip.

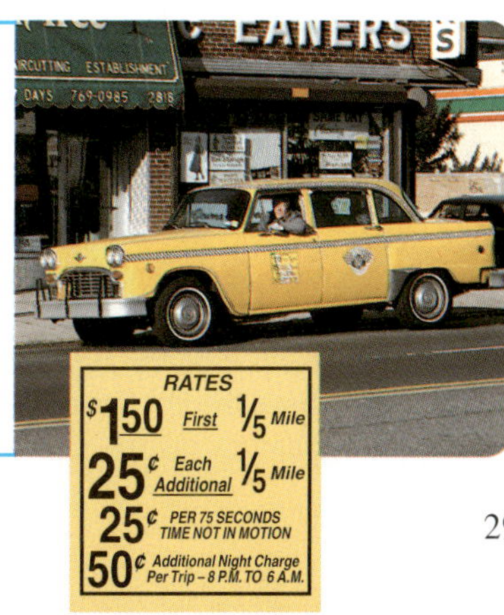

2 Text

"Hey, look at the gook."

The word hit Lan harder than a hand, harder than a stick or a stone.

Gook.

She began to cry, but she tried to smile politely and pretend that she had heard nothing. " And look at those clothes," said Wanda Potlowsky. "Where did she get them?"

Mother makes them, Lan thought. During the quiet hours at night, after she has worked ten hours for low wages in this wonderful country. That's where I get them. And she started to walk home, while the group of kids continued to laugh at her outside the school building. Oh, why had her parents decided to move to this area? Why had she been forced to move to a new school?

Maureen was leaving school at the same time and she heard what the students said. She recognized the new girl. "Another immigrant," one of the students said. "How many more are going to come before the government finally decides that the country is full?"

Maureen said nothing, although she had liked the girl when she had seen her in class. Like many Asians she moved beautifully and was so polite, always smiling. She smiled now, although the others were so cruel to her.

That evening Maureen said, "Mom, what does gook mean?"

"Where did you hear that expression?"

"We have a new girl in class. One of the kids said it to her."

Mrs Donovan started to get angry. "It was very stupid to say something like that. Gook was a rude name that was used for the Vietnamese who fought against the US during the Vietnam war. Is she Vietnamese?"

"I'm not sure. We've got a lot of immigrants at the moment. From Korea, the Philippines and other places. Some of the kids say they're taking away our jobs and our places at college, and that the government ought to stop them."

"Who said that?" asked her father.

"Frank Minetti."

"Frank Minetti! What does he know? His parents were immigrants, too. And his father still can't speak English properly. Whenever I say something to him, he answers in Italian. What a lot of your friends forget is that we were all immigrants once. Now they talk as if they own the place. They should ask that girl why her family came here before they shut the door in her face."

Lan was very good at school. In art she was the best in class. It seemed obvious that in a few years she would win a place in a good college. Maureen wanted to talk to Lan, but a lot of her friends didn't like Asians, and Maureen didn't want to be the first who broke the ice. But then one day she went into the art room and found Wanda Potlowsky there. She was holding a picture that Lan had painted for a school competition.

"I hate this picture," said Wanda. "And Mrs Warburton says she's so good at art. How can she say that? It's terrible."

"What are you going to do with it?" asked Maureen.

"What am I going to do with it? Maybe I'm going to throw it out of the window."

"No," shouted Maureen. "You can't do that." She ran toward the girl to save the picture. The two girls fought until the picture fell on the floor. At once Wanda put her foot on it. The two girls stood opposite each other and their eyes met. Then Wanda turned around and left the room. Lan was standing at the door, but she said nothing as Wanda walked past her. Maureen picked up the picture. It showed a frightened family – the parents, two girls and a baby in the father's arms. They were running along a country road. The two girls were screaming. Behind them were the dark clouds of war. Wanda had stood on the faces of the children.

"I'm sorry," said Maureen. Lan took the picture. Her eyes were sad, but she smiled and said,

“Thank you. It was very kind of you to try and save it. My father always wanted to come to America. Everybody is free there, he told my mother. He never imagined that people might not want him.” The two girls continued to talk and then Lan said, “Would you like to come to my home and meet my family?”
“Yes, please,” said Maureen.
“I’ll ask my parents tonight. Perhaps we can go after school tomorrow.”

The next day Maureen got off the bus with Lan and a group of other Vietnamese in a part of Brooklyn she didn’t know very well. In the distance behind the large old buildings she heard a ship. She supposed they must be near the harbor. Maureen and Lan left the others and went alone down a long empty street. A small boy walked next to them.
Maureen began to get nervous. “Don’t worry,” said Lan. “My brother will look after us.”
Maureen looked down at the young boy. “This is a dangerous area. How can he look after us?”
“Binh is small, yes, but we’re safe with him.”
Binh looked up at Maureen and smiled confidently with his huge white teeth.
Lan’s family lived on the fifth floor of a very old building. To get to the stairs you had to go down a long dark passage. The floor was covered with old boxes, newspapers and bottles; the smell was terrible. Suddenly Lan’s brother stopped and listened. He said something quickly to his sister, and Lan pushed Maureen into a dark corner between a lot of old boxes. “Don’t move,” she said. They waited, and very soon a gang of kids ran past, followed a moment later by another gang. She heard shouts, glass broke, boxes fell over, and the whole time they stood still and never moved. Minutes passed and then Binh went down the passage as quietly as a cat. When he came back he said, “We can go now.”
“What was that?” asked Maureen. Binh smiled. “Dangerous place,” he said.

Maureen was surprised how comfortable they had made their apartment with so few things.
“My father had a good business in Vietnam,” said Lan. “My mother was a teacher. At the moment Dad works in the harbor. Mom works in a food factory. I’ve told them what happened at school. They say we must work hard and be patient.”
Lan’s father offered Maureen a cup of tea. “Nothing here is as bad as what we left behind.”
Lan’s mother had cooked a Vietnamese meal, and while they ate it Maureen heard how Lan’s parents had lived through years of war. They had spent all their money to buy places in a boat so that they could leave their country, but the captain had put too many families into a boat that was too small. They had spent weeks on the open sea; they had been attacked by pirates; they hadn’t had enough food and water. Many died before they were finally found by a German boat. They had suffered all this to get to America. Just as her own Irish ancestors had probably suffered, Maureen thought.
“In your picture,” she said, “there were two girls and a baby.”
“My three sisters all died on the journey,” said Lan. “I never knew them. My brother and I were born here.”
When it was time to go, Maureen thanked Lan and her parents for the meal. As it was already dark, she called her mother. Mrs Donovan shouted, “*Where* did you say you are? Don’t try and walk! I’ll be there in half an hour.”
“My father will go down to the street with you,” said Lan, “so that you’ll be safe.”
Maureen thanked everybody again and left the apartment.
“You didn’t say she lived *here*,” said Mrs Donovan as they drove away toward their own neighborhood. Maureen looked out of the window at the kind, smiling man. “They’re very nice people,” she said.
“That isn’t an answer,” said Mrs Donovan, but Maureen wasn’t listening. She was thinking of her father’s words: we were all immigrants once.

Working with the text

a Finish these sentences in your own words:

One day after school Maureen heard how ...
She knew at once that the word ...
The kids also laughed ...
But Maureen didn't ...

That evening Maureen talked ...

They explained the word ...
And Mr Donovan said, "What a lot of you ..."

Some time later Wanda Potlowsky ...
Maureen tried to ...
The picture showed a frightened family ...

Now try to tell the story to the end.

b Let's talk about some people in the story:

1. What do Wanda, Lan, Maureen, Mr and Mrs Donovan do and say in the story?

   At the beginning of the story ... / At first ...
   Later (in the story) ...
   At the end of the story ...

2. What do you think of these people? Choose one or two and explain your opinion about them in a short text. Try to use some of the expressions on page 21.

   ... seems to be ... / ... doesn't seem to be ...
   impolite – nice – (un)reasonable – stupid – sad – (un)friendly – tolerant – confident – (un)fair – (un)happy – silly

c What does the text say about ...

1. ... this family's life in Vietnam?
2. ... the reasons why they left their home country?
3. ... how they came to the USA?
4. ... the reasons why they chose to go to the USA?
5. ... their life in the USA at the moment?
6. ... their ideas for their future?
7. ... reasons why Maureen wasn't listening to her mother at the end of the story?

d Some time later Frank wanted to start an argument with Lan. Maureen stopped him and said, "Look, Frank, ..." – Write a dialog between Maureen and Frank. Use some of the expressions on page 21.

e 1. Try to express in a picture how you imagine Lan, the neighborhood where she lives, the room where they had the meal, or the picture that Lan had painted. Then write a short text to explain your picture.
2. How would you feel if somebody destroyed one of your pictures? What would *you* do?

In New York there are between 50,000 and 100,000 people without a home. Homeless people are everywhere in Manhattan. They walk along the streets; they stand like ghosts outside hotels and in the doors of expensive stores. It is difficult to look away, and even more difficult to forget how lucky we are.

The discovery of America by the Europeans

1 Columbus was not the first European who reached America. The Vikings probably landed there in the ninth century. It seems certain that Leif Ericson landed on the northeast coast of America in the year 1000. He called the country Vinland.

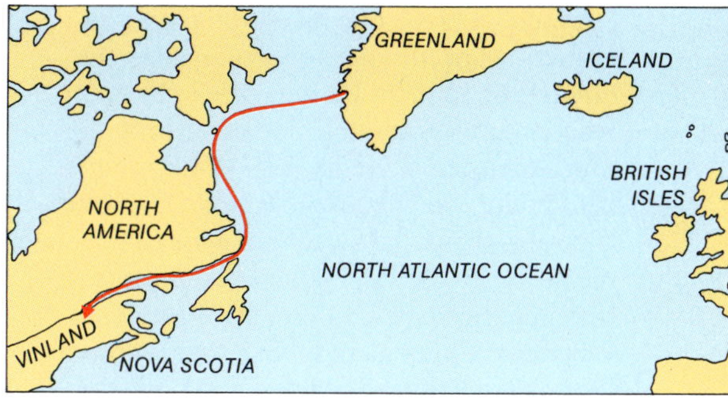

2 When Christopher Columbus sailed from Spain, he was really looking for a sea route to India. He found America instead. Just imagine, in the 15th century people in Europe did not even know that the American continent existed. In fact, when Columbus landed on an island near the southeast coast of North America, he really believed he *was* in India. That is why he called the people there "Indians".

◁ *Columbus on San Salvador, 1492*

3 The first Europeans who settled in North America were English. Jamestown, the first permanent English settlement, was founded in Virginia in 1607. It did not start well. The crossing was long and dangerous. The boats were too small for the number of passengers – all men. Many died on the journey. To make things worse, they chose a very bad place to build a settlement. It was already late December, but the men did not build proper houses and they did not start to grow food. Instead, they ate the food they had brought with them from England or stole food from the Indians. Others began to look for gold. They had heard and believed the stories about Indian girls who fell in love with the settlers and offered them gold.

The reconstructed Jamestown settlement

4 By the end of the first year, fewer than half the settlers were still alive. And they only survived because the Indians brought them food and helped them in other ways – and because a man called John Smith had become their leader. He was very strict and forced the men to work. His rule was, "No work, no food!" The men worked, and the colony survived. What saved it was, in fact, a plant that the Indians grew and used as medicine and for religious ceremonies: tobacco. Soon the colonists started to sell their tobacco to England. Thirteen years later, in 1620, there were over 1,000 colonists in Virginia and most of them were growing tobacco. Hundreds of women went from England to the colony in this year to marry the settlers and to start families.

5 Many of the people who emigrated to America in the 17th century were both "pulled" and "pushed". On the one hand, they saw the attractions of life in a new colony. On the other, they found it hard to stay in England where there was no religious freedom.
Since the time of Henry VIII (1491-1547), who broke away from the Roman Catholic Church because he no longer wanted to accept the power of the Pope, there had been trouble between the leaders of the new Protestant Church of England and those who were still Roman Catholics. Each new king or queen wanted to have only one official religion in the country for everybody. People with the "wrong" religion lost their jobs or were not allowed to go to university. Many were put in prison or were killed.
In 1604, the Protestant King James I said he would persecute those who did not conform, i.e. belong to the Church of England. In 1605, some Catholics, including Guy Fawkes, tried to blow up the King and his parliament. Other people who were being persecuted decided to leave England and go to a colony in America.

In 1620 a group of Nonconformists who became famous as the "Pilgrims" sailed to America in the Mayflower.

Compare the first settlers with the first astronauts. Who do you think was braver?
Imagine you were born in about 1590.
Why might you have decided to go to America?

William Penn (1644-1718)

Look quickly through the information about William Penn here and on the next page. Make a list of the dates you find.
Read the information again, this time in detail, use your list of dates to make notes, then write a short summary.

1 In the middle of the 17th century a new group of Nonconformists, the Quakers, were soon persecuted because they did not think armies or bishops or church taxes were necessary. The Quakers (or Friends) wanted to live very simple lives . Unusually, at their meetings both men and women were allowed to speak. They wore plain clothes, with no bright colors, and did not sing or dance. In those days English had another word for "you" – *thou* – (just like *du* in German) and the Quakers called everybody *thou*. They also refused to take off their hats when they met an important person. Sometimes they had to go to prison because of this, but they said: "We only take off our hats when we talk to God." One of their most famous leaders, William Penn, went to prison several times. But even as a prisoner in the Tower, in 1668-69, he continued to write a book about his beliefs. It was called: *No cross, no crown.*
He was in the Tower for eight months, and was only given his freedom after his father, Admiral Sir William Penn, had spoken to the King, Charles II (1630-1685). The Admiral had been a great help to the King in earlier years and the King also owed him a lot of money.

2 Charles II did not forget his debt to the Admiral, and in 1681 he gave William Penn a huge area of land between New York and Maryland. Penn wanted to call it New Wales. But, in memory of Penn's father, the Admiral, the King called it Pennsylvania (Latin for *Penn's woods*). Penn hoped it would become a place where everybody would be able to enjoy religious freedom. He wrote to a friend: "There may be room there [= Pennsylvania], though not here [= England], for such a holy experiment."

(From a painting by Benjamin West, 1771)

William Penn (middle of picture, arms held out) making peace with the Indians

3 Although Penn visited America only twice, from 1682 to 1684 and 1699 to 1701, he played a big role in his colony. He wrote its laws, designed its parliament and planned its first capital, Philadelphia (Greek for *loving your brother*). Here, at last, everybody who believed in God was allowed to worship as they wanted, there were free elections, and any man who believed in Jesus Christ was allowed to play a part in them.
Penn made peace with the Native Americans who lived on the land the King had given him. This was important to him. But not everyone was happy there. Slavery was allowed, and many settlers wanted to play a bigger part in government. Finally, Penn decided to sell his "holy experiment" back to the British government. He died in 1718 before this could be done, however, and Pennsylvania belonged to his family until the American War of Independence (when the colonies in America broke away from England and founded the USA). Then, Penn's laws served as a model for the men who met in Philadelphia in 1776 to write the American Constitution.
Today, "Penn's woods" continue to be a home for large groups of Nonconformists. Many are of German origin: the "Pennsylvania Dutch".

○A visit to Plimoth[1] Plantation

PLIMOTH PLANTATION

– A living-history museum –

The Pilgrims who sailed to America in the *Mayflower* in 1620 landed at a place in today's Massachusetts which was called Plimoth. They found a land of rolling hills, rocky coasts and thick forests. Not far from where they landed, they discovered an abandoned Indian village. They made this village their home.
Today, close to the original site, visitors can walk around a reproduction of the original Pilgrims' village.

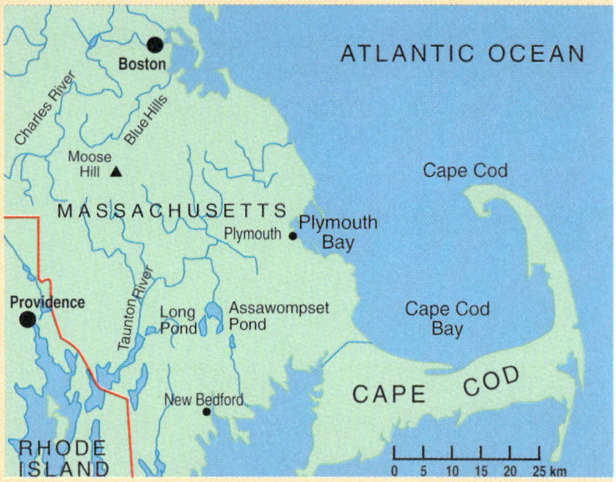

"It was like being in a time machine. In one house the people asked me where I was from and I said, 'Germany'. They looked at my jeans and asked me if that was the latest fashion there. My clothes looked very strange to them."

"It makes learning about history more interesting than reading books. You can really get an impression of what it was like to live in 17th-century America."

At Plimoth Plantation, one hour south of Boston, houses have been constructed from original materials, and the land is farmed just as it used to be almost 400 years ago. Actors who are wearing costumes play the parts of the settlers. The actors have taken over the names and identities of the men and women who actually lived there. They live and work just as the Pilgrims did and speak a variety of old English and Dutch dialects. Visitors can meet and talk to Captain Myles Standish, Master Isaac Allerton, Mistress Elizabeth Warren and many others. Visitors are encouraged to walk into the houses and join in the daily life of the community. The Plimoth actors are very well trained and expect visitors to imagine they have traveled back in time and that they, too, live in that period.

Find out from this page
… what you can learn about American history at Plimoth Plantation.
… what a living-history museum is.

Collect information about one of the following and present it to the class:
– the Pilgrims and the *Mayflower*,
– the Pennsylvania Dutch.

[1] 'Plimoth' is the original 17th-century spelling.

GOLDEN KANSAS

Debbie Thomas and her family live on a farm in Kansas. Kansas is often called the "Wheat State" or the "breadbasket of the nation" because much of the land is flat and covered with wheatfields. From the middle of June to the middle of July it looks like a huge sea of gold.
However, the state has little water – something that was a problem for the early farmers. Most of the lakes today are artificial.

Find Kansas on a map of the USA and say where it is. Compare its size and population with Germany (see p.6).

One of the most famous cities in Kansas is Dodge City, the "Cowboy City of the World". During the days of the Wild West it was the largest cattle market in the world. Today this old cowboy town – like many others – has been restored and is a tourist attraction, so you can see Dodge City as it was a hundred years ago. Other cow towns in Kansas are Abilene and Wichita.

Before the railways came to the west, the mail was carried by the Pony Express riders. Their route took them through Kansas. They rode night and day, and when they reached one of the Pony Express stations, they jumped off one tired horse and onto a fresh one that was waiting there. It took 75 ponies and 10½ days to reach California!

Imagine you have met somebody from Kansas. Work with a partner and interview him or her about the state. Ask about the countryside, its size, population and history.

An American teenager's life

Debbie Thomas lives on a farm about 30 minutes from the small town of Tonganoxie, Kansas. She, her brother Kenny, and most of her friends go to Tonganoxie High School. An American high school is similar to a German *Gesamtschule*.

While you are reading the text and looking at the pictures on these two pages, make notes about
– an average day for Debbie
– Tonganoxie High School
– the role of sports in American high schools.

MONDAY
Pizza Palace (4 p.m. - 7 p.m.)
Visit Nancy on the way home

TUESDAY
Drama Club (3 p.m. - 5 p.m.)
Meet Jerry, Rob and Ray in Dino's Ice-Cream Parlor

WEDNESDAY
Cheerleader practice (3 p.m. - 4:30 p.m.)
Meet Tommy (5 p.m. at Dino's)

THURSDAY
Pizza Palace (4 p.m. - 7 p.m.)

FRIDAY
Cheerleader practice (5 p.m. - 6 p.m.)
School basketball game (6:30 p.m.)
Choir practice (8 p.m.)

SATURDAY
Tennis with Tommy (10 a.m.)
Pizza Palace (4 p.m. - 7 p.m.)
Miranda's party (8 p.m.)

SUNDAY
Church

My school day starts at eight o'clock in the morning and finishes at three. During the week I often stay at school for an hour or two after classes. At most American high schools there's a huge choice of sports, clubs and activities like music or drama. We also have regular school dances and parties.
In Kansas a lot of students drive to school as you can get a driver's license when you are 16. Some students arrive at school in their own cars. There are sometimes more students' cars in the parking lot than teachers'. …

… On three days a week I work at a restaurant in town. (Nearly all my friends have part-time jobs.) After that I sometimes meet some of my friends, so it can be late before I finally get home to do my homework.

Sports are very important in American schools, especially football and basketball. The students who are chosen for the school teams are very popular. Games between two schools are big events. There's usually one every Friday night. Everybody comes to watch them: students, teachers, parents – even people from the town. Reports about the games and star players – girls and boys – appear in the local newspapers. The school band plays fight songs and the cheerleaders make sure there's a really good atmosphere. The people have a great time and really enjoy themselves.

My boyfriend Tommy plays basketball for our school. I myself am one of the cheerleaders. Cheerleaders are a group of students, mostly girls, who wear uniforms with the school colors. At Tonganoxie High they're black and white. Cheerleaders appear before each game. It's our job to make sure the crowd is excited and cheering wildly. But first, before the game starts, everybody stands and sings the national anthem. Then the cheerleaders dance and lead the cheering during the game.

When I have some free time – that is after school, after clubs, after sports and work – I visit my friends at their houses. We often meet in "Dino's Ice-Cream Parlor" in town, where we sit and talk, or we go for a ride in somebody's car. A lot of my friends have their own cars. (That's why they all have jobs – to pay for them!) We go cruising. That means we don't drive anywhere special.

Use your notes about Debbie's average day, Tonganoxie High School and the role of sports. Compare your life to Debbie's. Would you like to lead a life like hers?

Focus on GRAMMAR: Bedingungssätze: Typ II (Conditional sentences II)

In September Debbie's Welsh cousin Megan visited her, so Debbie and her parents drove to Kansas City airport to meet her. As they left the city behind them, Megan said, "I've heard so much about the traffic in America. But this road is almost empty."
"It's only quiet now because it's Saturday afternoon," Debbie said. "**If** it **was** Monday today, you **would see** far more cars."
When they got to Tonganoxie, Debbie laughed. "Well, this is it, Megan, the center of the universe. A main street, a few shops, two churches, my school – and that's about all."
"That's our church on the left," Mr Thomas said.
"Oh yes, I recognize it from the photos Debbie sent me," Megan said. "And you said you sing in the choir there, Debbie?"
"She does, sometimes, but she doesn't practice enough," Mrs Thomas said. "**If** she **practiced** more, she**'d sing** a whole lot better."

What **would happen if** things **were** different?

If-Satz (*if*-clause)	Hauptsatz (main clause)
If it **was** Monday, Wenn es Montag wäre,	they**'d** (= they **would**) **see** more cars. würden sie mehr Autos sehen.
If Debbie **gave up** her part-time job, Wenn Debbie ihre Teilzeitstelle aufgeben würde, / aufgäbe,	she **could go** to choir practice more often. könnte sie öfter zur Chorprobe gehen.
If the town **had** a movie theater, Wenn die Stadt ein Kino hätte,	they **might go** and see a movie. würden sie sich vielleicht einen Film ansehen.

In diesen Nebensätzen mit *if* steht das *simple past.*

Wir drücken mit dem *if*-Satz im *simple past* Bedingungen aus,
a) deren Erfüllung unmöglich ist. (Heute ist Samstag. Es ist unmöglich, dass heute Montag ist.)
b) deren Erfüllung wir für zweifelhaft halten. (Wir bezweifeln, dass Debbie ihre Stelle aufgibt.)
Man nennt diese Bedingungen daher irreal *(unreal).*

Im Hauptsatz stehen *would, could* oder *might* + Infinitiv.

Wir drücken mit dem Hauptsatz aus, was geschehen würde oder könnte, falls die genannten Bedingungen erfüllt würden. („Was wäre, wenn ...?")

Manchmal wird statt *was* im *if*-Satz *were* gebraucht. *Were* ist meist förmlicher: If it **were** Monday, ...
Für Ratschläge verwenden wir *if I were you ...*: If I **were** you, I'd phone your parents now.

Das *simple past* im *if*-Satz bezieht sich auf die Gegenwart oder die Zukunft, nicht auf die Vergangenheit. Diesem *simple past* entsprechen im Deutschen „würde", „wäre", „hätte" oder ein anderer Konjunktiv (z. B. „aufgäbe").

⚠ Kein *would* im *if*-Satz!

Game

Make two groups. Pupils in group A imagine an unusual situation and ask pupils in group B:

What would you do
- if an elephant came into our classroom?
- if you met the US President?
- if you saw a little green man from Mars?

Pupils in group B must try to say what they would do. For example:
I would hide under the table./I think I would ...

→ Ex 1-4

Focus on GRAMMAR: Bedingungssätze: Typ III (Conditional sentences III) 4 A

As they drove through Tonganoxie, Megan said, "Is that Dino's Ice-Cream Parlor, Debbie, where all those cars are parked?" "Yes, it is," Debbie said. "Mom, can you stop here, please, and let us out? I'd like to introduce Megan to all my friends. I know they're in there, because I can see their cars." "But how will you get home if we leave you here?" her mother said. "You already missed the last bus that goes our way." "Tommy will drive us to the farm, I'm sure," Debbie said. Megan liked Tommy at once, but there was another boy at Dino's she liked even more. He liked her, too. He was from Germany and had just spent a year in the US on an exchange. But this was his last day. "I'm flying home tomorrow, Megan – I'm afraid," Rolf said. Megan thought: "He's really nice. Perhaps we'll meet again in Europe?"

Of course, Megan **wouldn't have met** Rolf **if** her uncle **had taken** a different route. **If** he **had taken** the usual route, they **wouldn't have driven** through Tonganoxie. **If** they **hadn't driven** through town, Megan **wouldn't have seen** the cars outside Dino's and …

If-Satz (*if*-clause)	Hauptsatz (main clause)
If Rolf **had taken** an earlier flight, Wenn Rolf einen früheren Flug genommen hätte,	Megan **would have missed** him. hätte Megan ihn verpasst.
If Megan **hadn't seen** all the cars, Wenn Megan nicht all die Autos gesehen hätte,	she **wouldn't have noticed** Dino's. hätte sie Dinos nicht bemerkt.
If Debbie **hadn't sent** any photos, Wenn Debbie keine Fotos geschickt hätte,	Megan **couldn't have recognized** Dino's. hätte Megan Dinos nicht erkennen können.
If Megan **had arrived** a week earlier, Wenn Megan eine Woche früher angekommen wäre,	she **might have seen** more of Rolf. hätte sie Rolf vielleicht öfter gesehen.
In diesen Nebensätzen mit *if* steht das Verb im *past perfect (= had + past participle).*	Im Hauptsatz stehen *would/could/might + have + past participle.*
Die mit diesen *if*-Sätzen ausgedrückten Bedingungen beziehen sich auf die Vergangenheit. Mit ihnen stellen wir uns etwas vor, das in Wirklichkeit nicht geschehen ist oder nicht so war. Man nennt diese Bedingungen daher – wie bei Typ II – irreal *(unreal).* Vergleiche:	Wir drücken mit dem Hauptsatz aus, was gewesen wäre, falls diese Bedingungen in der Vergangenheit erfüllt worden wären. („Was wäre gewesen, wenn …?")

Megan **arrived** on Saturday. (So war es in Wirklichkeit.)
If she **hadn't arrived** on Saturday, … (Das stellen wir uns nur vor.)

Im Hauptsatz können auch *would/could/might* + Infinitiv stehen. Wir drücken damit aus, was in der Gegenwart (oder Zukunft) der Fall wäre, falls die Bedingung im *if*-Satz erfüllt worden wäre, z. B.:

If Debbie **had saved** more of her wages, Wenn Debbie mehr von ihrem Lohn gespart hätte,	she **would have** more money (now). hätte sie (jetzt) mehr Geld.
If Megan **hadn't gone** to Kansas, Wenn Megan nicht nach Kansas gefahren wäre,	she **wouldn't know** anything about Rolf (now). wüsste sie (jetzt) nichts von Rolf.

⚠ *'d* kann Kurzform von *had* oder von *would* sein:
If she**'d** (= she **had**) arrived a day later, she**'d** (= she **would**) have missed Rolf.

→ Ex 5-8

4A

Exchange visits

Many tourists who go to the USA have a good vacation but find out little about the people who live there.
Teenagers have other possibilities. You can go on an exchange program – for a few weeks perhaps or even for a year. You can stay with a family and share their daily lives. You will find out much more than a normal tourist can, as these reports show. They were written for *Amerika-Haus* by two teenagers from Germany.

"In April, 22 girls and boys from my school took part in an exchange program with a high school in North Carolina. The school had sporting grounds, a big parking lot for the school buses, and an even bigger parking lot for the students' cars!
Kay, my exchange partner, was a Korean American and 17 years old. We went to school together and on trips. She gave me her room and slept with her sister.
We visited an Indian village, watched a baseball game, made a birthday cake, swam in the ocean, went to church, ate Easter eggs, rode on a huge roller coaster, had fun … It was all over much too quickly. In July the Americans are coming to Germany to visit us and to see how we live."

Ute Dorfner, Halle

"On the third evening of my year in Kansas, Ricky and Carol, the people I was staying with, introduced me to their neighbors' son and he invited me to go out to Dino's Ice-Cream Parlor with him. It was the first time I'd ridden in a car that was driven by a sixteen-year-old!
At school I talked with a guidance counselor about which six classes I'd like to take. A day has six periods and you have the same six subjects every day, in the same order, five days a week. Everyone has American history, English and a sport (I chose swimming). And I decided to take art, typing and math. No geography for me this year, no German, no …
There was a flag in every classroom, and before the first class every day, all the students had to stand up, put their right hands on their hearts and say the 'Pledge of Allegiance'.
The most beautiful part of my visit was when Ricky and Carol took me on a trip to the Rocky Mountain National Park.
But the most exciting part of my visit was when I left them and went to summer camp for a month. It was near a lake and we did a lot of water-skiing. I also went to a class on computers, and in the evenings we had camp fires. Most of the other kids were from big cities in the East, but some came from abroad. They wanted to have fun and learn English at the same time."

Rolf Rosenberger, Passau

At summer camp

Working with the text

a 1. Look at page 42 and make notes of things that may have been surprising and new for Ute or Rolf. 2. Choose one or two of these things and say what you like/don't like about them. 3. Imagine a young American has come to visit you. What would she/he perhaps find surprising or new about the area where you live and the way of life there? 4. Imagine you are this American teenager. Write some lines in your diary about your feelings and thoughts on your first day in Germany.

b **Writing a formal letter**

One of Debbie's friends, Sue Baker, was interested in a visit to Germany. At school she was given the address of AFS in New York. She wrote to them, and this is the letter she got back.

AFS INTERCULTURAL PROGRAMS USA

313 EAST 43rd STREET
NEW YORK, NEW YORK 10017
(212) 949-4242

Miss Sue Baker
164 Opeka Street
Tonganoxie, KS 66086

5/20/95

Dear Sue,

Thank you for your letter and your questions on our Intercultural Programs. We are glad that you are interested in our exchange programs to Germany.

I see from your letter that you are 16 and in the 10th grade. The information I am sending you will show you that there are several possibilities for exchange visits. If you have further questions, please write to us again. We would be pleased to help you.

Thank you again and best wishes.

Sincerely,

Tara Texiera

Tara Texiera
Program Information Assistant

Try to imagine you are Sue and write the letter she originally wrote to AFS in New York. Introduce yourself and say what you would like to do.
Here's some important information about formal letters:

- How to start your letter:
  If you don't know the person's name: Dear Madam *or* Dear Sir *or* Dear Sir or Madam,
  If you know the person's name: Dear Mr/Mrs/Miss/Ms Smith
  ⚠ In AE a colon is used in business letters (Dear Madam: ...)
  Generally, a period is used in AE with Mr., Mrs., Dr., and Ms.
- Use long forms, e.g. We are ... (Short forms, e.g. We're . . . , are used in informal letters.)
- How to end your letter:
  AE Sincerely (yours),
  BE Yours faithfully,
  Yours sincerely, (if you've written the person's name at the beginning of the letter)
- ⚠ In *AE* the month is put before the day, e.g.: 4/3/95 = April 3rd, 1995
  3/4/95 = March 4th, 1995.

Focus on WORDS: Traveling and vacation

About 40 years ago only very few young Germans like Rolf had a chance to spend a year as an exchange student in the US or other foreign countries. In those days hardly any people could afford a vacation abroad. Since then things have changed a lot. In fact, we wouldn't be surprised if Rolf and Megan met in Munich or Leipzig, at Frankfurt airport, at a youth hostel in Amsterdam or at an international youth camp in France. Traveling abroad means +among many other things meeting new people of different nationalities, a chance to practice your +knowledge of a foreign language, to learn about different cultures, traditions and ways of life.

1 Collecting and arranging words: Here's a list of words and phrases you'll find helpful when you're making vacation plans and going on vacation. Put as many words as you can in one of the three groups a-c. You may add more words.

abroad airport arrive +baggage beach bed and breakfast bike tour boat +book a flight +brochure bus by plane camp site car caravan cathedral change money charter flight city climate clothes coach coast country cross crowded do pottery fare farm ferry festivals flight fly +flying time go by car go by ferry go camping go fishing go sailing guest house hotel international youth camp island journey land leave lie in the sun meals meet at the airport meet friends mountains museum (un)pack picnic rain relax resort +return fare return flight road rock climbing room route safari park +sightseeing tour skiing souvenirs station stay subway summer sunny sunshine swimming taking photos taxi ticket tour travel agency trip underground unload winter youth hostel

a **Planning and booking a vacation**
Places to go: abroad, …
Type of vacation: beach vacation, …
Weather: climate, …
+Accommodation: hotel, …
Transportation: fare, …

b **+Preparations for a trip**
pack suitcases, ask neighbor or friend to …, call…, …

c **At the vacation resort**
Attractions: safari park, …
Activities: do pottery, …
Souvenirs: clothes, …

2 Words in use

a Translate the combinations into German and use them in sentences.
Example: You look very tired. I think you need a vacation.

need/take/afford/have/spend/enjoy <u>a vacation</u>
go on/be on/return from <u>vacation</u>
a short/long/four-week/family/skiing <u>vacation</u>
<u>vacation</u> activities/guides/centers/apartments

b Discuss one of these two statements:
1. A trip to a foreign country can open your eyes and change your views.
2. Modern tourism is a danger to health and the environment.

1 A difficult time for everybody *Practice conditional sentences I and II.*

a Life isn't much fun for Ed at the moment. At school he doesn't work hard and doesn't get good grades. He doesn't listen and so he doesn't remember things. Although he likes football, he doesn't practice much and doesn't play as well as other people. He doesn't try hard enough and so he isn't chosen for the school team. He never brushes his hair and so he looks untidy. He doesn't have a bath very often and so he can't find a girlfriend.
His sister wants to help him. She is sure that he can change and sometimes says to him:
"If you work harder, you will get better grades. If you listen, you … . If you practice …" *Go on.*

b Ed's parents are less sure than their daughter. They don't really believe that Ed will change. So, when they speak to him, they say: "If you worked harder, you would get …" *Go on.*

c Why does Ed's sister use conditional I while his parents use conditional II? Can you say what the difference is between conditional I and conditional II?

2 If I had a magic wand, … *Practice conditional sentences II.*

If I had a magic wand,
I would/could/might …

… help the hungry in …

… stop the war in …

…

… invent a machine that would do my homework!

In all parts of the world there are problems, big ones and little ones. All that anyone would need to solve these problems is a magic wand. What would *you* do if you had a magic wand?

Choose four things you would/might do. Then, alone or with a partner, describe your ideas to the class and discuss them.

3 What would you do in these situations? *Practice conditional sentences II.*

You win $200 – lose your passport – see an accident on a country road – find a bag of money in the park – hear strange noises during the night – play football and break a window – …

I don't really know. But I think … / I imagine … Perhaps … I'm sure …	I would …

Example:
I don't really know. But I think if I won $200, I would invite my friends to a pizza in an Italian restaurant. I'm sure we would all have a good time.

4 Imagine you had a time-machine …
Practice conditional sentences II.

If you had a time-machine, and if you were allowed to stop three times – in the past or in the future – where would you stop? What would you do there? Who would you meet?

Example:
If I had a time-machine, I would first fly back to the year 1492. I would land on Columbus's ship Santa Maria before he reached America. Then I would suggest that he …

5 William Penn *Look back at Unit 3 and make sentences that begin with "If ...".*

1. Penn's father went to sea and became an admiral.
   If Penn's father hadn't gone to sea, he wouldn't have ...
2. Admiral Penn helped the King, so the King helped him.
3. Because he was a Quaker leader, Penn was put in the Tower.
4. The Admiral spoke to the King and Penn was given his freedom.
5. The King owed the Penns money, so he gave Penn a colony.
6. Penn didn't choose the colony's name, so it wasn't called New Wales.
7. Penn didn't stay in England, so he couldn't be put in prison again.
8. Not everybody was happy, so Penn decided to sell the colony.
9. Penn became ill and died, so he didn't sell Pennsylvania.

6 The right decision? *Say whether you would have done the same. Begin "If I had ...".*

1. Robin Hood stole money and gave it to the poor. He didn't keep it for himself.
   If I had been Robin, I would (not) have ...
2. When he landed in America, Columbus called the people he met "Indians".
3. When the soldiers caught Guy Fawkes, they took him to the Tower of London.
4. John Smith didn't ask the first Jamestown settlers to work, he forced them to work.
5. Some people had a chance to emigrate to America with the Pilgrims but didn't go.
6. William Penn decided to sell Pennsylvania back to the British government.
7. Dr Martin Luther King fought and died for equal rights.

Discuss your answers in class. Explain why you would have acted as you described.

7 We wouldn't have to learn English now if ... *Practice conditional sentences III.*

During the War of Independence, many colonists discussed the kind of flag they wanted for their new republic. They also talked about a new national language. In Pennsylvania, where 25% of the settlers were from Germany, some people suggested German. But German settlers were only 6% of the whole white population of America. Most settlers were of British origin – as was shown in 1790, when the population of the USA was first counted – so English was chosen. For the many colonists who spoke little English, and for future Americans, help came from Noah Webster. He wrote an English grammar book in 1784, and a dictionary soon followed. A book on spelling that he wrote was almost as popular as the Bible.

If most settlers had been German, what might have happened or wouldn't have happened?

If most settlers had been German, ... *Go on.*

8 In English, please:

1. Wenn das Wetter morgen gut ist, gehen wir zum Strand. 2. Ich könnte mit dir kommen, wenn ich mehr Zeit hätte. 3. Wenn du dich beeilt hättest, hätten wir den Bus vielleicht noch bekommen. 4. Ich würde dir sagen, wie spät es ist, wenn ich eine Uhr hätte. 5. Wenn ich mehr Zeit gehabt hätte, hätte ich dir jeden Tag eine Karte geschickt. 6. Wenn du nicht zu müde bist, können wir uns einen Film ansehen. 7. Ich wäre früher da gewesen, wenn ich nicht so viele Fotos gemacht hätte. 8. Wir könnten jetzt essen, wenn du unser Picknick nicht vergessen hättest.

9 Revision: Adjective or adverb?

Lan did not want to defend herself (public). She just walked away, first (slow), then she started running (fast). Inside she felt (terrible). And she cried (quiet), so that nobody would notice. She felt as if she had been attacked (violent). She had never expected such a (rude) word from the students in her class. She had been (nice) to them. She had not spoken (bad) of them or their country although life here was very (hard) for her family. For her it was (unimaginable) that anybody could be so (cruel). She wondered if they would ever be able to live (happy) in this country.

10 Revision: Relative clauses

Explain the following words to somebody who does not know what they mean. Use relative clauses with "who", "that", "which" or contact clauses.

ambulance bike messenger carrot cheerleader inventor thieves exchange partner computer guidance counselor

machine person vegetable vehicle (young) people

...

Example: An ambulance is a vehicle which takes sick people, or people who have had an accident, to a hospital.

11 "Mamas, don't let your babies grow up to be cowboys" (Willie Nelson/Waylon Jennings)

Try to rewrite part of an article that originally appeared in the American newspaper, Chicago Tribune, with the help of the following phrases.

Although many American mothers know this song by Willie Nelson and Waylon Jennings, many men – USA today – live with – cowboy inside them / cowboy – still – important figure – them / that figure – no more real – many of the figures – find in legends – stories
cowboy – 19th century – not – lonely hero on a horse – have many adventures / in fact – work – in a group of men – not often wear a gun / winter months – go home – cities – train – because often – not even own – horse
there – still cowboys today – but – not always ride – horse / often fly – helicopter – watch – cattle – sky

12 Listening comprehension: "Ridin' along in my automobile ..."

9 *Listen to the cassette, then answer these questions.*

1. What's "cruising"? 2. Who do Debbie and Megan meet? 3. Why do most American teenagers want to have their own car? 4. What's a "drive-in restaurant"? 5. What's special about a mobile home?

13 Say it in English: *Asking for and giving advice*

Some weeks before Megan came, Debbie went to see her guidance counselor, Mrs Wells.

My Welsh cousin Megan is coming to visit me soon. She'd like to come to school with me while she is here. Who should I see?

Well, I suggest that you discuss it first with the principal. I'm sure he'll be very pleased to have your cousin at the school.

All right. I'll do that today. What classes could she go to?

Why don't you leave that with me? I can work something out for her. Is she the same age as you?

Make a list of the expressions Debbie and Mrs Wells use to ask for or give advice. Here are some more:

Asking for advice:

Can you advise me what I should do (about . . .)?
I'd like to . . . . What should I do?
What should I do if . . . ?

Accepting advice:

I suppose you're right.
OK. Thanks very much.
Thanks for the advice.

Giving advice:

I think you should/ought to . . .
My advice would be to . . .
It might be a good idea to . . .
If I were you, I'd . . .

Rejecting advice:

I don't think . . .
Are you sure that's a good idea?
I don't really know if . . .
That doesn't sound like (such) a good idea.

a Now finish Debbie's conversation with Mrs Wells.

Debbie: a year younger
Mrs Wells: What subjects – Megan – at her school?
Debbie: don't know / letters – not much about school / Welsh comprehensive school
Mrs Wells: My advice – write – ask her
Debbie: I – do that / Thanks – advice

b Write and practice two more short dialogs. Use some of the expressions from above, too.

Debbie: have to work – evening – 4-7 / school – finish – 3 / What – do?
Mom: . . . come home – school bus – do homework / take you – later
Debbie: . . . / By the way – Tommy's party – Saturday / Tommy – drive me home
Mom: . . . – good idea? / . . . our car / Then – leave when you want
Debbie: . . .

Sue: . . . Mrs Wells, I – go – Germany next year / give me – information?
Mrs W.: Sure. . . . – write – two or three exchange organizations
Sue: Can they find – school?
Mrs W.: school – family – stay
Sue: think – good – go – foreign country?
Mrs W.: Well, if I – student today – go / great chance – meet people

14 WORDS WORDS WORDS

a Organize your words

ability	cheerleaders	death	member	poverty	tax
advice	choice	fare	musician	price	team
army	choir	feeling	nervousness	principal	thought
band	class	gang	organization	risk	tourist
bill	club	guidance counselor	pension	soldier	wages
change	crowd		population	student	

The underlined words are new in this Unit. Here are some ways to put words together. You will find that it is a good way to revise and learn words.

1. *Looking for nouns*
   (to) advise – advice
   (to) think – ?
   (to) choose – ?
   nervous – ?
   dead – ?
   poor – ?
   …

2. *Looking for people*
   school – students
   – ?
   – ?
   club – ?
   army – ?
   band – ?
   …

3. *"Money words"*
   bill: paper money, not coins
   tax: … *Go on.*

4. *People in groups*
   band: An army band played the national anthem when the President arrived.
   choir: … *Go on.*

b Trouble spot Spelling: SINGLE or DOUBLE consonant?

Fill in the missing consonants: "l" or "ll"? "m" or "mm"? "s" or "ss"? "t" or "tt"?

a- a-most Sco-land deve-oped intere-ting nece-ary promi-ed a-ways fu- i-agine ti- Sco-ish i-igrant ro-e we-come usua-y di-appointed a-owed pla-form Bri-ain bu-iness carefu- ca-endar co-ect fe-t po-ible di-agree a-one gla- unti-

c WORD BUILDER'S CORNER Adjectives which end in "-ful" or "-less"

success		successful	end		endless	help		helpful/helpless
peace		peaceful	worth		worthless	use	-ful	useful/useless
youth	-ful	youthful	sleep	-less	sleepless	care	-less	careful/careless
wonder		wonderful	home		homeless	hope		hopeful/hopeless
beauty		beautiful	time		timeless	power		powerful/powerless

Combination exercise

Use an adjective in "-ful" or "-less" with each of these nouns or noun phrases.

old lady writer sight night family orphan invention engine government information driver long winter handbook argument baby instrument fool park signs of peace

Write the phrases in your exercise book like this: a helpless old lady – eine hilflose alte Dame

○ Getting along in the USA: Using the telephone

The phone has just rung in the Thomases' house and Kenny has gone to answer it. Put the dialog in the right order.

– Sure.

– Hello?

– No, thanks. I'll go to the Pizza Palace later. Can you pick me up there at 8 o'clock?

– I'm still here at school. I've decided to stay and work on my history project with Carol.

– Thanks, Mom. See you later.

– OK, dear. Bye.

– Debbie, dear. Where are you?

– Wait a minute … Hey, Mom. It's Debbie.

– Have you had anything to eat yet? Shall I make dinner for you?

– Hi, Kenny. Can I talk to Mom, please?

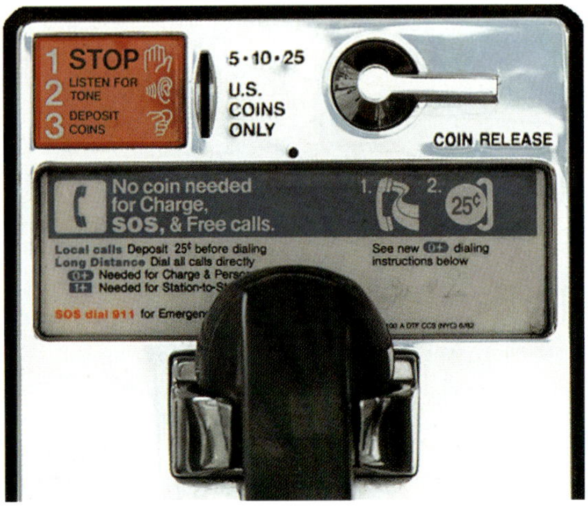

Debbie is at home and the phone has just rung.

Debbie: Hello? Debbie Thomas speaking.
Ms Alviar: Good morning. This is Rita Alviar from Blackwells'. Can I speak to Mr Thomas, please?
Debbie: I'm sorry. He's not home. Can I take a message?
Ms Alviar: Yes, please. Tell him his new tractor has arrived. If he wants to call me back, I'll be in my office until 5:30.
Debbie: OK. What did you say your name was?
Ms Alviar: Rita Alviar.
Debbie: Can you spell that, please?
Ms Alviar: Sure. A-l-v-i-a-r.
Debbie: Thanks. Bye.
Ms Alviar: Bye.

Collect as many "telephone" words and expressions as you can.

Role Play Work with a partner and practice making phone calls. You can reserve a hotel room, rent a car or book a flight, for example.

Did you know . . . ?

- *In the USA you cannot make phone calls at the post office. You have to use a public phone booth.*
- *If you want to make a long-distance phone call, you will need a lot of coins. So it is better to go to a bank first.*
- *A lot of companies and hotels have "toll-free numbers". That means they pay for the call when you call them. These numbers begin with 1-800.*

FOR MORE INFORMATION
or to ORDER BY PHONE
CALL TOLL FREE
1 (800) 634-6301
24 hours a day, 7 days a week

29 The star player

"We, we will succeed! We've got the power, the power we need!"
"We, we will succeed! We've got the power, the power we need!"

It was Friday night and the crowd in the Tonganoxie High School gym was shouting and cheering wildly for the school basketball team, the Chieftains. Debbie and her team of cheerleaders were jumping up and down excitedly and leading the cheering, while the band was playing as loudly as it could. The atmosphere was really exciting. Megan was in the crowd with her uncle and aunt. Mr Thomas was shouting the whole time. "Come on, Chieftains. Just one more basket, pl-e-e-ease."
The Chieftains *had* to win this game against St John's High School. They had lost their last three games, but now at last they had a real chance to win. There were only a few seconds left and the score was Chieftains 91: St John's 92 – and the Chieftains had the ball. One more basket, and the game was theirs! As the Chieftains' players ran across the floor, Debbie's eyes never left her boyfriend, Tommy Green. Tommy was the star player on the Tonganoxie team. He always made the most baskets.
The ball came to Tommy. He caught it, but at once he was surrounded by St John's players. "Here, Tommy, here!" shouted Steve Hitchcock from a good position near the basket. Tommy was in no position to shoot, but he didn't pass the ball to Steve. Instead, he jumped high into the air and threw the ball. It hit the edge of the basket and was caught by a St John's player.
Two more seconds and the game was over. The Chieftains had lost again.
As soon as Sid Lawrence, the team coach, saw Tommy after the game he shouted at him, "How many times do I have to tell you, Tommy? The plan was that you draw the St John's players away from the basket and then pass the ball to Eddie or Steve, so that they could score. But you don't listen! You think only of yourself, never of the team."
Tommy usually had a lot of respect for Mr Lawrence, but today he couldn't control himself. "What are you talking about? I *am* this team! Without me this team would be nothing."
"Shut your big mouth, Tommy," said Steve, Tommy's greatest rival. "Why didn't you pass the ball?"
"Steve is right, Tommy," said Rick. "You might be the top banana, but it's your fault that we lost today."
"Look, you guys, I took a chance. So what? It was our only chance to make that basket. Don't you see that?"
"That's where you're wrong, Tommy," said Mr Lawrence. "Steve was in a much better position. If you had passed the ball to him, he could have scored. You didn't even look at him – your eyes were only on the basket. Basketball is a team sport, Tommy. When are you going to learn that?"

Tommy took his things and walked to the door. "Okay," he said. "If you all know better – I'm quitting. You're playing against Weston next week. Let's see how good you are without me. I'll be there when you lose." The door shut behind him.

The next day everybody knew that Tommy Green had quit the school basketball team. Tommy was glad that the students and teachers were talking about him. He felt important. And he liked that, in or out of the gym.

"Who do these guys think they are?" he said as he drove away from school with Debbie. "Just wait till they play Weston. They have no chance." "Don't be too sure," said Debbie. "You're not the only player on the team."

"I'm the best," he said.

They drove along the main street and Tommy parked outside the ice-cream parlor. Tommy asked Debbie if she wanted to come in for a few minutes. Debbie said she still had some time as she didn't start work till four. Inside, their friends were sitting at different tables, where they were laughing and talking about school.

"Hi," said Tommy, and everybody turned around as he came through the door. He sat down with Debbie at an empty table. "You don't seriously think this team will get better without me, do you? Weston will walk all over them. Just wait. They'll soon ask me to come back. They'll be on their knees after the second game."

Debbie smiled at some of her friends. "Open your ears, Tommy. All the kids are saying the same thing: that you think the other players are only there to make sure you get the ball. Some are even enthusiastic about Steve and think he'll be a much better captain. At least if he was captain, it would be a team and not a one-man show."

Tommy looked at her angrily. "Whose side are you on anyway?"

"I'm not on anybody's side," she said. "The truth sometimes hurts."

"Come on, finish your drink. We're going."

"Maybe I don't want to go," she said.

"Okay, then stay here."

He got up and started to leave. "Hi, Sue," he called to another girl. "Are you going to be at the dance tomorrow night?"

"Sure," she said.

He looked back at Debbie and walked out to his car.

It seemed as if Tommy was right. The basketball team was easily beaten by Weston, and by the next team, too. But the third game finished with the score Tonganoxie Chieftains 74 : Benjamin Franklin High School 63. The fourth game, too, was won by the Chieftains. Steve Hitchcock, the new captain, was doing his job well. The whole team was now playing better with him as captain. Suddenly, people were no longer talking about Tommy Green. A few weeks before, he had been one of the most popular students. He had had a good chance to be the next Drama Club president; now he had no chance at all. Everybody had wanted to invite him to parties; now the other students were laughing and talking about parties he knew nothing about. Tommy was no longer so sure of himself. He no longer enjoyed the prestige he had had, and he missed it. Even more, he missed playing basketball – something that was more important to Tommy than anything else.

Everybody in Tonganoxie was happy that the basketball team seemed to be back in form again. Everybody except Tommy Green. Tommy did not feel happy. He only felt bitter. Then the team played – and won – again. This time the students decided to organize a dance to celebrate.

What was Tommy going to do now? He couldn't go and celebrate with the others. If he went, he would certainly feel bad. But if he stayed away, wouldn't he feel worse? Finally he decided to talk to Debbie, although she had avoided him since he had walked out of the ice-cream parlor. But she was still his girlfriend. Or was she? The next day after math, when all the other students had gone for lunch, he asked her if she was going to the dance on Saturday.

"Sure," she said.

"I thought maybe we could go together." She didn't say anything. "I'm sorry for the way I was," he added. "It was stupid of me. What do you say?" She looked up at him, thought for a second and said, "I'm sorry. I'm already going with somebody." And she walked away.

Working with the text

1 Summary writing

If you match the halves of the sentences correctly, you will get part of a summary. The endings of the sentences are in the right order.

1. Steve and Rick, two other players,	a) there's a fantastic atmosphere in the gym.
2. He throws the ball himself	b) the Chieftains have the chance to win the game.
3. During the game against St John's	c) the ball, but he is in a bad position.
4. After the game Mr Lawrence,	d) it to another player.
5. Debbie, his girlfriend, tells him	e) and misses the basket.
6. But he doesn't pass	f) the Chieftains' coach, shouts at Tommy.
7. Because of all this, Tommy	g) are angry with Tommy, too.
8. A few seconds before the end	h) leaves the team.
9. Tommy Green gets	i) that he is wrong.

Now tell the story to the end in your own words.

2 Why . . . ?

Try to answer these questions on the text. The phrases in the basket will help you.

1. . . . is everybody so excited that Friday night?
2. . . . doesn't Tommy pass the ball to Steve or Eddie?
3. . . . is Mr Lawrence so angry after the game?
4. . . . do Tommy and Debbie sit down at an *empty* table in the ice-cream parlor?
5. . . . does Tommy say "Hi" to Sue when he leaves the ice-cream parlor?
6. . . . does Tommy no longer have a chance to be the next Drama Club president?
7. . . . does Tommy want to go to the dance with Debbie?

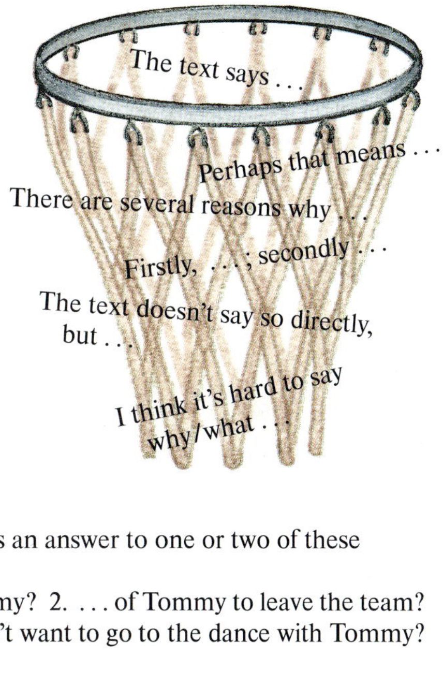

3 Is it right . . . ?

Discuss your opinions in class and then write a short text as an answer to one or two of these questions. Give reasons for your opinion, too.
1. . . . of Mr Lawrence and the others to be angry with Tommy? 2. . . . of Tommy to leave the team? 3. . . . of Debbie to tell him the truth? 4. . . . that she doesn't want to go to the dance with Tommy?

4 What do you think?

1. Should school sports have such importance as in the USA? 2. Why can stars sometimes be a problem for others? 3. Some people become stars when they are still very young. Why can that be a problem for them? 4. What should a good captain of a team be like? What should/shouldn't he/she do?

Unit 5 Young people in Britain and America

London, UK
pop.: 6,680,000
Asians: 635,000
Chinese: 53,000
Caribbeans: 294,000

New York, NY
pop.: 7,323,000
Hispanics: 1,787,000
Black Americans: 2,102,000

San Francisco, CA
pop.: 724,000
Asian Americans: 211,000

"The arrival after the 1940s of large numbers of immigrants from Third World countries ... was a break with the past."

Washington, D.C.
pop.: 607,000
Black Americans: 399,000

Birmingham, UK
pop.: 961,000
Asians: 138,000
Caribbeans: 45,000

Leicester, UK
pop.: 270,000
Asians: 68,000

Miami, FL
pop.: 359,000
Hispanics: 224,000

Leeds, UK
pop.: 681,000
Asians: 25,000

"Remember, always, that all of us, and you and I especially, are descended from immigrants."

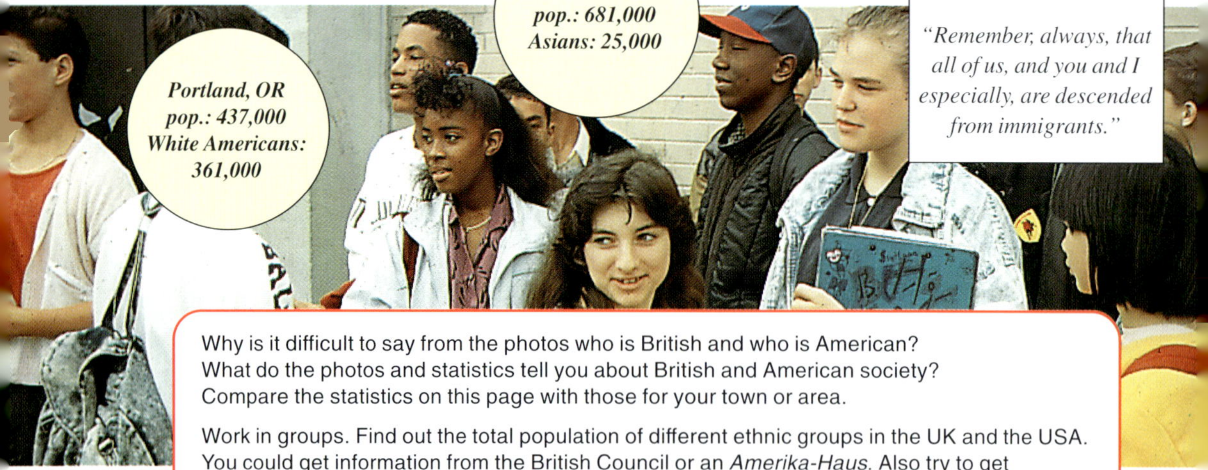

Portland, OR
pop.: 437,000
White Americans: 361,000

Why is it difficult to say from the photos who is British and who is American?
What do the photos and statistics tell you about British and American society?
Compare the statistics on this page with those for your town or area.

Work in groups. Find out the total population of different ethnic groups in the UK and the USA. You could get information from the British Council or an *Amerika-Haus*. Also try to get information about the total population and about ethnic groups in one or two German cities.

GROWING UP IN BRITAIN AND AMERICA

Before you read the texts, write a few sentences about one of the following:
- how you get along with your parents,
- what you think about politics and politicians,
- what job you would like to have,
- your money problems,
- the kind of things you are worried about.

Now read the texts and look at the illustrations. What kind of things are the teenagers talking about? Compare what you have written with what the five teenagers have written.

I just don't know where my money goes. I have a part-time job in a supermarket where I work after school and at the weekends, and I get money from my parents. But it's never enough. Life is one big financial disaster.
(Matthew, 15 – Birmingham, England)

Like a lot of my friends, I'm worried about the future of the world. When I see the wars and how people are suffering in other countries, I wonder whether there will ever be peace in the world.
(Maria, 14 – Columbia, South Carolina, USA)

I get along quite well with my parents. I sometimes think they are too strict, but most of the time they are helpful and we can talk about any problems I have. We have arguments regularly. But what kids don't argue with their parents?
(Jody, 14 – Denver, Colorado, USA)

I'm interested in politics, but I don't support any political party. I don't think the major parties really care about young people, possibly because we are too young to vote. I support a number of environmental groups. I believe the government should do more to protect the environment. I go to meetings and do all I can to help. *(Annabel, 14 – Exeter, England)*

I know that one day I'll leave school and then I'll have to look for a job. A lot of my friends know what they want to do. One of them already has plans for a firm of his own. But I have no idea what I could do. I'd like to do something useful, but I haven't found anything yet. I certainly don't want to find myself in a boring office job.
(Robin, 16 – Coventry, England)

Focus on GRAMMAR: Das Gerundium II (The gerund II)

a

In the USA over 1000 teenagers from 13 to 17 were recently asked about their ideas about family life. Most of the boys said they would like to get married, and they hoped that their wives would do the housework and be good **at cooking**. The boys said they might **consider washing** the dishes or **cutting** the grass, and they wouldn't **mind playing** games with the children, especially when the children were older. But few of them could **imagine staying** at home and **not going** out to work five days a week …

Rev. b

Du weißt schon lange, dass man die *-ing*-Form als Satzteil in der Rolle eines Nomens (d. h. als Gerundium) verwenden kann. Wie ein Nomen kann das Gerundium an verschiedenen Stellen im Satz stehen:

Cooking is easy. (subject)	I love **cooking**. (object)	I'm good at **cooking**. (preposition + gerund)

Das Gerundium kann durch ein Objekt oder eine adverbiale Bestimmung, z. B. eine Zeit- oder Ortsangabe erweitert werden.

Cooking omelettes is fun.	**Swimming at night** is fun.	**Swimming underwater** is fun.

Game

How far can you go? *One of you makes a sentence with a gerund. Then the next person adds something to it. How many more people can add something to it?*

Example: Choose/be a problem

Choosing a present can be a problem.
Choosing a birthday present can be a problem.
Choosing a birthday present for a friend can be …
Choosing an unusual birthday present for a friend can …
Choosing an unusual birthday present for a friend who …

Now try the same with these words:

1. Go/be exciting
2. Interview/be fun
3. Sell/be difficult
4. Ride/be dangerous

→ Ex 1, 2

c **Gerundium und *to*-Infinitiv nach bestimmten Verben**
(Gerund and *to*-infinitive after certain verbs)

1. Wie du weißt, steht nach gewissen Verben die *-ing*-Form. Beispiele für solche Verben sind: *admit* (= zugeben), *avoid, carry on* (= weitermachen), *consider, dislike* (= nicht mögen), *enjoy, finish, give up, imagine, keep, mention* (= erwähnen), *mind, miss, practise, risk, suggest.* → Ex 3

2. Nach folgenden Verben kann entweder das *gerund* oder der *to*-Infinitiv stehen: *begin, start, continue, like, love, prefer, hate, intend* (= vorhaben).

   My brother **likes to cook** exciting meals, but he doesn't **like washing** the dishes.

   ⚠ Nach *would like/love/hate/prefer* kann nur der *to*-Infinitiv stehen, z.B. **I'd like to get** married. → Ex 4

3. Nach *forget, remember, try* und *stop* kann zwar entweder das *gerund* oder der *to*-Infinitiv stehen, aber die Bedeutung ist jeweils unterschiedlich:

I'll never **forget arriving** in New York. Ich werde nie vergessen, wie ich in New York ankam.	I won't **forget to write** to you. Ich werde nicht vergessen an dich zu schreiben.

→ Ex 5

d The girls who were interviewed in the survey **believed in sharing** all the jobs in the home. Only 7% were **interested in staying** at home all day, while 86% wanted a career. Most of the girls wanted to have children, but **after staying** at home until their children started school, they wanted to have the **choice of going** back to work. So, if the men of tomorrow hope to avoid cooking and cleaning **by marrying**, it seems they are in **danger of being** disappointed. Most boys may **be against their wives having** jobs outside the home, but the girls of today have quite different ideas.

e **Das Gerundium nach Präpositionen** (The gerund after prepositions)

Are you **good at cooking**?
Kannst du gut kochen?

A lot of girls are not **interested in cooking**.
Viele Mädchen interessieren sich nicht fürs Kochen.

Have you got a **reason for asking** that?
Hast du einen Grund das zu fragen?

Rita **apologized for being** late.
Rita entschuldigte sich, dass sie zu spät kam.

Wie du weißt, steht ein Verb nach einer Präposition immer in der *-ing*-Form. Die Präposition kann verbunden sein:
- mit einem Adjektiv: *afraid of, crazy about, excited about, famous for, frightened of, good/bad at, interested in, proud of* (= stolz auf), *sorry about, worried about, wrong with*
- mit einem Nomen: *chance of, choice of, danger of, hope of, reason for*
- mit einem Verb: *apologize for, argue about, be against, believe in, complain about, consist of, decide against, dream of, hear of, succeed in, talk about, think about/of, worry about.*

⚠ Beachte, dass nach *look forward to* kein Infinitiv, sondern ein Gerundium steht:

My sister **is looking forward to meeting** you.

→ Ex 6-8

Lots of boys hope to avoid housework **by marrying** a woman who will do it.
…, indem sie/dadurch, dass sie eine Frau heiraten, …

Most girls want to have a career **instead of working** in the home all day.
… anstatt … zu arbeiten.

Das Gerundium steht auch nach bestimmten, allein stehenden Präpositionen (z. B. *after, before, by, instead of, without*). Im Deutschen verwenden wir dafür meist Nebensätze, die mit *nachdem, indem, dadurch dass, anstatt zu* usw. eingeleitet werden.

→ Ex 9

f **Das Gerundium mit eigenem „Sinnsubjekt"** (The gerund with its own subject)

Mrs Smith doesn't **like watching** TV late at night.
Mrs Smith sieht nicht gern spätabends fern.

Mrs Smith doesn't **like Tom/him watching** TV late at night.
Mrs Smith mag es nicht, wenn Tom/er spätabends fernsieht.

Vor das Gerundium kann man ein Nomen oder Pronomen stellen, um deutlich zu machen, dass sich das Gerundium nicht auf das Subjekt des Satzes bezieht, sondern ein eigenes Subjekt hat. Im formellen Englisch wird für das Subjekt des Gerundiums auch der *s*-Genitiv bzw. ein *possessive adjective* verwendet:

Formelle Form: Mrs Smith doesn't like **Tom's/his watching** TV late at night.

→ Ex 10

A problem for some teenagers is who to ask for advice when they need it: parents, teachers, the youth club leader, a sister or brother. Sometimes teenagers write to a magazine.

A·D·V·I·C·E

from Melanie

■ There's a girl in my class that I really like. But I'm sure she likes another boy. Two of my friends say that this girl likes me a lot and wants to meet me at the next school disco. I don't believe them. I'm quiet and shy, and they're lively and very popular. I don't believe what they say, because they played the same trick last Christmas and made a fool of me. What should I do?
(Chris, 14 – Oxford)

Don't listen to your friends and listen to yourself. You say you like this girl. Well, go and talk to her at the next school disco. You'll soon notice whether she likes you or not.

■ I come from an Asian family. Recently my parents bought a shop with a flat where we now live. It is in a neighbourhood where the majority of people are white. Most of the people are really nice and come to our shop. However, for the past few weeks a gang of youths has been attacking our home and they have been breaking the windows in the shop. The police come whenever we call them, but the gang comes back again the next night. What can we do? *(Rita, 15 – Leicester)*

My suggestion is to write to your MP. She or he can ask the police for a report and make sure that you are protected better. I am also sending you a list of addresses of different groups who help minorities if they feel they are threatened. Someone should be able to help you.

■ Mark and I have been going out for nine months and it's been really great, except that there's one problem: he's always jealous. When he has to work on Saturday night, he thinks I should stay at home. He even calls from work, and if I'm not there, he gets very angry. His behaviour is driving me crazy. How can I convince him he needn't worry about anything?
(Kelly, 15 – Manchester)

The year's most "popular" problems

When I read your letters from the past twelve months again, you seem to be especially worried about the following things:

- **Your parents have got or are getting divorced.**
- **You fall in love with somebody who is older than you are.**
- **You don't feel you are attractive to members of the other sex.**
- **Your best friend is going out with your girl-/boyfriend.**
- **You have a hopeless crush on a media star.**

Read and discuss the first two letters and answers. What do you think of Melanie's advice? Would you have given the same advice?
Now write an answer to the third letter.
Write your own letters. They can be about real or imaginary problems, funny or serious.
Your teacher will collect the letters and give you someone else's. Write an answer to it.
Read out some of the letters and the answers in class and talk about them.

Pocket-money

How much pocket-money do you think young people of your age should get?
Do your friends get more pocket-money than you?
How do you spend your pocket-money?
Do you save any?

Read the texts on this page and decide with a partner where the following numbers belong: 4, 4, 4.80, 11, 12, 16, 16, 85, 2000, 2000. The places for the numbers are marked with ◗.

Have you ever been told by your children that all their friends get more pocket-money than they do? – Last year ◗ parents were interviewed by our reporters. All the information was then put together and you will be able to read about the results next week in our

POCKET-MONEY SURVEY.

All in next week's PARENTS' MAGAZINE.

How much pocket-money do young people save? What is all the pocket-money spent on? **Nicholas Martin** reports.

The great pocket-money myth

Almost all parents are told by their children that their friends get more pocket-money. The results from PARENTS' MAGAZINE's big "Pocket-Money Survey" show that this is a myth. More than ◗ parents took part in our survey. Here are some of the questions we asked:

- How much pocket-money do you give your child?
- What does your child do with his or her money?
- How much of it is saved?
- Do you tell your child what the money should be spent on?

And here are some of the results that came out of the survey:

- Most children are not given very much.
- Younger children (between ◗ and ◗) save quite a lot. Not very much is saved by teenagers.
- The amount of "advice" gets less for children over the age of ◗, and young people over ◗ are no longer normally told by their parents what their money should be spent on.
- Many parents use pocket-money to influence children's behaviour.

For all those parents whose children are teenagers the "Pocket-Money Survey" is a must.

More about the survey:

- ◗% of all teenagers up to the age of ◗ get pocket-money.
- The average amount is £◗.
- Young people in London get the most pocket-money: £◗.
- Most pocket-money is spent on evenings out.

Discuss your decisions about the numbers in the text. Do you all agree where each number belongs?
Do you think what the article says is true for Germany, too? Think about what it says about saving, parents' "advice", parents using pocket-money to influence behaviour.
Do you find anything surprising in the results of the survey? If so, what?
What do you think about the average amounts of pocket-money that are mentioned?

Focus on WORDS: Talking about people

Each of us lives in a +network of +human +relations. We belong to a certain +race, a nation and a +social class. We are members of a club, a choir, a band, a political party or other groups. Every day we meet lots of people in different situations: other members of the family, relatives, pupils, friends, neighbors, immigrants, teachers at school. With all these people we +communicate: with some we have friendly conversations, with others we argue. How we get along with each other +depends on our own +character and our behavior towards each other. It's easy to get along with friendly, kind and tolerant people. With jealous, impatient or rude people we often feel unhappy.

1 Collecting and arranging words: Here's a list of words you can use to describe people. Put the words in the groups a-d. (Some words may go in more than one group.)

Afghans Africans agree with alone angry with annoy annoyed argue bitter bored boss careless care about comfortable convince crazy about defend disappointed drive sb. crazy Europeans excited feel sorry for make a fool of frightened gang +get on sb.'s nerves happy hate helpful Hispanics hopeless immigrants impolite influence jealous lazy neighbors nervous parents party patient with peaceful persecute pleased with polite proud of rough safe shy +tense threaten tolerant +upset worried about

a **Groups you can belong to**
- Germans, …
- ancestors, teenagers, …
- family, team, …

b **People's +attitudes towards other people**
They can
- like, love, … other people.
- dislike, … other people.

They can be
- friendly, nice, … towards other people.
- strict with, cruel to, … other people.

c **People's behavior towards other people**
They can
- understand, help, advise, protect, apologize to, … other people.
- complain about, fight with, defeat, … other people.

d **How people can feel in the company of others**
They can be/feel
- confident, relaxed, …
- sad, lonely, afraid, …

2 Words in use

a Write a short text about Ayntye, using the information and notes given below.

BACKGROUND
Ayntye •15-year-old girl •lives with her parents in Schweinfurt •pupil at a local school •younger brother •parents came from Turkey •parents own a shop •Ayntye born in Turkey •5 years in Germany •Ayntye helps in shop

OFTEN FEELS
•sad •lonely •bitter

FRIENDS MUST BE
•fair •tolerant •patient •nice towards other people

CHARACTER
•jealous •helpful •shy •not very sure of herself

DISLIKES PEOPLE WHO ARE
•unfair •not tolerant •stupid

b Make a similar "network" for yourself or somebody you know very well.

1 Revision: Spelling the *-ing* form

How do you spell the -ing form of each of the following verbs?

be eat get give hope leave lie make run say see sit stop try

2 Revision: The gerund as subject and object

a *Make comparisons. Your partner must say if he/she agrees.*

Examples:
1. Playing tennis is more exciting than watching TV.
– That's true. Especially if you win!
2. I find saying hallo easier than saying goodbye.
– I agree. It's usually much easier.

play tennis – watch TV
say hallo – say goodbye
be a girl – be a boy
feel happy – look beautiful
lie on a beach – sit in school
prepare a meal – eat a meal
sail a boat – swim 400 m
learn English – learn Greek

You could use these adjectives:

boring dangerous difficult easy exciting hard important interesting nice useful

b *Make three more comparisons of this kind, but use your own ideas (not the ones in part 2a).*

3 Last summer *Peter is telling a friend about his holiday in Wales. Complete the text with these verbs.*

ask drive lose pay sit smoke spend take travel unload

Grandad suggested … our holiday in Kenya, but he didn't mention … for it, so we just went to Wales. Getting there was boring. I don't enjoy … by car, as I dislike … still for hours and hours. I kept … Mum to stop for a break, but she just carried on … until we got there.
Our caravan was on a lovely site and, after we'd finished … all our things from the car, I said I wouldn't mind … a few photos. The girl from the next caravan came with me. She was very nice, but she had a bad cough. I noticed that she smoked. I knew I risked … my new friend at once, but I said: "Perhaps you ought to give up … ." "I'm trying to," she said.
I got a postcard from her yesterday. "Stopped smoking," it said, "I feel great. See you next summer?"

4 Maria's pen-friend

a *Complete Maria's sentences with gerunds or to-infinitives. (Sometimes you can use both.)*

My pen-friend, Cathy, dislikes (fly), but she loves (travel) by train. She enjoys (play) basketball, but she prefers (swim). She has begun (learn) German, but she is carrying on (do) Spanish, too. She would like (leave) school, but she is considering (go) to college. She wants (be) a dancer.

b *Say what your own pen-friend (or another friend) dislikes, loves, enjoys, prefers, has begun …*

5 Gerund or infinitive?

As you know, some verbs can be followed by a gerund or a *to*-infinitive with little or no change in meaning (e.g. Alex **likes reading** travel magazines, while Pat **likes to read** computer magazines).
However, a few verbs can be followed by either **a gerund or a *to*-infinitive** with a **difference of meaning**:

– **forget doing** sth.	vergessen, dass/wie man etwas getan hat
forget to do sth.	vergessen etwas zu tun
– **remember doing** sth.	sich daran erinnern, dass/wie man etwas getan hat
remember to do sth.	daran denken, etwas zu tun
– **try doing** sth.	etwas ausprobieren, es mit etwas probieren
try to do sth.	versuchen/sich bemühen etwas zu tun, was schwierig ist

⚠ Be careful: *stop* is followed by the gerund when it means "mit etwas aufhören", e.g.

Stop **talking**. (= Hör auf zu reden!)

But, like other verbs, *stop* can be followed by a *to*-infinitive (... um zu ...), e.g.

I stopped **(in order) to buy** a paper. (= Ich hielt an um eine Zeitung zu kaufen.)

Use the correct form of the first verb in the brackets together with the gerund or to-infinitive of the second verb. Then translate the sentences into German.

1. You left the lights on all night. Don't (forget/switch) them off when you go to bed tonight.
2. I feel so tired, but I really must (try/finish) my homework before I go to bed.
3. I'll never (forget/cross) the Channel in a heavy storm.
4. I'll always (remember/fly) for the first time.
5. Don't (forget/take) your raincoat. It hasn't (stop/rain).
6. Phil arrived at the party a little late, because he'd (stop/buy) some flowers.
7. If the door isn't open, (try/knock).
8. Oh dear, I didn't (remember/buy) tickets.
9. Don't (forget/buy) some milk when you go to the supermarket.
10. The shop on the corner has (stop/sell) fireworks.
11. If Sue isn't in her office, (try/phone) her home number.
12. Please (remember/phone) us as soon as you've arrived safely.

6a My family *Say it in one sentence, not two. Use a gerund.*

Example: Dad prepares our picnics. He's good at it.
Dad is good at preparing (our) picnics.

1. Dad might lose his job. He's worried about it.
2. Mum is Welsh. She's proud of it.
3. I tell terrible jokes. I'm famous for it.
4. I'm going on TV. I'm excited about it.
5. My sister dances a lot. She's crazy about it.
6. My brother can't read maps. He's bad at it.
7. He broke my camera. He's sorry about it.
8. I don't like flying. I'm afraid of it.

"I'm sick and tired of making you endless cups of tea."

b *What are you (or your family or friends) good at doing or bad at doing? What are you afraid of doing or not afraid of doing? What are you worried about?*
Make five sentences with gerunds, one for each of these expressions: afraid of *(doing)*, bad at *(doing)*, good at *(doing)*, proud of *(doing)*, worried about *(doing)*.

7 a A break from learning *Add a preposition and a gerund. Use:* about (2×), against, of (2×), to.

Tina needn't worry … (fail) her exams. She is in no danger … (do) that. She has got every chance … (get) good marks, as she has worked very hard. Now she is thinking … (have) a break from her books. She visited her grandparents only last week, so she has decided … (visit) them again. She is looking forward … (spend) a weekend at her aunt's in Leeds.

b *Now ask your partner:* What are you looking forward … (do) at the weekend/next week?

8 A trip to New York. In English, please – with gerunds

1. Es hat mir nichts ausgemacht, so lange am Flughafen zu warten. – I didn't mind …
2. Ich würde es nicht riskieren, nachts allein in New York spazieren zu gehen.
3. Einige aus unserer Gruppe waren besorgt ihre Pässe zu verlieren.
4. Während des Flugs waren einige nur daran interessiert, den Film zu sehen.
5. Ich habe aus dem Fenster geschaut in der Hoffnung die Küste zu sehen.
6. Ich freue mich darauf, Manhattan zu sehen.
7. Ich habe immer davon geträumt, nach Amerika zu fliegen.
8. In New York nicht in ein Musical zu gehen ist fast ein Verbrechen.
9. Für mich sind die Musicals ein Grund viel Zeit in New York zu verbringen.

I ♥ NY

9 At summer camp *Make one sentence out of two. Use a preposition with a gerund.*

Example: Janet will arrive at her camp tomorrow. Then she will choose her courses. (After …)
After arriving at her camp tomorrow, Janet will choose her courses.

1. At this camp many teenagers choose water sports. They don't try drama or art. (… instead of …)
2. The campers get up at about 6.30. Then they have a quick shower. (After …)
3. They always have a good breakfast. Then they begin the day's main activities. (… before …)
4. Some teenagers do as much sport as possible. They hope to get fitter or thinner. (By …)
5. In the evening most campers are tired. They have run or swum all day. (… after …)
6. The campers go to bed at 10. This is after they have sung songs round a camp fire. (Before …)
7. Last night one boy, Dan, went into his tent and fell asleep. He didn't say good night. (… without …)
8. Early this morning Dan woke everybody. He sang his favourite song. (… by …)

10 I hate it!

a *Make ten sentences that say what you like or don't like doing.*

Examples:
1. I like getting up late.
2. I don't like arriving late.
3. I like eating in the cinema.

b *Now say how you feel when your friends or other people do those things.*

Examples:
1. I don't mind other people getting up late.
2. I hate my friends arriving late.
3. I don't really like …

c *What do your family or your friends think about you? Write down six sentences.*

Examples:
1. Our cat doesn't like me playing the piano.
2. Dad worries about me failing my …

d *Exchange papers with a partner. Tell the class about your partner.*

Examples:
1. Uschi's cat doesn't like her playing the …
2. Ali's Dad worries about him failing his …

11 Revision: Possessive adjectives with parts of the body

Remember: In English possessive adjectives are used with parts of the body and with clothes, where we would use the definite article in German.

Example: I took off **my** gloves and rubbed **my** hands.
Ich zog **die** Handschuhe aus und rieb mir **die** Hände.

"I've got this constant buzzing in my ears."

(buzzing ['bʌzɪŋ] = *Summen*)

Translate these sentences into English.

1. Während ich auf den Bus wartete, rieb ich mir die Hände, denn es war kalt. 2. Die Füße taten mir auch weh. 3. Und ich hatte etwas im Auge. 4. Der Mann vor mir an der Haltestelle hatte einen warmen Hut auf dem Kopf und er hatte einen Ring *(= ring)* im Ohr. 5. Nach ein paar Minuten bemerkte ich, dass er sich den Arm gebrochen hatte. 6. Die junge Frau hinter mir sagte mindestens zehnmal zu einem kleinen Jungen: „Nimm die Hände aus der Tasche.“ 7. Sie war vielleicht seine Tante. Als wir im Bus saßen, bemerkte ich, dass sie keinen Ring am Finger hatte.

12 Revision: Possessive adjectives + *own*

Translate these sentences into English. Remember to use a possessive adjective before "own".

1. Ich habe ein eigenes Zimmer, weil mein Bruder jetzt eine eigene Wohnung hat. 2. Ich habe sie mit eigenen Augen gesehen. 3. Sie ist nicht teuer, da sie keine eigene Küche hat. 4. „Martin muss auf eigenen Füßen stehen“, sagt meine Mutter. 5. „Ja“, sagt mein Vater. „Er hat eigene Vorstellungen, wie er leben möchte. Es ist gut, dass er jetzt beginnt ein eigenes Leben zu führen.“

13 Revision: The article *Put in "the" or "a" where necessary.*

Mary Bell lived in … village in … north-west of England in … early 19th century. Like … most people in … village, … Bells were very poor. So, for Mary, going to … work was soon more important than going to … school. When she was only 12, she had to work in … factory for nine hours … day. … conditions in … factory were bad. There was little light, … air was full of smoke … most of … time, and … noise was terrible. Of course, … situation was … same for … most other children of Mary's age. Many of her friends stole … money or … food, and some had to go to … prison. Mary herself was often ill and died as … young woman of 17.

4 WORDS WORDS WORDS

a Collocations

Collocations are regular combinations of words. If you learn words in collocations you can avoid many mistakes. Here are some examples of English collocations:

A	have an accident	*(verb + noun)*
B	a serious accident	*(adjective + noun)*
C	a crowd of people	*(noun + noun)*
D	badly injured	*(adverb + adjective/ participle)*
E	drive carefully	*(verb + adverb)*

A

1. worship	a) pain
2. make	b) God
3. change	c) an exam
4. suffer	d) a battle
5. fail	e) mistakes
6. fight	f) trains

B

1. weak	a) potatoes
2. true	b) presents
3. public	c) taxes
4. useful	d) tea
5. high	e) transport
6. boiled	f) friends

Which words go together in the groups A-E? Add more collocations to each group.

C

1. pedestrian	a) stations
2. shop	b) information
3. travel	c) stop
4. a bus	d) boots
5. police	e) assistants
6. football	f) crossings

D

1. bitterly	a) packed
2. seriously	b) quiet
3. highly	c) disappointed
4. completely	d) ill
5. deadly	e) wrong
6. tightly	f) interesting

E

1. rain	a) brightly
2. complain	b) easily
3. share	c) equally
4. burn	d) bravely
5. win	e) bitterly
6. fight	f) heavily

b Trouble spot: of mine, of yours, of his, of hers, of ours, of theirs

Compare: Jeff is **my friend**. = I've got a friend. His name is Jeff.

Jeff is **one of my friends**.
Or: Jeff is **a friend of mine** (⚠ *not:* ~~of me~~). } = I've got several friends. Jeff is one of them.

Change the following sentences by using *of mine*, *of yours, etc*.

1. One of my cousins has been to Colorado. 2. When Maureen needed help, she called one of her friends. 3. Maureen's brother is meeting some of his friends tonight. 4. Is Mrs Warburton one of your teachers? 5. I want you to meet two of my friends. 6. Do Maureen and Scott know Mrs Black? – Yes, she's one of their relatives. 7. We haven't been to Washington. But some of our school friends were there on an exchange visit last year. 8. John doesn't know much about computers. But one of his friends is a computer expert.

c WORD BUILDER'S CORNER — Nouns and verbs with the same form

love Liebe	end Ende	call Anruf	rule Herrschaft
(to) love lieben	(to) end (be)enden	(to) call anrufen	(to) rule (be)herrschen

Here are more words of this kind. (You know either the noun or the verb or both.) Write them down in your exercise book.

dance dream escape fight hate paint promise race repair report sail sleep start switch test

Make two sentences with each of these words. Use each word as a noun and as a verb.

answer change cook crash escape help paint promise race test travel visit

Getting along in the USA: Information in local papers

On a short visit to the USA, you might just want to visit some of the most famous sights. If you have a little more time, it might be a good idea to read the local newspaper. It will tell you what is going on, and you might find something you want to buy. Look at these ads from the *Los Angeles Times* and find out:

- who sells cheap clothes,
- where you can go riding,
- when, where and how you could see the Rolling Stones,
- who to call if you want to take part in a TV game show.

COLLECTIBLES 1095

★ **CHUCK JONES** - IN PERSON ★ Book signing and show Dec 1 & 2 Gage Gallery 714/854-5697

PUBLIC AUCTION – 100's of collectible toys, cars, trains, comics etc. Sun 11/6 at 1 pm. Call 213/941-8602 for details.

★ ***RECORD ALBUM COLLECTION*** $275. 714/886-2476

ROUTE 66 orig road sign, blk/wht 2'x2', $300, 619-551-0753

ENTERTAINMENT 1265

GRATEFUL DEAD 2 tix 12/9, sect. 29, $40 ea, 818/889-5530

★ **JOHNNY MATHIS** ★ Dec 1 & 2, rows A & B, 6 tix at $45 each 213-733-3859

LAKERS vs New York 2 good seats 11/26 $75 Call Steve 818/548-3495

★ **PAUL MC CARTNEY** ★ 11/27 2 tix cntr sec B row 14 $375 ea 818-449-5017

ROLLING STONES 2 tix 12/6 Indianapolis. $200 213-397-1471

TV CONTESTANTS 1270

★ **WIN BIG MONEY & PRIZES** ★ TV contestants wanted. Call Family Feud 213/965-9999

★ **'RODEO DRIVE'** ★ New Game Show. FUN! CASH! PRIZES! Call 213/465-5413 Mo-Fr 10am-5pm

★ **'SCRABBLE'** Needs energetic contestants. Call 213/284-8644

SEA KAYAK THE CHANNEL ISLANDS

EXPLORE THE WORLD'S LARGEST SEA CAVE

- The ultimate wilderness adventure
- Paddle with dolphins and whales
- One & two day trips

No experience needed (you won't even get wet unless you want to).

Santa Barbara Watersports 119 State St., Santa Barbara, CA 93101. · Reservations: 805 / 564-8815

"THE MOST UNIQUE ADVENTURE IN SOUTHERN CALIFORNIA"

HOT AIR BALLOON RIDES

HIGH ADVENTURES

Flying out of Moorpark & Lancaster

(818) 891-8864

- ★ $1 off per hour, (Mon-Fr) with coupon*
- ★ Night/moonlight rides
- ★ Riding lessons
- ★ Open 7 days a week

SUNSET RANCH
3400 North Beachwood Dr. in Griffith Park

(213) 464-9612 • (213) 469-5450

*One coupon per person

AMERICAN CLASSICS

USED LEVI JACKETS $45
2ND HAND COWBOY BOOTS $99
NEW & USED LEATHER JACKETS
HARLEY DAVIDSON MOTORCYCLE BOOTS $79
COLLECTIBLES & JEWELRY

7368 Melrose Ave., Los Angeles, CA 90046 (213) 655-9375

1. What do you think the following abbreviations mean in the ads at the top of the page on the right: orig, blk/wht, tix, ea, cntr?
2. Work with a partner. You both work for Santa Barbara Watersports. Decide the following things: How big are the groups you take on trips? Are your kayaks for one, two or three people? How many instructors go with each group? How much do the one-day and two-day trips cost? Do you provide special clothes? Does this cost extra? How much? Do you provide sleeping arrangements for people on the two-day trips? Decide the arrangements.
3. Now work with another pair of students. Take it in turns to be tourists who want some information about kayak trips.

"Chocolate City"

Marvin Mitchell lives in Detroit with his father. His parents are divorced, and his mother lives with Marvin's sister in another part of the city. Like many other students in cities with large ethnic populations, he is bused to school every morning.

I get up at six o'clock. Dad works for one of the automobile companies. He helps to develop the models that people buy two or three years later. We always have breakfast together before he leaves. This morning he said, "Hey, I got an idea. Let's go out for dinner tonight. What do you say?" I said, "That's only because you don't want to cook. It's your turn tonight. Remember?" Since Mom left last year, we've had this problem about who does what in the apartment. I usually do most of the housework, because Dad doesn't come home till after six in the evening, and then he expects to find a meal on the table. Last night I said, "Listen. You haven't learned a thing. You really annoy me. If you carry on like this, *I'm* going to leave you, too." "Don't be so cruel, Marv," he said. "You're worse than Gale ever was." I said, "Mom wasn't bad. You just didn't understand her problems." He really looked at me then, I can tell you.

Although there's a school only ten minutes from where I live, I have to travel 30 minutes to a school on the other side of town. I get on the bus at the end of the street. As we drive along, more and more kids get on till the bus is full. When Elliot sees me, he always makes jokes about me and Dad. "Hey, what's on the menu tonight, Marv? You know, one day you'll make somebody a wonderful wife." Elliot is the star player on the school basketball team, but he can hardly read or write. He says school is a waste of time, and he'll only escape from the world he lives in by becoming a successful athlete. He lives in one of the poor areas of Detroit with his mother, two sisters and three brothers. But two of his brothers are in prison right now.

At Redford High School half the students are black. The other half seem to come from almost every country in the world. We have Greeks, Italians, Puerto Ricans, Vietnamese, Afghans – to mention just a few. Altogether, I think over 20 languages are spoken at our school. For Elliot, they're all Puerto Ricans, no matter where they come from. One day a teacher brought in a world map. Everybody had to show where they came from. I can remember Elliot shouting, "Hey, Mr Welsh, let me show them where I come from." He went to the map, looked hard at it, and put his finger on Australia. "That's it. Chocolate City." Several kids laughed until a Vietnamese girl took his big hand and put it on the USA. "You mean here, man," she said. "You from here."

The only time the whole school is all together is in the cafeteria. Then it's like the United Nations. It's always crowded and noisy, and sometimes it's very tense. Only two days ago a group of Afghans were in the line. They were laughing and making jokes, when two Afghan girls came and joined them. A big athletic girl called Melissa Stephens shouted at the two girls because they hadn't gone to the back of the line. One of the Afghan girls said, "We're staying." A fight started, but it was over before a teacher could get between them. Melissa is real tough, but the girl she fought with was a karate expert!

School is over at three o'clock. As Dad doesn't get home till six, the apartment is empty and I sometimes get a bit lonely. So I often go to Mom's apartment to do my homework or I visit some of my friends. Dad hates me hanging around with Elliot. "Are you crazy?" he shouts at me then. "You stay away from those areas, do you hear me? The only place you'll go is prison if you hang around there." The problem is: I like playing basketball and I love music. Elliot and his friends often meet in one of the parks downtown, where they play music and practice basketball. I don't know why it upsets Dad so much. I mean, Detroit is the home of some of the best sports teams and black musicians in the United States.

Both Mom and Dad say I have to do well at school and go to college. I try to explain to them that I find school boring and I'd like to quit – get a job or maybe play music. But Dad only gets angry again. "Why do you think we fought so hard in the past?" he said to me once. "So that you can drop out of school? Why do you think so many people went on the streets and died? Do you want to know? It was so that kids like you can go to school and college like any white kid. Do you hear me? It was so that you can sit on a bus and nobody can say, 'Hey, man, you go and sit at the back. This seat is for whites only.' You want to play music, that's fine. But finish school first. You're just as good as anybody else in this world. Remember that."

(Based on *Tales out of school* by Patrick Welsh)

INFO BOX

Blacks in the USA suffer because of inner-city problems like unemployment, poverty, crime far more than whites. One third of all black Americans live in poverty.
Almost half of all the women and men in prison are black, although blacks are only about 12% of America's population. Almost half of all black teenagers are out of work.
Most inner-city black children grow up in broken homes. Many do not know what it is like to have a father who has a job and who lives at home.
But not all blacks are underprivileged. There is also a black middle class with people who are not exactly rich, but certainly not poor, who have good jobs and whose children go to university.

Working with the text

1a 1. How does Marvin get to school? 2. Why does Marvin have to do so much housework? 3. Who is Elliot? 4. What is special about Redford High School? 5. Why did Melissa and the Afghan girl fight with each other? 6. Why does Mr Mitchell sometimes get angry with Marvin? What does he say to Marvin then? 7. Why did black Americans fight so hard in the past?

b 1. Collect information and then write about
- the Mitchell family,
- Marvin's day or
- Elliot and his family.

2. What do you think of the way Marvin talks to his father at the beginning of the text?

c 1. What do you do with your friends in your free time? 2. Have you ever had problems with your parents because of friends? Why?/Why not? 3. What jobs around the house do you have to do? Do you think children should help their parents with the housework? Why?/Why not?

2 **Say it in English:** *Being annoyed or angry – apologizing – reacting to an apology – defending yourself – answering back*

Apologizing:

I'm (very) sorry (that) . . .
(Sorry,) I didn't mean/want to annoy/upset you.
I'd like to apologize.

Reacting to an apology:

That's all right/ OK (,then).
Don't worry about it.
It doesn't matter./ Never mind.

Being annoyed or angry:

I'm (so) angry/annoyed (with you because/that . . .)
. . . is/are (really) annoying (me).
. . . is/are getting on my nerves.
I'm (very) upset (that/ because . . .)

Defending yourself:

What's wrong? I haven't done anything.
I don't understand why . . . .
I haven't done anything wrong.

Answering back:

But can't you see . . . ?
If that's the case, then please tell me . . .

a Now try to complete this short dialog with expressions from above.

Mr Welsh:
Elliot, you – my nerves / know – not like it – when – silly.

Elliot:
What's …? I …

Mr Welsh:
But can't … – make a fool of yourself – lesson?

Elliot:
Oh – mean – joke about Chocolate City?

Mr Welsh:
Yes – think – stupid joke.

b Work with a partner: Mr Mitchell has been informed that Marvin has gotten worse in several subjects at school. Mr Mitchell is talking to Marvin: he is very angry that Marvin spends a lot of his time with Elliot; he thinks Elliot is bad company for him. Marvin is trying to defend himself. He apologizes for his bad grades but doesn't believe that they have anything to do with Elliot. He mentions other reasons. Write a dialog between Marvin and his father and try to use phrases from this page and from page 21.

c Think of a situation in which a teacher or a friend was annoyed or angry with you because you had done something wrong. Write a letter to the person and apologize. Explain why you made the mistake or defend yourself and explain why you think you did not make a mistake.

Unit 6

Britain – then and now

Stonehenge and the Celts

You can find out about Britain's history by visiting museums.
You can also find evidence of the past by looking around you. And, if you stay with a family and help them in the garden, you might even dig up a piece of Britain's history!

1 Stonehenge

In 1993 archaeologists found evidence of people who lived in England about 500,000 years ago, but nobody knows who these people were. The oldest monument in Britain is Stonehenge, a circle of huge stones that was finished over 3500 years ago. The stones were possibly brought from an area in Wales 250 km away, but nobody knows who put them up or how – or why. The sun shines on certain stones at the winter and summer solstices, so Stonehenge might have been a temple or a kind of calendar. Later, some believe, it was used by the Druids (the priests of the Celts). In their religion the sun was very important.

JANET'S GARDEN GOLD

What looked like an old button lying in the garden has turned out to be a gold coin of Celtic origin, about 2000 years old and worth up to £750.
"My husband was planting a rosebush at the time," said Janet Barber, a typist. "This small object came out of the soil and Frank thought it was probably a button or something off a children's toy. But after we had cleaned it, a friend of ours recognized it in a coin catalogue."
An archaeologist dug up the rest of the garden, but no more buried treasure was discovered, so Janet and Frank sent the coin to the British Museum, who confirmed that it was a coin from between 30 BC and AD 10 . It will be sold at an auction in London in six weeks' time.

Can you find any more information about Stonehenge, e.g. how big the stones are?
Until recently, tourists were allowed to walk around the monument, but now the authorities want to stop this, because some people climbed on the stones and broke off pieces as souvenirs. Are the authorities right?

Stonehenge, near Salisbury in England and …

… Pentre Ifan, a megalith 250 km away in Wales

2 The Celts

Over 2000 years ago, several Celtic tribes moved from the continent of Europe and settled on a group of islands in the North Sea. One tribe, the Britons, gave their name to the islands: the British Isles. (Great Britain, the largest of these, is the biggest island in Europe, but there are over 900 islands in the group.) The different tribes often fought each other and, as we can see from the evidence in museums, they made strong swords and other weapons. They also loved music, and they made beautiful jewels and fine clothes. However, these early Celts left no written records.

Examples of Celtic jewels

> What can you find out about the Celts in Germany?
> Before you read the text below, look at the photos. What seems unusual on the signs?
> Can you guess why the Celtic cross has its unusual shape?

3 Pushed from the centre to the fringe

After the Celts arrived, Britain was invaded many times – at first by the Romans, then (c. 450-600) by the Angles, Saxons and Jutes (who came from northern Germany and Denmark; the name England is a form of *Angle*land). Later, the Vikings invaded too. The Romans and Celts lived together more or less peacefully. But the Angles, Saxons and Jutes attacked the Celtic villages, so the Celts were forced to leave the eastern and central parts of Great Britain. They escaped to the west and north, to Cornwall and the hills of Wales and Scotland; and Celts survived in Ireland too.

Today, evidence of Britain's Celtic past can still be found in the language and culture of the "Celtic fringe". Among the things you can see are examples of the Celtic cross, a combination of the sun and the Christian cross. The Celts, in the early fourth century, were the first people in Britain who became Christians.

A Celtic cross

Signs of Britain's past in Wales

... in Scotland

... in Ireland

- **c.700 BC** Celts arrive
- **55 and 54 BC** Julius Caesar leads Roman expeditions to Britain
- **43** Romans invade Britain
- Christianity arrives
- **409** The last Romans leave
- **c.450-600** Angles, Saxons and Jutes invade
- **787** Vikings start to arrive
- **878** Led by King Alfred, the Saxons defeat a Viking army

... 100 BC | 0 | AD 100 | 200 | 300 | 400 | 500 | 600 | 700 | 800 | 900

The Romans in Britain

1

Race against time for Roman town

Archaeologists at Heybridge in Essex have discovered what they believe is one of the best examples of a Roman town in the country, but are working against time before 400 houses are built over it.
"The more we dig, the more we find, but we have so little time," said project manager Mark Atkinson.

The GUARDIAN June 9 1994

Read the newspaper article and then say what has been found and why there is a problem.
Discuss the situation in two groups. Group A takes the part of the archaeologists, group B the part of the building firm.

Now read the rest of pages 72-73 and find out:
- when and in what way Britain was invaded by the Romans,
- who ruled Britain before the Romans arrived,
- who Boudicca was and why she is remembered,
- what Hadrian's Wall is and why it was built,
- how long the Romans stayed in Britain,
- what the Romans left behind as their legacy.

2 From a history project at a British school

The Romans came to Britain for a short time in 55 and 54 BC. They were led by Julius Caesar and they won some battles but, each time, storms damaged many of their ships, so they were afraid to stay. Later, a Roman army under the Emperor Caligula got as far as the English Channel but did not cross it. Of course, there was no Channel Tunnel in those days! It was not till AD 43, under the Emperor Claudius, that the Romans invaded and stayed.
At that time Britain was divided among hundreds of small tribes. The Romans soon captured the capital of southeast Britain – Camulodunum in Latin, or Colchester as we call it today – and they captured eleven kings from different tribes. They made the land a Roman province and called it Britannia. Jamie Cooper

The Iceni, a tribe that lived north of Camulodunum, lived in peace with the Romans until their king died. Then the Romans plundered their area and raped the king's daughters. So the queen, Boudicca, collected together a huge army and in AD 61 totally destroyed Camulodunum and two other Roman towns: Londinium (London) and Verulamium (St Albans).
A report by Tacitus, a Roman historian, says Boudicca's army killed 70,000 Romans before the Romans finally defeated them. Boudicca killed herself.
Sarah McCormack

It was in the north that the Romans had to fight the hardest. So, when the Roman Emperor Hadrian visited Britannia in AD 122, he decided to build a wall 80 miles long from coast to coast to keep the "barbarians" out and protect his Roman province in the south. Annie Carpenter

A statue of Boudicca outside the Houses of Parliament in London

3 The Roman legacy

The Romans were in Britain for over three centuries, from AD 43 to 409, and during that time British life and culture changed very greatly.
The Romans built towns and cities and over 6000 miles of roads. They developed trade and started several new industries.
Much of Hadrian's Wall still stands, and you can see Roman remains in many other places too. You can see beautiful mosaic floors, for example, or the city walls and gates in Chester and Colchester, and you can visit the Roman baths – at Bath, of course.
The Latin word for camp – *castra* – can be found in many place names, e.g. Manchester, Worcester ['wʊstə], Lancaster.
The old Roman roads were built very straight so that soldiers could be moved quickly from one place to another. Many modern roads follow more or less the same routes.

Hadrian's Wall

Unit 6

Medieval Britain (1066-1485)

What do you know about Robin Hood?
Do you know who the Normans were and where they came from?
Why is 1066 (ten sixty-six) an important date in British history?
Where do the English words 'autumn' and 'parliament' come from?
Now read pages 74-75. What do they tell you?

A statue of Robin Hood, outside Nottingham Castle

1 Robin Hood

You have probably read a story or seen a film about Robin Hood and a group of Saxon outlaws who lived in a forest near Nottingham 800 years ago. If you go to Nottingham today, you can visit an interesting exhibition about Robin Hood and learn a lot about his adventures. You'll also find out that Nottingham Castle, where Robin's great enemy, the Sheriff of Nottingham, lived, was built by the Normans in 1068 – two years after a famous date in British history.

2 Harold and William

1066 was the last time England was successfully invaded. William of Normandy (Normandy is in northern France) and his army arrived on the south coast in October and defeated the English army that had come to fight them.
The Battle of Hastings lasted all day. When it was over, King Harold II, the last Saxon King of England, lay dead. One of Europe's oldest and richest kingdoms now belonged to the Normans. On Christmas Day 1066 William – or William the Conqueror as he later became known – was crowned William I, King of England, in Westminster Abbey.
With William the English didn't just get a new king but also a new culture and a new language. From 1066 until 1327, no king of England spoke English as his first language. Those with power in the land spoke French, or Latin, and over the next few centuries many new words came into the English language, words like 'autumn' (Latin: *autumnus*; Old French: *autompne*), and 'parliament' (Old French: *parlement* from *parler*).

This is part of a huge embroidery, the 'Bayeux tapestry' (Bayeux is in Normandy). About 50 cm high and 68 m long, it tells the story of how first Harold became King of England, then William.

3 The Saxons under Norman rule

A statue of Richard I outside the Houses of Parliament in London

The Normans quickly built several castles, including the White Tower, the central part of the Tower of London, and they ruled England very strictly. The Saxons hated them because William divided all the land among his Norman lords, and the Saxons had to do all the work for them. The Saxons were also no longer allowed to hunt wild animals in any of England's forests. If they killed any animals and were caught, the Normans hanged them or cut off a hand or arm. The Saxons had few rights. If they broke a law, their only hope was to run away and hide in the forests. According to the legend of Robin Hood, he was the leader of some Saxon outlaws in the late twelfth century. At this time the King of England, Richard I (1189-1199), was often away in the Middle East on crusades against the Muslims. While he was away, his younger brother John ruled the country very cruelly. Until Richard returned, Robin Hood – at least in legend – was the hero who robbed the rich and protected the weak.

4 The Norman legacy

In 1215 King John (1199-1216) was forced by some barons to sign the Magna Carta ('Great Charter'), a document that limited his power. This is often seen as a first step towards democracy in Britain. Today, the legacy of the Normans that is easiest to see is their influence on British architecture. Some of the country's finest churches and castles were built during the Norman period.

St David's Cathedral, Wales

The White Tower, the oldest part of the Tower of London

Unit 6

Tudor Britain (1485-1603)

1 Defender of the faith

Henry VIII

If you look at a British coin, you will see a Latin abbreviation on it: *Fid Def* or just *FD*. This stands for the Latin words *fidei defensor*, 'defender of the faith'. It is a title that every British monarch has used since 1521, when the Pope gave it to Henry VIII to thank him for criticizing the Protestant Martin Luther. And Henry kept it, even after breaking with Rome in 1534 and making himself the head of a new church, the Church of England.

2 The monarch's religion

This statue in Oxford is in memory of three bishops who were killed (in 1555 and 1556) after refusing to break with the Church of England. One of the three was Thomas Cranmer, the Archbishop of Canterbury who had allowed Henry VIII's divorce.

In fact, Henry VIII became head of the Church of England not because he wanted to change the church, but because he wanted a divorce from his first wife and the Pope refused to allow this.

As head of his own Church, Henry was able to get his divorce, of course. But religion and state politics stayed married. Henry persecuted those, like Thomas More, who continued to support the Pope – and he destroyed Catholic monasteries all over the country. Later his first daughter, Mary I, persecuted those who would not go *back* to the Catholic church. Then Mary's half-sister Elizabeth I supported Protestants again.

In a TV interview in 1994, the heir to the throne, Prince Charles, said Britain was now a multi-cultural society with many faiths. So, when he became King, he would like to be a "defender of faith" (not "of *the* faith").

This caused quite a storm, with big headlines in the papers and discussions on radio and TV – because the British monarch is still head of the Church of England and by law is not even allowed to be a Catholic.

Daily Express

INSIDE TODAY

Ross Benson: The truth about the Prince and Camilla

STARTS PAGE 24

Charles: I will still be King

As the Prince's marriage to Lady Diana Spencer had broken down, other questions were asked too. Ought Prince Charles to become King at all, especially if he became divorced? Was he a fit person to defend *any* faith at all?

3 Elizabeth I

Elizabeth I was the fifth and last English monarch from a Welsh family, the Tudors, who ruled from 1485-1603. She said: "I know I have the body of a weak and feeble woman, but I have the heart and stomach of a king."

The House of Tudor	
1485-1509	Henry VII
1509-1547	Henry VIII
1547-1553	Edward VI
1553-1558	Mary I
1558-1603	Elizabeth I

During the Tudor period Columbus landed in America (in 1492) and navies became very important. What can you remember from Book 3 about two of Britain's most famous sailors, Sir Francis Drake (1540-96) and Sir Walter Raleigh (1554-1618)?

Elizabeth I

Sir Walter Raleigh

Under Elizabeth I, England grew richer and more powerful – in spite of religious problems and battles with Catholic countries (including France, Ireland, Scotland and Spain) – and her reign is often talked of as a 'golden age'. Many of Britain's sailors were not very different from pirates, and some were active in the slave trade, including Francis Drake, later a hero in the battle against the Spanish Armada. These sailors brought all kinds of new things home with them, e.g. potatoes and tobacco, and they made their country richer.
Some fine buildings were built under the early Tudors, for example Hampton Court Palace near London, and several of the colleges in Oxford and Cambridge. But now some new theatres were added and some wonderful plays written. It was in the reign of Elizabeth I that Britain's greatest writer was born: William Shakespeare (1564-1616).

The building in Stratford-upon-Avon where Shakespeare was born

St John's College, Cambridge

911 Vikings settle in Normandy as Normans

1066 Battle of Hastings – William of Normandy becomes King of England

1215 King John signs the Magna Carta

1337-1453 Hundred Years' War with France

1534 Henry VIII breaks with Rome

1588 Spanish Armada defeated

1000 – 1100 – 1200 – 1300 – 1400 – 1500 – 1600

1 In Germany today, especially in adverts, you often see words that have been taken over from English.
1500 years ago it was the other way round. People in Britain were using words that had come from Germany and Denmark.

The following words came to Britain via the Angles and Saxons: *eight, house, mouse, night, pound, thick.* What are their equivalents in modern German?
Other words came into English from Latin or French. Try to find the English words that correspond to these words:

a) *accipere, certus, destruere, difficilis, Germania, machina, pagina, parens, persona, serius, signum, theatrum*
b) *activité, adresse, appartement, automne, dictionnaire, découvrir, grand-mère, hôpital, idée, introduire, leçon, prix, prononciation, survivre, véhicule, vocabulaire.*

2 When the last Romans left Britain in AD 409, there was no longer a strong army there and the island was soon invaded, at first by the Angles and Saxons. These tribes both spoke similar Germanic dialects; so, after they had driven the Celts to the west and north, a mixture of their dialects became the main language in the country. It was called Anglo-Saxon.
In the ninth century Vikings started settling in Britain, especially in the north and east. They introduced many of their own words, but the language remained basically Anglo-Saxon.
After the Normans had conquered Britain in 1066, their form of French became its official language for 300 years. However, Anglo-Saxon remained the language of the ordinary people. Most of them learned French words only when they had to.
By the 14th century English had become a mixture of Anglo-Saxon and Norman French.

We gave Britain a lot of place names ending in *-chester, -cester, -caster.*

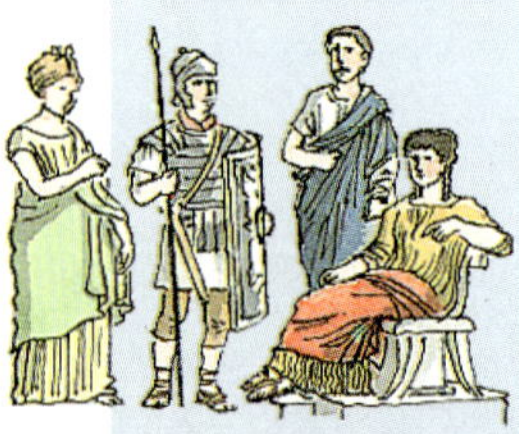

Romans

From us came the word *English* and words like *mother, brother, father; eat, sleep, drink; cow, cat, fish, field.*

Angles and Saxons

We added *egg, leg, sky, knife, take, hit, same, skirt, they, them, their.*

Vikings

We introduced *government, parliament, minister, science, religion, crime, defend.*

Normans

of the English language

From us came *bungalow, guru, jungle, pyjamas, shampoo.*

Indians

We added *koala* and *kangaroo.*

Aborigines

From us came *moccasins* and place names like *Manhattan.*

Native Americans

We keep making up expressions like *computerize, down-size, megastore.*

Americans today

Under the Tudors, English continued to develop and to accept words from other languages. As British explorers sailed back from different countries in the 15th and 16th centuries, they introduced 'shampoo' and 'pyjamas' from India and 'tea' from China. And it has continued to accept more and more new words: 'anorak' from the Inuit (Eskimos) and 'moccasins' from Native Americans. Today, the English language has over 500,000 words, although an average speaker perhaps uses only 15,000 of them. English has more words than any other language – and more words are created every day, especially in the USA.

3

I gave the world 'ghoti'.

G. B. Shaw

Another feature of English is the difference between spelling and pronunciation. English pronunciation has changed a lot since the 14th century, when written English became more common, but spelling has not kept up with it.

The writer George Bernard Shaw (1856-1950) wanted to make English spelling simpler. To show how crazy it can be, he made up the 'word' *ghoti*. This is how you could spell [fɪʃ] if you took the right parts of *cou**gh***, *women* and *nation*!

When the English tongue we *speak*
Why is *break* not rhymed with *weak*?
Won't you tell me why it's *true*
We say *sew*, but also *few*?
And the maker of a *verse*
Cannot rhyme his *horse* with *worse*?

Think of *blood* and *food* and *good*;
Mould is not pronounced like *could*.
Why is it *done*, but *gone* and *tone* –
Is there any reason *known*?
To sum it up, it seems to me
That sounds and letters don't agree.

4 A lot of English jokes are based on words that sound the same but have different meanings.

Q: Why is 6 afraid of 7?
A: Because 7, 8, 9.

Customer: What's this?
Waiter: It's bean soup, sir.
Customer: I don't want to know what it was. What is it now?

Unit 7

Mazes in fact and fiction

1 Hampton Court

Hampton Court Palace was built in 1515 for Thomas Wolsey (c.1475-1530), the son of a butcher, who became the second most powerful man in England. Wolsey gave the palace to Henry VIII in1526 as a sign of his friendship.
Today the palace is a popular tourist attraction and its gardens are the home of Britain's most famous maze.

△ *Hampton Court palace*

▽ *Hampton Court maze*

Have you ever been in a real maze?
Or have you played a computer maze? Did you like it? Why (not)?
What is the purpose of a maze?
Look at the photo of Hampton Court maze.
Do you think you could find your way through it?

Read the magazine article on the opposite page and answer these questions:
– How old is Hampton Court maze?
– Is it the oldest maze in Britain?
– How big is it?
– Is it the biggest maze in Britain?
– How many visitors visit it each year?

Amazing mazes

For thousands of years, mazes have been designed in all shapes and materials, and many stories have been told about them. Near Blenheim Palace, just north of Oxford, one story says, are the ruins of a special maze that was built for Henry II (1154-89). It had thick walls and doors and was the secret home of the King's mistress, Rosamund – until 1176, when Queen Eleanor found a way inside and gave her rival a choice: a cup of poison or the rest of her life in a nunnery. What did she do? It is said she chose the cup.

The new maze at Blenheim Palace, opened in 1993

Nowadays, the most popular kind of maze in Britain is the hedge maze, for it combines the British love of gardens with the equally strong love of any kind of puzzle: a detective story, a quiz, a jigsaw, a crossword puzzle or even, today, a multi-maze computer game.

The world's largest hedge maze is at Longleat House, just south of Bath. However, it is Hampton Court Palace – 24 km south-west of Central London – where the world's most famous hedge maze can be found. Hampton Court maze, the oldest maze in England, was planted in 1690. Its non-rectangular shape was dictated by some paths that were already in the gardens. The longest side of the maze is 68 metres, its total area about 1000 square metres. It is a popular tourist attraction and over 500,000 visitors go there every year. America's best-known maze, at Williamsburg, Virginia, is based on the maze at Hampton Court; and it has been copied in other countries too.

It is often said that the centre of any maze can be reached quite easily by the "hand-on-wall" method – that is, by keeping to the left (or right) all the way, even in and out of dead ends, without ever taking your hand off the hedge. In fact, it is not always so easy.

A coward's guide to Hampton Court maze

For those who don't want to get lost, here's the correct way into and out of the famous maze at Hampton Court. Turn left when you enter the maze, then right, right again, left, left, left and right. Then you will be at the centre. To leave the maze, without getting lost, turn right, then right three more times, left twice, and then you reach the exit!

Read the article again. There is a mistake somewhere near the end. Can you find it?

3 It's absurd to call it a maze

Hampton Court maze is described in Jerome K. Jerome's novel *Three Men in a Boat* (1889), and this book and the film of the same name (1957) have helped to make it famous all over the English-speaking world.
The following text is an extract from Jerome K. Jerome's book. The man who is telling the story is enjoying a holiday with his dog and two friends, George and Harris. They have hired a boat and are rowing up the Thames from London to Oxford. On the way they go past Hampton Court.

Look at the picture on the next page. What do you think the story is about?
Now read the story and find out. (The text has been simplified a little, but it still contains some words that are new. The difficult unknown words are explained at the foot of the page. You should be able to guess the others from the context.)

Harris asked me if I'd ever been in the maze at Hampton Court. He said he went in once to show somebody else the way. He had studied it in a map, and it was so simple that it seemed foolish – hardly worth the twopence admission. Harris said he thought the map must have been done as a joke, because it wasn't at all like the real thing, and only misleading. It was a cousin that Harris took in. He said to his cousin:
"We'll just go in here so that you can say you've been, but it's very simple. It's absurd to call it a maze. You just take the first turning to the right all the time. We'll walk round for ten minutes, and then go and get some lunch."
They met some people soon after they had got inside who said they had been there for three quarters of an hour, and had had about enough of it. Harris told them they could follow him if they liked; he was just going in, and then would turn round and come out again. They said it was very kind of him, and followed.
They picked up various other people, as they went along, until they had collected all the people in the maze. People who had given up all hopes of ever getting either in or out, or of ever seeing their home and friends again, plucked up courage at the sight of Harris and his party, and joined the procession. Harris said he thought there must have been twenty people following him, in all; and one woman with a baby, who had been there all the morning, insisted on taking his arm, so that she didn't lose him.
Harris took the turning to the right all the time, but it seemed a long way, and his cousin said he supposed it was a very big maze.
"Oh, one of the largest in Europe," said Harris.
"Yes, it must be," said the cousin, "because we've walked a good two miles already."
Harris began to think it a little strange himself, but he carried on until, at last, they passed half a penny bun on the ground that Harris's cousin swore he had noticed there seven minutes ago. Harris said: "Oh, impossible!" but the woman with the baby said, "Not at all," as she herself had taken it from the child, and thrown it down there, just before she met Harris. She also added that she wished she had never met Harris, and expressed an opinion that he was an impostor. That made Harris mad, and he produced his map, and explained his theory.
"That map may be all right enough," said one of the party, "if you know whereabouts in it we are now."
Harris didn't know, and suggested that the best thing to do would be to go back to the entrance and begin again. For the beginning-again part of it there was not much enthusiasm; but with regard to the advisability of going back to the entrance there was complete agreement, and so they turned and trailed after Harris again, in the opposite

(line 6) admission *Eintritt* (l. 9) misleading *irreführend* (l. 25) (to) pick up *einsammeln, aufnehmen* (l. 29) (to) pluck up courage *Mut fassen* (l. 34) (to) insist (on) *bestehen (auf)* (l. 45) bun *süßes Brötchen* (l. 53) impostor *Schwindler, Hochstapler* (l. 63) with regard to *im Hinblick auf* direction. About ten minutes more passed, and then they found themselves in the centre. Harris thought at first of pretending that that was what he had been planning; but the crowd looked dangerous, and he decided to pretend it was an accident.

Anyhow, they had got something to start from then. They did know where they were, and the map was once more consulted, and the thing seemed simpler than ever, and off they started for the third time.

And three minutes later they were back in the centre again.

After that they simply couldn't get anywhere else. Whatever way they turned brought them back to the middle. It became so regular that some of the people stopped there, and waited until the others took a walk round, and came back to them. Harris drew out his map again, after a while, but the sight of it only made the crowd angry, and they told him to go and curl his hair with it. Harris said that he couldn't help feeling that, to a certain extent, he had become unpopular.

They all got crazy at last, and shouted for the keeper, and the man came and climbed up the ladder outside, and shouted out instructions to them. But they were, by this time, so confused that they were unable to understand anything, and so the man told them to stop where they were, and he would come to them. They huddled together, and waited; and he climbed down, and came in.

But he was a young keeper and new to the business; and when he got in, he couldn't get to them, and then *he* got lost. They caught sight of him, every now and then, running about the other side of the hedge, and he saw them, and ran to get to them, and they waited there for about five minutes, and then he reappeared again in exactly the same place, and asked them where they had been.

They had to wait until one of the old keepers came back from his dinner before they got out.

Harris said he thought it was a very fine maze; and we agreed that we would try to get George to go into it, on our way back.

Different text types: fiction and non-fiction

Think about the differences between the first text (*Amazing mazes*, p. 81) and the second text (the extract from *Three Men in a Boat*). These questions may help you:

1. Which of the texts is easier to read? Why?
2. How many names are used in each text and what effect does this have?
3. Which text can you remember better?
4. Which text gives you the better idea of what it feels like to be in a maze? How?
5. Which text gives you more information about mazes?
6. Which text is easier to summarize?
7. What tense is used most in each text?
8. Which text uses the passive more, which direct speech?

(l. 1) direction *Richtung* (l. 21) (to) curl *locken, kräuseln* (l. 22) couldn't help …ing *konnte nicht umhin zu …* (l. 23) extent *Grad* (l. 32) (to) huddle *kauern, hocken*

Unit 8

CROESO I GYMRU
WELCOME TO WALES

Sandy beaches on the South Wales coast near Swansea

29 A letter from Wales

Do you remember Megan, who visited her cousin Debbie in Kansas and met a German boy, Rolf, there? He has written to her in Wales. Here is her reply.

11 Gower Road
Swansea
SA99 1AB
February 2nd

Dear Rolf,

Diolch am dy lythyr o Passau. Do, cefais amser bendigedig gyda'm cefnither yng Nghansas. Ni fyddaf fyth yn ei anghofio. Ac ydw, rydw i'n gallu sôn ychydig am Gymru ac am ein hiaith.

I'm sure you didn't understand that – it was in Welsh. So here it is again in English: Thank you for your letter from Passau. Yes, I had a wonderful holiday at my cousin's in Kansas. I'll never forget it. And, yes, I can tell you something about Wales and our language.

About half a million people in Wales (about one fifth of the population) still speak Welsh. But most of them live in villages and small towns in north and west Wales. Here in Swansea it's mostly the older people who speak Welsh. We learn Welsh at school, but my Welsh isn't very good. Mum is from Cardiff. She doesn't speak Welsh either. But my dad speaks the language very well. (He helped me with the first part of the letter!) When we visit my grandparents in Aberystwyth, he speaks Welsh all the time. I can't understand a lot and it's really annoying.

My parents moved to Swansea when Dad got a job as an engineer in a big steel factory. But the factory closed down and now Dad is out of work. He hasn't found another job yet, so he's at home all day now. He's fed up with the situation. Fortunately, Mum is a nurse in a big hospital, so it isn't that bad. And Dad now does most of the housework.

Unemployment is a huge problem in this part of Wales. Once, the main industries here were steel and coal. But the coal mines have been closed and every year more and more factories close down. Thousands of men and women have lost their jobs and become unemployed. And there aren't enough jobs in farming or tourism or in new industries like micro-electronics. It's very difficult.

I'm sending you some photos with this letter.

If you come to Wales in your summer holidays, I'd be very happy to see you again and show you some of the places in the photos.

Megan

Write a similar letter to a new friend about your family and the job situation in your area.

Focus on GRAMMAR: Der Infinitiv mit *to* (The infinitive with *to*)

a Rolf made plans for a visit to Wales. When he finally arrived, Megan was very **pleased to see** him. She was at the station **to meet** him, and they laughed as they remembered how they had first met.
"Now," Megan said, "what **would** you **like to see** first? We've had to sell our car, I'm afraid, so my parents can't drive us anywhere; but it's **easy enough to get** to most places by bus."
Rolf smiled. "Well, I'm **too tired to go** up a mountain – or even up a church tower." It had been a long journey.

Swansea

Rev. b **Der *to*-Infinitiv nach Verben, Adjektiven und Nomen**
(The *to*-infinitive after verbs, adjectives and nouns)

Du weißt, dass der *to*-Infinitiv nach Verben, Adjektiven und Nomen stehen kann:

Verb + *to*-Infinitiv: Megan **had hoped to get** a letter from Rolf.
Adjektiv + *to*-Infinitiv: Megan was very **happy to see** Rolf again.
Nomen + *to*-Infinitiv: Megan had a **chance to show** him her photos of Kansas.

Rev. c **Der *to*-Infinitiv zum Ausdruck eines Zwecks** (The *to*-infinitive to express purpose)

Megan went to Kansas **(in order) to visit** her relatives and have a holiday.
Megan reiste nach Kansas um ihre Verwandten zu besuchen und Ferien zu machen.

Rolf went to America **(in order) to improve** his English.
Rolf reiste nach Amerika um sein Englisch zu verbessern.

Der *to*-Infinitiv kann zur Angabe einer Absicht oder eines Zwecks verwendet werden. Die Absicht wird durch die Verwendung von *in order to* besonders betont.

→ Ex 1

d **Der *to*-Infinitiv zum Ausdruck einer Folge** (The *to*-infinitive to express result)

Rolf didn't run **quickly enough to catch** the bus.
Rolf lief nicht schnell genug um den Bus zu erreichen.

It's **too hot to play** tennis today.
Es ist heute zu heiß um Tennis zu spielen. (..., als dass wir Tennis spielen könnten.)

Zur Angabe einer Folge steht der *to*-Infinitiv nach einem Adjektiv/Adverb + *enough* bzw. nach *too* + Adjektiv/Adverb.

→ Ex 2

e The next day Megan showed Rolf Swansea. In the harbour they saw a car ferry and Rolf noticed that **the first car to drive on** was from Ulm.
Then they walked around the busy market. Most of the traders spoke fast and had a Welsh accent. Rolf wondered if he was **the only one** there **not to understand** their jokes. There was **nobody** there **to explain** them to him at first.
Then Megan found one of her neighbours, Mr Evans, and he was just **the person to help**. He knew some of the traders personally, and he **asked them to speak** more slowly or repeat things – until everyone was laughing.
Megan's parents **had invited Rolf to stay** with them for the weekend. In fact, there was so much **for him to see** around Swansea that he stayed longer. Most of all, Megan **wanted him to visit** one of the sandy beaches of the Gower Peninsula. When he left Swansea in order to join a cousin on a tour of other parts of Wales, Rolf didn't really want to go.

f **Der *to*-Infinitiv anstelle eines Relativsatzes** (The *to*-infinitive instead of a relative clause)

There was **nobody** | **to help** Rolf at first.
who could help Rolf at first.

Mr Evans was **the person** | **to talk to**.
he should/might talk to.

Nach *someone, something, nobody* usw. sowie nach bestimmten Nomen kann der *to*-Infinitiv statt eines Relativsatzes mit Modalverb stehen.

I was **the last** | **to arrive**.
who arrived.

The only person/The only one | **not to laugh** was Rolf.
who didn't laugh …

The youngest person | **to speak** Welsh was a boy of five.
who spoke Welsh …

Ebenfalls statt eines Relativsatzes kann der *to*-Infinitiv nach *the first/last/next/only* oder nach einem Superlativ + Nomen stehen. (Auf *the only* muss immer ein Nomen oder *one/ones* folgen). → Ex 3, 4

g **Der *to*-Infinitiv nach bestimmten Verben + Objekt**
(The *to*-infinitive after certain verbs + object)

Rolf **asked Megan to write** to him again.
Rolf bat Megan ihm wieder zu schreiben.

Megan **wanted him to enjoy** his visit to Wales.
Megan wollte, dass er seinen Besuch in Wales genießt.

Megan **advised Rolf to bring** boots and an anorak with him if he wanted to walk up Snowdon.

Nach Verben zum Ausdruck eines Wunsches oder einer Aufforderung (z. B. *ask, expect, tell, want, would like*) kann ein Objekt + *to*-Infinitiv stehen. Das Objekt ist „Sinnsubjekt" des *to*-Infinitivs.
Weitere Verben dieser Art sind z. B. *advise, encourage* (= ermuntern, ermutigen), *force, help, invite, remind* (= erinnern), *teach, warn.*

⚠ Nach *want* und *would like* darf kein Nebensatz mit *that* stehen.
Beachte die unterschiedliche Bedeutung der folgenden Sätze:

Megan **wanted to help** her neighbour.
Megan wollte ihrem Nachbarn helfen.

Megan **wanted** her neighbour **to help** her.
Megan wollte, dass ihr Nachbar ihr half. → Ex 5, 6

h **Der *to*-Infinitiv nach *for* + Nomen/Pronomen** (The *to*-infinitive after *for* + noun/pronoun)

It's important **to come**.

It's important **for Megan to come**.
Es ist wichtig, dass Megan kommt.

It's the last chance **to meet** Rolf.

It's the last chance **for Megan to meet** Rolf.
Es ist die letzte Chance für Megan Rolf zu treffen.

It's too hot **to play** tennis.

It's too hot **for anybody to play** tennis.
Es ist zu heiß, als dass irgendjemand Tennis spielen könnte.

Beachte, dass der *to*-Infinitiv in den Sätzen rechts ein eigenes „Sinnsubjekt" hat, das nach der Präposition *for* steht.

Megan is waiting **for him to phone**.
Megan wartet darauf, dass er anruft.

Auch nach Verben, die mit *for* verbunden sind, kann ein Objekt + *to*-Infinitiv stehen. Zu diesen Verben gehören *wait for* (= darauf warten, dass), *arrange for* (= dafür sorgen, dass) und *ask for* (= darum bitten, dass). → Ex 7

8A Wales and the Welsh

Megan Thomas, Year 10

The information and the pictures on these two pages are part of a project that Megan did at school.

1 Wales is a small country. It is only about a quarter the size of Scotland. It is a country of small farms and sheep. (There are three sheep for every person in Wales!) And you are never very far from the sea. This is Tenby, a popular holiday centre in the southwest.

2 *Snowdon is the highest mountain in Wales. It is 3,560 feet high (1,085 metres). There is a little mountain railway which carries visitors from Llanberis to the top, but my father and I walked up Snowdon last year. It took us four hours! I was really tired. But on a clear day you can see for miles from the top.*

3

The Brecon Beacons National Park

In a small and crowded island like Britain National Parks are necessary and important. The countryside there is protected against development. In Wales there are three National Parks: Snowdonia in the northwest, the Pembrokeshire Coast in the southwest and the Brecon Beacons in the south. Together they cover about one fifth of the whole of Wales. People visit the National Parks to go walking, climbing, pony-trekking or just to enjoy the beautiful countryside.

How can we help to look after the National Parks?

Don't make fires.

Stay on the paths.

Close all gates.

Don't pick flowers and plants.

Don't take birds' eggs.

Take your litter home.

PS The name Brecon comes from the name of an Irish king, Brychan, who came here in the Middle Ages. He had 12 sons and 24 daughters. I'm glad I wasn't his wife! 'Beacon' is another word for hill, by the way.

4

At the beginning of the twentieth century, Wales was the largest coal-exporting area in the world. One third of the world's coal was produced in South Wales. Today coal is no longer an important industry, and the mines have now closed down. But this has had some advantages. Coal-mining areas which were once black with coal and smoke are turning green again.

5

New industries – are they helping Wales?

There are many successful new industries in Wales. The Japanese, for example, have built new factories. But often the new industries do not bring enough jobs. And sometimes they are in areas where people want to protect the countryside, so there is a conflict between jobs and the environment. Under the mountains around Snowdon there are important minerals. But should new mines be opened here and should the countryside be destroyed just because of a few thousand jobs?

In a Japanese television factory in South Wales

6

The Welsh love music and they are famous as singers. Every July there is a huge festival of music and poetry: the International Eisteddfod in Llangollen, North Wales. People come from all over the world to play, sing – or just listen.

I hope to go there next year with the school choir.

Project work

Work in groups and collect information and pictures about your area and do the same as Megan.
Put everything together and make a poster in English for a British friend.

Focus on GRAMMAR: *some, any, each, every*

a Wales, England and Scotland were **each** independent countries once, with their own languages. But in 1536, after the English had conquered Wales, the Welsh were ordered to speak English as their official language. This policy continued into the 19th century, when **any** pupil who used Welsh at school was punished by having to wear a sign around the neck that said "WELSH NOT". But now things are different. You see Welsh on signs everywhere, and it now has a fresh status. About 30% of schoolchildren can speak at least **some** Welsh – and there is even a Welsh TV channel, S4C. Is Welsh difficult? If you visit a school in Wales **some** day, perhaps you will be able to find out. Welsh is now taught as a subject in almost **every** school in the country. A quarter of the schools even use it as their only or main teaching language.

Rev. b Du weißt schon lange, dass man *some* vor allem in bejahten Aussagesätzen verwendet, aber auch in Fragen, wenn man etwas anbietet oder um etwas bittet.
Du weißt auch, dass *any* und seine Zusammensetzungen (*anyone, anything* usw.) in verneinten Sätzen und in Fragen verwendet werden.

I'd like **some** postcards. Would you like **some**, too? – Yes, and shall I buy **some** stamps?
I do**n't** know **any** Welsh. Do you know **any**? – No, and I do**n't** know **anybody** who does.

c ***any*** **in der Bedeutung „irgendein beliebiger, jeder x-beliebige"**

You can come **any** time. – Can I bring my cousin? – You can bring **anyone** you want.
Du kannst jederzeit kommen. Du kannst jeden mitbringen, den du willst.

I can talk to my parents about **anything**. If **anybody** has **any** questions, please ask.
If I talk about **anything** that has to do with my band, my parents get bored.

any hat auch die Bedeutung „irgendein beliebiger, jeder x-beliebige, ganz gleich welcher". In dieser Bedeutung werden *any* und seine Zusammensetzungen auch in bejahten Aussagesätzen verwendet.

⚠ Vergleiche: **any** day = Monday **or** Tuesday **or** ...
every day = Monday **and** Tuesday **and** ...

If **anything** goes wrong, ... Wenn **irgendetwas** schief geht, ...
If **something** goes wrong, ... Wenn **etwas** schief geht, ...
If **everything** goes wrong, ... Wenn **alles** schief geht, ...

→ Ex 8

d ***every*** **und** ***each*** **im Vergleich**

Rolf would like to visit **every** castle in Wales. Rolf möchte jede Burg (= alle Burgen) in Wales besuchen.
Each castle is interesting in a different way. Jede (einzelne) Burg ist auf eine andere Art ...

Every und *each* stehen beide vor zählbaren Nomen im Singular und bedeuten „jeder". Oft sind *every* und *each* austauschbar. Wenn man jedoch jedes einzelne Mitglied der Gruppe für sich betrachtet, zieht man *each* vor.

⚠ Nur *each* kann vor einer *of*-Fügung stehen oder einem (Pro-)Nomen nachgestellt werden.
Each of the tourists in the group asked a question. **They each** asked a hard question.

Focus on WORDS: Talking about the +economy

In her letter from Wales Megan writes about the +economic situation of the part of Wales she lives in. The situation in Wales is similar to that in the Ruhr district in Germany, and in many other parts of the world.
In the past the economies of many countries were generally based on +raw materials like oil, gas and coal, on farming, hunting and fishing, or on heavy industry. But modern economies are based very much on high technology (microelectronics, computers, new +communications systems, +robots, etc.) and on service industries. Of course, we still need +workshops, factories and +machinery to produce +goods from materials like metal, +leather, wood, etc. And we need +tools like +hammers or +pliers. And of course we need farmers, teachers, painters and +carpenters. But we also need people who are trained in "future technologies" like +biotechnology, +medical electronics or other +fields. If the economy and +consumers, too, do not change, problems like unemployment, +energy supply and +protection of the environment cannot be solved.

1 Collecting words

advise airport assistant astronaut baker borrow boss buy check chemist coal company competition control crane customer debt doctor electronics engine engineer exchange expert export factory farmer improve instructor invent invention inventor ladder lend machine mechanic mine miner minerals nurse office oil platform organize port produce repair reporter restore rival sell serve shop silver spend supermarket support teacher trader waiter work full-time work part-time

Collect all the words that are related to the field "economy" in the text above. Add them to one of the groups a-c. Also add the words from the box and any other "economy" words that you know.

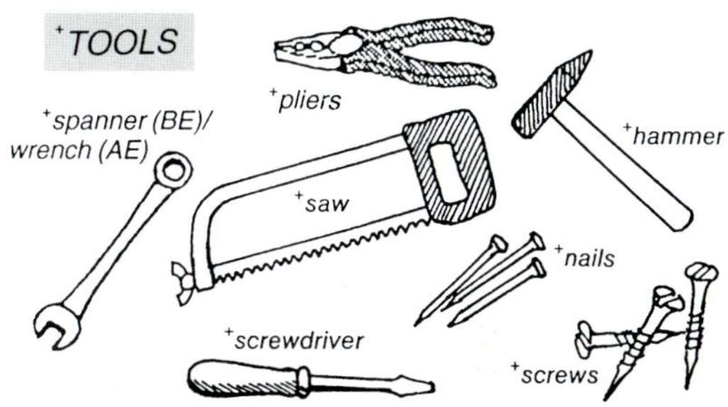

a **Different jobs and job-related activities**
architect, boss, …
(to) invent/develop/offer/sell … a product
(to) work 40 hours a week …
(to) make/offer/+supply …

b **What is needed to produce or do things**
raw materials: coal, …
places of work: shop, firm, …
tools and machinery: hammer, crane, …

c **Words related to business**
business, competition, market, sell, …
boss, worker, +employer, +employee, consumer, …
(to) trade with sb., export/import goods, …

2 Arranging words

a How many products can you think of which are made of paper, glass, steel, plastic, wood or a mixture of these materials? Try to make a network with a material as the starting word.

b Choose a job like "architect" and make a network to describe the job. Which materials does he/she need? Where might he/she work? …

3 Words in use

a Imagine you have a foreign visitor. Tell him/her about the economic situation in your region: important employers, main industries, the jobs people do, etc.

b Invent a new product. Describe it to your class and find as many reasons as possible why people should buy it. Make an advert or a funny poster for your product.

1 Revision: The *to*-infinitive

Answer these questions with an infinitive with "to" (which you must find yourself) and a phrase from this list:

ears / equal rights / freedom / merry Christmas / route to India / the other side! / the poor

1. Why did the Pilgrim Fathers go to America?
   – They went (in order) to practise their religion in freedom.
2. Why did Robin Hood steal from rich people?
3. Why did Columbus sail across the Atlantic?
4. Why did Dr Martin Luther King march through the USA?
5. Why do people send their friends Christmas cards?
6. Why did the wolf wear Grandmother's hat?
7. Why did the chicken cross the road?!

"We're here to escape prejudice, intolerance and persecution in England. Why are you here?"

2 What could you say or ask in these situations? *Use "too" or "enough" with a to-infinitive.*

1. Your friend asks how the film will end. You aren't sure yet. *(soon/say)* 2. You're very thirsty, but the water in the river looks dirty. *(clean/drink)* 3. Your friend wants to go to the beach, but it isn't very warm. *(cold/go)* 4. You want to go to the cinema, but the film is only for people over 18. *(old/see)* 5. You always go to school by bus. *(far/walk)* 6. You're ill and can't go to the concert.

Examples: 1. It's too soon to say. 2. Is it clean enough …?

3 A postcard from Talyllyn, Mid-Wales

Complete Rolf's postcard with the to-infinitive of these verbs:

answer choose explain live talk visit

Dear Megan,
I know you think the best place in the world … in is South Wales. But Mid-Wales is great, too, with lots of nice places … and so many interesting activities … from.
Yesterday I went on the Talyllyn railway. I asked the train driver about the history of the line and he called a friend of his over to us … how the line was built. She was a really interesting person … to.
Please don't forget we said we would write to each other. I hope there will be a letter for me … when I get back to Germany.
Rolf

4 In English, please. *Use a noun/pronoun + to-infinitive.*

1. Es muss interessant sein, in Swansea zu leben. *(Swansea must be an interesting place to … .)* 2. Manche Jugendliche haben niemanden, mit dem sie reden können. 3. Ich brauche jemanden, der mir bei den Hausaufgaben hilft. 4. Anne dachte, sie würde die Einzige sein, die die Prüfung nicht besteht *(pass)*. 5. Dort ist die Person, die Sie fragen sollten. 6. Die älteste Frau, die diesen Berg bestieg, war 86 Jahre alt.

5 Teenagers! – Parents! *Use infinitives to say what John's parents told him (not) to do when …*

a 1. … his room was untidy. 2. … his shoes were dirty. 3. … his school bag was lying in the kitchen. 4. … his clothes were lying on the floor of his room. 5. … his radio was very loud and the door to his room was open. 6. … his friends phoned him in the middle of the night. 7. … he came home very late at night. 8. … he felt tired.

Example: 1. They told him to tidy …

b *Can you think of five things your parents have told/asked you to do in the last few days?*

Examples: 1. Yesterday my parents asked me to … . 2. On Sunday my father told me to …

6 Sponsored activities

Translate the head teacher's message into German. You will find some examples of verb + object + to-infinitive that often cause problems. Which verbs are the "trouble-makers"? Try to explain why they cause problems.

To all teachers

As pupils, parents and teachers agreed before the holidays, we would like each class to take part in at least one sponsored activity this term. Classes must decide if they themselves want to organize an activity or if they will take part in an activity which is organized by another class.
I don't expect classes to decide before the end of the month. Would all sports teachers please tell their classes to collect ideas? (Warn pupils not to take part in too many things.)
If pupils want parents to help, we should allow them to ask parents.
50% of the money we collect will go to OXFAM, the other 50% will be used for books for the school library.

7 One of Ireland's most famous present-day writers

Read the following text, then translate it into German. (Perhaps you can use it for your school magazine.) In the text there are a number of "for" + noun/pronoun + to-infinitive constructions. Look at the context carefully to see how to translate them. For example:

… impossible for him to express himself.	… unmöglich für ihn sich auszudrücken./… ihm unmöglich sich auszudrücken.
… a typewriter for him to use.	… eine Schreibmaschine, die er benutzen konnte.

Christopher Nolan was eleven years old before anybody knew he could write. It was hardly possible for his family to communicate with him. His physical handicap was so bad that it was hard for people to believe that there was a quite normal mind inside his body. To most people 'Chrissy' was just a person they could pity.
But when he was eleven his life changed totally. A new medicine made it possible for him to control the movements of his head for short periods of time. His doctors made a

'unicorn' stick for him to fit on his forehead. Everybody was surprised when Christopher was able to use a typewriter with this stick. His doctors had found a way for him to express himself and to write down everything he had had inside him for so many years. At first it took ten to fifteen minutes for him to write one word, but he didn't give up.
Only five years later, in 1981, Christopher's first book, *Dam Burst of Dreams,* was published and made him known as a talented young writer.

(based on the introduction to C. Nolan, *Dam Burst of Dreams*)

physical handicap *körperliche Behinderung* mind *Geist* (to) pity *bemitleiden*
unicorn ['ju:nɪkɔ:n] *Einhorn* forehead ['fɒrɪd] *Stirn* (to) publish *veröffentlichen, herausgeben*

8 In English, please. *Use "any", "anything", etc. or "some", "something", etc.*

1. Ich habe noch keine Pläne für den Sommer. 2. Ich fahre mit dir überallhin. Aber es muss ein Land sein, wo die Sonne scheint. 3. Einige meiner Freundinnen dürfen fast überall allein hingehen. 4. Ich darf nirgendwo ohne meine große Schwester hingehen. 5. Sie darf alles tun, was sie will, was auch immer es ist. 6. Sie weiß die Antwort auf jede Frage, die meine Eltern stellen. 7. Wenn irgendetwas schief geht, ist sie nie schuld. 8. Ich muss jetzt Schluss machen *(go)*, weil irgendjemand an die Tür klopft.

9 Revision: *s*-genitive and *of*-phrase. In English, please.

1. Megans Mutter hat mir gestern einige Fotos von Megans Urlaub gezeigt. 2. Megan war *(stayed)* letztes Jahr bei ihrer Cousine in Kansas. 3. Dann zeigte mir Megans Vater die Sehenswürdigkeiten Swanseas. 4. Ich konnte mich nicht an die Größe der Stadt erinnern. 5. Frau Thomas' Beruf bringt es mit sich *(means)*, dass sie manchmal nachts arbeiten muss. 6. Megan und ich fuhren mit dem Bus, weil das Auto ihrer Eltern verkauft werden musste. 7. Die Zahl der Kinder an Megans Schule, die Walisisch sprechen, ist nicht groß. 8. Aber der alte Nachbar der Familie spricht Walisisch. 9. Der morgige Ausflug bringt mich in ein Gebiet, wo mehr Walisisch gesprochen wird.

Statue of Dylan Thomas (1914-53), a famous poet born in Swansea

10 Revision: Mixed tenses

a
1. I need a new bike. My old one is too small.
   – When / buy a new one?
2. We live in Cardiff.
   – How long / live there?
3. What do you think of my new anorak?
   – It looks expensive. How much / cost?
4. There's a tourist office in St David's.
   – know the exact address?
5. I can't come with you. My bike still has a puncture.
   – Why / not repair yet?
6. Hugh was busy when I phoned him.
   – Oh, what / do?
7. I don't really want to stop reading now. My book is too exciting.
   – What / read?

b *Choose one example from part 10a and develop it into a longer dialogue with a partner.*

○ **11 Listening comprehension: A National Park warden**

Listen to the cassette, then answer these questions.

1. Who is John Roberts? 2. Why do people sometimes think he is a policeman? 3. What does he think is his most important job? 4. What silly things do tourists sometimes do? 5. Do you think John enjoys his job? Try to say why.

12 WORDS WORDS WORDS

a The infinitive after verbs of perception

After verbs like *see, hear, notice* or *watch* you can often find an object plus an infinitive without *to*. Example:
I watched the woman jump out of the window. – Ich sah die Frau aus dem Fenster springen.
Ich sah, dass die Frau aus dem Fenster sprang.

Use these verbs to make phrases.

SEE somebody pick up the money/ …
HEAR a boy shout for help/ …
NOTICE a car stop at the bank/ …
WATCH a man jump out of a car/ …

Now find at least one infinitive to complete the following sentences.

1. I think I heard somebody … a window. 2. Did you notice a woman … out of the bank a few minutes ago? 3. I just saw something … past the window, but I don't know what it was. 4. No one saw the robber … the bank. 5. She heard someone … her name behind her. 6. I'm sure I noticed him … the money on the table, but nobody knows who took it away.

b Trouble spot: Do or make?

Add "do" or "make" to the words and phrases in the box and write them in your exercise book.

50 mph – an exam – an exercise – an offer – business – butter from cream – tea – magic – one's own clothes – sb. seasick – sb. a favour – the best of a situation – the housework – the next sentence – the shopping – well at school – a phone call – your homework – debts – a good impression – a lot of damage – a discovery – a mistake – tricks – a suggestion – a test

c WORD BUILDER'S CORNER Adjectives that are made from verbs

If you add **-able** to the verb **drink**, you can make an adjective: **drinkable**. ['drɪŋkəbl]
If you put **un-** in front of it, you can make its opposite: **undrinkable** = not drinkable.

Here are some more adjectives. Write them down in your exercise book together with the verbs they are made from.

acceptable avoidable countable eatable enjoyable readable understandable unacceptable unanswerable unavoidable unbelievable unbreakable uncountable uneatable unexplainable unforgettable unimaginable unpronounceable unsingable unsinkable unthinkable washable

Use these adjectives in collocations. Examples:
an avoidable accident – an enjoyable evening – a very readable article.

Now complete the following sentences with the right verb and adjective.

1. You'll get ill if you … that polluted water from the river. It's quite … . 2. I didn't … the film very much. But perhaps you'll find it more … than I did. 3. I find it very difficult to … all these silly questions. In fact, I think, some are quite … . 4. Careful! Don't … these glasses. They're not …, you know. 5. The Titanic … in 1912, although everybody thought that the ship was … . 6. Is this pullover…? – Yes, but you must … it separately. 7. Some pop songs are easy to … . Others are quite … . 8. I'll never … what happened that night. And my friends agree that it was an … night.

Getting along in Britain: Bed & breakfast

When Rolf left Swansea and joined his cousin, they travelled by train and bus to St David's, 100 km to the west. The tourist office was closed when they arrived, so they had to find a bed for the night without any official help. And it had to be somewhere that wasn't too expensive for them. But it wasn't difficult. Megan had told Rolf that there were bed-and-breakfast places all over Britain, usually large private houses which had been converted to make bedrooms for guests. Rolf and Georg saw lots of places with "B & B" signs outside. And it didn't take them long to work out the difference between "Full", "No Vacancies", "Rooms available" and "Vacancies".

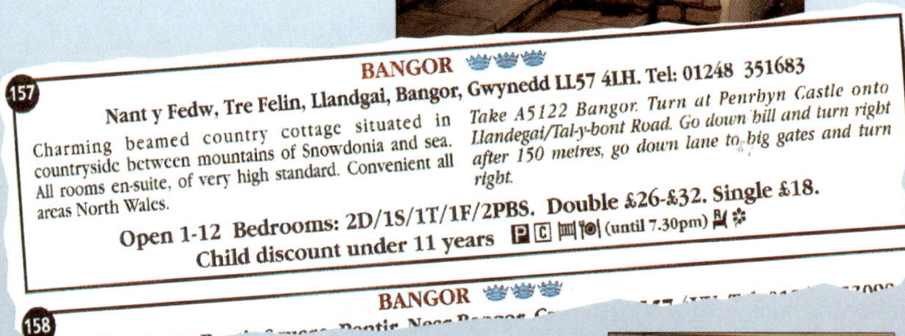

157 BANGOR

Nant y Fedw, Tre Felin, Llandgai, Bangor, Gwynedd LL57 4LH. Tel: 01248 351683

Charming beamed country cottage situated in countryside between mountains of Snowdonia and sea. All rooms en-suite, of very high standard. Convenient all areas North Wales.

Take A5122 Bangor. Turn at Penrhyn Castle onto Llandegai/Tal-y-bont Road. Go down hill and turn right after 150 metres, go down lane to big gates and turn right.

Open 1-12 Bedrooms: 2D/1S/1T/1F/2PBS. Double £26-£32. Single £18.
Child discount under 11 years (until 7.30pm)

158 BANGOR

Woman: Hello. Can I help you?
Rolf: I see that you've got some vacancies.
Woman: Yes. Is it for two?
Rolf: Yes. This is my cousin Georg.
Woman: How many nights is it for?
Rolf: Just for tonight. How much is that?
Woman: It's £13 a night, per person. That includes a cooked breakfast. But you can have a continental breakfast if you prefer. It's the same price.
Georg: We'll have a cooked breakfast, please.
Woman: Fine. Breakfast is from 7.30 to 9.30. I'll show you your room. It's on the first floor.

Work with a partner. Make up several different dialogues, for example reserving a room by phone, discussing your requirements in a tourist office, asking for a room in a bed-and-breakfast place. Make notes first and decide what you want to know. Begin with these ideas:

- You want a room for you and your parents and your brother and sister. (How about a double room and a room with three beds?)
- Ask how much the rooms cost. (It is cheaper if you stay two nights or more.)
- You want to stay three nights. (These rooms are only free for two nights.)
- Find out more about the rooms. (The double overlooks the road; the other room is quieter, en suite, and has satellite TV.)

A Welsh Legend

There is only one man in British legends who is as famous as Robin Hood: King Arthur. While nobody knows whether Arthur really existed, most stories say he was born in Tintagel in southwest England in the fifth century. Most agree that he was much loved; that he led his people in battles against Saxon invaders; and that he was helped by Merlin, a magician.

There is also a Welsh legend that says Arthur and the Knights of the Round Table are not dead. They are only sleeping in a secret cave – in the mountains of Snowdonia or perhaps in a cave in Glamorgan, South Wales. One day, when the country is in great danger, they will wake up again to save the situation. This is why Arthur is sometimes called "the once and future king".

29

Is it the day?

A young man called Huw set off from his farm in South Wales to sell some of his black cattle in the great city of London. To protect himself from thieves, and to guide the cattle as he rode along on his pony, he carried a thick hazel staff. He knew the route well, because he had ridden it many times before. But it was a long, slow journey, and he was pleased when it was over.

Huw sold his cattle and was riding back across London Bridge, when he met an old man. "That white staff of yours is most unusual," the stranger said. "You didn't get it here in London, did you?"

In fact, Huw had cut the staff from a tree near his farm only a few weeks before, and he told the old man. "As I thought," the old man said. "And, if I'm right, that tree grows where some treasure lies hidden."

Huw was excited to hear this. So he invited the stranger to ride back to Glamorgan with him. Together they went to the hill where the young man had cut his staff and there, under some leaves, they found a big flat stone – and under this they found a tunnel.

As they went along the tunnel, deep into the heart of the hill, they came to a narrow part, where a bell hung from the wall. It was just wide enough for them to get past. Then, suddenly, they were in a huge cave, where thousands of knights in armour were sleeping in a circle. Each of them had a sword, and next to one of them lay a golden crown.

On the floor, inside the circle, was a pile of gold and a pile of silver. The old man told Huw he could take either gold or silver. But he warned him not to touch the bell on the way out. If he did, one of the knights would wake up and ask, "Is it the day?" Then, if Huw wanted to escape misfortune, he would have to answer, "No, not yet! Sleep on!"

Huw filled his pockets with gold, but the old man took nothing. "I only came to find out if the old stories were true. That's enough for me," he said. "We should leave now."

On their way out, Huw was too excited to be careful – and hit the bell. At once a voice like

thunder called out, "Is it the day?" But the knight went back to sleep when Huw gave him the right answer: "No, not yet! Sleep on!"
Once outside again, Huw helped the old man to put back the stone and cover it with leaves. Then they said goodbye to each other.

Huw did not spend his gold wisely. He wasted it. Soon, it was gone. "Well," he said to himself, "I know what to do." And he made his way to the hazel trees on the hill. He took a bag with him, and in the cave he filled it greedily with both gold and silver. On the way out, he hit the bell heavily with the bag. "Is it the day?" a knight asked. And then another: "Is it the day?" Huw could hear the sound of metal on metal. But he had forgotten the right answer. "No, it isn't," he said, "not at all." In a moment, a dozen knights were chasing him along the tunnel …

How do you think the story ends?
Try and write your own ending.

Working with the text

a **It's true that …, but …**

Each of these sentences is only partly true. Say what is right, and correct what is wrong. Add information from the text if possible.

1. Huw had a farm in North Wales. 2. He took some sheep to London to sell them. 3. He told a stranger to ride back with him. 4. The old man advised Huw to ring the bell in the tunnel. 5. The old man took no gold, because he was rich. 6. After Huw had said goodbye to the stranger, he spent all his gold wisely.

b 1. Read the text that is upside down. Compare it with your own ending. 2. Describe Huw. What kind of a man is he? 3. What would you do if you were shown a secret cave as Huw was? 4. Huw's character is tested. Say how. 5. Is Huw treated fairly, do you think? 6. Do you feel sorry for him? Why/Why not? 7. Does the story try to teach us anything about how we should behave?

c 1. Look at the definition of a legend and say which parts of it are true for *Is it the day?*
2. Do you know any other famous (English or German) legends? Say what they are about.

A definition

legend ['ledʒənd] (n.): an old story which lies between myth and historical fact. Early legends were about the lives of saints.
A legend is usually about somebody who may or may not have existed and describes adventures or events from his or her life. If the character is a real historical figure, further stories are often made up about him or her.

This is how the legend ends:

They caught him before he could reach the end of it and beat him. Then they took his bag from him and threw him out on to the hill.
From this day, Huw's health was not good and, although he looked under all the hazel leaves on the hill, he was never again able to find the tunnel to King Arthur's cave.

Quiz page

Quiz 1: **Who am I?**

First you ask a pupil to leave the room. The class then decides who she/he is. You may choose a character from the book or a historical person mentioned in the book. Then call the pupil back into the room. She/he must make statements about the person she/he thinks the class has chosen. The class tells the pupil if the statements are right or wrong.

Example:

I live in New York.	– That's right.
I've got a brother.	– That's right.
I go to work on the subway.	– Sorry, that's wrong.

Some different ways of playing:
1. You can decide on a certain number of statements. If the person guessed her/his name with that number of statements, she/he has lost.
2. The person who must guess her/his identity must ask yes/no questions, e.g. Do I live in New York? …
3. One person chooses an identity and the class must make statements or ask questions.
4. Make two groups. Each group chooses an identity, the other group must find out who they are.

Quiz 2: **How's your history?**

One pupil chooses a historical event mentioned in the book. The class has to find out which one it is by asking yes/no questions.
For the first few events you can allow 10-12 questions; later on try to guess in no more than five or six questions.

Working with an English-German dictionary[+]

Some general information

1. In a dictionary you will usually find words at the top of a page (① and ⑨). They tell you the first and/or the last word on the page. If you look at these words, you will know at once if your word is on the page.
   Find out how this is done in different dictionaries.

2. Words that "belong" to a headword (②) can often be found in the entry (③) which goes with a headword. But sometimes words have their own entry although they "belong" to another headword. *Compare:* far – faraway – far-fetched
   Compare how words are arranged in different dictionaries.

3. In the entry you will find the phonetic transcription and German translations. And you will often find information that helps you to decide which German word is best in a certain context. You will also find information on British and American English. It is important to know the most important symbols and abbreviations used in your dictionary (④-⑧, ⑩-⑬, ⑮).
   Find out what symbols and abbreviations other dictionaries use and where they are explained. Which ones are the same in different dictionaries, which ones are different?

① first headword on page

② headword

③ entry

④ The phonetic transcription gives you the pronunciation.

⑤ Small numbers after headwords tell you that one word has two (or more) completely different meanings.

⑥ The ⚠ tells you that you must be careful with the German translation.

⑦ The tilde is used so that a word – or a part of a word – does not have to be repeated.

⑧ A dot in a word tells you where the word can be divided.

family 116

fam·i·ly ['fæməlɪ] **1.** Familie *f*; **2.** Familien..., Haus...; ***be in the ~ way*** F in anderen Umständen sein; **~ al'low·ance** → ***child benefit***; **'~ name** Familien-, Nachname *m*; **~ 'plan·ning** Familienplanung *f*; **~ 'tree** Stammbaum *m*

fam|·ine ['fæmɪn] Hungersnot *f*; Knappheit *f* (***of*** an *dat.*); **'~·ished** verhungert; ***be ~*** F am Verhungern sein

fa·mous ['feɪməs] berühmt; ⚠ *nicht* ***famos***

fan¹ [fæn] **1.** Fächer *m*; Ventilator *m*; **2.** (***-nn-***) (zu)fächeln; an-, *fig.* entfachen

fan² [fæn] (*Sport- etc.*)Fan *m*

fa·nat|·ic [fə'nætɪk] Fanatiker(in); **~·i·cal** [fə'nætɪkl] fanatisch

'fan belt *tech.* Keilriemen *m*

fan·ci·er ['fænsɪə] (*Tier-*, *Pflanzen-*) Liebhaber(in), (-)Züchter(in)

fan·ci·ful ['fænsɪfl] fantastisch

'fan club Fanklub *m*

fan·cy ['fænsɪ] **1.** Fantasie *f*; Einbildung *f*; plötzlicher Einfall, Idee *f*; Laune *f*; Vorliebe *f*, Neigung *f*; **2.** ausgefallen; Fantasie...; **3.** sich vorstellen; sich einbilden; ***~ that!*** stell dir vor!, denk nur!; sieh mal einer an!; **~ 'ball** Kostümfest *n*, Maskenball *m*; **~ 'dress** (Masken)Kostüm *n*; **~-'free** frei u. ungebunden; **~ 'goods** *pl.* Modeartikel *pl.*, -waren *pl.*; **'~·work** feine Handarbeit, Stickerei *f*

fang [fæŋ] Reiß-, Fangzahn *m*; Hauer *m*; Giftzahn *m*

'fan mail Fan-, Verehrerpost *f*

fan|·tas·tic [fæn'tæstɪk] (***~ally***) fantastisch; **~·ta·sy** ['fæntəsɪ] Fantasie *f*

far [fɑː] (***farther, further; farthest, furthest***) **1.** *adj.* fern, entfernt, weit; **2.** *adv.* fern; weit; (sehr) viel; ***as ~ as*** bis; ***in so ~ as*** insofern als; **~·a·way** ['fɑːrəweɪ] weit entfernt

fare [feə] **1.** Fahrgeld *n*; Fahrgast *m*; Verpflegung *f*, Kost *f*; **2.** *gut* leben; ***he ~d well*** es (er)ging ihm gut; **'~ dodg·er** Schwarzfahrer(in); **~'well 1.** *int.* lebe(n Sie) wohl!; **2.** Abschied *m*, Lebewohl *n*

far-'fetched *fig.* weit hergeholt, gesucht

farm [fɑːm] **1.** Bauernhof *m*, Gut *n*, Gehöft *n*, Farm *f*; ***chicken ~*** Hühnerfarm *f*; **2.** *Land*, *Hof* bewirtschaften; **'~·er** Bauer *m*, Landwirt *m*, Farmer *m*; **'~·hand** Landarbeiter(in); **'~·house** Bauernhaus *n*; **'~·ing 1.** Acker..., landwirtschaftlich; **2.** Landwirtschaft *f*; **'~·stead** Bauernhof *m*, Gehöft *n*; **'~·yard** Wirtschaftshof *m* (*e-s Bauernhofs*)

far|-off [fɑːr'ɒf] entfernt, fern; **~ 'right** *pol.* rechtsgerichtet; **~'sight·ed** *bsd. Am.* weitsichtig, *fig. a.* weitblickend

far|·ther ['fɑːðə] *comp. von* ***far***; **~·thest** ['fɑːðɪst] *sup. von* ***far***

fas·ci|·nate ['fæsɪneɪt] faszinieren; **'~·nat·ing** faszinierend; **~·na·tion** [fæsɪ'neɪʃn] Zauber *m*, Reiz *m*, Faszination *f*

fas·cis|·m *pol.* ['fæʃɪzəm] Faschismus *m*; **~t** *pol.* ['fæʃɪst] **1.** Faschist *m*; **2.** faschistisch

fash·ion ['fæʃn] Mode *f*; Art *f* u. Weise *f*; ***be in ~*** in Mode sein; ***out of ~*** unmodern; **2.** formen, gestalten; **~·a·ble** ['fæʃnəbl] modisch, elegant; in Mode; **'~ pa·rade, '~ show** Mode(n)schau *f*

fast¹ [fɑːst] **1.** Fasten *n*; **2.** fasten

fast² [fɑːst] schnell; fest; treu; echt, beständig (*Farbe*); flott; ⚠ *nicht* ***fast***; ***be ~*** vorgehen (*Uhr*); **'~·back** *mot.* (Wagen *m* mit) Fließheck *n*; **~ 'breed·er, ~ breed·er re'ac·tor** *phys.* schneller Brüter

fas·ten ['fɑːsn] befestigen, festmachen, anheften, anschnallen, anbinden, zuknöpfen, zu-, verschnüren; *Blick etc.* richten (***on*** auf); sich festmachen *od.* schließen lassen; ⚠ *nicht* ***fasten***; **'~·er** Verschluss *m*

'fast| food Schnellgericht(e *pl.*) *n*; **~-food 'res·tau·rant** Schnellimbiss *m*, -gaststätte *f*

fas·tid·i·ous [fə'stɪdɪəs] anspruchsvoll, heikel, wählerisch, verwöhnt

'fast lane *mot.* Überholspur *f*

fat [fæt] **1.** (***-tt-***) fett; dick; fett(ig), fetthaltig; **2.** Fett *n*; ***low in ~*** *pred.* fettarm

fa·tal ['feɪtl] tödlich; verhängnisvoll, fatal (***to*** für); **~·i·ty** [fə'tælətɪ] Verhängnis *n*; tödlicher Unfall; (Todes)Opfer *n*

fate [feɪt] Schicksal *n*; Verhängnis *n*

fa·ther ['fɑːðə] Vater *m*; **♀ 'Christ·mas** *bsd. Brt.* der Weihnachtsmann, der Nikolaus; **'~·hood** Vaterschaft *f*; **~-in-law** ['fɑːðərɪnlɔː] (*pl.* ***fathers-in-law***) Schwiegervater *m*; **'~·less** vaterlos; **'~·ly** väterlich

[+]All new words are in the mini-dictionary.

How to work with a dictionary

1. Find the word you are looking for. *Remember:* You may have to read the whole entry to find it. *Examples:* family tree, father-in-law, feathery, feeder road
2. If you want to find an expression which consists of several words, decide which word is the "most important" one in the expression. In the entry for this word you will probably find the expression. If you can't find it in that entry, look up another word in the expression. *Examples:* out of **fashion**, birds of a **feather**
3. When you have found the word, check which German translation fits best in your text. *Remember:* The additional information in the entry will help you to decide.

Here are some things you can do to become successful dictionary users: Ask each other …

1. … how to pronounce "new" words with the help of the phonetic transcription. "Page 116, first column. How do you pronounce the eighth headword?" ("fancier")
2. … what the symbols and abbreviations mean. *Example:* "What does *pl.* in the entry 'feet' mean?"
3. … which of the German words in an entry is best for the translation of an English sentence. *Example:* "There's a **fault** in the car engine."

117 **fellow**

fath·om ['fæðəm] **1.** *naut.* Faden *m* (*Tiefenmaß*); **2.** *naut.* loten; *fig.* ergründen; **'~·less** unergründlich
fa·tigue [fə'ti:g] **1.** Ermüdung *f*; Strapaze *f*; **2.** ermüden
fat|·ten ['fætn] dick *od. contp.* fett machen *od.* werden; mästen; **'~·ty** (***-ier, -iest***) fett(ig)
fau·cet *Am.* ['fɔ:sɪt] (Wasser)Hahn *m*
fault [fɔ:lt] Fehler *m*; Defekt *m*; Schuld *f*; ***find ~ with*** et. auszusetzen haben an (*dat.*); ***be at ~*** Schuld haben; **'~·less** fehlerfrei, -los; **'~·y** (***-ier, -iest***) fehlerhaft, *tech. a.* defekt
fa·vo(u)r ['feɪvə] **1.** Gunst *f*; Gefallen *m*; Begünstigung *f*; ***in ~ of*** zu Gunsten von *od. gen.*; ***do s.o. a ~*** j-m e-n Gefallen tun; **2.** begünstigen; bevorzugen, vorziehen; wohlwollend gegenüberstehen; *Sport*: favorisieren; **fa·vo(u)·ra·ble** ['feɪvərəbl] günstig; **fa·vo(u)·rite** ['feɪvərɪt] **1.** Liebling *m*; *Sport*: Favorit *m*; **2.** Lieblings...
fawn¹ [fɔ:n] **1.** *zo.* (Reh)Kitz *n*; Rehbraun *n*; **2.** rehbraun
fawn² [fɔ:n]: ***~ on*** (*dat.*) (vor Freude) an *j-m* hochspringen *etc.* (*Hund*); *fig.* katzbuckeln vor (*dat.*)
fax [fæks] **1.** Fax *n*; **2.** faxen; ***~ s.th.*** (***through***) ***to s.o.*** j-m et. faxen; **'~ (machine)** Faxgerät *n*
FBI [ef bi: 'aɪ] *Abk. für* ***Federal Bureau of Investigation*** FBI *m, n* (*Bundeskriminalpolizei der USA*)
fear [fɪə] **1.** Furcht *f* (***of*** vor *dat.*); Befürchtung *f*; Angst *f*; **2.** (be)fürchten; sich fürchten vor (*dat.*); **'~·ful** furchtsam; furchtbar; **'~·less** furchtlos
fea·si·ble ['fi:zəbl] durchführbar
feast [fi:st] **1.** *rel.* Fest *n*, Feiertag *m*; Festessen *n*; *fig.* Fest *n*, (Hoch)Genuss *m*; **2.** *v/t.* festlich bewirten; *v/i.* sich gütlich tun (***on*** an *dat.*)
feat [fi:t] große Leistung; (Helden)Tat *f*
fea·ther ['feðə] **1.** Feder *f*; *a.* **~s** Gefieder *n*; ***birds of a ~*** Leute vom gleichen Schlag; ***birds of a ~ flock together*** gleich u. gleich gesellt sich gern; ***that is a ~ in his cap*** darauf kann er stolz sein; **2.** mit Federn polstern *od.* schmücken, *Pfeil* fiedern; **~ 'bed** Matratze *f* mit Feder- *od.* Daunenfüllung; ⚠ *nicht* ***Federbett***; **'~·bed** (***-dd-***) verhätscheln; **'~·brained** F hohlköpfig; **'~ed** gefiedert; **'~·weight** *Sport*: Federgewicht(ler *m*) *n*; Leichtgewicht *n* (*Person*); **~·y** ['feðərɪ] gefiedert; feder(art)ig, leicht
fea·ture ['fi:tʃə] **1.** (Gesichts)Zug *m*; (charakteristisches) Merkmal; *Zeitung, Rundfunk, TV*: Feature *n*; Haupt-, Spielfilm *m*; **2.** groß herausbringen *od.* -stellen; *Film*: in der Hauptrolle zeigen; **'~ film** Haupt-, Spielfilm *m*; **'~s** *pl.* Gesichtszüge *pl.*
Feb *nur geschr. Abk. für* **February** Febr., Februar *m*
Feb·ru·a·ry ['februərɪ] (*Abk.* **Feb**) Februar *m*
fed [fed] *pret. u. p.p. von* **feed** 2
fed·e·ral *pol.* ['fedərəl] Bundes...; **°~ Bureau of In·ves·ti'ga·tion** (*Abk.* ***FBI***) Bundeskriminalpolizei *f* (*der USA*); **°~ Re·pub·lic of 'Ger·man·y** *die* Bundesrepublik Deutschland (*Abk.* ***BRD***)
fed·e·ra·tion [fedə'reɪʃn] *pol.* Bundesstaat *m*; Föderation *f*, Staatenbund *m*; *econ., Sport etc.*: (Dach)Verband *m*
fee [fi:] Gebühr *f*; Honorar *n*; (Mitglieds)Beitrag *m*; Eintrittsgeld *n*
fee·ble ['fi:bl] (***~r, ~st***) schwach
feed [fi:d] **1.** Futter *n*; Nahrung *f*; Fütterung *f*; *tech.* Zuführung *f*, Speisung *f*; **2.** (***fed***) *v/t.* füttern; ernähren; *tech. Maschine* speisen, *Computer*: eingeben; weiden lassen; ***be fed up with*** *et. od. j-n* satt haben; ***well fed*** wohlgenährt; *v/i.* (fr)essen; sich ernähren; weiden; **'~·back** *electr., Kybernetik*: Feed-back *n*, Rückkoppelung *f*; *Rundfunk, TV*: Feed-back *n* (*mögliche Einflussnahme des Publikums auf den Verlauf e-r Sendung*); Zurückleitung *f* (*von Informationen*) (***to*** an *acc.*); **'~·er** Esser *m*; **'~·er road** Zubringer(straße *f*) *m*; **'~·ing bot·tle** (Säuglings-, Saug)Flasche *f*
feel [fi:l] **1.** (***felt***) (sich) fühlen; befühlen; empfinden; sich anfühlen; ***~ sorry for s.o.*** j-n bedauern *od.* bemitleiden; **2.** Gefühl *n*; Empfindung *f*; **'~·er** *zo.* Fühler *m*; **'~·ing** Gefühl *n*
feet [fi:t] *pl. von* **foot** 1
feign [feɪn] *Interesse etc.* vortäuschen, *Krankheit a.* simulieren
feint [feɪnt] Finte *f*
fell [fel] **1.** *pret. von* ***fall*** 2; **2.** niederschlagen; fällen
fel·low ['feləʊ] **1.** Gefährt|e *m*, -in *f*,

F

(9) last headword on page

(10) *Am.* tells you that "faucet" is an AE word.

(11) The brackets tell you that the AE spelling is "favor".

(12) The circle over the tilde shows that the word is spelt with a capital letter ("Federal Republic of Germany").

(13) Numbers in an entry are used for different word classes (nouns, verbs, etc.).

(14) an expression which "belongs" to the headword "feed"

(15) Additional information and abbreviations are used to help you with translation.

Songs

Unit 2: **New York, New York**

Start spreadin' the news, I'm leavin' today,
I want to be a part of it, New York, New York.
These vagabond shoes are longing to stray
Right through the very heart of it, New York, New York.
I wanna wake up in a city that doesn't sleep
And find I'm king of the hill, top of the heap.
These little town blues are melting away,
I'll make a brand new start of it in old New York.
If I can make it there, I'll make it anywhere,
It's up to you, New York, New York.

New York, New York,
I want to wake up in a city that never sleeps
And find I'm A number one, top of the list,
King of the hill, A number one.
These little town blues are melting away,
I'm gonna make a brand new start of it
In old New York,
And if I can make it there I'm gonna make it anywhere,
It's up to you, New York, New York, New York.

Written by F. Ebb, J. Kander, sung by Frank Sinatra

- *Who, do you think, is "I"? What is his/her past?*
- *What do you think about his/her hopes and dreams?*

Unit 4: **Small town**

1. Well, I was born in a small town
And I live in a small town
Prob'ly die in a small town
Oh, those small communities

2. All my friends are so small town
My parents live in the same small town
My job is so small town
Provides little opportunity

3. Educated in a small town
Taught the fear of Jesus in a small town
Used to daydream in that small town
Another boring romantic that's me

4. But I've seen it all in a small town
Had myself a ball in a small town
Married an L.A. doll and brought her to this small town
Now she's small town just like me

5. No, I cannot forget where it is that I come from
I cannot forget the people who love me
Yeah, I can be myself here in this small town
And people let me be just what I want to be

6. Got nothing against a big town
Still hayseed enough to say
Look who's in the big town
But my bed is in a small town
Oh, and that's good enough for me

7. Well I was born in a small town
And I can breathe in a small town
Gonna die in this small town
And that's prob'ly where they'll bury me

Written and sung by John Mellencamp

- *What impression of life in a small town do you get from the song?*
- *What are the singer's feelings about it?*

"Hey, New York! I'm Orville Foteman just off the bus from Horse Cave, Kentucky, and I'm going to turn you upside-down!"

Unit 6: **Scarborough Fair**

Are you goin' to Scarborough Fair:
Parsley, sage, rosemary and thyme.
Remember me to one who lives there.
She once was a true love of mine.

Tell her to make me a cambric shirt:
    On the side of a hill in the deep forest green.
Parsley, sage, rosemary and thyme;
    Tracing of sparrow on snowcrested brown.
Without no seams nor needle work,
    Blankets and bedclothes the child of the mountain.
Then she'll be a true love of mine.
    Sleeps unaware of the clarion call.

Tell her to find me an acre of land:
    On the side of the hill in a sprinkling of leaves.
Parsley, sage, rosemary and thyme;
    Washes the grave with silvery tears.
Between the salt water and the sea strands,
    A soldier cleans and polishes a gun.
Then she'll be a true love of mine.
    Sleeps unaware of the clarion call.

Tell her to reap it with a sickle of leather:
    War bellows blazing in scarlet battalions.
Parsley, sage, rosemary and thyme:
    Generals order their soldiers to kill.
And gather it all in a bunch of heather,
    And to fight for a cause they've long ago forgotten.
Then she'll be a true love of mine.

Traditional, arranged and sung by Simon and Garfunkel

Unit 8: **Cosher Bailey** *(Welsh traditional)*

Cosher Bailey had an engine, but it always needed mending,
And whenever he repaired her, there was no one who could catch her.
Chorus: Did you ever see, did you ever see, did you ever see such a funny thing before?

Cosher bought her second-hand and he painted her so grand.
And every time he oiled her, she nearly burst her boiler.

When downhill or on the level, well, she went just like the devil.
When she stopped inside a tunnel, Cosher climbed out through the funnel.

Cosher drove her through the Gower and he did four miles an hour.
When they rattled through the station, well, they frightened half the nation.

Cosher had a sister Anna and she played the grand 'pianna'.
She also played the fiddle up the sides and down the middle.

In the chapel Sunday night Cosher sings with all his might.
And his version of "Cwm Rhondda" makes the angels dance up yonder.

So then here's to good old Wales, where they brew the best of ales.
If you want to get some Sunday, you will have to wait till Monday.

Unit 8: **Cwm Rhondda** *(Possibly the most famous of all Welsh hymns)*

Guide me, O thou great Jehovah,
Pilgrim through this barren land;
I am weak, but thou art mighty;
Hold me with thy powerful hand:
Bread of heaven, bread of heaven,
Feed me now and evermore,
Feed me now and evermore.

Last chorus in Welsh:
O! am aros, O! am aros,
Yn ei gariad ddyddiau f'oes,
Yn ei gariad ddyddiau f'oes.

EXTRA READING

Look at the picture and try to explain what you think is happening there. It will help you to understand the beginning of the story better.

Unit 3: **Widow's Walk**

"Have a nice day in the office," she said with a smile.
"Don't worry, I'll enjoy every minute," he said. From the door of the house he watched his wife help their two children Troy and Cindy into the car. He waved as she got into the driver's seat.
"You'll bring them home from school this afternoon?" he asked.
She nodded. "You've got a whole day, all to yourself. So get some work done."

Steven Hillman watched his wife Cathy drive away from the house and down the street with their two young children. He turned around and shut the door. With his coffee cup in his hand, he walked up the stairs of the empty house and into his new office.
Steven and Cathy had bought the large old house on the New England coast some weeks ago, as Steven had decided he wanted to leave his firm in Boston and work from home. They had decorated it and organized his office in one of the best rooms with a beautiful view over the sea.
Steven sat down at his desk and leaned back. His computer, his fax, telephone, answering machine, printer, copier were all in position. No more city noise, no more traffic jams, no more complaints that the kids couldn't play anywhere. Here they had the beach, and he had his job.
The phone rang. It was Jerry, a good friend from his old firm in Boston.
"Have you started work yet?" he asked.
"Thinking about it," said Steven. "How's Boston?"
"Hot, noisy, full of tourists. Nothing you'd want to come back to."
Steven looked out at the quiet sea. "You can say that again."
"Listen," said Jerry. "I've got a couple of new clients I could send to you. Are you interested?"
"I sure am," said Steven.
"OK. I'll fax you the details."
"Thanks, Jerry."

Steven put down the phone and started his daily routine of work. At lunchtime he heard somebody move in the house. Cathy wasn't due back with the kids until after three. He listened carefully, but it was difficult to hear if somebody was downstairs in the kitchen or not. He got up from his desk and went down the stairs.
"Cathy, are you back?" he called. But there was no answer.
He went into the kitchen and found that it was empty. He walked through the other rooms, but there was nobody there. It must be the wood in the old house, he thought. Sometimes it can make strange sounds.
He made a sandwich and went back up the stairs. It was such a fine day that he decided to go onto the roof. The old New England houses along the coast had, on their roofs, a small square platform with a railing where you could stand and look out to sea. In the 19th century the wives of the sailors used to stand on these platforms and look for the ships that would bring their husbands back. The platforms were known as the Widow's Walk as many men were lost at sea, and sometimes ships never came back.
Steven climbed the steep ladder, opened the door and climbed onto the platform. Their house was on a small hill and now from the roof he could see for miles, both along the coast and out to sea. He imagined how it must have been for women and

their families as they were waiting for a ship to appear on the horizon, with no news when it would return or whether the crew was safe.

Steven turned to go back down to his office and suddenly felt something against his body. It came as a shock. For a moment he thought a seagull had flown into him, attracted by his sandwich, but there weren't any on the roof. It had been a strange feeling. Steven returned to his office and soon forgot the whole thing.

Several days later Steven's wife Cathy said, "Did you know we've got a ghost?"

"Where?" he asked.

"Here in the house."

She said it in such an ordinary way as if she had discovered a cat in the garage.

Steven suddenly remembered his experience on the roof. With a smile, he said. "Yes, I walked into her."

"How did you know it was a woman?" Cathy asked.

"I didn't," he said. "I just said that."

"Her name is Mrs Thomas. She stands on the Widow's Walk."

Steven became serious. "Who told you that?"

"A neighbor three houses away. She's a wonderful person. You must meet her."

"Who? The ghost?"

"No. Our neighbor. Mrs Evans. I've invited her for coffee tomorrow afternoon."

Mrs Evans was a friendly woman, possibly about sixty years old. Her family had lived in Bedford for generations. What she didn't know about New England, Steven thought, wasn't worth knowing.

"I believe we have a ghost in the house," said Steven.

"Yes, but don't be frightened. Mrs Thomas is a very nice person. She lived in this house about 150 years ago. I first heard the story as a child. Her husband was the captain of a whaling ship and the ship never came back. She never found out what happened to the ship or her husband. For years she stood on the Widow's Walk when the sky was clear and the stories say she will never rest until she knows where he lies."

"That's great news for us. Nobody told us about her when we bought this place. Do the kids know?"

Just then the door flew open and Steven and Cathy's two children ran into the house.

"Can we go up onto the roof, please?" Troy asked.

"Not without me," said Steven. "If you fall, it's a long way to the ground."

Steven got up as the children ran towards the stairs.

"I'll come with you," said Mrs Evans. "It's a beautiful day. The view must be wonderful."

From the Widow's Walk the sea below rested peacefully. Yachts were sitting like toys on the water; their white sails were not moving at all.

"Did the whaling ships really sail from here?" asked Cindy. "I can't imagine it."

"Yes," said Steven. "They were called the Nantucket Whalers. The ships sailed from here to Greenland to fish for whales. The men hunted the whales in small boats with harpoons. The dead whales were then pulled onto the large factory ships and processed. Later the ships sailed to England with the processed whales and unloaded their cargo in cities like Liverpool. After that they sailed back. Sometimes they were gone for over six months." Steven paused. "Did anybody ever find out what happened to the captain?" he asked Mrs Evans.

"I tried to," she said. "The people who lived here before you were quite worried about Mrs Thomas, especially as they wanted to sell the house. I offered to find out the name of the ship he was on and to discover its route." She stopped and seemed to listen to the gulls and breathe in the fresh air. "But you moved in before I got all the information. You see, the ship was called the *Eliza* and it sailed to Greenland and then later to the British Isles. It sailed to Milford Haven, a whaling port in South Wales that was actually founded by the Nantucket Whalers. The weather must have been very bad, because the ship hit the rocks near the Welsh coast and sank. The bodies were all found, and the captain was later buried in a small village."

Mrs Evans stopped and with a gentle smile on her face looked out over the quiet sea. Steve watched her curiously. "I think she'll rest peacefully now," she said.

She breathed out, as if happy about some good news she had just heard and said, "Well, shall we go down?"

Carl Taylor

EXTRA READING

Poem pages

Unit 3: **In the States**

With half a heart I wander here
As from an age gone by
A brother – yet though young in years,
An elder brother, I.

You speak another tongue than mine,
Though both were English born.
I towards the night of time decline,
You mount into the morn.

Youth shall grow great and strong and free,
But age must still decay:
Tomorrow for the States – for me,
England and Yesterday.

Robert Louis Stevenson

- *This poem was written in the second half of the 19th century. What has happened since then? Have things developed as Stevenson predicted?*
- *R. L. Stevenson is the author of a very famous children's book. Do you know its name in English?*

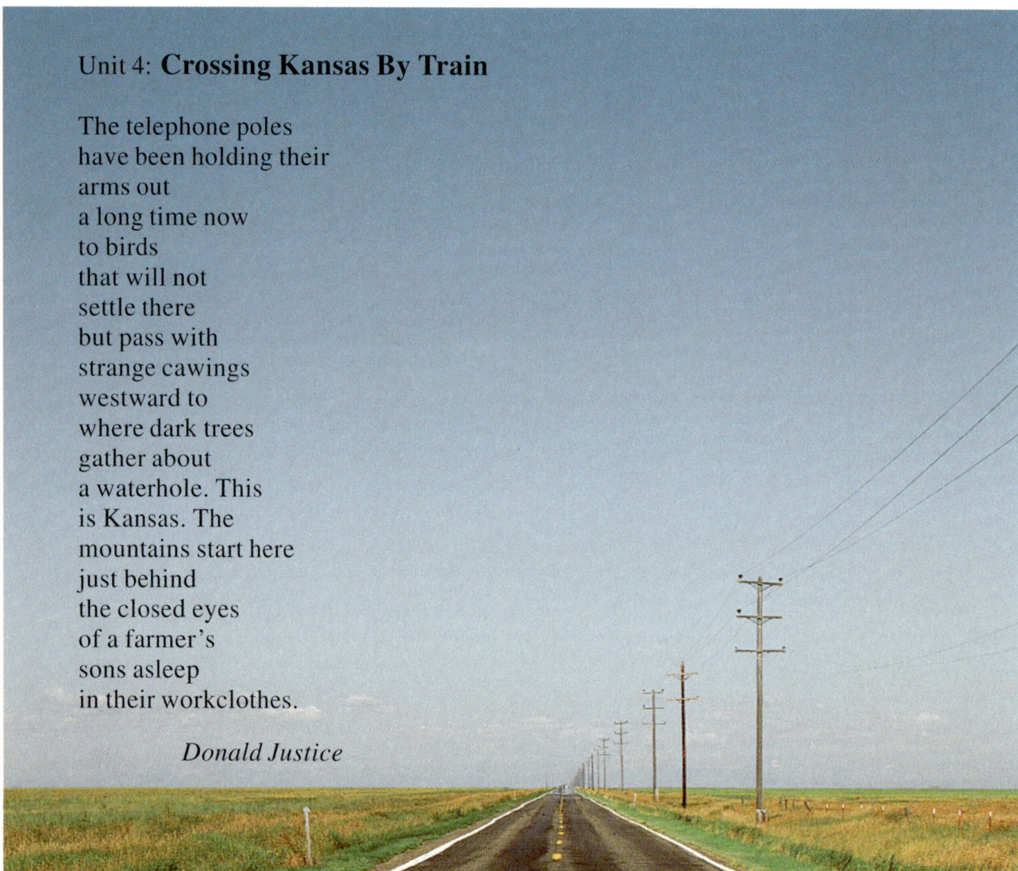

Unit 4: **Crossing Kansas By Train**

The telephone poles
have been holding their
arms out
a long time now
to birds
that will not
settle there
but pass with
strange cawings
westward to
where dark trees
gather about
a waterhole. This
is Kansas. The
mountains start here
just behind
the closed eyes
of a farmer's
sons asleep
in their workclothes.

Donald Justice

EXTRA READING

Unit 5: **Poem**

I loved my friend.
He went away from me.
There's nothing more to say.
The poem ends,
Soft as it began –
I loved my friend.

Langston Hughes

Unit 5: **Friends**

I fear it's very wrong of me,
And yet I must admit,
When someone offers friendship
I want the *whole* of it.
I don't want everybody else
To share my friend with me.
At least, I want *one* special one,
Who, indisputably,
Likes me much more than all the rest,
Who's always on my side,
Who never cares what others say,
Who lets me come and hide
Within the shadow, in his house –
It doesn't matter where –
Who lets me simply be myself,
Who's always, always there.

Elizabeth Jennings

Unit 5: **Mother to Son**

Well, son, I'll tell you:
Life for me ain't been no crystal stair.
It's had tacks in it,
And splinters,
And boards torn up,
And places with no carpet on the floor –
Bare.
But all the time
I'se been a-climbin' on,
And reachin' landin's,
And turnin' corners,
And sometimes goin' in the dark
Where there ain't been no light.
So, boy, don't you turn back.
Don't you set down on the steps
'Cause you finds it kinder hard.
Don't you fall now –
For I'se still goin', honey,
I'se still climbin',
And life for me ain't been no crystal stair.

Langston Hughes

EXTRA READING

Unit 5: *The fun they had*

Margie even wrote about it that night in her diary. On the page headed May 17, 2157 she wrote, "Today Tommy found a real book!"

It was a very old book. Margie's grandfather once said that when he was a little boy *his* grandfather told him that there was a time when all stories were printed on paper. They turned the pages, which were yellow and crinkly, and it was awfully funny to read words that stood still instead of moving the way they were supposed to – on a screen, you know. And then, when they turned back to the page before, it had the same words on it that it had had when they read it the first time.

"Gee," said Tommy,"what a waste. When you're through with the book, you just throw it away, I guess. Our television screen must have had a million books on it, and it's good for plenty more. I wouldn't throw *it* away."

"Same with mine," said Margie. She was eleven and hadn't seen as many telebooks as Tommy had. He was thirteen.

She said, "Where did you find it?"

"In my house." He pointed without looking, because he was busy reading. " In the attic."

"What's it about?"

"School."

Margie was scornful. "School? What's there to write about school? I hate school."

Margie always hated school, but now she hated it more than ever. The mechanical teacher had been giving her test after test in geography and she had been doing worse and worse until her mother had shaken her head and sent for the County Inspector.

He was a round little man with a red face and a whole box of tools. He smiled at her and gave her an apple, then took the teacher apart. Margie had hoped that he wouldn't know how to put it together again, but he knew how all right, and, after an hour or so, there it was again, large and black and ugly, with a big screen on which all the lessons were shown and the questions were asked. That wasn't so bad. The part she hated most was the slot where she had to put homework and test papers. The mechanical teacher calculated the mark in no time.

The inspector had smiled after he was finished and said to her mother, "It's not Margie's fault, Mrs. Jones. I think the geography sector was geared a little too quick. These things happen sometimes. Actually, her progress is quite satisfactory."

Margie was disappointed. She had been hoping they would take the teacher away altogether. They had once taken Tommy's teacher away for nearly a month because the history sector had blanked out completely.

So she said to Tommy, "Why would anyone write about school?"

Tommy looked at her with very superior eyes. "Because it's not our kind of school, stupid. This is the old kind of school that they had hundreds and hundreds of years ago." He added, pronouncing the word carefully, *"Centuries* ago."

Margie was hurt. "Well, I don't know what kind of school they had all that time ago." She read the book over his shoulder for a while, then said, "Anyway, they had a teacher."

"Sure they had a teacher, but it wasn't a *regular* teacher. It was a man."

"A man? How could a man be a teacher?"

"Well, he just told the boys and girls things and gave them homework and asked them questions."

"A man isn't smart enough."

"Sure he is. My father knows as much as my teacher."

"He can't. A man can't know as much as a teacher."

"He knows almost as much, I betcha."

Margie said, "I wouldn't want a strange man in the house to teach me."

Tommy screamed with laughter. "You don't know much, Margie. The teachers didn't live in the house. They had a special building and all the kids went there."

"And all the kids learned the same thing?"

"Sure, if they were the same age."

"But my mother says a teacher has to be adjusted to fit each boy and girl it teaches, and that each kid has to be taught differently."

"They didn't do it that way then. If you don't like it, you don't have to read the book."

"I didn't say I didn't like it," Margie said quickly. She wanted to read about those funny schools.

They weren't even half-finished when Margie's mother called, "Margie! School!"
Margie looked up. "Not yet mamma."
"Now!" said Mrs Jones. "And it's probably time for Tommy, too."
Margie said to Tommy, "Can I read the book some more with you after school?"
"Maybe," he said. He walked away, the dusty old book beneath his arm.

Margie went into the schoolroom. It was right next to her bedroom, and the mechanical teacher was on and waiting for her. It was always on at the same time every day except Saturday and Sunday, because her mother said little girls learned better if they learned at regular hours.
The screen said: "Today's lesson is on the addition of fractions. Please insert yesterday's homework."
Margie did so with a sigh. She was thinking about the old schools they had when her grandfather's grandfather was a little boy. All the kids from the whole neighborhood came, laughing and shouting in the schoolyard, sitting together in the schoolroom, going home together at the end of the day. They learned the same things, so they could help one another on the homework and talk about it.
And the teachers were people.
The mechanical teacher was flashing on the screen: "When we add the fractions $^{1}/_{2}$ and $^{1}/_{4}$ –"
Margie was thinking about how the kids must have loved it in the old days. She was thinking about the fun they had.

Isaac Asimov (adapted)

- *Would you like to live in the world described in the story? Why/Why not?*

Unit 6: **Roman Wall Blues**

Over the heather the wet wind blows,
I've lice in my tunic and a cold in my nose.

The rain comes pattering out of the sky,
I'm a Wall soldier, I don't know why.

The mist creeps over the hard grey stone,
My Girl's in Tungria; I sleep alone.

Aulus goes hanging around her place,
I don't like his manners, I don't like his face.

Piso's a Christian, he worships a fish;
There'd be no kissing if he had his wish.

She gave me a ring but I diced it away;
I want my girl and I want my pay.

When I'm a veteran with only one eye
I shall do nothing but look at the sky.

W. H. Auden

The story of St. Alban

During the first and second centuries neither the Romans nor the British were Christians. In Verulamium, for example, the Romans and the British each worshipped their own pagan gods in their own temples. And in other parts of the Empire, the Romans tolerated all the different pagan religions. But with Christianity it was different. The Romans persecuted all the men and women who followed this religion, not only in Rome, but all over their Empire.

One day in the year 209, a Christian priest arrived at Verulamium. His name was Amphibalus and he was hiding from Roman soldiers. A man called Alban gave him shelter in his house. Alban was British and a pagan, but he was moved when the priest talked about his religion. Finally he, too, decided to become a Christian. When the Roman soldiers heard that the priest was hiding in Alban's house, they came to look for him. They marched down the narrow streets towards Alban's house and knocked loudly on the wooden door. Alban wanted to save the priest's life, so he quickly put on the priest's cloak and ran out of the house. The soldiers followed him until they caught him. And so the real priest, Amphibalus, was able to escape.

The soldiers took Alban to a Roman judge. When the judge asked Alban who he was, he said "I am Alban. I worship the true God who created all things." The judge ordered Alban to give up the Christian religion. But Alban refused. He ordered Alban to kill an animal and offer it to the Roman gods, but still he refused. So the Romans tortured him and finally he was sentenced to death.

It was the custom in those days that Christians were killed by gladiators or wild animals in a large arena. But this was not possible with Alban. He was rich and what was more important: although he was British, he was also a Roman citizen. On June 22nd in the year 209 Roman soldiers marched Alban out of Verulamium to a hill half a mile from the city walls.

Stories say that so many people followed Alban from the town that they could not all cross the bridge over the river. Alban stopped, looked up to heaven and the river suddenly went dry, and so they were all able to cross over. When the executioner saw this, he threw his sword on the ground and refused to kill Alban. He wanted to die instead of Alban or with him.

From the river Alban walked to the top of the hill. It was a beautiful day in early summer and the ground was covered with flowers of many different colours. There Alban asked God for some water and a fountain suddenly came up from the ground. Then Alban was executed, and so he became the first Christian martyr who died for his religion in Britain. But the man who executed him was punished. As Alban's head fell off, the executioner's eyes fell from his head and onto the grass.

The soldier who had refused to kill Alban was also executed. But the judge was so surprised when he saw what had happened that he stopped persecuting Christians. In fact, after Alban's death Christians were never persecuted in Britain again, and the site of Alban's execution became a place that Christians remembered. First they built a simple wooden church. Today the cathedral stands on that site.

EXTRA READING

A 12th century Welsh legend:

The Three Blows (Unit 8)

One day a young shepherd called Gwyn was eating his bread beside a lake in the heart of the Black Mountains when he noticed a beautiful young woman. She was sitting on the waters of the lake and brushing her golden hair.

Gwyn fell in love with the fairy at once. But she refused to speak to him.

Day after day he returned to the lake and tried to get an answer. Each time he offered to share his bread with the woman, but she continued to ignore him – until one day she finally took some bread. "Your bread is hard and I am hard to hold," she said. Then she dived under the water.

Gwyn came back the next day with some unbaked bread. This time he was told, "Soft is your bread – you and I won't wed."

The young shepherd was not sure what to do now, so he asked his mother to help him and she baked some bread that was just right. This time, when Gwyn offered his bread to the fairy, she took it and said, "Return tomorrow and we can be married."

***

The next day, Gwyn saw nobody at first. Then an old man appeared in the middle of the lake, together with two young women. As they came across the water towards him, the old man spoke, "Young man, my daughter that you love will be your wife if you can tell me which is she and which her sister."

The shepherd looked into the faces of the two beautiful women and realized that they were twins. Eyes, hair, hands, even the clothes they wore were the same.

"Speak, which do you love?" the old man said. Gwyn did not know who to choose, and

EXTRA READING

his eyes fell. Then he noticed a breadcrumb on one of the girls' shoes. Quickly he turned towards the father and cried, "I love the one you hold with your right hand!"

"Well chosen. She will be your wife and you will prosper. However, know this. If you ever strike her without reason, at the third blow she will return to me and you will never again see the daughter I now give to you."

* * *

As Gwyn walked down the mountain with his bride, out of the lake there appeared five times five of the finest sheep the young man had ever seen, then five times five goats, then cows and horses – as a dowry. The shepherd and his wife lived happily, and they had three sons. And thanks to the dowry of a hundred animals, they grew richer as each year passed.

* * *

One day, however, when it was time to go to church for their eldest son's confirmation, the lady hesitated, so Gwyn gave her a gentle push in the back.

Later, when a friend's son was married, she had tears in her eyes, so he patted her on the arm and told her not to cry. Each time, she warned him not to strike her again without good reason, and he tried to remember.

However, on the day of a neighbour's funeral, the shepherd could not understand why his wife was smiling, so he grabbed her wrist and shook it. "If you knew more about the world of the dead, you would understand," she said, "for they have no problems." But she stopped smiling, and now tears came into her eyes.

"Ah, Gwyn!" she cried. "Three times you have struck me without good reason. I must now return to where I came from."

Gwyn could only watch as she climbed the mountain towards the lake, where she disappeared into the dark waters and all the sheep, goats, horses and cattle of the farm followed her. He was no longer rich now, and had to give up the farm and work as a simple shepherd.

He often went up to the lake and stared into its waters until the sun went down. But, as her father had promised, the lady never came back. Months and years passed by. Gwyn refused to give up hope, but he never saw his wife again.

- *Is Gwyn treated fairly, do you think? Do you feel sorry for him?*
- *What do you think of his wife? Why do you think she acted as she did?*

Additional material

Revision exercise pool

After Unit 2:

1 *Find the right places for all these little words.*

one mine any (2×)
theirs yours there
some ones their

1. You can't find your hairbrush? Why don't you use . . . ?
2. We've still got some soap, you needn't buy . . . .
3. I've put your towel in the washing machine. You can take a clean . . . .
4. What do you think of that skirt over . . . ?
5. You can try on my jacket if you let me try . . . on.
6. I don't like those brown trousers. I prefer the black . . . .
7. Feed the cats, please. And remember, the Millers are on holiday. We've got to feed . . . , too.
8. I must have . . . chips with ketchup today. I haven't had . . . for such a long time.
9. Most of the food in that new restaurant is good. Only . . . pizzas aren't so nice.

2 **Asking for more information** *Practise questions in different tenses.*

a
1. I need a new car. It would be too expensive to repair the one I've got now.
   – When/buy a new one?

2. We live in New York.
   – How long/live there?
3. Have a look at my new CD-player.
   – Oh, it looks expensive. How much/cost?
4. Mrs Silver's office is in Manhattan.
   – How/get there?
5. My bike still has a puncture.
   – Why/not repair it yet?
6. Tom was busy when I phoned him. He couldn't help me.
   – Oh, what/do?
7. I don't want to stop reading now. This book is so exciting.
   – What/read?

b *Practise dialogues with a partner: Choose statements from above or make up your own statements. First your partner asks for more information. Then you give her/him an answer.*

After Unit 4:

1 **My brother John** *Decide if you need an indefinite or a definite article or no article at all.*

My brother John is … teacher in … small town of Willmington, Ohio. … life of … teacher isn't easy in America. Many American teachers don't earn enough to live comfortably. That's why, like many other American teachers, he has … second job. He works as … car mechanic. Some years ago he still had a job as … window-cleaner.
John visits us here in Detroit twice … year. He says he likes Detroit, but just for … week. At … end of … week he feels he has had enough of … town life. He doesn't like … noise you get in big towns, especially … noise of … traffic. He prefers … quiet life he has in Willmington.

Revision exercises

2 The new car *Use the right form of the verb in brackets.*

Every year Lothar from Würzburg (visit) his aunt and uncle in Nashville, Tennessee. When Aunt Marilyn (meet) him at the airport last July, he (be) surprised to see her with a new car.

I see you (have got) a new car. When (you/buy) it, Aunt Marilyn?

Oh, we (decide) to get a new one about two months ago. So we just (go) out and (get) one.

And your old car? It still (look) quite good last year.

It (still stand) in the garage. We (not sell) it yet.

Then I (can) drive it while I'm on vacation. I (really look forward) to that.

Oh, no you . . . . And anyway, it (not be) there very long.

What (you/do) with it?

One of our friends (fetch) it next week.

(he/be) that car-crazy friend of yours who (collect) old cars?

That's right, Al (collect) old cars for several years now. But please (not ask) me what he (do) with them – I really (not know).

After Unit 5:

1 Problems of early settlers *Active or passive?*

The History of Plimoth Plantation (write) by William Bradford between 1620 and 1651. It is a kind of diary in which he (write) about the life of the Pilgrims. After the Pilgrims had landed in Plimoth harbour, they (unload) the *Mayflower*. Then all their things (put) in a dry place. Later, cottages (build) for everybody. They also (discuss) things and (make) laws for their small group of people.
In the winter months of 1620/21 over half of the Pilgrims (die) and over 40 (become) ill. For some time all the work (have to/do) by only six or seven people. They (have to/work) day and night to help those who (not be able to) look after themselves.

2 What different people said to Marvin *Practise reported speech.*

1. *Mrs Mitchell:* It's Wednesday, Marvin, so I won't be back from work before five.
2. *Mr Mitchell:* It really annoys me that you don't work harder in class.
3. *Elliot:* Do you want to come with me to Mr Feldman's shop?
4. *Mrs Mitchell:* Don't hang around with Elliot all the time.
5. *Joe McDowell:* Don't tell anybody or you'll be in trouble.
6. *Mrs Stone:* Somebody saw a black boy in the alley, Marvin.

Examples: 1. His mother reminded him that it was . . . . 2. His father said that . . . . *Go on.*

After Unit 8:

1 Just imagine … *Practise conditional sentences. Find three or more endings to the following sentences.*

1. We'll be on the front page of all the newspapers if …

2. I'll write to the President of the USA if …

3. If I had known …

4. If you were older …

2 A phone call from Ms Alviar

Check your tenses. In some cases more than one tense can be used.

Where (you/be) all afternoon?

Where (you/think) I (be)? In the fields, of course. Why (you/ask)?

A Ms Alviar (phone) about an hour ago. She (want) to talk to you.

Alviar? Oh, she (be) from Blackwells'. What (she/say) about our new tractor? (it/arrive) yet?

Yes. Ms Alviar (give) me the telephone number of her office. She (say) she (be) there till 5.30.

Well, I (try) to phone her for several days, but whenever I (phone) she (not be) there. I must phone her at once. Maybe we (be able to) fetch the tractor before the weekend.

"It's your boss. He wants to know why you're not at work."

○Interpreting and translation practice

After Unit 2:

1 **Macy's – it's still the largest of them all** (Adapted from an article in *Where Magazine*)

In 1858, people thought Rowland Hussey Macy was either a fool or a genius. History proved he was a genius. He had had the life of an adventurer; he had been a whaler and he had been an unsuccessful businessman – twice in Massachusetts and once in California. Three times he had gone bankrupt. But he was a man who believed in the maxim "If at first you don't succeed, try, try again."
He tried again – this time in New York, where he started a small store on 14th Street. The store did so well that in 1902 it was time to move to a different place, to where the store now stands in Herald Square. . . .

a **Interpreting:** Imagine a German friend would like to know what this article says. If your friend only wants to know the important pieces of information you can interpret for her/him. Then you don't have to express things in the same way as the original text. You can leave out the information which you think is not so important.
Here are some expressions you will need when you interpret
– a written text: „Hier steht …", „Dann steht hier noch …", „Hier heißt es, dass …"; "At the beginning the text says …", "And then it says …".
– a spoken text (e.g. a conversation): „Frau/Herr … meint/sagt, dass …/möchte wissen …"; "Mr/Mrs … says/thinks …/would like to know if/why/how …".

Now interpret what the text says. The following words are new: genius, (to) prove, adventurer, whaler, unsuccessful, businessman, (to) go bankrupt, maxim. You will be able to guess what some of the words mean from the context or because they are similar to English words you know, to German words or words you know from another foreign language. The word-building rules you have learnt will also help you. The rest you can look up in a dictionary.

b **Translating:** If your friend wants to know exactly what the text says, you will have to translate it. In a translation it is important to keep to the original text as much as possible. Translate the text above and then compare the two German texts.

2 Interpret what the following text says. New words: in the meantime, (to) take over, (to) remain, (to) expand, addition, symbol, success, profit, (to) return sth., (to) sponsor, firework display, Thanksgiving Day Parade.

… In the meantime Isidor and Nathan Straus, Germans who had come to New York in 1852, had become business partners of the Macy family. They finally took over the store, but kept the name. And the store has remained in their family until today.
In the 1920s the Straus brothers expanded the business through a number of additions to the building so that Macy's covered almost the whole area between 34th and 35th Streets, Broadway and 7th Avenue. In its more than 130-year history, Macy's has become a symbol of success, an example of an American success story.
Every year part of Macy's profit is returned to New Yorkers and to visitors to New York. The store sponsors the big firework display that can be seen from along the East River on July 4, and there is Macy's famous Thanksgiving Day Parade in November.

After Unit 4:

Remember: The English words "one" or "you", or a passive can often be translated into German as "man".

New words in the sentences on the left and in the text below: short wave, radio talk, audience; journalist, weekly, (to) do a programme, (to) receive, (to) tune in to, the (BBC) World Service, aim, (to) unite, Texan. Guess what these words mean from the context or look them up in a dictionary.

a Translate these sentences:

1. In the USA *you can* only *hear* Alistair Cooke's programme on short wave.
2. *One can say* that a radio talk is made for a friend sitting in his room, not for a large audience.
3. *Americans are* sometimes *thought to be* very different from Europeans.

This is how you can begin: 1. „In den USA kann man ..." 2. „Man kann sagen, dass ..." 3. „Man glaubt manchmal, dass ..."

b Now translate the following text and use German "man" where possible.

LETTER FROM AMERICA

by Alistair Cooke

(Based on "A note to the reader" in A. Cooke, *The Americans*)

During the Second World War Alistair Cooke, a journalist from Manchester, started a weekly radio programme from America for the BBC. Originally Cooke was expected to stop his talks after the end of the war. But in 1946 he was asked to do another weekly programme with the title *Letter from America*. This 15-minute programme about America could be received in Britain and in many other parts of the world.

It seems unbelievable, but even today, more than 50 years after the first *Letter from America,* you can switch on your radio, tune in to BBC Radio 4 or the World Service and listen to the programme. (You can listen to A. Cooke on Sunday mornings on Radio 4 and on Monday morning in the World Service.)

One can learn things about America from Cooke's talks which one would never read about in newspapers and never see on television. That is why in many countries Cooke is thought to be an expert on America.

He says his aim is still what it was when the talks began: to show what life is like in America, to show that there are many things which unite a Texan and a person from Britain or Germany, Africa or Asia.

Interpreting and translation practice

After Unit 5:

a *Remember:* Preposition + gerund in English must often be translated into German by a subordinate clause.

St Louis

One of the attractions of St Louis is Union Station, once an important station on the way west. It was finally shut down in 1978 after having served over 100 000 passengers a day from the 1920s to the 1950s. Instead of demolishing it, the city of St Louis restored the station. By restoring it as a tourist attraction, the city wanted to remind visitors of its importance as a railroad center in the 19th century and the first half of the 20th century.

Translate this text for a German friend. Use a subordinate clause in German for preposition + gerund in the English text. Here is some help: *St Louis, eine dynamische Stadt:*
Die Union Station .... Dieser Bahnhof wurde schließlich ..., nachdem er .... Anstatt ihn ...

After Unit 8:

Remember: Some verbal expressions in English can be translated into German as adverbs.

a
1. I'm afraid I can't go on holiday with you to California.
2. We hope to see you soon after you've come back.
3. I suppose it's the fresh air which makes many tourists hire bikes and ride along the beach.
4. Others prefer exploring the area when they jog.
5. This peaceful area seems to be paradise for many tourists.
6. If you like eating seafood, you must go to one of the waterfront restaurants in Monterey.

Translate the sentences above and use adverbs in your German sentences for the underlined English verbal expressions. Here is some help: 1. Leider ... 2. Hoffentlich ... 3. Vermutlich ... 4. ... lieber ... 5. ... anscheinend ... 6. ... gern ...

b Now translate this text and use adverbs for verbal expressions where possible.

Exploring the California coast

(Based on an article in *Adventure Road*)

If you like eating, drinking fine wines, looking at fantastic scenery, then I suppose Carmel and the Monterey Peninsula, 120 miles south of San Francisco, are the "good life" for you. The area has so much to offer that you will certainly have problems deciding what to do. If you like playing golf, you can go to Pebble Beach; if you prefer shopping or visiting galleries, then go to Carmel-by-the-Sea, an artists' colony since the 1920s.
Carmel is a sleepy little town with trees along the streets, and lots of art galleries and shops. Clint Eastwood, famous star of many westerns, seems to like Carmel, too. He was once mayor of the town.

Grammar at a glance

Unit 2

▶ Der bestimmte Artikel (The definite article)

	OHNE bestimmten Artikel stehen	MIT bestimmtem Artikel stehen
1	How did **life** begin? … das Leben? **Children** like animals. Kinder … Every animal needs **water**. … Wasser.	We read about **the life** of Robin Hood. … das Leben … Where are **the children** I talked to? … die Kinder … **The water** in our town is not polluted. Das Wasser …
	– abstrakte Nomen, zählbare Nomen im Plural und Stoffnamen, wenn sie ganz allgemein gebraucht werden.	– abstrakte Nomen, zählbare Nomen im Plural und Stoffnamen, wenn sie näher bestimmt sind.
2	**Little Joan** couldn't see the film. Die kleine Joan … **Fifth Avenue** has many fine shops. Die Fifth Avenue … We met our friends in **Times Square**. … am Times Square.	**The Claytons** are our new neighbours. (Die) Claytons … **The United States** is a huge country. Die Vereinigten Staaten … **The Bronx** is in the north of New York. Die Bronx …
	– Personennamen und die meisten Namen von Straßen und Plätzen.	– Familiennamen im Plural und einige geographische Namen.
3	My parents have gone to **church**. … in die Kirche.	This is a good photo of **the church**. … von der Kirche.
	– *church, hospital, prison, school, university* usw., wenn an den Verwendungszweck des Gebäudes gedacht wird.	– *church, hospital, prison, school, university* usw., wenn an den Ort oder an das Bauwerk gedacht wird.
4	**Lincoln Center** **Rockefeller Center**	**the Empire State Building** **the World Trade Center**
	Bei Gebäudenamen ist die Verwendung des bestimmten Artikels unterschiedlich.	

→ Unit 2, p. 19

▶ Der unbestimmte Artikel (The indefinite article)

Der unbestimmte Artikel *a/an* steht

Francis Drake was **an Englishman**. … war Engländer.	– vor Nationalitätsbezeichnungen,
My sister wants to become **a teacher**. … möchte Lehrerin werden.	– vor Berufsangaben,
I used my shoe as **a hammer**. … als Hammer.	– nach *as* (= als),
The tomatoes are 90p **a pound**. … 90p pro Pfund.	– in der Bedeutung „pro/je“ vor Zeit-, Maß- und Mengenangaben.

→ Unit 2, p. 22

▶ **Bedingungssätze** (Conditional sentences)

1 Mit einem Bedingungssatz lassen sich unterschiedliche Arten von Bedingungen ausdrücken:

Reale Bedingungen: – Die Bedingung ist erfüllbar oder bereits erfüllt (Bedingungssatz I):
If Tom wins the race tomorrow, I'll be happy.

Irreale Bedingungen: – Die Bedingung ist nicht erfüllbar oder wird höchstwahrscheinlich nicht erfüllt (Bedingungssatz II):
If Tom won the race tomorrow, I'd be happy.

– Die Bedingung bezieht sich auf die Vergangenheit und ist daher nicht mehr erfüllbar (Bedingungssatz III):
If Tom had won the race yesterday, I'd have been happy.

2 Bedingungssatz I („Was ist, wenn …?")

If-Satz (*if*-clause)		Hauptsatz (main clause)	
simple present	If the sun **shines**,	we**'ll go** to the beach.	*will-future*
	If you **want** to,	we **can play** tennis.	modales Hilfsverb + Inf.
	If you **see** Megan today,	**ask** her to ring me.	Imperativ
simple present	If you **eat** too much,	you **get** fat.	*simple present*
present progressive	If it**'s raining**,	we can't play outside.	
present perfect	If you**'ve been** to York,	you'll know how beautiful it is.	
modales Hilfsverb + Inf.	If you **can't come**,	we'll go without you.	

3 Bedingungssatz II („Was wäre, wenn …?")

If-Satz (*if*-clause)		Hauptsatz (main clause)	
simple past	If I **was** on holiday,	I **would sleep** till 11.	*would* + Inf.
	If Mr Lee **won** $150,000,	he **could buy** a house.	*could* + Inf.
	If we **hurried**,	we **might catch** the bus.	*might* + Inf.

→ Unit 4, p. 40

4 Bedingungssatz III („Was wäre gewesen, wenn …?")

If-Satz (*if*-clause)		Hauptsatz (main clause)	
past perfect	If you **had asked** me,	I **would have helped**.	*would have* + Part. Perf.
	If you **had told** me earlier,	I **could have come**.	*could have* + Part. Perf.
	If Sue **had shouted**,	I **might have reacted**.	*might have* + Part. Perf.
past perfect	If Pete **had got up** earlier,	he **wouldn't be** late now.	*would* + Inf.

→ Unit 4, p. 41

Unit 5

▶ Das Gerundium (The gerund)

1 Das Gerundium nach bestimmten Verben

a Do you **enjoy reading**?
Liest du gern?

Mrs Sands **gave up smoking** last year.
Mrs Sands gab letztes Jahr das Rauchen auf.

Nach bestimmten Verben steht das Gerundium als Objekt. Beispiele: *admit*, *avoid*, *carry on*, *consider*, *dislike*, *enjoy*, *finish*, *give up*, *imagine*, *keep*, *mention*, *mind*, *miss*, *practise*, *risk*, *suggest*.

b My father **hates driving**./My father **hates to drive**.
Mein Vater fährt sehr ungern Auto.

Nach folgenden Verben kann entweder das Gerundium oder der *to*-Infinitiv verwendet werden: *begin*, *start*, *continue*, *like*, *love*, *prefer*, *hate*, *intend*. Die Bedeutung ändert sich dabei nicht.

c Can't you **remember seeing** Mr Brown last summer?
Kannst du dich nicht daran erinnern, dass wir Mr Brown letzten Sommer getroffen haben?
Please **remember to write** to Mr Brown.
Vergiss bitte nicht an Mr Brown zu schreiben!

Die Verben *forget*, *remember*, *stop*, *try* haben unterschiedliche Bedeutungen, je nachdem ob sie mit dem Gerundium oder dem Infinitiv verbunden werden.

→ Unit 5, p. 56, 62

2 Das Gerundium nach Präpositionen

a Tony's team is **afraid of losing** the match.
Tonys Mannschaft befürchtet das Spiel zu verlieren.
Frank had no **chance of escaping** the storm.
Frank hatte keine Möglichkeit dem Sturm zu entkommen.
Cathy **apologized for being** late.
Cathy entschuldigte sich, dass sie zu spät kam.

Verben, die auf eine Präposition folgen, stehen im Gerundium. Die Präposition kann mit einem Adjektiv, Nomen oder Verb verbunden sein.

b Mike has been playing all afternoon **instead of doing** his homework.
... anstatt seine Hausaufgaben zu machen.
After swimming we were tired.
Nach dem Schwimmen .../Nachdem wir geschwommen waren, ...

Das Gerundium kann zusammen mit bestimmten, allein stehenden Präpositionen (z.B. *after*, *before*, *by*, *instead of*, *without*) eine adverbiale Bestimmung bilden.

→ Unit 5, p. 57

3 Das Gerundium mit eigenem „Sinnsubjekt“

Mrs Smith doesn't **mind her daughter/her coming** home late.
Mrs Smith macht es nichts aus, wenn ihre Tochter/sie spät nach Hause kommt.

Ein Nomen oder Pronomen vor dem Gerundium zeigt an, dass das Gerundium sich nicht auf das Subjekt des Satzes bezieht, sondern ein eigenes Subjekt hat.

→ Unit 5, p. 57

Unit 8

▶ Der Infinitiv mit *to* (The infinitive with *to*)

1 Der *to*-Infinitiv nach bestimmten Verben, Adjektiven und Nomen

I'm sorry, but I **forgot to post** your letter.
It's **difficult to find** our house.
Sue's **decision to leave** school surprised everybody.

Der *to*-Infinitiv kann nach bestimmten Verben, Adjektiven und Nomen stehen. → Unit 8, p. 86

2 Der *to*-Infinitiv zum Ausdruck eines Zwecks

We stayed at home **(in order) to watch** TV.
Wir blieben zu Hause um fernzusehen.

Der *to*-Infinitiv dient häufig zum Ausdruck einer Absicht oder eines Zwecks. → Unit 8, p. 86

3 Der *to*-Infinitiv zum Ausdruck einer Folge

This time Mary didn't swim **fast enough to win** the race.
Diesmal schwamm Mary nicht schnell genug um das Rennen zu gewinnen.

It's **too windy to sit** in the garden today.
Es ist heute zu windig um im Garten zu sitzen.

Zum Ausdruck einer Folge steht der *to*-Infinitiv nach einem Adjektiv/Adverb + *enough* bzw. nach *too* + Adjektiv/Adverb. → Unit 8, p. 86

4 Der *to*-Infinitiv anstelle eines Relativsatzes

I don't know **anyone to ask**. = … anyone who I can ask.
Ich kenne niemanden, den ich fragen kann.

Aldrin and Armstrong were **the first men to land** on the moon. = … the first men who landed …
Aldrin und Armstrong waren die ersten Menschen, die auf dem Mond landeten.

Nach *someone*, *anyone* usw., nach bestimmten Nomen, nach *the first/last/next/only* oder nach einem Superlativ + Nomen kann der *to*-Infinitiv anstelle eines Relativsatzes stehen. → Unit 8, p. 87

5 Der *to*-Infinitiv nach bestimmten Verben + Objekt

I don't **want the children to play** football in the street.
Ich möchte nicht, dass die Kinder auf der Straße Fußball spielen.

Nach bestimmten Verben (z.B. *ask*, *expect*, *want*, *would like*) kann ein Objekt + *to*-Infinitiv stehen.

→ Unit 8, p. 87

6 Der *to*-Infinitiv nach *for* + Nomen/Pronomen

It's very important **for Tom to talk** to the boss.
Es ist sehr wichtig, dass Tom mit dem Chef spricht.

We're waiting **for you to start**.
Wir warten darauf, dass du anfängst.

Der *to*-Infinitiv steht häufig nach *for* + Nomen/Pronomen. Die Präposition *for* kann mit einem Verb verbunden sein (z.B. *wait for*). → Unit 8, p. 87

▶ Zusammenschau 1: Die Verwendung der modalen Hilfsverben
(Summary 1: The use of the modal auxiliaries)

1 Fähigkeit: *can, could, be able to*

My sister **can** repair/**is able to** repair a computer.	Present: *can, be able to*
John **couldn't** come/**wasn't able to** come yesterday.	Past: *could, was/were able to*
In a few years you**'ll be able to** speak English well.	Zusammengesetzte Zeitformen: *be able to*

2 Erlaubnis: *can, may, be allowed to*; Verbot: *can't, mustn't, be not allowed to*

You **can** see/**are allowed to** see the patient now.	Present: *can, be allowed to*
You **can't** smoke/**aren't allowed to** smoke now.	
Can/Could/May we have a look at the pets, please?	Bitte um Erlaubnis: *Can/Could/May I/we …?*
You **mustn't** cross the street here.	Ausdrückliches Verbot: *mustn't*
We**'ve** never **been allowed to** watch TV late at night.	Zusammengesetzte Zeitformen: *be allowed to*

3 Zwang, Notwendigkeit: *must, have to, needn't*

We **must** choose/**have to** choose four of the questions.	Present: *must/needn't, have to/don't have to*
We **needn't** answer/**don't have to** answer all of them.	
Why **did** you **have to** leave so early?	Past und zusammengesetzte Zeitformen: *have to*

4 Verpflichtung, Ratschlag: *should, ought to*

You **should** stop/**ought to** stop smoking.

5 Bitte, Aufforderung: *Can/Could/Would you …?*

Can/Could/Would you do the shopping for me today?

6 Vorschlag, Angebot: *Shall I/we …?*

Shall we have an ice-cream?

7 Möglichkeit, Wahrscheinlichkeit: *can, may, might, could, should, ought to*

Where **can** Derek be now? – He **may** be/**might** be/**could** be at his office.
The children left an hour ago. They **should** be/**ought to** be at home by now.

8 Modale Hilfsverben + *have* + Partizip Perfekt

We **should have told** the police about the accident.
You **could have asked** me before you took the car.
Ashraf is late. He **may have missed/might have missed** the bus.

Grammar at a glance/Zusammenschauen

▶ Zusammenschau 2: Die Zeitformen der Vollverben
(Summary 2: The tenses of the main verbs)

1 Simple present

Aktiv: **ask/asks** Passiv: **am/is/are asked**

John **works** at the airport.
I **know** the Blacks quite well.
The first bus **leaves** at 5.20 tomorrow morning.
Send me a postcard when you **get** to Rome.

- wenn etwas regelmäßig, oft oder nie geschieht;
- wenn man (gegenwärtige) Zustände beschreibt;
- wenn etwas Zukünftiges durch einen Zeit- oder Fahrplan festgelegt ist;
- in Nebensätzen der Zeit und der Bedingung, die sich auf die Zukunft beziehen.

Present progressive

A: **am/is/are asking** P: **am/is/are being asked**

I **am writing** letters at the moment.
Jill **is having** a party on Saturday.

- wenn eine Handlung/ein Vorgang gerade im Gange ist und noch nicht abgeschlossen ist;
- wenn eine Handlung fest für die Zukunft geplant oder vereinbart ist.

2 Present perfect (simple)

A: **has/have asked** P: **has/have been asked**

We **have** only **met** Paul once.

I **have known** the Blacks since 1972.

- wenn man sagt, dass (nicht: wann!) etwas geschehen ist;
- wenn man sagt, wie lange ein Zustand schon andauert.

Present perfect progressive

A: **has/have been asking**

The girls **have been playing** football since lunch.

- wenn man sagt, seit wann oder wie lange eine Handlung/ein Vorgang schon andauert.

3 Simple past

A: **asked** P: **was/were asked**

When **did** you last **see** Mark? – It **was** three days ago.

- wenn man sagt, wann etwas geschah oder wann jemand etwas getan hat.

Past progressive

A: **was/were asking** P: **was/were being asked**

When Sue arrived, we **were having** lunch.

- wenn eine Handlung/ein Vorgang zu einer bestimmten Zeit in der Vergangenheit gerade im Gange war.

4 Past perfect (simple)

A: **had asked** P: **had been asked**

All the things in the bag **had been stolen**.

- wenn eine Handlung/ein Vorgang bereits vor einem Zeitpunkt in der Vergangenheit stattgefunden hatte.

Past perfect progressive

A: **had been asking**

We **had been working** for some time when we noticed that it was 12.30.

- wenn eine Handlung/ein Vorgang vor einem Zeitpunkt in der Vergangenheit begonnen hatte und zu diesem Zeitpunkt noch andauerte.

5 Will-future

A: **will ask**	P: **will be asked**

I don't think you**'ll like** it here.
You look tired. I**'ll carry** the bags for you.

– wenn man Vorhersagen oder Vermutungen über die Zukunft äußert;
– wenn man spontane Entschlüsse oder Versprechen äußert.

Future progressive

A: **will be asking**

This time next week I**'ll be taking** my last test.

– wenn eine Handlung/ein Vorgang zu einem Zeitpunkt in der Zukunft im Gange, d.h. noch nicht abgeschlossen sein wird.

Future perfect

A: **will have asked**	P: **will have been asked**

Wait a moment, I**'ll have finished** in 10 minutes.

– wenn eine Handlung/ein Vorgang zu einem Zeitpunkt in der Zukunft geschehen sein wird.

6 Going to-future

A: **am/is/are going to ask**	P: **am/... going to be asked**

What **are** you **going to do** tonight?

– wenn man Absichten, Pläne oder Vorhaben ausdrücken will.

▶ Zusammenschau 3: *s*-Genitiv und *of*-Fügung
(Summary 3: *s*-genitive and *of*-phrase)

1 Bildung des *s*-Genitivs

Singular	regelmäßige Pluralform	unregelmäßige Pluralform
my **sister's** cat **Tom's** boss	our **neighbours'** dog the **Webbs'** house	the **children's** mother the **men's** voices

2 Gebrauch des *s*-Genitivs

a This is **my brother's** girlfriend.
Is that **the children's** ball?
We ought to see **the lions'** cage.

Der *s*-Genitiv wird für Personen und häufig auch für Tiere verwendet.

b Is there **a baker's** (shop) near here?
We met Rose at **Robert's** (house).

Bei bestimmten Ortsangaben wird das Nomen nach dem *s*-Genitiv (z.B. *shop, house*) meist weggelassen.

c **Last month's** business was bad.
Do you know **yesterday's** football results?

Bestimmte Zeitangaben (z.B. *last month, today, yesterday, an hour*) können als *s*-Genitiv stehen.

3 Gebrauch der *of*-Fügung

a Can you tell me the name **of the street**?
The doors **of the room** were wide open.

Die *of*-Fügung wird für Sachen verwendet.

b six **litres of paint**
two **bottles of lemonade**

Die *of*-Fügung wird für Maß- und Mengenangaben verwendet.

→ Unit 8, Ex 9

Grammar at a glance/Zusammenschauen

▶ Zusammenschau 4: Mengenbezeichnungen (Summary 4: Quantifiers)

1 Übersicht

a **some – any**
a lot (of)/lots (of)
much – many
(a) little – (a) few

every – each
all
both
no

Some, *any*, *a lot (of)* usw. sind Mengenbezeichnungen. Von *some*, *any*, *every* und *no* gibt es Zusammensetzungen mit *-body*, *-one* und *-thing*, z.B. *somebody*, *anyone*, *everything*.

b Do you need **some money**? – Just **a little**.

Mengenbezeichnungen können entweder als Bestimmungswort *(determiner)* vor einem Nomen stehen oder als Pronomen, d.h. allein stehend, verwendet werden. Nur *every* und *no* stehen immer vor einem Nomen.

2 *some – any*

a We've still got **some** lemonade.
Is there **any** milk left?
There are**n't any** people here.

There's **somebody** at the door.
Can you see **anybody**?
I ca**n't** see **anything**.

Some, *somebody* usw. werden vor allem in bejahten Aussagesätzen verwendet.
Any, *anybody* usw. werden vor allem in Fragen und in verneinten Sätzen verwendet.

b Would you like **some** bread? Do you want **something** to drink, too?
Can I ask you **some** questions?

Some, *something* usw. werden in Fragen verwendet, wenn man etwas anbietet oder um etwas bittet.

→ Unit 8, p. 90

3 *a lot of/lots of, much – many, (a) little – (a) few*

a

mit nicht zählbaren Nomen	mit zählbaren Nomen im Plural
a lot of/lots of butter **much work** **(a) little time**	**a lot of/lots of oranges** **many jobs** **(a) few days**

b I haven't got **much** money.
How **many** cars did you count?

My friend has got **a lot of** British coins.
We saw **lots of** cars.

Much und *many* werden meist in verneinten Aussagesätzen und in Fragen verwendet.
In bejahten Aussagesätzen ist *a lot of/lots of* gebräuchlicher.

4 *every – each – any*

Every house was dark. — *every* = jede(r,s) ohne Ausnahme, alle
Each of my friends wrote a letter. — *each* = jede(r,s) einzelne
You can ask **anybody**. — *any* = jede(r,s) beliebige, irgendeine(r,s)

Every/Each child has to take three tests. — *Every* und *each* sind oft austauschbar (außer vor *of*).

→ Unit 8, p. 90

Grammatical terms

abstract noun [ˌæbstrækt 'naʊn]	abstraktes Nomen, Abstraktum
collocation [ˌkɒlə'keɪʃn]	Kollokation, (feste) Wortverbindung
consonant ['kɒnsənənt]	Konsonant, Mitlaut
determiner [dɪ'tɜːmɪnə]	Bestimmungswort
(phonetic) transcription [fəˌnetɪk træn'skrɪpʃn]	(phonetische) Umschrift
prefix ['priːfɪks]	Vorsilbe, Präfix
transitive verb [ˌtrænzətɪv 'vɜːb]	transitives Verb, Verb mit direktem Objekt
unreal condition [ʌnˌrɪəl kən'dɪʃn]	irreale Bedingung
verb of perception [ˌvɜːb‿əv pə'sepʃn]	Verb der (Sinnes-)Wahrnehmung
vowel ['vaʊəl]	Vokal, Selbstlaut

Vocabulary

Im folgenden Wörterverzeichnis (Vocabulary) sind die **neuen Wörter jeder Unit** aufgeführt. **Eingerückte Wörter** sollen mit dem vorausgehenden Wort mitgelernt werden, obwohl sie nicht an der betreffenden Stelle der Unit vorkommen. **Eigennamen** stehen nach dem Mini-dictionary auf den Seiten 185-187. **Grammatische Fachausdrücke** stehen am Ende der Grammatikübersicht auf Seite 129.

Die **fett gedruckten Wörter** gehören zum Grundwortschatz.

Die wenigen **normal gedruckten Wörter** gehören zum so genannten ‚Situationswortschatz'.
Es sind Wörter, die zwar zum Thema einer bestimmten Unit gehören, aber weniger gebräuchlich sind und daher in den folgenden Units nicht als bekannt vorausgesetzt werden.

Die **kursiv gedruckten Wörter** sind aus fakultativen Abschnitten. Sie werden außerhalb dieser fakultativen Abschnitte nicht als bekannt vorausgesetzt.

Die **Tilde** (~) in der dritten Spalte steht anstelle des Wortes oder der Wendung aus der ersten Spalte. Pro Tilde muss ein Wort eingesetzt werden.

sb. = somebody, sth. = something; jd. = jemand, jm. = jemandem, jn. = jemanden
adj. = adjective, adv. = adverb, n. = noun, prep. = preposition, sing. = singular, pl. = plural
AE = American English, BE = British English
infml. = informal (umgangssprachlich), nonstandard (nicht hoch- oder schriftsprachlich)

Kurz-Unit 1: Introduction and Revision

The United States of America

p. 5	**flag** [flæg]	Fahne, Flagge	The American ~ …
	the Stars and Stripes *(sing.)* [ˌstɑːz‿n ˈstraɪps]	das Sternenbanner *(Nationalflagge der USA)*	… is called the ~ *and* ~.
	stripe [straɪp]	Streifen	

The USA

p. 6	**federal** [ˈfedrəl]	Bundes-	Berlin is the capital of the *F*~ Republic of Germany.
	sq. = square [skweə]	Quadrat-; quadratisch, viereckig	My room is not very big, it's only 8 ~ meters.
	c. = circa [ˈsɜːkə]	ca. = circa	*c.* 60 million people = about 60 million people
	distance (from … to) [ˈdɪstəns]	Entfernung (von … bis, nach); Ferne	The ~ from San Francisco to Denver is about 1,500 km. In the ~ means far away.
	(to) **cross** [krɒs]	überqueren, kreuzen	You mustn't ~ the road when the light is red.
	(to) **realize** [ˈrɪəlaɪz]	erkennen, sich klarmachen; einsehen, merken	Michael ~*d* when he got home that he'd left his bag in the shop.
	surprising [səˈpraɪzɪŋ]	erstaunlich, überraschend	I'm really surprised that you've never been in a plane. I find it really ~.
	within [wɪˈðɪn]	innerhalb, in	Different languages are spoken ~ the USA.
	zone [zəʊn]	Zone	When we arrive in the USA it'll be 3 o'clock ~ time.
	local [ˈləʊkl]	Orts-, Lokal-; örtlich	Find out what's happening in your town! Buy your ~ paper!
p. 7	**such (a)** [sʌtʃ]	solch (ein/e), so	The USA is ~ a large country that it's necessary to have a car to travel around. You've got ~ lovely hair. What shampoo do you use?

such a/an + (adjective) + **noun**		**so** + **adjective**	
He's **such a fool.**	= **so** ein Dummkopf	He's **so stupid.**	= **so** dumm
Your sister is **such a** nice **person.**	= **so** ein netter Mensch	Your sister is **so nice.**	= **so** nett
It was **such a** good **book** that I read it twice.	= **so** ein gutes Buch	The book was **so good** that I read it twice.	= **so** gut

(to) **cover** [ˈkʌvə]	bedecken, zudecken	The countryside is all white. It's ~*ed* with snow.
valley [ˈvælɪ]	Tal	A ~ is low land, often with a river, between hills or mountains.
desert [ˈdezət]	Wüste	large areas of sand, stones and rocks in hot, dry climates
(to) **last** [lɑːst]	(an-, fort)dauern; (aus)reichen	The film ~*ed* for three hours. Will the bread ~ until tomorrow? – Yes, I think so. ⚠ Es wird nicht lange *dauern.* = It won't *take* long.
death [deθ]	Tod	A friend died in a car accident. His ~ was an awful shock.
degree [dɪˈgriː]	Grad	It's very hot. The temperature is 40 ~*s*.

Temperatures

°**Fahrenheit** [ˈfærənhaɪt]	°F = °C × $\frac{9}{5}$ + 32	–4 °F	14 °F	**32 °F**	50 °F	68 °F	86 °F	104 °F	**212 °F**
°**Celsius** [ˈselsɪəs]	°C = (°F – 32) × $\frac{5}{9}$	–20 °C	–10 °C	**0 °C**	10 °C	20 °C	30 °C	40 °C	**100 °C**

Water freezes at 0 °C or 32 °F. = … at **zero** [ˈzɪərəʊ] **degrees** Celsius or **thirty-two degrees** Fahrenheit.
What's the temperature today? = Wie viel Grad sind/hat es/haben wir heute?
It's –5 °C. = It's **minus** [ˈmaɪnəs] **five degrees** Celsius./It's **five degrees below zero.**
It's **in the 90s.** = Es sind über 90 Grad (Fahrenheit).

Hi!

p. 8	**ancestor** [ˈænsestə]	Vorfahre	Maureen is American, but her ~*s* came from Ireland.
	in those days	damals	The first immigrants came to America by boat. Of course, they weren't able to fly there *in* ~ ~.
	poverty [ˈpɒvətɪ]	(die) Armut	India is a very poor country. There's much ~ in India.
	African American [ˈæfrɪkən əˈmerɪkən]	Afro-Amerikaner	His ancestors were from Africa, so he's an ~ ~.
	willing [ˈwɪlɪŋ]	bereit(willig), gewillt	Mr Smith has to work 50 hours a week. He doesn't do this ~*ly*.
	Jew [dʒuː]	Jude, Jüdin	Many ~*s* had to leave Germany in the 1930s.
	Jewish [ˈdʒuːɪʃ]	jüdisch; Jude, Jüdin	My friend Rebecca is ~. She's got lots of relatives in Israel [ˈɪzreɪl].
	political [pəˈlɪtɪkl]	politisch	Sarah is very interested in ~ questions. She reads the newspaper every day.
	religious [rəˈlɪdʒəs]	religiös, Religions-	I go to church regularly. I'm very ~.
	religion [rəˈlɪdʒn]	Religion	
	freedom [ˈfriːdəm]	Freiheit (⚠ *nicht:* Frieden = peace)	In prison you lose your ~.
	(to) **persecute** sb. [ˈpɜːsɪkjuːt]	jn. verfolgen *(aus politischen oder religiösen Gründen)*	The Romans ~*d* the Christians many years ago.
	grocery store [ˈgrəʊsərɪ stɔː]	Lebensmittelgeschäft	a shop which sells all kinds of food
	(to) **look forward to** sth. [ˌlʊk ˈfɔːwəd]	sich auf etwas freuen	We'*re* really ~*ing* ~ *to* our holiday as our last one was three years ago.

Unit 1

p. 9	**nurse** [nɜ:s]	Krankenschwester, Krankenpfleger/in	Doctors and ~*s* work in hospitals.
	engineer [endʒɪˈnɪə]	Ingenieur/in, Techniker/in	A person who designs machines is an ~.
	unemployed [ˌʌnɪmˈplɔɪd]	arbeitslos	Someone who doesn't have a job is ~.
1 Ex 3	**development** [dɪˈveləpmənt]	Entwicklung; Erschließung	Something has happened in the story. There's a new ~.
	so far [səʊ ˈfɑ:]	bis jetzt, bisher	*S~ ~* means "till now".
	computer science [kəmˌpju:tə ˈsaɪəns]	Informatik	*C~ ~* is the science of computers. It can be the name of a subject at school or university.
4	(to) **meet** sb. [mi:t]	jn. (vom Zug usw.) abholen	Her friend was waiting at the station to ~ her.
5	(to) **hold** [həʊld]	veranstalten, abhalten	We *are ~ing* a meeting for all members tomorrow evening.
7	(to) **cost – cost – cost** [kɒst]	kosten	How much do the tickets ~? - $34.

⚠ These words sound similar – don't mix them up!

obwohl	**Although** [-ˈ-] I'm tired, I can't sleep.	→ I'm tired, and I'm **also** [ˈ--] hungry.	auch
mindestens	George waited **at least** one hour, …	→ then the boss arrived **at last.**	endlich
kosten	How much does it **cost** [kɒst] …	→ to go to the **coast** [kəʊst]?	Küste
tot	My grandparents are both **dead**.	→ What happened after Arthur's **death**?	Tod
fühlte	Tim **felt** a hand on his arm, …	→ then he **fell** to the ground.	fiel
Essen	Do you like French **food** [fu:d]?	→ I've broken my left **foot** [fʊt].	Fuß
interessiert	I'm **interested** in old maps.	→ I find old maps **interesting**.	interessant
jetzt	Can we go **now** [naʊ]?	→ I don't **know** [nəʊ].	wissen
Preis	What **price** [praɪs] did you pay?	→ Who won the first **prize** [praɪz]?	Preis
ganz	Tim is **quite** [kwaɪt] nice, …	→ but he's very **quiet** [ˈkwaɪət].	ruhig
retten	George tried to **save** [seɪv] Tim.	→ Keep your money in a **safe** [seɪf] place.	sicher
dann	First think, **then** [ðen] write.	→ Greg can run faster **than** [ðən] Tim.	als
wo(hin)	**Where** [weə] can he be?	→ Your parents **were** [wɜ:, wə] here.	waren

8	**period** [ˈpɪəriəd]	Zeitspanne, Zeitraum; Epoche	An hour, or a week is a ~ of time.
	(to) **practice** (AE) [ˈpræktɪs]	üben	BE: to practise
	(to) **study** (for an exam) [ˈstʌdɪ]	(für eine Prüfung) lernen, sich vorbereiten; studieren	I'*m ~ing* hard for the next English test.
	dialog (AE) [ˈdaɪəlɒg]	Dialog	BE: dialogue
p. 14	(to) **introduce** [ˌɪntrəˈdju:s]	einführen	The firm decided to ~ longer holidays for everyone.
	general [ˈdʒenrəl]	allgemein, generell	*~ly* = mostly, usually
	earth [ɜ:θ]	Erde; Boden	The ~, the moon and the sun are three planets.
	(to) **advise** [ədˈvaɪz]	(be)raten	What should I do? What do you ~ me to do?

British English – American English

). 16	**pronunciation** [prəˌnʌnsɪˈeɪʃn]	Aussprache	the way in which words are pronounced ⚠ *spelling:* (to) pronounce – pronunciation
	vocabulary item [vəˈkæbjʊlərɪ ˌaɪtəm]	Vokabel	A ~ ~ is a word.
	spelling [ˈspelɪŋ]	Rechtschreibung, Orthographie	English ~ is much more difficult than German ~.
	boot [buːt]	Stiefel; BE *auch:* Kofferraum (⚠ *nicht:* Boot = boat)	something you might wear on your foot when it rains BE also: space at the back of a car for bags and boxes
	trunk [trʌŋk] (AE)	Kofferraum	BE: boot

Kern-Unit 2: New York

2 A New York, New York

). 17	**somewhere/anywhere else** [ˌsʌmweər‿ˈels]	(irgendwo) sonst, (irgendwo) anders	~ ~ = some other place
	excellent [ˈeksələnt]	ausgezeichnet, hervorragend	good, first-class
	gateway (to) [ˈgeɪtweɪ]	Tor(weg), Einfahrt (zu)	
	(to) **enter** [ˈentə]	betreten; einreisen in	Please knock before you ~ the room. ⚠ Not: … before you ~~enter into~~ the room.
	homeless [ˈhəʊmləs]	obdachlos	A ~ person doesn't have a home.
	subway [ˈsʌbweɪ] (AE)	U-Bahn	BE: Underground, tube (in London)
). 18	mouth (of a river)	(Fluss-)Mündung	
	(to) **name** [neɪm]	(be-, er)nennen, taufen	to ~ sth. = to say the name of sth.

The five New York boroughs

the Bronx [brɒŋks]	– *der nördlichste Stadtbezirk, der als einziger auf dem Festland liegt*
Manhattan [mænˈhætn]	– *Insel zwischen dem Hudson und dem East River, berühmt für ihre Wolkenkratzer*
Queens [kwiːnz]	– *Stadtbezirk an der Südwestspitze der Insel Long Island, vor allem Wohngebiet (ohne Wolkenkratzer)*
Brooklyn [ˈbrʊklɪn]	– *wie Queens auf Long Island gelegen; eine Stadt für sich*
Staten Island [ˌstætn‿ˈaɪlənd]	– *Insel an der Einfahrt zum Hafen von New York, mit Manhattan durch Fährbetrieb verbunden*

dialect [ˈdaɪəlekt]	Dialekt, Mundart	form of a language used in a part of a country
suspension bridge [səˈspenʃn brɪdʒ]	Hängebrücke	
that is (i. e.) [ˌðæt‿ˈɪz, ˌaɪ‿ˈiː]	das heißt (d. h.)	in other words
origin [ˈɒrɪdʒɪn]	Ursprung, Entstehung; Herkunft	the beginning or start of something Nobody knows the true ~ of the world.
one/one's	man/sein	*O*~ should clean ~*'s* teeth at least once a day.

Unit 2

(p. 18)

German "man"

1. **One** should wash **oneself/one's** hair regularly. 2. **You** should wash **yourself/your** hair regularly.	**Man** sollte **sich/seine** Haare regelmäßig waschen.
3. **They/People** say that this weather won't last.	**Man** sagt, dass dieses Wetter nicht andauern wird.
4. This colour **isn't worn** often today. *(passive)*	Diese Farbe trägt **man** heute nicht oft.

One wird vor allem im formellen Englisch gebraucht. In der Umgangssprache werden eher **you** oder **they** bzw. **people** verwendet.

nationality [ˌnæʃəˈnælətɪ]	Nationalität, Staatsangehörigkeit	My husband and I have different ~*ies*. He's French and I'm Spanish.
fact [fækt]	Tatsache, Information	It's a well-known ~ that Canada is larger than the USA.

2 A Focus on GRAMMAR

p. 19	**environment** [ɪnˈvaɪrənmənt]	Umwelt, Umgebung	Pollution is destroying the ~.
	love [lʌv]	Liebe	She loved him a lot. = Her ~ for him was great.

2 A The rock concert

p. 20	**quite a** [kwaɪt]	ein(e) ziemlich(er, -e, -es)	Pollution is ~ *a* problem for all big cities. Scott is ~ *a* good basketball player.

The indefinite article after "quite", "such", "half" and "what"

quite a good film	**ein recht** guter Film	**half a** kilo of apples	**ein halbes** Kilo Äpfel
such a cold night	**eine so/so eine** kalte Nacht	**What a** big dog!	**Was für ein** großer Hund!

(to) **run – ran – run**	verkehren, fahren *(Zug, Bus)*	In New York the subway ~*s* all night.
criminal [ˈkrɪmɪnl]	Verbrecher/in, Kriminelle/r	Al Capone was a famous ~. He lived in Chicago.
weapon [ˈwepən]	Waffe	Guns, swords and knives are ~*s*.
(to) **sit/stand still** [sɪt ˈstɪl]	still sitzen/stillstehen	Don't move. Just ~ ~.
(to) **catch** (a bus/train) **– caught – caught**	(einen Bus/Zug) erreichen, nehmen	We had to run to ~ the bus. We don't have to walk. We can ~ a bus.
cab [kæb]	Taxi	usual word for taxi in AE, less usual in BE
crowd [kraʊd]	(Menschen-)Menge	a large group of people
(to) **appear** [əˈpɪə]	erscheinen; auftauchen	Jack *didn't* ~ at the party until 10 pm.
(to) **scream** [skriːm]	schreien, kreischen	He ~*ed* loudly when the gang attacked him.
wonderful [ˈwʌndəfəl]	wunderbar	*W*~ is another word for very nice or fantastic.
peaceful [ˈpiːsfʊl]	friedlich, friedfertig	The countryside was lovely – no noise, no traffic. It was very ~.
peace [piːs]	Friede(n)	War is the opposite of ~.
musician [mjuːˈzɪʃn]	Musiker/in	The Beatles were four famous ~*s* from Liverpool.

Manhattan (1)

Broadway [ˈbrɔːdweɪ] *längste Straße New Yorks (26 km); berühmt vor allem durch seine Theater*
Brooklyn Bridge [ˌbrʊklɪn ˈbrɪdʒ] *alte, eindrucksvolle Hängebrücke, die seit 1883 Manhattan mit Brooklyn verbindet*
Carnegie Hall [ˌkɑːnəgɪ ˈhɔːl] *Konzerthalle*
Central Park [ˌsentrəl ˈpɑːk] *größter Park Manhattans*
Chinatown [ˈtʃaɪnətaʊn] *Chinesenviertel*

20)

Manhattan (2)

Ellis Island [ˌelɪs‿ˈaɪlənd] *Insel vor der Südspitze Manhattans, von 1892-1954 Kontrollstelle für 12 Mill. Einwanderer*
the Empire State Building [ˌempaɪə ˈsteɪt ˌbɪldɪŋ] *zweithöchster Wolkenkratzer New Yorks (381 m)*
Fifth Avenue [ˌfɪfθ‿ˈævənjuː] *große Straße mit exklusiven Geschäften und Wohnungen*
Grand Central (Station) [ˈgrænd ˌsentrəl ˈsteɪʃn] *einer der zwei großen Bahnhöfe New Yorks*
Greenwich Village [ˌgrenɪtʃ ˈvɪlɪdʒ] *Künstlerviertel im Süden Manhattans*
Lincoln Center [ˌlɪŋkən ˈsentə] *Kulturzentrum mit Konzertsälen, Theatern, Bibliotheken und Oper*
Madison Square Garden [ˈmædɪsn ˌskweə ˈgɑːdn] *Veranstaltungszentrum für Sport, Musik, Zirkus etc. (20000 Sitzplätze, über Pennsylvania Station erbaut)*
Rockefeller Center [ˌrɒkəfelə ˈsentə] *riesiges Geschäfts- und Unterhaltungszentrum in Midtown Manhattan*
the Statue of Liberty [ˌstætʃuː‿əv ˈlɪbətɪ] die Freiheitsstatue *auf Liberty Island südlich von Manhattan*
Times Square [ˌtaɪmz ˈskweə] *Platz am Broadway im Zentrum des Vergnügungsviertels*
the United Nations [juːˌnaɪtɪd ˈneɪʃnz] = **the UN** die Vereinten Nationen *(bzw. deren Verwaltungsgebäude)*
Wall Street [ˈwɔːl striːt] *Finanzviertel mit der New Yorker Börse*
Washington Square [ˌwɒʃɪŋtən ˈskweə] *Platz im Zentrum von Greenwich Village*
the World Trade Center [ˌwɜːld ˈtreɪd ˌsentə] *höchster Wolkenkratzer New Yorks (411 m hohe Doppeltürme)*

). 21 (to) **disagree** (with sb./sth.) [ˌdɪsəˈgriː]	nicht übereinstimmen (mit jm./etwas), anderer Meinung sein (als)	not to agree with Do you really think that? I'm sorry but I ~ with you.
someone, anyone, everyone, no one		= somebody, anybody, everybody, nobody

everyone / someone / anyone / no one + they (them, their)

Everyone in Marvin's class had to show where **they** (= he or she) came from.
Someone has parked **their** car (= his car or her car) in front of ours.
If **anyone** phones, tell **them** (= him or her) I'll be back soon.

so do I [səʊ dʊ ˈaɪ]	ich auch	I like sport. – *S~ ~ I.* (= I like it, too.)
neither/nor do I [ˈnaɪðə dʊ ˈaɪ]	ich auch nicht	I don't like sport. – *N~/N~ do I.* (= I don't like it either.)

***so* + auxiliary + subject = German "auch"**

Jan **is** good at languages and **so is Carl.** (= … and Carl is too.)	… und Carl auch.
I've done my homework. – **So have I.** (= Me too.)	… – Ich auch.
My brother **lives** in Exeter. – Really? **So do I.** (= I do too.)	… – Wirklich? Ich auch.
Karen **reads** the daily newspaper and **so does Pat**.	… und Pat auch.

***neither/nor* + auxiliary + subject = German "auch nicht"**

I can't help you with this problem and **neither/nor can my father**. (= … and my father can't either.)	… und mein Vater auch nicht.
Jim **didn't** watch the programme and **neither/nor did Tina**. (= …and Tina didn't either.)	… und Tina auch nicht.

***but* + subject + auxiliary = German "… aber/aber …"**

I **don't** like this cheese. – **But I do**. (= But I like it.)	… – Ich aber.
I **like** this ham. – **But I don't**. (= But I don't like it.)	… – Ich aber nicht.
Ann **can** speak Spanish. – **But Philip can't**. (= But Philip can't speak it.)	… – Aber Philip nicht.

Unit 2

(p. 21)	**advantage** [əd'vɑ:ntɪdʒ]	Vorteil	Tim can run very fast. This is an ~ when he plays hockey.
	disadvantage [ˌdɪsəd'vɑ:ntɪdʒ]	Nachteil	I have very large feet. This is a great ~ when I buy shoes.
	discussion (about sth.) [dɪ'skʌʃn]	Diskussion, Besprechung (über etwas)	⚠ You *discuss something,* but you have a *discussion about something.*

2 A Focus on GRAMMAR

p. 22	(to) **come true** [-'-]	wahr werden	Ann's dream *came ~:* she won the tennis competition.
	hairdresser ['heədresə]	Friseur/in, Friseuse	A ~ cuts people's hair.
	mayor [meə]	Bürgermeister	A ~ is an important public person in a town.
	magnet ['mægnət]	Magnet	
	pioneer [paɪə'nɪə]	Pionier, Vorkämpfer/in	A ~ is one of the first people who does something in a new area.
	genetics [dʒə'netɪks]	Genetik	
	synagogue ['sɪnəgɒg]	Synagoge	A Jewish 'church' is called a ~.
	waiter ['weɪtə]	Kellner, (Herr) Ober	A ~ is a man who brings food to your table in a restaurant.
	including [ɪŋ'klu:dɪŋ]	einschließlich	There were five students and a teacher. There were six people ~ the teacher.
	(to) **dream** (about/of sth.) – **dreamed/dreamt – dreamed/dreamt** [dri:m]	träumen (von etwas)	to ~ = to have a dream

2 A Focus on WORDS

p. 23	(public) **transportation** (AE) [ˌtrænspɔ:'teɪʃn]	(öffentliche) Verkehrsmittel	BE: transport
	gas (AE) [gæs]	Benzin	BE: petrol
	traffic jam ['træfɪk dʒæm]	(Verkehrs-)Stau	
	thief [θi:f], *pl.* **thieves** [θi:vz]	Dieb/in	Help! A ~ has stolen my bag.
	vehicle ['vi:ɪkl]	Fahrzeug	Cars, buses and lorries, for example, are *~s.*
	(bike) **messenger** ['mesɪndʒə]	(Fahrrad-)Bote/-in	A bike ~ takes messages to people by bike. ⚠ *spelling:* messenger – message
	truck [trʌk]	Lastwagen	a ~ 
	lorry (BE) ['lɒrɪ]	Lastwagen	*L~* is another word for truck.
	motorcycle (AE) ['məʊtəsaɪkl]	Motorrad	My brother had a bike, then a ~, then a car.
	motorbike ['məʊtəbaɪk]	BE: Motorrad; AE: Moped, Mofa	In Britain ~ is another word for motorcycle.
	engine ['endʒɪn]	Motor; Maschine	The ~ is what makes a car go.
	horn [hɔ:n]	Hupe	a thing in a car that makes a loud noise
	seatbelt ['si:tbelt]	Sicherheitsgurt	You should always wear a ~ when you travel by car.
	(to) **miss** [mɪs]	verpassen, verfehlen; vermissen	I got up too late today, so I *~ed* the bus. My friend has moved to America. I really ~ her. Now that I live in the country I ~ going to the shows on Broadway.

23)	(an) **intersection** [ˈɪntəˌsekʃn] (AE) (a) **crossroads** *(sing.)* [ˈkrɒsrəʊdz] (BE)	(eine) Kreuzung	An ~ is where two roads cross. Excuse me, do you know where the nearest bank is? – Yes, it's at the ~.
	pedestrian crossing [pɪˌdestrɪən ˈkrɒsɪŋ]	Fußgängerüberweg	It's safest to cross the road at a ~ ~.
	sidewalk [ˈsaɪdwɔ:k] (AE) **pavement** [ˈpeɪvmənt] (BE)	Gehweg	It's much safer to walk on the ~ than on the road.
	(to) **improve** [ɪmˈpru:v]	(sich) verbessern; besser machen/werden	If you practice your vocabulary regularly, you can ~ your English.
Ex 1	(to) **choose to do sth.** [tʃu:z]	es vorziehen, etwas zu tun; beschließen etwas zu tun	(to) ~ *to do sth.* = (to) prefer or decide to do sth.
3	(to) **express** [ɪkˈspres]	äußern, (sich) ausdrücken	I can't ~ myself very well in a foreign language.
	expression [ɪkˈspreʃn]	Ausdruck; Äußerung	"Have a nice day" is an ~ you hear very often in America. He had a terrible ~ on his face.
5	**student** [BE: ˈstju:dənt, AE: ˈstu:dənt]	Student/in; AE *auch:* Schüler/in	a person at university; AE also: a pupil
6	**pound** [paʊnd]	engl./amerik. Pfund (= 454 g)	Carrots are 50¢ a ~ (= 50¢/lb.), madam.
10	**class, classes**	*hier:* Unterricht(sstunde)	= lesson, lessons
	maybe [ˈmeɪbi:]	vielleicht	*M~* is another word for perhaps.
13	abstract [ˈæbstrækt]	abstrakt (= begrifflich, nicht gegenständlich)	The word "hunger" is an ~ noun.

○ Getting along in the USA: In Manhattan

29	*avenue* [ˈævənju:]	Allee; Boulevard	*token* [ˈtəʊkən]	Marke *(als Fahrausweis)*
	on 42nd street	in der 42. Straße		

2 T The new girl

30	gook [gu:k] (AE, infml.)	*amerik. Schimpfwort für einen Asiaten/eine Asiatin*	
	stick [stɪk]	Stock; (trockener, abgebrochener) Zweig	a ~ 
	(to) **pretend** [prɪˈtend]	so tun, als ob; vortäuschen	Simon didn't want to go to school, so he *~ed* he was ill.
	(to) **recognize** [ˈrekəgnaɪz]	erkennen; anerkennen	Look, there's Kevin! He's much older. I almost *didn't* ~ him.
	cruel [ˈkru:əl]	grausam	The ~ man hit his dog.
	rude [ru:d]	unhöflich, grob; unanständig	very impolite
	Vietnamese [vjetnəˈmi:z]	Vietnamese/-in; vietnamesisch	A ~ is a person from Vietnam.
	as if [əz ɪf]	als ob	It looks ~ ~ it's going to snow soon.
	(to) **own** [əʊn]	besitzen	If you ~ something it belongs to you. You're the owner.
	(to) shut the door in sb.'s face	jm. die Tür vor der Nase zuschlagen	
	obvious [ˈɒbvɪəs]	offensichtlich	She drank a whole bottle of coke. She was *~ly* thirsty.
	(to) **hold** [həʊld]	(hoch)halten	What is that you *are ~ing* in your hand?
	(to) **turn (a)round** [tɜ:n]	(sich) (um)drehen	I *~ed* ~ quickly when I heard the noise.
	(to) **pick sth. up** [pɪk‿ˈʌp]	etwas (vom Boden) aufheben	Can you ~ ~ that pen from the floor, please?
	frightened [ˈfraɪtənd]	verängstigt, erschrocken, ängstlich	A ~ animal is an animal that's afraid.

Unit 2/Unit 3

p. 31	**kind** (of you) [kaɪnd]	nett, freundlich (von dir)	It was ~ of you (= nice of you) to help me yesterday.
	floor [flɔː]	Stock(werk)	A skyscraper has many *~s*.

floor (Stockwerk)

BE		AE
second floor	← zweiter Stock →	**third floor**
first floor	← erster Stock →	**second floor**
ground floor	← Erdgeschoss →	**first floor**

⚠ Ich wohne **im** zweiten Stock.
= I live **on** the second (BE)/ third (AE) floor.

	passage [ˈpæsɪdʒ]	Gang	a narrow way between two buildings, for example ⚠ *gang* = Bande (*nicht:* ~~der Gang~~)
	(to) **pass** [pɑːs]	*(Zeit)* vergehen	(of time) to go by
	(im)patient (with sb.) [ɪmˈpeɪʃnt]	(un)geduldig (mit jm.)	You have to be very *p~* to catch fish. You have to be *p~* with young children.
	(to) **suffer** sth./ from sth. [ˈsʌfə]	etwas ertragen; unter/an etwas leiden	I'm not very well. I'*m ~ing from* a bad cold.
	(to) **thank** sb. [θæŋk]	jm. danken, sich bei jm. bedanken	To ~ somebody means to say "thank you" to them.
p. 32	**reasonable** [ˈriːznəbl]	vernünftig	Please be ~: I can't take you to the station because I'll be at work.

American English and British English (1)

AE:	BE:		AE:	BE:	
apartment	**flat**	Wohnung	**student**	**pupil**	Schüler/in
apartment house	**block of flats**	Mietshaus	(student	student	Student/in)
first floor	**ground floor**	Erdgeschoss	**subway**	**Underground**	U-Bahn
gas	**petrol**	Benzin	**truck** [trʌk]	**lorry, truck**	LKW
gas station	**petrol station**	Tankstelle	**trunk**	**boot**	Kofferraum
intersection	**crossroads**	(Straßen-)Kreuzung	(trunk	trunk	Baumstamm)
mom [mɑːm]	**mum**	Mama, Mutti	(boot	boot	Stiefel)
sidewalk	**pavement**	Bürgersteig	**vacation**	**holiday(s)**	Ferien, Urlaub

Kurz-Unit 3

The discovery of America by the Europeans

p. 33	(to make a) **discovery** [dɪˈskʌvərɪ]	(eine) Entdeckung (machen)	When was America discovered? = When was the ~ of America?
	Viking [ˈvaɪkɪŋ]	Wikinger/in	
	instead [ɪnˈsted]	stattdessen, dafür	Sue couldn't find a clean skirt, so she wore a dress ~.
	instead of	(an)statt, anstelle von	Let's have tea in the garden ~ ~ in the kitchen.
	(to) **exist** [ɪɡˈzɪst]	existieren, vorhanden sein	Some people think that the Loch Ness monster *doesn't ~*.
	permanent [ˈpɜːmənənt]	dauerhaft, (be)ständig	opposite of temporary
	settlement [ˈsetlmənt]	Siedlung	
	crossing [ˈkrɒsɪŋ]	Überfahrt	The journey across a sea from one port to another is the ~.
	to make things worse [meɪk θɪŋz ˈwɜːs]	was die Dinge noch schlimmer machte	It started to rain, and *to ~ things ~*, we didn't have coats.

33)	(to) **grow** sth. – **grew** – **grown** [grəʊ]	(Gemüse, Wein usw.) anbauen, anpflanzen	We ~ vegetables in our garden.
	settler ['setlə]	Siedler/in	A ~ is a person who goes to settle in a colony or a new country.
	plant [plɑ:nt]	Pflanze	a ~ 
	ceremony ['serəmənɪ]	Zeremonie; Feier(lichkeit)	The royal wedding ~ was shown on TV.
	colonist ['kɒlənɪst]	Kolonist/in, Siedler/in	a settler
	(to) **start a family**	eine Familie gründen	To ~ ~ ~ means to have children.
34	(to) **emigrate** (to) ['emɪgreɪt]	auswandern, emigrieren (nach)	to leave your country to live in another
	(to) **pull** [pʊl]	ziehen	*To* ~ is the opposite of to push.
	on the one hand/on the other hand [hænd]	einerseits/andererseits	*On* ~ *one* ~ I like living in a city because there's so much to do. *On* ~ *other* ~, I hate the pollution.
	power ['paʊə]	Macht, Kraft, Gewalt; Befugnis	A mayor has the ~ to decide things.
	(the) **Pope** [pəʊp]	(der) Papst	The *P*~ is the man with the most power in the Catholic church.
	no longer ['lɒŋgə]	nicht mehr, nicht länger	If you say that you *no* ~ do something, you mean that you did it but don't do it now.
	Protestant *(n., adj.)* ['prɒtɪstnt]	Protestant/in; protestantisch, evangelisch	Are you ~ or Catholic?
	the Church of England [tʃɜ:tʃ əv 'ɪŋglənd]	die anglikanische Kirche	
	(to) **conform** [kən'fɔ:m]	(sich) anpassen; sich (ein)fügen	*To* ~ means to act in the way everybody is expected to act.
	Nonconformist [nɒnkən'fɔ:mɪst]	Angehörige(r) einer protestantischen Freikirche	
	brave [breɪv]	tapfer, mutig (⚠ nicht: ~~brav~~)	A ~ person isn't easily frightened.

False friends

brave	**brav**	**freedom**	**Frieden**	**play**	**Spiel**	**high school**	**Hochschule**
mutig	good	Freiheit	peace	Theaterstück	game	amerik. Oberschule	university, college

would/should/could/might/needn't + have + past participle

I would have failed without your help.	Ich **wäre** ohne deine Hilfe **gescheitert.**
You **shouldn't have made** all this food for me.	Du **hättest nicht** all das Essen für mich **machen sollen.**
You **could have asked** me before you took my bike.	Du **hättest** mich **fragen können**, ehe du mein Rad nahmst.
You **shouldn't have swum** in that river. You **might have drowned.**	Du **hättest nicht** in dem Fluss **schwimmen sollen.** Du **hättest ertrinken können.**
I needn't have hurried. There was plenty of time.	Ich **hätte mich nicht beeilen müssen./Ich hätte mich nicht zu beeilen brauchen.** ...

William Penn

(in) **detail** ['di:teɪl]	(im) Detail; Einzelheit	I know a little about the plan, but tell me about it *in* ~ now, please.
summary ['sʌmərɪ]	Zusammenfassung	What happens in the film? Can you give me a quick ~?

Unit 3

(p. 34)	Quaker ['kweɪkə]	Quäker	(= Mitglied der Religionsgemeinschaft der *Society of Friends)*
	(arch)bishop ['bɪʃəp]	(Erz-)Bischof	A ~ is above a priest, but below an *arch~*.
	tax [tæks]	Steuer	All wage earners have to pay *~es.*
	plain [pleɪn]	einfach, klar	*P~* is the opposite of bright and colourful.
	(to) **dance** [dɑ:ns]	tanzen	At Jenny's party we *~d* for hours.
	(to) **refuse** (to do sth.) [rɪ'fju:z]	sich weigern (etwas zu tun); verweigern, ablehnen	He *~d* to help her, although she had a lot of problems.
	God [gɒd]	Gott	
	prisoner ['prɪznə]	Gefangene(r)	A ~ is someone who is in prison.
	belief (in), *pl.* **beliefs** [bɪ'li:f]	Glaube (an), (religiöse) Überzeugung	What are their *~s*? = What do they believe in?
	cross [krɒs]	Kreuz	a ~ 
	(to) **owe** [əʊ]	schulden	How much do I ~ you? – £27.
p. 35	**debt** [det]	Schuld	A ~ is money that you owe someone.
	in memory of [ɪn 'memərɪ əv]	in Erinnerung an	They called the hospital Mother Teresa Hospital *in ~ of* her.
	Latin ['lætɪn]	Latein	The letters "i.e." stand for the ~ words "id est".
	(even) though *(conj.)* [ðəʊ]	obwohl	*T~* is the same as although.
	holy ['həʊlɪ]	heilig, geweiht	The Bible is sometimes called the *H~* Book.
	experiment (on, with) [ɪk'sperɪmənt]	Experiment, Versuch (mit)	In our science lessons we often do *~s.*
	(to) **worship** ['wɜ:ʃɪp]	(an)beten; seine Andacht verrichten	To ~ means to go to church and speak to God.
	election [ɪ'lekʃn]	(politische) Wahl	Which political party won the last ~?
	any ['enɪ]	jeder/jede/jedes (beliebige)	It's so easy, ~ child could do it!
	(to) **serve** [sɜ:v]	(be)dienen; servieren	When you do the exercise, the letter on page 20 can ~ as a model.
	constitution [ˌkɒnstɪ'tju:ʃn]	Verfassung	the (system of) laws of a country

○ A visit to Plimoth Plantation

p. 36	*plantation* [plɑ:n'teɪʃn]	(historische) Siedlung; Plantage	*costume* ['kɒstju:m]	Kostüm, Tracht
	rolling hills ['rəʊlɪŋ]	sanfte Hügel	*identity* [aɪ'dentɪtɪ]	Identität
	(to) abandon [ə'bændən]	verlassen, im Stich lassen	*actually* ['æktʃʊəlɪ]	tatsächlich; eigentlich
	close (to) [kləʊs]	nahe (bei/an)	*variety* [və'raɪətɪ]	Vielzahl, Vielfalt
	originally [ə'rɪdʒənəlɪ]	ursprünglich	*Master* … ['mɑ:stə]	„der junge Herr …" *(förmlicher Titel für Jungen; veraltet)*
	reproduction [ˌri:prə'dʌkʃn]	Reproduktion, Nachbildung	*Mistress* ['mɪstrəs]	*etwa:* Herrin *(veraltet)*
	(to) construct [kən'strʌkt]	bauen, konstruieren	*(to) encourage* [ɪn'kʌrɪdʒ, ɪn'kɜ:ridʒ]	ermutigen; ermuntern; fördern
	material [mə'tɪərɪəl]	Material, Stoff	*(to) join in (sth./doing sth.)* [ˌdʒɔɪn‿'ɪn]	mitmachen (bei etwas), sich beteiligen (an etwas)
	(to) farm [fɑ:m]	(Land) bebauen	*community* [kə'mju:nətɪ]	(politische) Gemeinde, Kommune; Gemeinschaft
	it used to be … ['ju:stə]	es war früher (immer) …	*fashion* ['fæʃn]	Mode
	actor ['æktə]	Schauspieler/in	*(to) present* [prɪ'zent]	präsentieren, darlegen

Kern-Unit 4: Kansas

4 A Golden Kansas

.37	**wheat** [wi:t]	Weizen	*W*~ is used to make bread.
	artificial [ɑ:tɪ'fɪʃl]	künstlich, Kunst-	Are those flowers real? – No, they're ~.
	cattle *(pl.)* ['kætl]	(Rind-)Vieh	Cows and bulls are ~. ⚠ The *cattle* are in the field. = Das Vieh ist …
	(to) **restore** [rɪ'stɔ:]	wiederherstellen; restaurieren	It costs a lot of money to ~ old historical buildings.
	(to) **risk** [rɪsk]	riskieren, wagen	A lot of people ~ their lives when they drink and drive. We ~ missing the train if we wait here any longer.
	risk	Risiko, Wagnis	It's safer to wear a helmet. Don't take any ~*s*.
	orphan ['ɔ:fən]	Waise, Waisenkind	a child whose parents are dead
	(to) **apply** (to sb. for sth.) [ə'plaɪ]	sich (bei jm. um etwas) bewerben; (etwas) beantragen	Did you get the job? – No, I *didn't* even ~ for it.

4 A An American teenager's life

.38	**average** ['ævərɪdʒ]	Durchschnitts-; Durchschnitt	The ~ temperature in July is 20 degrees.
	ice-cream parlor (AE) ['aɪskri:m pɑ:lə]	Eisdiele	The ~-~ ~ on Elm Street has the best ice-cream in town.
	cheerleaders ['tʃɪəli:dəz]	*Mädchen (selten auch Jungen), die die Zuschauer zum Beifall anfeuern.*	
	choir ['kwaɪə]	Chor	A ~ is a group of people who sing together.
	choice (of) [tʃɔɪs]	(Aus-)Wahl (an)	There's a ~ of three different meals.
	driver's license (AE)/ **driving licence** (BE) ['-- ˌlaɪsns]	Führerschein	You have to have a ~ ~ to drive a car.
	parking lot ['---] (AE)/**car park** ['--] (BE)	(großer) Parkplatz; Parkhaus	Where shall we park the car? In the ~ ~? – Yes. We should be able to find a parking space there.
	part-time [ˌpɑ:t'taɪm, 'pɑ:ttaɪm]	Teilzeit-; halbtags	Many students have to work ~-~ because they don't have enough money. I've got a ~-~ job. I just work in the mornings.

(Zusammengesetzte) Wörter mit wechselndem Betonungsmuster

Hauptbetonung auf der Endsilbe, wenn das Wort **allein** steht	Keine Betonung auf der Endsilbe, wenn das Wort **vor einem Nomen** steht
Mr Green works **part-time** [ˌpɑ:t'taɪm].	Mr Green has a **part-time job** [ˌ-- 'dʒɒb].
Let's go **downtown** [ˌdaʊn'taʊn].	Let's take the **downtown bus** [ˌ-- 'bʌs].
She's **well-known** [ˌwel'nəʊn] in Italy.	She's a **well-known singer** [ˌ-- 'sɪŋə].
I'm **thirteen** [ˌθɜ:'ti:n].	The war lasted **thirteen years** [ˌ-- 'jɪəz].
Hyde Park [ˌhaɪd 'pɑ:k], **Heathrow** [ˌhi:θ'rəʊ]	**Hyde Park Corner** [ˌ-- 'kɔ:nə], **Heathrow Airport** [ˌ-- 'eəpɔ:t]
Waterloo [ˌwɔ:tə'lu:], **Vietnam** [ˌvjet'næm]	**Waterloo Bridge** [ˌ--- 'brɪdʒ], **Vietnam War** [ˌ-- 'wɔ:]

39	(American) **football** ['fʊtbɔ:l]	*dem Rugby ähnliches amerikanisches Mannschaftsspiel*	American ~ is quite different from what we call "Fußball". The football is not even round.

Unit 4

(p. 39)	(to) **make sure** [ʃʊə]	sich vergewissern; darauf achten, dafür sorgen (, dass)	to check
	atmosphere ['ætməsfɪə]	Atmosphäre	The ~ at a football match can be very exciting.
	national anthem [ˌnæʃnəl‿'ænθəm]	Nationalhymne	At international football matches the ~ ~ of each country is played before the match starts.
	(to) **cheer** (sb.) [tʃɪə]	jn. anfeuern; klatschen, jubeln	The boys *~ed* their football team (on). Everybody *~ed* when the pop star arrived. …
	(to) **go for a ride** [raɪd]	herumfahren, eine Spritztour machen	My mother has just bought a new car. We *went ~ a ~* in it last night.
	(to) cruise [kru:z] (AE)	eine Spazierfahrt machen	

4 A Focus on GRAMMAR

p. 40	**universe** ['ju:nɪvɜ:s]	Universum	
	if I were you	(ich) an deiner Stelle	How should I travel? – Well, ~ *I ~ you*, I'd go by train.

an/the [ðɪ] before **u-** [ʌ-]	an untidy room an Underground train	the underlined words the unemployment situation in Germany
a/the [ðə] before **u-** [ju:-]	a university town a unit about Scotland	the universe the United Kingdom

4 A Exchange visits

p. 42	**sporting ground** (AE) **sports ground** (BE) ['spɔ:tɪŋ ˌgraʊnd]	Sportplatz	Where do you play football? – On the school ~ ~.
	roller coaster ['rəʊlə ˌkəʊstə]	Achterbahn(wagen)	
	(to) **be over** ['əʊvə]	vorüber sein, zu Ende sein	The party *is* ~. Everybody has gone home.
	guidance counselor ['gaɪdns ˌkaʊnsələ] (AE)	*Beratungslehrer/in an einer amerikan. High School, berät Schüler/innen über Schullaufbahn und Beruf*	teacher in an American High School who helps students with their problems
	period ['pɪərɪəd]	(Unterrichts-)Stunde; (AE auch:) Punkt (am Satzende)	another word for lesson
	(to) **type** [taɪp]	tippen, Maschine schreiben	Don't write the letter by hand. I think you should ~ it.
	Pledge of Allegiance (AE) [ˌpledʒ əv ə'li:dʒəns]	*(amerikanischer) Treueeid*	
p. 43	**way of life** [ˌweɪ‿əv 'laɪf]	Lebensart, Lebensweise	the way people live
	feeling ['fi:lɪŋ]	Gefühl	
	thought [θɔ:t]	Gedanke, Einfall	Do you know what he's thinking? Can you read his *~s*?
	(in)formal [ɪn'fɔ:məl]	(in)formell, (nicht) förmlich	It was a very *f~* event. The men had to wear a tie. Hi is a less *f~* word for hello.
	AFS [ˌeɪ‿ef 'es] = American Field Service ['sɜ:vɪs]	*amerikanische Organisation, die Schüleraustauschprogramme organisiert*	
	(to) **be pleased** (with) [pli:zd]	sich freuen (über), zufrieden sein (mit)	You look very happy! – Yes, I'*m* very ~ because I've just passed my math exam.
	best wishes ['wɪʃɪz]	mit den besten Wünschen	
	Sincerely (yours), … [sɪn'sɪəlɪ] (AE)	Mit freundlichen Grüßen …, Mit herzlichen Grüßen …	BE: Yours, sincerely, …
	original [ə'rɪdʒənl]	ursprünglich; Original-	The ~ letter has been lost. This is only a copy.

43) **Dear Sir/Dear Madam** [dɪə sɜː/dɪə ˈmædəm]	Sehr geehrter Herr/ Sehr geehrte Dame	
Dear Sir or Madam, …	Sehr geehrte Damen und Herren, …	
colon [ˈkəʊlən]	Doppelpunkt	

Punctuation marks [ˌpʌŋktʃʊˈeɪʃn mɑːks] (Satzzeichen)

. full stop (BE)/period (AE)	**,** comma	**;** semi-colon [ˌsemɪˈ- -]	**:** colon
! exclamation mark [ˌekskləˈmeɪʃn mɑːk]	**?** question mark [ˈkwestʃən mɑːk]	**-** hyphen[1] [ˈhaɪfən]	**—** dash[2] [dæʃ]
() parentheses, BE *also:* brackets [pəˈrenθɪsiːz, ˈbrækɪts]	**“ ”** quotation marks [kwəʊˈteɪʃn mɑːks]	**’** apostrophe [əˈpɒstrəfɪ]	[1] Bindestrich [2] Gedankenstrich

Yours faithfully, … [ˈfeɪθfʊlɪ] (BE)	Mit freundlichen Grüßen …, Hochachtungsvoll …	a polite, formal way to end a letter

Dates

You write:		You say:
BE: 12/4/1995 12.4.1995	= April 12(th), 1995 *or:* 12(th) April 1995	**April the twelfth**, nineteen ninety-five **the twelfth of April**, nineteen ninety-five
AE: 12/4/1995	= December 4, 1995	**December fourth**, nineteen ninety-five

in the 1960s, in the sixties — in den Sechzigerjahren (des 20. Jahrhunderts)
in the early/late 1870s — Anfang/Ende der Siebzigerjahre (des 19. Jahrhunderts)

4 A Focus on WORDS

44 **among** [əˈmʌŋ]	(mitten) unter, zwischen (mehreren Personen oder Dingen)	There are several reasons. *A*~ other things, it's very expensive.
knowledge (of) *(sing.)* [ˈnɒlɪdʒ]	Wissen (über); Kenntnis(se)	Your ~ of English is quite good. ⚠ *pronunciation:* to know [nəʊ] – knowledge [ˈnɒlɪdʒ]
baggage [ˈbægɪdʒ]	Gepäck	They're just unloading the ~ from the plane.
(to) **book** [bʊk]	buchen	I'*ve* already ~*ed* and paid for my ticket.
brochure [ˈbrəʊʃə, AE: brəʊˈʃʊər]	Broschüre, Prospekt	Write to the tourist office and ask them to send some ~*s* about the town.
flying time [ˈflaɪɪŋ taɪm]	Flugzeit	The flight leaves at 10:00 and arrives at 11:00, so the ~ ~ is one hour.
return fare	Fahrpreis hin und zurück	The ~ ~ is the price for a ticket there and back.
return flight [rɪˈtɜːn]	Rückflug	The ~ ~ is the flight back.
sightseeing tour [ˈsaɪtsiːɪŋ]	Besichtigungstour, Rundfahrt	If you go on a ~ ~, you'll be shown all the sights in a place.
accommodation [əˌkɒməˈdeɪʃn]	Unterkunft	I need some ~. = I need a place where I can stay.
preparation [ˌprepəˈreɪʃn]	Vorbereitung, Zubereitung	Can I help you with the ~*s* for the party, Sam?
suitcase [ˈsuːtkeɪs]	Koffer	When you go on a trip, you put your clothes in a bag or a ~.
health [helθ]	Gesundheit	Sarah's ~ is very bad. She's always ill.

Unit 4

4 Ex 1	**grade** [greɪd]	(Zeugnis-)Note, Zensur; (AE auch) Jahrgangsstufe, Klasse	~ = mark (at school)
2	magic wand [wɒnd]	Zauberstab	
	(to) **solve** [sɒlv]	*(Aufgabe, Problem)* lösen	to find the answer to (a problem etc.)
6	(to make a) **decision** [dɪ'sɪʒn]	(eine) Entscheidung (treffen)	to make a ~ = to decide
	equal ['i:kwəl]	gleich, gleichberechtigt	There's an ~ number of boys and girls in this class: 15 boys and 15 girls.
7	(to) **count** (to) [kaʊnt]	zählen (bis)	Do you speak French? – Well, I can ~ to ten in French.
	dictionary ['dɪkʃənrɪ]	Wörterbuch	If you don't know what a word means, you can look in a ~.
	Bible ['baɪbl]	Bibel	
9	(to) **defend** [dɪ'fend]	verteidigen	A country's soldiers ~ the country in times of war.
	violent ['vaɪələnt]	gewaltsam, gewalttätig; heftig	I never hit anyone. I'm not a ~ person. Some films on TV are very ~.
	(un)imaginable [ˌʌnɪ'mædʒɪnəbl]	(un)vorstellbar	If you can't imagine something is possible, it is ~.
10	**inventor** [ɪn'ventə]	Erfinder/in	a person who invents something
11	(to) **rewrite** sth. [ˌri:'raɪt]	etwas neu schreiben, noch mal schreiben	to write something again
	gun [gʌn]	(Schuss-)Waffe	British policemen don't usually carry ~*s*.
°12	*ridin'* ['raɪdɪn]	= riding	
	drive-in restaurant [ˌ-- '--] (AE)	*Restaurant, wo Kunden im Auto bedient werden*	
13	**advice** *(sing.)* [əd'vaɪs]	Rat, Ratschläge	to advise someone = to give them some ~ ⚠ *Never:* ~~an advice~~
	principal (AE) ['prɪnsɪpl]	Schulleiter/in, Direktor/in	the "boss" of a school
	(to) **reject** [rɪ'dʒekt]	ablehnen, zurückweisen	opposite of to accept
	organization [ˌɔ:gənaɪ'zeɪʃn]	Organisation	The United Nations is a very large ~ which meets to discuss world problems.
14	(to) **revise** [rɪ'vaɪz] (BE)	*(den Lernstoff)* wiederholen	Have you started ~*ing* irregular verbs for the test tomorrow? – No, I haven't looked at them yet.
	single ['sɪŋgl]	einzig; einzeln, Einzel-; ledig, unverheiratet	a ~ room = a room for one person. Are you married? – No, I'm ~.
	double ['dʌbl]	doppelt, Doppel-	Would you like a single or a ~ bedroom?
	consonant ['kɒnsənənt]	Konsonant, Mitlaut	The letters b, k, s and v, for example, are ~*s*.
	vowel ['vaʊəl]	Vokal, Selbstlaut	The letters a, e, i, o, u are ~*s*.

○ Getting along in the USA: Using the telephone

p. 50	*(to) pick up* [pɪk 'ʌp]	abholen
	This is Rita.	Hier spricht/ist Rita.
	Can I take a message (for him)? ['mesɪdʒ]	Kann ich (ihm) etwas ausrichten?
	tractor ['træktə]	Traktor
	(to) reserve [rɪ'zɜ:v]	buchen, reservieren (lassen)
	(to) rent [rent]	mieten, leihen
	(tele)phone booth (AE) [BE: bu:ð, AE: bu:θ] / *(tele)phone box* (BE)	Telefonzelle
	long distance call [ˌlɒŋ ˌdɪstəns 'kɔ:l]	Ferngespräch
	toll-free (call) [ˌtəʊl fri: 'kɔ:l]	gebührenfrei(er Anruf)

4 T The star player

51	(to) **succeed** [sək'si:d]	Erfolg haben; gelingen	If you try hard enough, you'll ~.
	(to) **be left** [left]	übrig sein	The match was almost finished, there *were* only a few seconds ~.
	score [skɔ:]	Spielstand; Ergebnis	The ~ is 92:91 to St John's.
	(to) **score**	*(einen Punkt/Treffer)* erzielen, *(ein Tor)* schießen	St John's won the basketball game. They ~*d* the most baskets.
	(to) make a basket	einen Korb erzielen *(beim Basketball)*	
	(to) **surround** [sə'raʊnd]	umgeben	He was sitting on the floor ~*ed* by books.
	position [pə'zɪʃn]	Lage; Position	a place where a person, thing, etc. is or stands
	(to) **pass** (the ball)	(den Ball) abspielen, abgeben	to throw the ball to a member of one's own team
	edge [edʒ]	Rand, Kante	Be careful. There's a glass at the ~ of the table.
	(to) **draw** [drɔ:]	ziehen	*D*~ your chair nearer the table.
	(to) **control** [kən'trəʊl], **-ll-**	beherrschen; die Kontrolle haben über, steuern (⚠ *nicht:* kontrollieren, überprüfen = to check)	The pupils don't listen to their teacher. He finds it difficult to ~ them. Susan was so angry that she found it difficult to ~ herself.
	rival ['raɪvl]	Rivale/-in, Konkurrent/in	someone you try very hard to beat, e.g. in a race
	the top banana [ˌ– –'– –] (AE, infml.)	das „große Ass", der/die Größte	the "big star"
	fault [fɔ:lt]	Schuld, Fehler	It's your ~ that I'm late because you hid my bike.
	(to) **take a chance** [tʃɑ:ns]	ein Risiko eingehen, es darauf ankommen lassen	You've nothing to lose. Why *don't* you ~ *a* ~?
52	(to) **quit – quitting** *(-ing form)* – **quit – quit** [kwɪt]	aufhören; *(eine Stelle)* aufgeben	Mrs Brown didn't like her job, so she decided to ~. *Q*~ making that noise, I'm trying to read.
	(to) play a team	gegen ein Team spielen	= to play against a team
	(to) walk all over sb. (infml.)	jn. mit Leichtigkeit besiegen	
	knee [ni:]	Knie	
	enthusiastic(ally) [ɪnˌθju:zɪ'æstɪk(lɪ)]	begeistert, enthusiastisch	If you are ~ about something, you want to do it very much or like it very much.
	truth [tru:θ]	Wahrheit	Where did you go last night? Tell me the ~.
	(to) **be sure of oneself**	selbstsicher sein	to be quite sure that what one does is right
	except [ɪk'sept]	außer, bis auf	Everybody was tired ~ Don.
53	(to) **match** (two things) [mætʃ]	(zwei Dinge) passend zusammenfügen; zusammenpassen	In this exercise you must ~ a noun with an adjective. The color of your shirt doesn't go with the color of your trousers. The two colors don't ~.
	importance [ɪm'pɔ:təns]	Wichtigkeit	Is there anything important in the post? – No, there's nothing of any ~.

Kern-Unit 5: Young people in Britain and America

54	**West Indian** [ˌwest‿'ɪndɪən]	Westinder/in; westindisch	
	break with [breɪk]	Bruch (mit)	Last Christmas we had a ~ *with* tradition and didn't celebrate with all the familiy, as we usually do.
	(to) **be descended from** [dɪ'sendɪd]	abstammen von	His name is Shakespeare, but I don't think he'*s* ~ *from* the famous one.
	statistics *(pl.)* [stə'tɪstɪks]	Statistik	

Unit 5

(p. 54)	**society** [sə'saɪətɪ]	Gesellschaft; Verein, Arbeitsgemeinschaft	British ~ consists of people of many different nationalities, religions and races. ⚠ No article: *British society = die britische Gesellschaft*
	total ['təʊtl]	Gesamt-, gesamt; völlig, total	The ~ cost was much higher than had been expected.

5 A Growing up in Britain and America

p. 55	**politics** *(sing.)* ['pɒlɪtɪks]	Politik	Are you interested in ~ – the government, how we are ruled, how new laws are made?
	politician [ˌpɒlə'tɪʃn]	Politiker/in	Members of the government are ~*s*.
	illustration [ˌɪlə'streɪʃn]	Illustration, Bild, Abbildung	Pictures, photos etc. are ~*s*.
	(to) **support** [sə'pɔːt]	unterstützen; befürworten	Do you ~ the people who are against the new road?
	party ['pɑːtɪ]	Partei	The politician said that her ~ would do most for young people. ⚠ *party* = 1. Partei; 2. Party, Fest, Fete
	major ['meɪdʒə]	gewichtig, bedeutsam; Haupt-	(most) important
	(to) **care** (about) [keə]	sich kümmern (um); wichtig nehmen	Matthew isn't interested in politics. He doesn't ~ about politics.
	possibly ['pɒsəblɪ]	möglicherweise, vielleicht, eventuell	I don't know where we're going on holiday this year – ~ to France.
	(to) **vote for** [vəʊt]	(ab)stimmen für, wählen	Which political party would you ~ *for* if you were 18?
	environmental [ɪnˌvaɪrən'mentl]	Umwelt-	*E*~ groups are groups of people who want to protect the environment.
	financial [faɪ'nænʃl]	finanziell	He lost his job and now has serious ~ problems.
	disaster [dɪ'zɑːstə]	Katastrophe, Desaster, Fiasko	Earthquakes are examples of natural ~*s*. My cake was a real ~! It tasted really salty.
	a business **of** her **own** [əʊn]	ihre eigene Firma	She has her own business. = She has a business *of* her ~.

own (eigen)

I have **my own** room/a room **of my own.**	Ich habe **(m)ein eigenes** Zimmer.
I have **some** CDs **of my own.**	Ich habe **einige eigene** CDs.
I have **no** CD-player **of my own.**	Ich habe **keinen eigenen** CD-Spieler.
I have books **of my own.**	Ich habe **eigene** Bücher.

5 A Focus on GRAMMAR

p. 56	**recently** ['riːsntlɪ]	vor kurzem, neulich	Andy looks very fit. He's been on holiday ~.
	idea (about, of) [aɪ'dɪə]	Begriff, Vorstellung (von); Meinung (über, von)	The film gave us a good ~ of what life is like in a small town.
	(to) **consider** sth./doing sth. [kən'sɪdə]	über etwas nachdenken, etwas in Betracht ziehen	We'*re* ~*ing* going to France for our holiday, but we haven't decided yet.
	(to) **admit, -tt-** [əd'mɪt]	zugeben; zulassen, (hin)einlassen	Alan ~*ted* stealing the money. The college ~*s* 2000 new students each year. Joe *wasn't* ~*ted* into the restaurant because he was wearing shorts.
	(to) **carry on** [kærɪ 'ɒn]	weitermachen, fortfahren	to continue doing something Even after the film had started, people ~*ied* ~ talking.
	(to) **dislike** [dɪs'laɪk]	nicht mögen, nicht leiden können	opposite of to like I like my job, but I ~ getting up so early.
	(to) **keep ... ing**	etwas weiter tun, weiter-; etwas wiederholt tun	to carry on

56)

(to) keep

Here's your pen. – Oh, you can **keep** it. I've got another one.	… Du kannst ihn **behalten**. …
Butter is best **kept** in the fridge.	Butter **bewahrt** man am besten im Kühlschrank **auf**.
We **keep** a few chickens in our garden.	Wir **halten (uns)** ein paar Hühner im Garten.
Many American Indians want to **keep** their traditions **alive**.	Viele Indianer möchten ihre Traditionen **am Leben erhalten**.
We need a fence round the garden to **keep** the dogs **out**.	Wir brauchen einen Zaun um den Garten um die Hunde **draußen** zu **halten**.
Paul had to leave the Youth Hostel because he didn't **keep the rules**.	Paul musste die Jugendherberge verlassen, weil er **die Regeln** nicht **einhielt/befolgte**.
That's not fair. You must **keep your promise**.	… Du musst **dein Versprechen halten**.
Keep going till you get to the traffic lights.	**Geh (immer) weiter,** bis du an die Ampel kommst.

(to) **mention** [ˈmenʃn]	erwähnen	I forgot to ~ it, but it's Tom's birthday tomorrow.
(to) **intend** (to do sth.) [ɪnˈtend]	beabsichtigen, (fest) vorhaben (etwas zu tun)	I *~ed* to play tennis this afternoon, but I've hurt my foot and can't now.

English **"like/love doing – like/love to do"** = German **"gern tun"**

I **like** read**ing/to** read in bed.	Ich lese **gern** im Bett.
I'd **like to** know her name.	Ich würde/möchte **gern** ihren Namen wissen.
My cat **loves** watch**ing/to** watch TV.	Meine Katze sieht **sehr gerne** fern.
Do you want to see my cat? – Oh yes, I'd **love to**.	Willst du meine Katze sehen? – Oh ja, **sehr gern**.

57	**survey** [ˈsɜːveɪ]	Umfrage, Untersuchung	The recent government ~ on smoking shows that more and more people are giving it up.
	career [kəˈrɪə]	Beruf; Karriere; Laufbahn; Berufs-, Aufstiegs-	Alison hopes her new job will be the start of a successful ~.
	(to) **apologize** (to sb. for sth.) [əˈpɒlədʒaɪz]	sich (bei jm. für etwas) entschuldigen	to say sorry for something I *~ed* to the others for arriving late.
	(to) be **proud** (of sth.) [praʊd]	(auf etwas) stolz sein	She's very ~ of winning the competition.
	by (marry)**ing**	indem (sie heiratete)	

5 A Advice from Melanie

58	**shy** [ʃaɪ]	scheu, zurückhaltend	Oliver is very ~. He hates talking to strangers.
	(to) **make a fool of** sb. [fuːl]	jn. lächerlich machen	to make somebody look stupid
	majority [məˈdʒɒrətɪ]	Mehrheit	the ~ of the people = most of the people The ~ of the people are very friendly.
	MP = Member of Parliament [ˌemˈpiː]	*Mitglied des Unterhauses in der britischen Regierung*	a politician who has been voted by the people to be in parliament
	minority [maɪˈnɒrətɪ]	Minderheit	opposite of majority
	(to) **threaten** [ˈθretn]	(be)drohen	Mrs Simmons *~ed* to stop Brian's pocket-money if he didn't work harder at school.
	jealous (of) [ˈdʒeləs]	eifersüchtig (auf); neidisch (auf)	He's so ~ when I go out with other boys. John is ~ of his sister because she's good at school.
	behaviour (towards) [bɪˈheɪvɪə]	Verhalten, Benehmen (gegenüber)	Tim is behaving very strangely. His ~ towards me has changed in the last few months.
	(to) **behave** [bɪˈheɪv]	sich verhalten, sich benehmen	

Unit 5

(p. 58)	(to) **drive** sb. **crazy** (infml.) [draɪv]	jn. wahnsinnig, verrückt machen	Homework and tests *are driving* me ~. I have no free time.
	(to) **convince** (sb. of sth.) [kən'vɪns]	(jn. von etwas) überzeugen	Nobody believed what she said. = Nobody *was ~d.*
	(to) **get divorced** (from sb.) [dɪ'vɔ:st]	sich (von jm.) scheiden lassen	They had been married for 22 years when they *got ~.*
	divorce [dɪ'vɔ:s]	Scheidung	After their parents' ~ the children lived with their mother.
	attractive [ə'træktɪv]	anziehend, attraktiv, reizvoll	beautiful, good-looking Sarah is very beautiful. – Yes, she's a very ~ woman.
	sex [seks]	Geschlecht; Sex	What ~ is your cat? – It's a "he". There's a bigger risk of getting AIDS for people who have ~ with lots of different partners.
	(to) have a crush on sb. (infml.) [krʌʃ]	in jm. verschossen sein	
	the media *(pl.)* ['mi:dɪə]	(die) Medien	TV, radio and newspapers are all examples of *the ~.*
	(to) **read** sth. **out** [ri:d 'aʊt]	etwas vorlesen	Who wants to ~ their story ~ to the class?
	(to) **mark** [mɑ:k]	kennzeichnen, bezeichnen, markieren	Tourist attractions *are ~ed* on the map with a star.

5 A Pocket-money

p. 59	**myth** [mɪθ]	Mythos, Märchen	It's a complete ~ that it rains a lot more in England than in Germany. It's just not true.
	amount (of) [ə'maʊnt]	Menge; Summe, Betrag (von)	a large ~ of money = a lot of money
	(to) **influence** ['ɪnflʊəns]	beeinflussen	There was one teacher at her school who *~d* her life very much.
	if so	wenn ja	Have you got enough money with you? *I~ ~*, you can pay me now.

"so" and "not"

Is Alan here? – I **think so**./I **don't think so**.	Ich **glaube ja**./Ich **glaube nicht**.
Does Janet know? – I'm **afraid so**./I'm **afraid not**.	Ich **fürchte ja**./**Leider nicht**.
Will Dave come? – I **hope so**./I **hope not**.	Ich **hoffe ja**./Ich **hoffe nicht**.
Are you ready? **If so**, we'll start./ **If not**, please hurry up.	**Wenn ja**, fangen wir an./ **Wenn nicht**, beeilen Sie sich bitte.

5 A Focus on WORDS

p. 60	**network** ['netwɜ:k]	Netz(werk); Vernetzung	A railway ~ is a system of railway lines that cover a certain area.
	(in)**human** ['hju:mən, ɪn'-]	(un)menschlich	It's only ~ to make mistakes.
	relations (with) *(pl.)* [rɪ'leɪʃnz]	Beziehungen (mit)	International *~s* between the two countries are very good. There are no problems.
	race [reɪs]	Rasse	People of different nationalities and ~ live in Britain. ⚠ *race* = 1. Rasse; 2. (Wett-)Rennen
	social ['səʊʃl]	gesellschaftlich; sozial, Sozial-; gesellig	People who live in the same street often belong to the same ~ class.

30)	(to) **communicate** (with) [kə'mju:nɪkeɪt]	kommunizieren (mit), sich verständigen (mit)	I was able to ~ with Pedro because we both spoke English.
	(to) **depend on** [dɪ'pend]	abhängig sein von, abhängen von; sich verlassen auf	Can you come? – I'm not sure. It *~s on* how much work I've got. You can ~ *on* Jill. She will always help if there's a problem.
	character ['kærɪktə]	Charakter; Figur *(in einem Roman usw.)*	Tell me about his ~. Was he friendly, tolerant, impatient? What was he like?
	(to) **get on** sb.'s **nerves** [nɜ:vz]	jm. auf die Nerven gehen	He makes me so annoyed. He really *~s on* my ~.
	tense [tens]	(an)gespannt, nervös	Before an important test people are often very ~.
	(to) **upset** sb. – **upsetting** *(-ing form)* – **upset** – **upset** [ʌp'set]	jm. aus der Fassung bringen, verärgern, beunruhigen	She really ~ Mike when she said she didn't want to see him again.
	attitude (towards) ['ætɪtju:d]	Haltung, Einstellung (gegenüber, zu)	He has a very strange ~ towards work.
	Turkey ['tɜ:kɪ]	(die) Türkei	Ankara is the capital of ~.
Ex 2	**Greek** [gri:k]	Griechisch; griechisch; Grieche, Griechin	*G~* is the language spoken in Greece.
5	**meaning** ['mi:nɪŋ]	Bedeutung (⚠ *nicht:* Meinung = opinion)	What's the ~ of this word? – I don't know. Look in the dictionary.
11	**glove** [glʌv]	Handschuh	You'll get very cold hands if you don't wear *~s* in this weather.
14	(badly) **injured** ['ɪndʒəd]	(schwer) verletzt	After the accident Mr Carter was taken to hospital. Both his legs were broken. He was badly ~.

of + s-Genitiv als „doppelter Genitiv"

Jim is one of her friends.	= Jim is a friend of hers.	ein Freund von ihr
Jim is one of Rita's friends.	= Jim is a friend **of Rita's.**	ein Freund **von Rita**
I know some of his friends.	= I know some friends of his.	einige Freunde von ihm
I know some of my brother's friends.	= I know some friends **of my brother's.**	einige Freunde **von meinem Bruder**

O Getting along in the USA: Information in local papers

66	*(to) go on* [gəʊ 'ɒn]	los sein	*abbreviation (for)* [ə,bri:vɪ'eɪʃn]	Abkürzung (von)
	ad [æd]	Annonce, Anzeige, Inserat	*(to) provide* [prə'vaɪd]	zur Verfügung stellen, bereitstellen
	$1 off [ɒf]	$1 Rabatt	*extra* ['ekstrə]	zusätzlich; Extra-
	moonlight ['mu:nlaɪt]	Mondlicht, Mondschein	*arrangements* [ə'reɪndʒmənts]	Möglichkeit(en), Vorkehrungen
	vs (= versus) ['vɜ:səs]	gegen	*(to) take it in turns to do sth.* [,teɪk ɪt ɪn 'tɜ:nz]	der Reihe nach etwas tun, abwechselnd etwas tun
	row [rəʊ]	Reihe		
	contestant [kən'testənt]	(Wettkampf-)Teilnehmer/-in		
	kayak ['kaɪæk]	Kajak		
	experience [ɪk'spɪərɪəns]	Erfahrung(en), Erlebnis		

5 T "Chocolate City"

67	(to) bus sb. [bʌs]	*Schulkinder mit Bussen in andere Bezirke befördern, um gemischtrassige Schulklassen zu schaffen*	In some American cities, black children are taken by bus to schools in "white" areas and white children are *~ed* to schools in "black" areas.

Unit 5

(p. 67)	**auto(mobile)** (AE) ['ɔ:təʊ, 'ɔ:təməbi:l]	Auto, Wagen	another word for car, especially in the USA
	I got (an idea) (nonstandard)		= I've got (an idea)
	since [sɪns]	seit(dem)	*S*~ I've lived here, I've only seen them twice.
	not till six	erst um/nicht vor sechs	In Germany you ca*n't* learn to drive ~ you're eighteen.
	(to) **annoy** sb. [ə'nɔɪ]	jn. ärgern, belästigen	Ben always corrects my English. He really ~*s* me.
	You'll make a good wife.	Du wirst mal eine gute Ehefrau sein.	
	waste (of) [weɪst]	Verschwendung (von)	Sally doesn't watch TV. She thinks it's a ~ of time.
	athlete ['æθli:t]	(Leicht-)Athlet/in, Sportler/in	A basketball player is an ~. ⚠ athlete ['æθli:t] – athletic(s) [æθ'letɪks]

Check your stress! (⚠ Die folgenden englischen Wörter werden auf der **ersten** Silbe betont.)

accent	Akzent	character	Charakter	instrument	Instrument	pronoun	Pronomen
article	Artikel	colony	Kolonie	metal	Metall	record	Rekord
astronaut	Astronaut	conflict	Konflikt	parliament	Parlament	student	Student
athlete	Athlet	dialect	Dialekt	president	Präsident	temperature	Temperatur
atmosphere	Atmosphäre	industry	Industrie	product	Produkt	transport	Transport

	right *(adv.)*	gerade, direkt, genau	I'll help you in a minute, but I'm busy ~ now.
	Puerto Rican [ˌpwɜ:təʊ'ri:kən]	Puertoricaner/in	
	Afghan ['æfgæn]	Afghane(r)	
	no matter how/what/when/where [nəʊ 'mætə]	egal, wie/was/wann/wo	I'll find him, *no ~ where* he's hiding.
p. 68	**line** [laɪn] (AE)/ **queue** [kju:] (BE)	Schlange *(wartender Menschen)*, Reihe	There's often a long ~ at the bus stop. 
	(to) **join** [dʒɔɪn]	sich anschließen; mitmachen; eintreten in *(einen Klub usw.)*	I'm all alone. Can I ~ you? Are you a member of a tennis club? – No, I'm not, but I've always wanted to ~ one.
	athletic [æθ'letɪk]	athletisch, sportlich	A person with a strong, healthy body who is good at sports and other physical activities is an ~ person.
	tough [tʌf]	zäh, *hier:* stark, robust	I can't eat this meat. It's really ~. A mountain-climber must be ~.
	(to) hang around – hung – hung	sich herumtreiben, herumlungern	The kids didn't know what to do with their time, so they just *hung* ~ and did nothing.
	downtown [ˌdaʊn'taʊn] (AE)	(im/ins) Zentrum, (in der/die) Innenstadt	(in or to) the business centre of a town or city
	(to) **drop out** (of school) [ˌdrɒp‿'aʊt], **-pp-**	(die Schule) abbrechen, vorzeitig verlassen	to stop taking part Some children ~ ~ of school because they don't like school.
	(to) **be based on** sth. [beɪst]	auf etwas basieren; *hier:* nach, entnommen aus	The text on pages 67-68 *is ~ on* "Tales out of school" by Patrick Welsh.
	tale [teɪl]	Erzählung, Geschichte	
	inner city [ˌɪnə 'sɪtɪ]	innerstädtisches Wohngebiet *(mit sozialen und wirtschaftlichen Problemen)*	
	(to) **grow up**	aufwachsen; groß werden	to develop from a child to a man or woman
	the privileged/ the underprivileged [ˌʌndə'prɪvɪlɪdʒd]	die besser Gestellten/ die schlechter Gestellten	We say that people who don't have the same chances in life as other people, usually because they are poor, are ~.

SEITE 151

Verbs with a preposition

I **disagree with** you.	Ich **bin anderer Meinung als** du.
Divide the class **into** three groups.	**Teile** die Klasse **in** drei Gruppen **ein**!
The farmers are **hoping for** a change in the weather.	Die Bauern **hoffen auf** einen Wetterwechsel.
Some of the kids **laughed at** Lan's clothes.	Einige Kinder **lachten über** Lans Kleidung.
Don't **laugh at** him because he's so fat.	**Lach** ihn nicht **aus**, weil er so dick ist.
I'm really **looking forward to** your party.	Ich **freu mich** wirklich **auf** deine Fete.
How did Cindy **react to** your suggestion?	Wie hat Cindy **auf** deinen Vorschlag **reagiert**?
Tom is very ill. We must **send for** a doctor.	... Wir müssen einen Arzt **holen/kommen lassen**.
Maureen was so angry that she **shouted at** Wanda.	Maureen war so wütend, dass sie Wanda **anschrie**.
My father often **suffers from** headaches.	Mein Vater **leidet** oft **unter/an** Kopfschmerzen.

(to) answer (sb.) back	sich *(mit Worten)* verteidigen; (jm.) freche Antworten geben	
(to) **mean to** do sth.	etwas absichtlich tun, etwas tun wollen	to want to do something I'm sorry. I *didn't ~ to* upset you.
Never mind.	Das macht doch nichts.	I've forgotten to bring the CD you lent me. I'm sorry. – *Never ~*, you can give it me tomorrow.
upset (about sth.) [ʌp'set]	aufgeregt, aufgebracht; beunruhigt; betrübt (wegen etwas)	Dave was very ~ when he heard about his sister's accident.
case [keɪs]	Fall	I'm very disappointed with your work! – If that's the ~, then please tell me why. I don't often agree with you, but in this ~ I think you're right.
(to) **inform** [ɪn'fɔːm]	informieren, benachrichtigen	to tell somebody about something
company ['kʌmpənɪ]	Gesellschaft, Begleitung	Sue hates being alone. She loves ~. Helen was in the ~ of her husband.

American English and British English (2)

AE:	BE:	
bill	**note**	Geldschein
car, auto(mobile)	**car**	Auto, Wagen
driver's license	**driving licence**	Führerschein
fall, autumn	**autumn**	Herbst
grade	**class, form**	Klasse(nstufe)
line	**queue**	Schlange, Reihe
(line	line	Linie, Zeile)
mail	**post, mail**	Post(sendungen)
math	**maths**	Mathe
movie, film	**film**	Film
movie theater/movies	**cinema**	Kino
period	**full stop**	Punkt
(period	period	Zeitspanne; Schulstunde
principal	**headmaster/-mistress**	Schulleiter/in, Direktor/in
Sincerely (yours), ...	**Yours sincerely, ...**	Mit freundl./herzl. Grüßen
Z [ziː]	**Z** [zed]	Z *(Buchstabe)*

AE:	BE:
-or(-)	**-our(-)**
color	colour
neighbor	neighbour
favorite	favourite
-er	**-re**
center	centre
theater	theatre
-l-	**-ll-**
traveling	travelling
counselor	counsellor

Remember:
In AE *Mr., Mrs., Ms.* are usually written with a full stop.

The date 11/3/95 means '3 November 1995' in AE, but '11 March 1995' in BE.

Kurz-Unit 6

Stonehenge and the Celts

p. 70	**evidence** (of) *(sing.)* ['evɪdəns]	Beweis(e) (für); Beleg(e) (für); Zeugnis(se) (von)	Graham has stolen my money. – Do you have any ~ of this?
	(to) **dig** (up) – **dug** – **dug** [dɪg, dʌg]	(aus-, um)graben	They'*re ~ ging up* the road again. Last week it was the waterworks, this time it's the electricity company.

button ['bʌtn]	Knopf	*archaeologist* [,ɑ:kɪ'ɒlədʒɪst]	Archäologe/-in
(to) turn out to be [tɜ:n]	sich erweisen als	*(to) bury)* ['berɪ]	begraben
(to) plant sth. [plɑ:nt]	etwas (ein)pflanzen	*treasure* ['treʒə]	Schatz, Kostbarkeit
rosebush ['rəʊzbʊʃ]	Rosenbusch	*(to) confirm* [kən'fɜ:m]	bestätigen
at the time [æt ðə 'taɪm]	gerade	*BC* [,bi:'sɪ:]	v. Chr.
		AD [,eɪ'di:]	n. Chr.
typist ['taɪpɪst]	Schreibkraft	*auction* ['ɔ:kʃn]	Auktion, Versteigerung
object ['ɒbdʒɪkt]	Gegenstand	*in six weeks' time* [---'-]	in sechs Wochen
soil [sɔɪl]	(Mutter-)Boden, Erde		

	archaeologist [,ɑ:kɪ'ɒlədʒɪst]	Archäologe/-in	*A~s* discovered many important things when they opened the Pyramids in Egypt.
	circle ['sɜ:kl]	Kreis	some *~s* 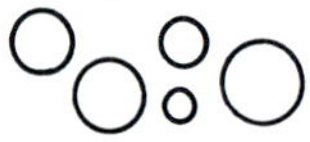
	solstice ['sɒlstɪs]	Sonnenwende	
	Druid ['dru:ɪd]	Druide	
	(the) **authorities** [ɔ:'θɒrətɪz]	Behörde(n)	the people or organizations that say what we can or cannot do
	megalith ['megəlɪθ]	Megalith	
p. 71	**tribe** [traɪb]	(Volks-)Stamm	a group of people who live together and share the same customs
	the **Britons** ['brɪtnz]	die Britannier	a tribe that settled in Britain and gave Britain its name (⚠ die Briten = the British)
	sword [sɔ:d]	Schwert	
	written record ['rɪtn 'rekɔ:d]	schriftliche Überlieferung	something that is written down We know this event must have happened, although there are no *written ~s.*
	shape [ʃeɪp]	Gestalt, Form	What ~ is the sun? – Round of course. (⚠ What shape/colour/size *is* ...?/= Welche Form/Farbe/Größe *hat* ...?)
	fringe [frɪndʒ]	Rand(gebiet, -zone)	the edge
	the **Jutes** [dʒu:ts]	die Jüten	one of the tribes that invaded Britain in the 5th–6th centuries
	54 **BC** [,bi:'sɪ:]	54 v. Chr.	54 ~ = 54 years before Christ [kraɪst]
	(to) **invade** (a country) [ɪn'veɪd]	einmarschieren, einfallen (in ein Land)	A foreign army last *~d* Britain over 900 years ago.
	eastern ['i:stən]	östlich	northern, southern, ~, western
	culture ['kʌltʃə]	Kultur	Every country has its own ~.
	expedition [,ekspɪ'dɪʃn]	Expedition	Who led the ~ that first climbed Mount Everest in 1953?

The Romans in Britain

72	**the …, the …** [ðə … ðə]	je …, umso/desto …	*The* more you practise, ~ better you become.
	legacy [ˈlegəsɪ]	Vermächtnis, Erbe	what people leave behind after they have died
	(to) **damage** [ˈdæmɪdʒ]	beschädigen	A storm can ~ trees and houses.
	emperor [ˈempərə]	Kaiser	the "king" of an empire
	AD 43 = 43 **AD** [ˌeɪˈdiː]	43 n. Chr.	~ 43 = 43 years after Christ ~ stands for "Anno Domini" [ˌænəʊ ˈdɒmɪnaɪ] ("im Jahre des Herrn")
	(to) **capture** [ˈkæptʃə]	erobern, erbeuten; gefangen nehmen	The foreign army ~*d* thousands of soldiers and took them prisoner.
	(to) **make sb./sth. sth** [meɪk]	jn./etw. zu etwas machen	They'll probably ~ Mark captain of the football team.
	province [ˈprɒvɪns]	Provinz	Countries that the Romans captured became ~*s* in the Roman Empire.
	barbarian [bɑːˈbeərɪən]	Barbar/in	people who are cruel and violent and have no culture
	(to) **plunder** [ˈplʌndə]	(aus)plündern	to steal things from a place, especially during a war
	(to) **rape** [reɪp]	vergewaltigen	The barbarians killed the men and ~*d* the women.
	historian [hɪˈstɔːrɪən]	Historiker/in	someone who studies or writes about history
73	**greatly** [ˈgreɪtlɪ]	sehr, außerordentlich, höchst	Your English has improved ~ since you were in England.
	remains [rɪˈmeɪnz]	(Über-)Reste	What shall I do with the ~ of the meal – throw them away?
	mosaic [məʊˈzeɪɪk]	Mosaik	

Medieval Britain

74	**medieval** [ˌmedɪˈiːvl]	mittelalterlich	from the Middle Ages The town has an old ~ castle, built in the 13th century.
	outlaw [ˈaʊtlɔː]	Geächtete(r)	*O~s* were people who broke the law and hid in lonely areas to avoid being caught.
	exhibition [ˌeksɪˈbɪʃn]	Ausstellung	There's an ~ of Celtic jewels and weapons at the city museum.
	(to) **learn** (about)	herausfinden (über), erfahren (über)	I didn't ~ about Ed's plans till yesterday.
	enemy [ˈenəmɪ]	Feind	Between 1939 and 1945 the British and the Germans were ~*ies*.
	kingdom [ˈkɪŋdəm]	Königreich	a country ruled by a king or queen
	conqueror [ˈkɒŋkərə]	Eroberer/in, Bezwinger/in	a person who conquers
	embroidery [ɪmˈbrɔɪdərɪ]	Stickerei(arbeit)	
	tapestry [ˈtæpəstrɪ]	Gobelin, Wandteppich	The castle had rooms with beautiful ~*ies* on the walls.
75	**rule** [ruːl]	Herrschaft, Regierung	Roman ~ in Britain lasted about 400 years.
	(to) **hunt** [hʌnt]	jagen	to kill wild animals for food or sport
	(to) **hang** sb. [hæŋ]	jn. (er)hängen	From that tree an outlaw *was ~ed.* ⚠ *(to) hang – hanged – hanged* = (er)hängen *(to) hang – hung – hung* = hängen, aufhängen (Bilder, Wäsche, …)
	the **Middle East** [ˌmɪdl ˈiːst]	der Nahe Osten	Israel, Syria and Jordan are three countries in the ~ ~.
	crusade [kruːˈseɪd]	Kreuzzug	

Unit 6

(p. 75)	**Muslim** *(n., adj.)* ['mʊzlɪm, 'mʌzlɪm]	Moslem; moslemisch	Iran and Saudi Arabia are two *M*~ countries.
	baron ['bærən]	Baron	a kind of lord
	(to) **sign** [saɪn]	unterschreiben	to write your name at the end of a letter or document
	charter ['tʃɑ:tə]	Charta, Urkunde	
	document ['dɒkjʊmənt]	Dokument, Urkunde	Passports and driving licences are ~*s* that people often carry around with them.
	democracy [dɪ'mɒkrəsɪ]	Demokratie	The workers complain that they have no rights and that there is no ~ in this firm.

Tudor Britain

p. 76	**faith** [feɪθ]	Glaube(n)	belief in God
	abbreviation (for) [ə,bri:vɪ'eɪʃn]	Abkürzung (von)	UN is the ~ for the United Nations.
	title ['taɪtl]	Titel	The title of her new book is "Goodbye to Africa".
	monarch ['mɒnək]	Monarch/in	another word for king or queen
	(to) **criticize** (for) ['krɪtɪsaɪz]	kritisieren (wegen)	The politician *was ~d* because she didn't inform Parliament.
	head [hed]	Oberhaupt	The ~ of a big organization is the boss of that organization.
	monastery ['mɒnəstrɪ]	Kloster	

heir to the throne [eə]	Thronfolger	*by law* [baɪ 'lɔ:]	per Gesetz, nach dem Gesetz
multi-cultural [,mʌltɪ'kʌltʃərəl]	multikulturell	*marriage (to)* ['mærɪdʒ]	Ehe (mit); Heirat
(to) cause [kɔ:z]	verursachen	*(to) break down* [,breɪk 'daʊn]	scheitern
headline ['hedlaɪn]	Schlagzeile	*fit* [fɪt]	(hier:) würdig, geziemend

p. 77	**feeble** ['fi:bl]	schwach	another word for weak
	in spite of [spaɪt]	trotz	The open-air concert took place *in ~ of* the bad weather.
	reign [reɪn]	Regierung(szeit)	Queen Elizabeth's ~ lasted from 1558 till 1603.
	active ['æktɪv]	rege, aktiv	She leads a very ~ life, even though she's 88.
	college ['kɒlɪdʒ]	College *(eigenständiger Teil der Universität)*	

The development of the English language

p. 78	**the other way round** [,ʌðə weɪ 'raʊnd]	andersherum	The table won't go through the door. – Yes, it will, we'll just have to turn it *the ~ ~ round.*
	via ['vaɪə]	über, per, via	I always travel from Munich to Frankfurt ~ Stuttgart, but you can go ~ Nuremberg.
	equivalent [ɪ'kwɪvələnt]	Entsprechung	The ~ of cup in German is "Tasse".
	(to) **drive – drove – driven** [draɪv, drəʊv, 'drɪvn]	(an)treiben	Can you help me ~ the cattle into that field over there?
	mixture ['mɪkstʃə]	Mischung	My new pullover is a ~ of different colours.
	Anglo-Saxon [,æŋgləʊ'sæksn]	Angelsachse; Angelsächsisch, angelsächsisch	People in England spoke *A*~ - ~ in the 8th century.
	(to) **remain** [rɪ'meɪn]	bleiben; übrig bleiben	another (more formal) word for to stay
	basically ['beɪsɪklɪ]	im Grunde, im Wesentlichen	There is not really a difference. = There is ~ no difference.
	ordinary ['ɔ:dɪnərɪ]	einfach, gewöhnlich, normal	normal, not unusual You don't have to wear anything special, just your ~ clothes.

78)	**sky** [skaɪ]	Himmel	If you look up into the ~, you can see the sun, or the moon and the stars.
79	**jungle** [ˈdʒʌŋgl]	Dschungel	The ~ was full of strange noises, wild animals and unusual plants.
	bungalow [ˈbʌŋgələʊ]	Bungalow	a house with just one floor
	(to) **make** sth. **up** [meɪk ˈʌp]	sich etwas ausdenken, etwas erfinden	If you don't know the answer, just ~ it ~.
	(to) computerize [kəmˈpju:təraɪz]	computerisieren, auf Computer umstellen	The whole system *has been ~d*. You now do everything – getting information, booking, paying – by computer.
	(to) downsize [ˈdaʊnˌsaɪz]	verkleinern	to make smaller He lost his job when the international firm he worked for *~d* the British part of its organization.
	megastore [ˈmegə]	(Einkaufs-)Markt	a very big store
	Aborigine [æbəˈrɪdʒəni:]	australische(r) Ureinwohner/in	The *A~s* were the people who lived in Australia before the Europeans came.
	(to) **create** [kri:ˈeɪt]	(er)schaffen	to make something new The company is so successful that it *has ~d* 100 new jobs in the last two years.
	feature [ˈfi:tʃə]	Merkmal, Eigenschaft	This new model has a number of very interesting new *~s*.
	common [ˈkɒmən]	üblich, normal	The word "baron" is not a very ~ word, because there aren't many barons today!
	(to) **keep up to date** (with), (to) **keep up** (with) [ki:p ˈʌp wɪð]	(sich) auf dem Laufenden/auf dem neuesten Stand halten (über)	It's important to ~ *up with* new developments if you're in the computer industry.

tongue [tʌŋ]	Sprache	*blood* [blʌd]	Blut
(to) rhyme [raɪm]	(sich) reimen	*mould* [məʊld]	Schimmel(pilz)
(to) sew [səʊ]	nähen	*tone* [təʊn]	Ton, Klang; Stimmung
verse [vɜ:s]	Strophe (eines Gedichtes oder Liedes), Vers	*(to) sum sth. up, -mm-* [sʌm‿ˈʌp]	etwas zusammenfassen

Kurz-Unit 7

Mazes in fact and fiction

80	maze [meɪz]	Irrgarten, Labyrinth	
	fact [fækt]	Wirklichkeit	Is the story a myth, or is it ~?
	fiction [ˈfɪkʃn]	Dichtung; Prosaliteratur; Fiktion	This book isn't based on real events. It's ~.
	friendship [ˈfrendʃɪp]	Freundschaft	They were very good friends, and their ~ lasted 20 years.
	purpose [ˈpɜ:pəs]	Zweck	Why do people build mazes? What are they for? What is their ~?
81	**amazing** [əˈmeɪzɪŋ]	erstaunlich	I can't believe that Janet of all people has won. I find it quite ~.
	material [məˈtɪərɪəl]	Material, Stoff	Wood, steel and paper are three examples of different *~s*.
	mistress [ˈmɪstrəs]	Geliebte	
	poison [ˈpɔɪzn]	Gift	They used ~ from an exotic plant to kill the king. ⚠ *poison* = Gift, *gift* = Geschenk

Unit 7/Unit 8

(p. 81)	**nunnery** ['nʌnərɪ]	Nonnenkloster	a "monastery" for nuns
	nowadays ['naʊədeɪz]	heutzutage	*N*~ most people have a telephone, even if they don't all have a computer.
	hedge [hedʒ]	Hecke	We didn't have a fence or a wall round the garden – we had a ~.
	(to) **combine** (with) [kəm'baɪn]	(sich) verbinden (mit), kombinieren (mit)	Mrs Stewart ~*d* a business trip to Rome with a few days holiday. ⚠ *(to) combine* [kəm'baɪn] *combination* [ˌkɒmbɪ'neɪʃn]
	jigsaw ['dʒɪgsɔː]	Puzzle	This ~ is a picture of an old ship and has 2000 pieces!
	non- [nɒn]	nicht-…; Nicht-…	People who don't smoke are ~-smokers.
	rectangular [rek'tæŋgjʊlə]	rechteckig	The box is not square, but ~.
	(to) **dictate** [dɪk'teɪt]	diktieren; vorschreiben, bestimmen	The size of the room will ~ how many chairs we'll be able to get in it.
	method ['meθəd]	Methode, Verfahren	way of doing something
	(to) **keep to** [kiːp tə]	sich halten an	When you drive in Britain you must always ~ *to* the left.
	dead end [ded 'end]	Sackgasse	
	coward ['kaʊəd]	Feigling	He wasn't brave. He was quite the opposite: a ~.
	(to) **be lost/get lost** [lɒst]	sich verlaufen haben/ sich verlaufen	When it's foggy in the mountains, walkers with little experience can easily ~ ~.
	exit ['eksɪt]	Ausgang; (Autobahn-) Ausfahrt	You enter the building through this door, but the ~ is that door over there.
p. 82	**absurd** [əb'sɜːd]	absurd	It's ~ to ask 47 other people to change their plans, just because the meeting is at the same time as your favourite TV programme.
	novel ['nɒvl]	Roman (⚠ *nicht*: ~~Novelle~~)	A ~ is a long written story, like "Die Blechtrommel" by Günter Grass.
	extract (from) ['ekstrækt]	Auszug (aus einem Buch)	some lines from a book or a diary, for example
	(to) **row** [rəʊ]	rudern	You have to ~ a small boat that hasn't got an engine or a sail.
	(to) **be about** [biː ə'baʊt]	handeln von	What *is* the book ~? – It'*s* ~ the writer's journey across Australia.
	(to) **simplify** ['sɪmplɪfaɪ]	vereinfachen	to make simpler
p. 83	**effect** (on) [ɪ'fekt]	(Aus-)Wirkung (auf)	Janet's father has lost his job. That will of course have an ~ on the family's holiday plans.
	(to) **summarize** sth. ['sʌməraɪz]	etwas zusammenfassen	to write a summary of something

Kern-Unit 8: Wales

8 A A letter from Wales

p. 85	**reply** (to) [rɪ'plaɪ]	Antwort, Erwiderung (auf)	another word for answer
	annoying [ə'nɔɪɪŋ]	ärgerlich, lästig	I've already got wet twice today. This rain is really ~.
	(to) **be fed up with** sth./sb. [ˌfed‿'ʌp]	etwas/jn. satt haben, die Nase voll haben von etwas/jm.	I'm ~ ~ *with* this weather. Rain, rain, rain all the time.
	fortunately ['fɔːtʃnətlɪ]	glücklicherweise	I thought I had missed the train. But ~ the train was late, too.

85)	(not) **that** bad [bæd]	(nicht) so schlimm	not ~ bad = not so bad
	micro-electronics *(sing.)* ['maɪkrəʊˌɪlek'trɒnɪks]	Mikroelektronik	People who design computers are experts in ~.

8 A Focus on GRAMMAR

). 86	**most of all** [məʊst‿əv 'ɔːl]	am allermeisten	Our cat likes fish and playing with balls of wool. But ~ *of* ~ it likes to sleep!
	peninsula [pə'nɪnsjʊlə]	Halbinsel	a piece of land surrounded by water on three sides
). 87	(to) **encourage** [ɪn'kʌrɪdʒ]	ermutigen; ermuntern; fördern	Ann isn't very interested in running on Saturday. We must ~ her to take part in the competition.
	(to) **remind sb.** (of sth.) [rɪ'maɪnd]	jn. (an etwas) erinnern	This photo ~*s* me of New York. Please ~ me to phone my parents. I mustn't forget. ⚠ *Ich erinnere mich* gut *an* New York. = *I remember* New York well.
	(to) **arrange for** [ə'reɪndʒ]	sorgen für	I have to leave very early tomorrow. Can you ~ *for* a taxi to come at 5.30, please?

8 A Wales and the Welsh

. 88	**clear** ['klɪə]	klar, deutlich	The teacher explained everything, so that it was ~ what to do.
	the **whole** of (Wales) [həʊl]	ganz (Wales)	There is snow all over Wales. = The ~ of Wales is covered with snow.
	(to) **pick** [pɪk]	pflücken	You mustn't ~ flowers in National Parks.
	litter ['lɪtə]	Abfall, herumliegendes Papier	After the open-air concert the field was covered with ~.
	the **Middle Ages** (pl.) [ˌmɪdl‿'eɪdʒɪz]	das Mittelalter	the period between about AD 1100 and AD 1500
. 89	(to) **export** [ɪk'spɔːt]	exportieren, ausführen	To ~ things means to sell them to another country.
	(to) **import** (from … to/into) [ɪm'pɔːt]	einführen, importieren (aus … in/nach)	the opposite of to export
	(to) **produce** [prə'djuːs]	produzieren, herstellen, erzeugen	Steel *is* ~*d* in a steel factory.
	(to) **turn** (brown, …) [tɜːn]	(braun, …) werden	Fields and trees ~ green in spring.
	minerals ['mɪnərəlz]	Mineralien, Bodenschätze	Coal and gold are ~.
	poetry ['pəʊɪtrɪ]	Dichtung, Dichtkunst	
	eisteddfod [aɪs'teðfɒd]	*walisisches Sänger- und Dichterfest*	

8 A Focus on GRAMMAR

. 90	(to) **order sb. to do sth.** ['ɔːdə]	jm. befehlen etwas zu tun; jn. damit beauftragen, etwas zu tun	The captain ~*ed* the sailors to clean the ship.
	policy, *pl.* **policies** ['pɒlɪsɪ]	Politik (= Verfahren, Richtlinien, Taktiken usw.)	What is the government's new foreign ~? ⚠ *politics* = (allgemeine) Politik, „Staatskunst" *policy* = Politik (als Taktik, Verfahren usw.); (Geschäfts-)Politik
	(to) **punish** ['pʌnɪʃ]	bestrafen	Sally didn't do her homework, and her teacher ~*ed* her by giving her extra work.

Unit 8

(p. 90)	**status** [ˈsteɪtəs]	Status	
	channel [ˈtʃænl]	Kanal, Programm	ARD and ZDF are two ~*s* on German TV.
	(to) **go wrong** [gəʊ ˈrɒŋ]	schief gehen	Everything *went* ~: the bus was late, I missed the train, then I found out that the match wasn't till the next day!

"any" (in positive sentences) = irgendein beliebiger, jeder x-beliebige, ganz gleich welcher

Marvin can go to college like **any** white kid.	... wie **jeder** weiße Jugendliche
You can come **any** day you like.	... an **irgendeinem** Tag, an **jedem beliebigen** Tag
You're just as good as **anybody** else.	... wie **jeder** andere, wie **irgendein** anderer
You can have **anything** you like for Christmas.	... **(alles,) was** du willst
More cars are made in Detroit than **anywhere** else in the USA.	... als **irgendwo** sonst, als an **jedem** anderen Ort

⚠ **any/anybody** etc. is often used after *if*: If **anybody** has **any** questions, I'll be happy to answer them.

8 A Focus on WORDS

p. 91	**economy** [ɪˈkɒnəmɪ]	Wirtschaft	industry and trade
	economic *(adj.)*, **economically** *(adv.)* [ˌiːkəˈnɒmɪk, ˌekəˈnɒmɪk]	(volks)wirtschaftlich, Wirtschafts-	The country's economy is strong. The country's ~ position is good. ⚠ *pronunciation*: economy [ɪˈkɒnəmɪ] economic [iːkəˈnɒmɪk]
	raw [rɔː]	roh, Roh-	The meat hasn't been cooked yet. It's still ~.
	communications *(pl.)* [kəmjuːnɪˈkeɪʃnz]	Nachrichtentechnik, Telekommunikation	Radio, television and the telephone are examples of ~ systems.
	robot [ˈrəʊbɒt]	Roboter, Fertigungsautomat	a machine which does several activities automatically
	workshop [ˈwɜːkʃɒp]	Werkstatt	a room where things are made or repaired
	machinery *(sing.)* [məˈʃiːnərɪ]	Maschinerie, Maschinen	a general word for machines New ~ was bought for the factory last year.
	goods *(pl.)* [gʊdz]	Waren, Güter	things that are produced, transported and sold
	leather [ˈleðə]	Leder	Most people wear ~ shoes, not plastic ones.
	tool [tuːl]	Werkzeug	What materials and ~*s* do you need to repair your bike?
	hammer [ˈhæmə]	Hammer	The thieves broke the shop window with a big ~.
	pliers *(pl.)* [ˈplaɪəz]	(eine) (Kombi-)Zange	a tool that you use to hold or cut things
	carpenter [ˈkɑːpɪntə]	Tischler/in, Schreiner/in	A ~ is a person who works with wood and makes things like chairs and tables.
	biotechnology [ˌbaɪəʊtekˈnɒlədʒɪ]	Biotechnik	technology that uses plants, bacteria etc.
	medical [ˈmedɪkl]	medizinisch, Medizin-; ärztlich	Alison is a ~ student. She is studying medicine.
	(in the) **field** (of) [fiːld]	(auf dem) Gebiet (von)	Her firm is one of the leading companies in the ~ of biotechnology.
	consumer [kənˈsjuːmə]	Verbraucher/in, Konsument/in	a person who buys goods or services
	energy [ˈenədʒɪ]	Energie	It's important to save ~, so please switch off all the machines when you are not using them.
	supply [səˈplaɪ]	Versorgung; Vorrat; Lieferung	Energy ~ to industry is very important. Without energy, industry can't work.
	(to) **supply** (with) [səˈplaɪ]	(be)liefern; versorgen (mit)	Who can ~ me ~ some information about the Scottish whisky industry?
	protection (against) [prəˈtekʃn]	Schutz (vor)	I wear this thick coat for ~ against the cold wind.

91)	(to) **be related** (to) [rɪ'leɪtɪd]	verwandt sein (mit); sich beziehen auf	The next question *is not* ~ *to* the one we have just discussed.
	spanner (BE) ['spænə], **wrench** (AE) [rentʃ]	Schraubenschlüssel	
	saw [sɔ:]	Säge	You cut wood with a knife or a ~.
	nail [neɪl]	Nagel	We need a hammer and ~*s* to join these two pieces of wood together.
	screwdriver ['skru:draɪvə]	Schraubenzieher	
	screw [skru:]	Schraube	If you haven't got a hammer and nails, you can join them with ~*s*.
	employer [ɪm'plɔɪə]	Arbeitgeber/in	The owner of a firm is the ~ of the people who work there.
	employee [,emplɔ'i: ɪm'plɔii:]	Arbeitnehmer/in, Angestellte(r)	someone who is paid to work
	made of (paper)	aus (Papier)	These plates are ~ ~ paper.
Ex 1	(to) **practise** (BE)/ (to) **practice** (AE) ['præktɪs]	*hier:* ausüben	You ~ your religion when, for example, you go to church.
	(to) **march** [mɒ:tʃ]	marschieren	Soldiers don't walk, they ~.
	prejudice (against) ['predʒʊdɪs]	Vorurteil, Voreingenommenheit (gegen[über])	My brother has a ~ against women. He doesn't think they're as brave as men.
	prejudiced	voreingenommen	He's ~ against women.
3	**mid-** [mɪd]	mittlere(r/s), Mittel-	The middle of March is ~-March.
6	**sponsored activity** ['spɒnsəd]	*Aktivität (meist sportlicher Art) um Geld für Wohltätigkeitszwecke zu sammeln*	
	head teacher [,hed 'ti:tʃə]	Schulleiter/in	the "boss" of a school
	(to) **cause** *(v.)*	verursachen	How did the accident happen? What ~*d* it?
	cause *(n.)* [kɔ:z]	Ursache	What was the ~ of the accident?
7	**present-day** ['prezənt ,deɪ]	heutig, gegenwärtig	That singer is one of today's pop idols. She's a ~-~ pop idol.
	typewriter ['taɪpraɪtə]	Schreibmaschine	a machine that you use to write letters, for example
11	*warden* ['wɔ:dn]	Aufseher/in	
12	**plus** [plʌs]	plus	Four ~ two is six.
	(to) **do business** (with) ['bɪznɪs]	Geschäfte machen (mit)	Which British companies *does* your firm ~ *business* ~?
	(to) **make a telephone call** [kɔ:l]	einen Anruf machen, ein Telefongespräch führen	Can I use your phone? I need to ~ *a* quick *call.*
	(to) **do damage** ['dæmɪdʒ]	Schaden anrichten	Storms sometimes ~ a lot of ~ to houses in the area.

Prefixes expressing the opposite

un-	**in-**	**im-** (before **p, b**)	**ir-** (before **r**)	**dis-**	**non-**
unfair	**in**correct	**im**patient	**ir**regular	**dis**agree	**non**-Indian
unable	**in**dependent	**im**polite		**dis**advantage	**non**-smoker
unhappy	**in**formal	**im**possible			**non**-stop

un- is the most usual prefix to make an opposite.

Unit 8

○ Getting along in Britain: Bed & breakfast

p. 96	*(to) convert (into)* [kən'vɜ:t]	umbauen (zu)
	(to) work out [wɜ:k 'aʊt]	(her)ausarbeiten, herausbekommen; ausrechnen
	vacancy ['veɪkənsɪ]	freies Zimmer; freie (Arbeits-)Stelle
	available [ə'veɪləbl]	verfügbar, vorhanden; vorrätig
	(to) include [ɪn'klu:d]	(mit) einschließen, enthalten, beinhalten
	continental breakfast [ˌkɒntɪ'nentl]	kontinentales Frühstück (= wie auf dem europäischen Festland üblich)
	(to) reserve [rɪ'zɜ:v]	reservieren (lassen); buchen
	requirement [rɪ'kwaɪəmənt]	(An-)Forderung
	(to) overlook [ˌəʊvə'lʊk]	überblicken
	en suite [ˌɒn 'swi:t]	mit eigenem Bad

8 T A Welsh legend

p. 97	**people** ['pi:pl]	Volk	The king ruled his ~ fairly.
	knight [naɪt]	Ritter	The legend of King Arthur and his *~s* is a famous one.
	Round Table ['raʊnd 'teɪbl]	Tafelrunde	
	once [wʌns]	*hier:* einstig	
	(to) **set off** [set 'ɒf]	aufbrechen	to leave somewhere and start a journey
	hazel [heɪzl]	Haselnuss(strauch)	
	staff [stɒ:f]	Stab, Stock	
	most (unusual) [məʊst]	höchst (ungewöhnlich)	~ unusual = very unusual
	treasure ['treʒə]	Schatz, Kostbarkeit	Where do you think the pirates hid their ~ — all that gold and silver?
	leaf, *pl.* **leaves** [li:f, li:vz]	Blatt (einer Pflanze)	In autumn the ~ on the trees turn brown and fall off.
	wide [waɪd]	breit	the opposite of narrow
	armour ['ɑ:mə]	Rüstung	
	pile [paɪl]	Haufen	a ~ of sand, a ~ of old newspapers
	misfortune [mɪs'fɔ:tʃu:n]	Unglück	
	(to) **sleep on** [sli:p]	weiterschlafen	to carry on sleeping
	thunder ['θʌndə]	Donner	
	(to) **go back to sleep** [bæk tə 'sli:p]	wieder einschlafen	I woke up, but when I saw it was only 4 am I turned over and *went* ~ *to* ~.
p. 98	**wise** [waɪz]	weise, klug	She was a very ~ woman to give you that advice.
	gone [gɒn]	weg	I've used all the paper and there's none left. It's all ~.
	greedy ['gri:dɪ]	(hab)gierig	A ~ person never has enough and always wants more.
	metal ['metl]	Metall	Gold is a kind of ~.
	dozen ['dʌzn]	Dutzend	a ~ eggs = 12 eggs
	(to) **chase** (away) [tʃeɪs]	(weg-, ver)jagen, verfolgen	The policeman *~d* the thief down the street and caught him outside the post office.
	partly ['pɑ:tlɪ]	zum Teil, teilweise	not completely Liz goes to the disco ~ because she likes the music, ~ because she meets her friends there.
	upside down [ˌʌpsaɪd'daʊn]	verkehrt (herum), mit dem Kopf nach unten	If you turn your cup ~ ~, you lose all the tea in it.
	(to) **treat** [tri:t]	behandeln	Tim *~s* Jane badly. He's often very unkind to her.
	definition [defɪ'nɪʃn]	Definition	A ~ of ice is "frozen water".
	saint [seɪnt]	Heilige(r)	a very holy person

○ Songs, poems and extra reading texts

New York, New York

102	*(to) spread* [spred]	verbreiten	*heap* [hi:p]	Haufen
	vagabond ['vægəbɒnd]	Vagabund/in	*blues* (infml.) [blu:z]	Melancholie
	(to) long (to do) [lɒŋ]	sich sehnen (danach zu tun)	*(to) melt* [melt]	schmelzen
	(to) stray [streɪ]	(herum)strolchen, (-)streifen	*(to) make it* (infml.)	es schaffen, es zu etwas bringen
	very	genau	*it's up to you*	es kommt auf dich an
	wanna (infml.)	= want to		

Small town

103	*prob'ly*	= probably	*had myself a ball*	amüsierte mich gut
	community [kə'mju:nətɪ]	Gemeinde, Gemeinschaft	*L. A.*	= Los Angeles
	(to) provide [prə'vaɪd]	bieten, liefern	*doll* [dɒl]	Puppe
	opportunity [ɒpə'tju:nətɪ]	Gelegenheit, Chance	*hayseed* ['heɪsi:d]	tölpelhaft, naiv
	I used to … ['ju:stə]	früher habe ich (immer) …	*(to) breathe* [bri:ð]	atmen
			gonna (infml.)	= going to
			(to) bury ['berɪ]	begraben

Scarborough Fair

104	*fair* [feə]	Kirmes, Jahrmarkt	*clarion call* ['klærɪən kɔ:l]	(Weck-)Ruf
	parsley ['pɑ:slɪ]	Petersilie	*acre* ['eɪkə]	Morgen *(Flächenmaß)*
	sage [seɪdʒ]	Salbei	*a sprinkling of …* ['sprɪŋklɪŋ]	ein paar (verstreute) …
	rosemary ['rəʊzmərɪ]	Rosmarin	*tear* [tɪə]	Träne
	thyme [taɪm]	Thymian	*strand* [strænd]	*(hier:)* Strand
	remember me to …	grüß … von mir	*(to) polish* ['pɒlɪʃ]	polieren
	cambric ['keɪmbrɪk]	Cambric *(lockeres Baumwollgewebe)*	*(to) reap* [ri:p]	*(Getreide usw.)* schneiden, ernten
	tracing ['treɪsɪŋ]	Zeichnung	*sickle* ['sɪkl]	Sichel
	sparrow ['spærəʊ]	Spatz *(Vogel)*	*(to) bellow* ['beləʊ]	brüllen
	snowcrested ['snəʊ,krestɪd]	mit einem Kamm aus Schnee	*(to) blaze* [bleɪz]	lodern, brennen, leuchten, stahlen
	seam [si:m]	Saum	*scarlet* ['skɑ:lət]	scharlachrot
	needle ['ni:dl]	(Näh-)Nadel	*(to) gather* ['gæðə]	(auf-, ein-)sammeln
	blanket ['blæŋkɪt]	(Woll-)Decke	*bunch of heather* [,bʌntʃ əv 'heðə]	Heidestrauß
	bedclothes ['bedkləʊðz]	Bettzeug, -wäsche	*cause* [kɔ:z]	Sache
	(to) be unaware of sth. [,ʌnə'weə]	sich etw. nicht bewusst sein, etw. nicht bemerken		

Cosher Bailey

105	*engine* ['endʒɪn]	Lokomotive	*grand pianna (= piano)* [grænd pi:'ænəʊ]	(Konzert-)Flügel
	needed mending ['mendɪŋ]	musste repariert werden	*fiddle* ['fɪdl]	Fiedel
	grand [grænd]	prächtig	*chapel* ['tʃæpl]	Kapelle, Kirche
	(to) burst [bɜ:st]	sprengen, zum Platzen bringen	*might* [maɪt]	Kraft
	boiler ['bɔɪlə]	Kessel	*angel* ['eɪndʒəl]	Engel
	level ['levl]	Ebene	*up yonder* ['jɒndə]	dort oben
	devil ['devl]	Teufel	*Here's to Wales.*	(Ein Prosit) Auf Wales!
	funnel ['fʌnl]	Schornstein	*(to) brew* [bru:]	brauen
	(to) rattle ['rætl]	rattern	*ale* [eɪl]	Ale, Bier
	(to) frighten ['fraɪtən]	erschrecken		

○ Extra reading

Cwm Rhondda

(p. 105)	*thou* [ðaʊ]	= you	*thy* [ðaɪ]	= your
	barren [ˈbærən]	öde, dürr, kahl	*heaven* [ˈhevn]	Himmel
	art [ɑ:t]	= are	*(to) feed* [fi:d]	(er)nähren
	mighty [ˈmaɪtɪ]	mächtig	*evermore* [ˈevəˌmɔ:]	ewig, immerfort

Widow's Walk

p. 106	*widow* [ˈwɪdəʊ]	Witwe	*complaint* [kəmˈpleɪnt]	Klage
	(to) wave [weɪv]	winken	*(I'm) thinking about it.*	ich überlege es mir
	all to yourself	ganz für dich	*You can say that again.* [---ˈ---]	Das kannst du laut sagen!
	Get some work done.	Arbeite mal schön!	*I sure am.* [--ˈ-]	Aber klar!
	(to) decorate [ˈdekəreɪt]	tapezieren, streichen	*(to) put the phone down*	auflegen
	(to) lean [li:n]	(sich) (an)lehnen	*(to) be due (back)* [dju:]	(zurück)erwartet werden
	answering machine [ˈɑ:nsərɪŋ məˌʃi:n]	Anrufbeantworter	*railing* [ˈreɪlɪŋ]	Geländer
	traffic jam [ˈtræfɪk ˌdʒæm]	(Verkehrs-)Stau	*used to stand* [ˈju:stə]	standen früher (immer)
			steep [sti:p]	steil
p. 107	*crew* [kru:]	Mannschaft, Besatzung	*(to) process* [ˈprəʊses]	verarbeiten
	seagull [ˈsi:gʌl]	Möwe	*cargo* [ˈkɑ:gəʊ]	Fracht
	(to) attract [əˈtrækt]	anziehen, anlocken	*(to) breathe (in/out)* [bri:ð]	(ein-/aus-)atmen
	ordinary [ˈɔ:dənrɪ]	gewöhnlich	*actually* [ˈæktʃʊəlɪ]	tatsächlich
	experience [ɪkˈspɪərɪəns]	Erfahrung, Erlebnis	*body* [ˈbɒdɪ]	Leiche
	whaling ship [ˈweɪlɪŋ ʃɪp]	Walfänger	*(to) bury* [ˈberɪ]	begraben
			gentle [ˈdʒentl]	zart, behutsam
	(to) rest [rest]	ruhen	*curious* [ˈkjʊərɪəs]	neugierig

In the States

p. 108	*yet though* [jet]	obwohl noch	*(to) mount* [maʊnt]	steigen
	elder [ˈeldə]	= older	*morn* [mɔ:n]	= morning
	tongue [tʌŋ]	Sprache	*(to) decay* [dɪˈkeɪ]	ver-, zerfallen
	(to) decline [dɪˈklaɪn]	sich neigen	*(to) predict* [prɪˈdɪkt]	vorhersagen

Crossing Kansas By Train

pole [pəʊl]	Stange	*cawing* [ˈkɔ:ɪŋ]	Krächzen
(to) pass [pɑ:s]	passieren, vorbeiziehen	*(to) gather* [ˈgæðə]	sich versammeln

Poem

p. 109	*soft* [sɒft]	weich, leise

Friends

yet [jet]	doch	*shadow* [ˈʃædəʊ]	Schatten
indisputably [ɪndɪsˈpju:təblɪ]	unstrittig	*it doesn't matter where* [ˈmætə]	egal wo

Mother to Son

109	*ain't been no* (infml.)	= hasn't been a	*landin' = landing* ['lændɪŋ]	Treppenabsatz
	tack [tæk]	(Nagel-)Stift, Zwecke	*(to) turn back*	umkehren
	splinter ['splɪntə]	(Holz-)Splitter	*'cause*	= because
	(to) tear – tore – torn [teə – tɔ: – tɔ:n]	reißen	*kinder = kind of* (infml.)	irgendwie, ein bisschen
	bare [beə]	nackt, bloß	*I'se still going* (infml.)	= I'm still going
	I'se been a-climbin' (infml.)	= I've been climbing	*honey* ['hʌnɪ]	Liebling

The fun they had

110	*headed* ['hedɪd]	mit Überschrift, betitelt	*slot* [slɒt]	Schlitz
	(to) print [prɪnt]	drucken	*(to) calculate* ['kælkjʊleɪt]	(aus)rechnen
	crinkly ['krɪŋklɪ]	zerknittert	*(to) gear* [gɪə]	einstellen
	(to) be supposed to ['səpəʊzd]	(tun) sollen	*actually* ['æktʃʊəlɪ]	tatsächlich, eigentlich
	screen [skri:n]	Bildschirm	*progress* ['prəʊgres]	Fortschritt(e)
	I guess (meist AE) [ges]	ich nehme an	*satisfactory* [,sætɪs'fæktərɪ]	befriedigend
	plenty (of) ['plentɪ]	eine Menge	*(to) blank out* [blæŋk]	aussetzen
	(to) point [pɔɪnt]	zeigen, deuten	*superior* [su:'pɪərɪə]	überlegen, überheblich
	attic ['ætɪk]	Dachkammer	*shoulder* ['ʃəʊldə]	Schulter
	scornful ['skɔ:nfʊl]	verächtlich	*regular* ['regjʊlə]	normal
	(to) shake – shook – shaken [ʃeɪk – ʃʊk – 'ʃeɪkn]	schütteln	*smart* [smɑ:t]	klug
	county ['kaʊntɪ]	*(etwa:)* (Land-)Kreis	*I betcha = I bet you* [bet]	ich wette
	apart [ə'pɑ:t]	auseinander	*(to) adjust* [ə'dʒʌst]	einstellen
111	*dusty* ['dʌstɪ]	staubig	*(to) insert* [ɪn'sɜ:t]	einschieben
	beneath [bɪ'ni:θ]	unter	*(to) flash* [flæʃ]	blinken
	fraction ['frækʃn]	Bruch(zahl)		

Roman Wall Blues

blues (infml.) [blu:z]	Melancholie	*(to) creep* [kri:p]	kriechen, schleichen
heather ['heðə]	Heidekraut	*(to) hang around* [hæŋ]	sich herumtreiben, herumlungern
lice [laɪs]	Läuse	*place* [pleɪs]	*hier:* Haus
tunic ['tju:nɪk]	Tunika, Waffenrock	*manners* ['mænəz]	Benehmen, Manieren
(to) patter ['pætə]	prasseln	*(to) dice* [daɪs]	würfeln, knobeln
mist [mɪst]	Nebel		

The story of St. Alban

112	*neither ... nor* ['naɪðə ... nɔ:]	weder ... noch	*(to) torture* ['tɔ:tʃə]	foltern
	pagan ['peɪgən]	heidnisch	*(to) sentence* ['sentəns]	verurteilen
	Christianity [,krɪstɪ'ænətɪ]	Christentum	*citizen* ['sɪtɪzən]	Staatsbürger/in
	shelter ['ʃeltə]	Obdach	*heaven* ['hevn]	(der) Himmel
	moved [mu:vd]	gerührt	*executioner* [,eksɪ'kju:ʃənə]	Henker, Scharfrichter
	cloak [kləʊk]	Cape, Umhang	*(to) execute* ['eksɪkju:t]	hinrichten
	judge [dʒʌdʒ]	Richter/in	*site* [saɪt]	Stätte, Stelle

○Extra reading

The three blows

p. 113	*blow* [bləʊ]	Schlag	*bride* [braɪd]	Braut
	shepherd [ˈʃepəd]	Schäfer	*goat* [gəʊt]	Ziege
	beside [bɪˈsaɪd]	neben	*dowry* [ˈdaʊrɪ]	Mitgift
	(to) fall in love (with) [fɔːl ɪn ˈlʌv]	sich verlieben (in)	*confirmation* [ˌkɒnfəˈmeɪʃn]	Firmung
	fairy [ˈfeərɪ]	Fee	*lady* [ˈleɪdɪ]	Dame
	(to) bake [beɪk]	backen	*(to) hesitate* [ˈhezɪteɪt]	zögern
	soft [sɒft]	weich	*gentle* [ˈdʒentl]	sanft
	(to) wed [wed]	heiraten	*tears* [tɪəz]	Tränen
	twin [twɪn]	Zwilling	*(to) pat* [pæt]	tätscheln
	breadcrumb [ˈbredkrʌm]	Brotkrümel	*funeral* [ˈfjuːnrəl]	Beerdigung
			(to) grab [græb]	(er)greifen
	(to) prosper [ˈprɒspə]	Glück/Erfolg haben	*wrist* [rɪst]	Handgelenk
	(to) strike [straɪk]	schlagen		
p. 114	*(to) shake - shook - shaken* [ʃeɪk - ʃʊk - ˈʃeɪkn]	schütteln	*(to) stare* [steə]	starren

Mini-dictionary

Alphabetical list of words (Books 1-4)

Die alphabetische Wortliste enthält den gesamten obligatorischen Wortschatz der Bände A1 bis A4. In der Regel wird nur die Schreibweise und Aussprache des britischen Englisch angegeben.

sb. = somebody, sth. = something, AE = American English, BE = British English, infml. = informal

A

a [ə] ein, eine; **50p a week** 50 Pence pro Woche
abbey ['æbɪ] Abtei, Kloster
abbreviation [əˌbriːvɪ'eɪʃn] Abkürzung
ability [ə'bɪlətɪ] Fähigkeit
able ['eɪbl]: **be able to** können, fähig sein
Aborigine [ˌæbə'rɪdʒəniː] australische(r) Ureinwohner/in
about [ə'baʊt] 1. über; 2. ungefähr, etwa; 3. wegen; **be about** handeln von; **What about ... ?** Wie steht's mit ... ?, Wie wär's mit ... ?
above [ə'bʌv] 1. über, oberhalb (von); 2. oben, darüber
abroad [ə'brɔːd] ins/im Ausland
absurd [əb'sɜːd] absurd
accent ['æksənt] Akzent
accept [ək'sept] annehmen, akzeptieren
acceptable [ək'septəbl] akzeptierbar
accident ['æksɪdənt] 1. Unfall; 2. Versehen
accommodation [əˌkɒmə'deɪʃn] Unterkunft
according to [ə'kɔːdɪŋ] entsprechend, gemäß, nach
accountant [ə'kaʊntənt] Buchhalter/in, Wirtschaftsprüfer/in
ache [eɪk] 1. Schmerz; **(a) stomach ache** ['stʌmək‿eɪk] Magenschmerzen, Bauchschmerzen; 2. wehtun, schmerzen
across [ə'krɒs] (quer) über, durch
act [ækt] 1. spielen, darstellen; 2. handeln; **action** ['ækʃn] Handlung, Tat; Handeln; **active** ['æktɪv] rege, aktiv
activity [æk'tɪvətɪ] Projekt, Beschäftigung
AD [ˌeɪ'diː] n. Chr.
add [æd] hinzufügen
additional [ə'dɪʃnəl] zusätzliche(r, s)
address [ə'dres] Adresse, Anschrift
admiral ['ædmərəl] Admiral
admit [əd'mɪt] 1. zugeben; 2. zulassen, (hin)einlassen
adult ['ædʌlt] Erwachsene(r)
advantage [əd'vɑːntɪdʒ] Vorteil
adventure [əd'ventʃə] Abenteuer
advert ['ædvɜːt] Anzeige, Reklame; **advertising agency** ['ædvətaɪzɪŋ ˌeɪdʒənsɪ] Werbeagentur
advice [əd'vaɪs] Rat, Ratschläge
advise [əd'vaɪz] (be)raten
afford [ə'fɔːd] sich leisten
afraid [ə'freɪd]: **be afraid (of)** Angst haben, sich fürchten (vor); **I'm afraid** leider
Africa ['æfrɪkə] Afrika; **African-American** [ˌæfrɪkən‿ə'merɪkən] Afro-Amerikaner/in; **African-Caribbean** [ˌæfrɪkən kærɪ'biːən] (Nachkomme der) Einwanderer aus Westindien; westindisch
after ['ɑːftə] 1. nach; 2. nachdem; 3. hinter ... her; **after that** danach
afternoon [ˌɑːftə'nuːn] Nachmittag; **Good afternoon.** Guten Tag! **in the afternoon(s)** am Nachmittag; **on that afternoon** an jenem Nachmittag; **this afternoon** heute Nachmittag
again [ə'gen, ə'geɪn] wieder; noch (ein)mal
against [ə'genst] gegen
age [eɪdʒ] (Lebens-, Zeit-)Alter
agency ['eɪdʒənsɪ] Agentur
ago [ə'gəʊ] vor; **not long ago** vor kurzem
agree (with) [ə'griː] übereinstimmen (mit); zustimmen, sich einigen, beschließen
air [eə] Luft; **airmail** ['eə meɪl] Luftpost
airport ['eəpɔːt] Flughafen
A-Level ['eɪ ˌlevl] **= Advanced Level exam** (BE) *etwa:* Abitur
alive [ə'laɪv] am Leben
all [ɔːl] 1. alle; alles; 2. ganz; **all of you** ihr alle; **all over** überall in/auf; **all right** gut, in Ordnung; **I'm all right.** Mir geht's gut. **It's all right for Liz.** Liz ist gut dran. Liz hat's gut. **If it's all right with Dad.** Wenn es Vati recht ist. **That's all right.** Schon gut. Nichts zu danken. **most of all** am allermeisten
alligator ['ælɪgeɪtə] Alligator
allow [ə'laʊ] erlauben; **be allowed to** dürfen
almost ['ɔːlməʊst] fast, beinahe
alone [ə'ləʊn] allein; **leave sb. alone** jn. in Ruhe lassen
along [ə'lɒŋ] entlang
Alps [ælps] Alpen
already [ɔːl'redɪ] schon, bereits
also ['ɔːlsəʊ] auch; **not only ... but also** nicht nur ..., sondern auch
although [ɔːl'ðəʊ] obwohl, obgleich
altogether [ˌɔːltə'geðə] insgesamt, alles zusammen
always ['ɔːlweɪz] immer
am [æm] bin
am [ˌeɪ‿'em] ... Uhr morgens/vormittags
amazing [ə'meɪzɪŋ] erstaunlich
ambulance ['æmbjʊləns] Krankenwagen; **ambulance man/woman** Sanitäter/in
America [ə'merɪkə] Amerika; **American** [ə'merɪkən] amerikanisch; Amerikaner/in
among [ə'mʌŋ] (mitten) unter, zwischen
amount [ə'maʊnt] Menge; Summe; Betrag
an [æn, ən] ein, eine
ancestor ['ænsestə] Vorfahre
and [ænd, ən(d)] und
Angles ['æŋglz] Angeln; **Anglo-Saxon** [ˌæŋgləʊ 'sæksn] 1. angelsächsisch; 2. das Angelsächsische
angry (with) ['æŋgrɪ] wütend, böse, zornig (auf)
animal ['ænɪml] Tier
annoy [ə'nɔɪ] ärgern, belästigen; **annoying** ärgerlich, lästig; **be annoyed** verärgert sein, sich ärgern
anorak ['ænəræk] Anorak
another [ə'nʌðə] 1. ein(e) andere(r, s); 2. noch ein(e)
answer ['ɑːnsə] 1. Antwort; 2. antworten, beantworten; **answer the (tele)phone** ans Telefon gehen
any ['enɪ] (irgend)welche(r, s); jede(r, s) (beliebige); **not ... any** (gar) kein, keine; keins; **anybody/anyone** (irgend)jemand; jede/r (Beliebige); **not ... anybody** niemand; **anything** (irgend)etwas; irgendetwas (x-Beliebiges); **Anything else?** Sonst noch etwas? **not ... anything** nichts; **anyway** außerdem, überhaupt; sowieso; jedenfalls; **anywhere** irgendwo(hin); **not ... anywhere** nirgendwo(hin)
apartment [ə'pɑːtmənt] (*meist* AE) Wohnung
apologize [ə'pɒlədʒaɪz] sich entschuldigen
apostrophe [ə'pɒstrəfɪ] Apostroph
appear [ə'pɪə] erscheinen, auftauchen; **appear (to be)** (zu sein) scheinen
apple ['æpl] Apfel
apply (for) [ə'plaɪ] sich bewerben (um), beantragen
April ['eɪprəl] April
aquarium [ə'kweərɪəm] Aquarium
archaeologist [ˌɑːkɪ'ɒlədʒɪst] Archäologe/-in
archery ['ɑːtʃərɪ] Bogenschießen
architect ['ɑːkɪtekt] Architekt/in
architecture ['ɑːkɪtektʃə] Architektur

are [ɑ:, ə] bist, sind, seid
area ['eərɪə] **1.** Gebiet, Gegend; **2.** Fläche
argue (about) ['ɑ:gju:] (sich) streiten, zanken (über/wegen); **argument** ['ɑ:gjʊmənt] **1.** Argument, Grund; **2.** Streit
ark [ɑ:k] Arche; **Noah's Ark** [ˌnəʊəz‿'ɑ:k] die Arche Noah
arm [ɑ:m] Arm
armchair [ˌɑ:m'tʃeə] Sessel
army ['ɑ:mɪ] Armee, Heer
around [ə'raʊnd] um … herum, im Gebiet um
arrange [ə'reɪndʒ] (an)ordnen; **arrange for** sorgen für
arrival [ə'raɪvl] Ankunft; **arrivals lounge** Ankunftshalle; **arrive** [ə'raɪv] ankommen, eintreffen
art [ɑ:t] Kunst
article ['ɑ:tɪkl] Artikel
artificial [ɑ:tɪ'fɪʃl] künstlich
as [æz, əz] **1.** als, während; **2.** da, weil; **3.** wie; **as if** als ob; **as late as …** erst um …; **as long as** solange, sofern; **(not) as fast as** (nicht) so schnell wie; **as soon as** sobald
Asia ['eɪʃə] Asien; **Asian** Asiat/in, asiatisch
ask [ɑ:sk] fragen; **ask about** fragen nach; **ask a question** eine Frage stellen; **ask for** bitten um
asleep [ə'sli:p]**: be asleep** schlafen; **fall asleep** einschlafen
assistant [ə'sɪstənt] Verkäufer/in; Assistent/in, Gehilfe/-in
astronaut ['æstrənɔ:t] Astronaut/in
at [æt, ət] bei, an; **at breakfast** zur Frühstückszeit, beim Frühstück; **at Dave's/my house** bei Dave/mir (zu Hause); **at Easter** zu Ostern; **at first** zuerst, anfangs; **at home** zu Hause; **at last** endlich; schließlich; **at least** mindestens; wenigstens, zumindest; **at night** nachts, bei Nacht; **at once** sofort, (so)gleich; **at school** in der Schule; **at the end** am Ende, am Schluss; **at the moment** im Moment, im Augenblick; zurzeit; **at the side (of)** an der Seite (von); **at the weekend** am Wochenende; **at 3 o'clock** um 3 Uhr; **at 22 Albert Road** in der Albertstraße Nr. 22; **at work** bei der Arbeit; **good/bad at** gut/schlecht in; **look at** anschauen; **(not) at all** überhaupt (nicht)
athlete ['æθli:t] (Leicht-)Athlet/in, Sportler/in; **athletic** [æθ'letɪk] athletisch, sportlich
Atlantic [ət'læntɪk] Atlantik; atlantisch
atmosphere ['ætməsfɪə] Atmosphäre
attack [ə'tæk] angreifen
attitude ['ætɪtju:d] Haltung, Einstellung
attraction [ə'trækʃn] Attraktion, Anziehungspunkt; **attractive** anziehend, attraktiv, reizvoll
August ['ɔ:gəst] August
aunt [ɑ:nt] Tante
Australia [ɒs'treɪlɪə] Australien
Austria ['ɒstrɪə] Österreich
authorities [ɔ:'θɒrətɪz] Behörde(n)
automatic(ally) [ˌɔ:tə'mætɪklɪ] automatisch
auto(mobile) ['ɔ:təʊ, 'ɔ:təməbi:l] (AE) Auto, Wagen
autumn ['ɔ:təm] Herbst; **in (the) autumn** im Herbst
average ['ævərɪdʒ] Durchschnitt; Durchschnitts-
avoid [ə'vɔɪd] (ver)meiden; ausweichen; **avoidable** vermeidbar
away [ə'weɪ] **1.** weg, fort; **2.** entfernt; **go away** verreisen; **throw away** wegwerfen

B

baby ['beɪbɪ] Baby
back [bæk] **1.** Rückseite, hinterer Teil; Rücken; **2.** hintere(r, s), Hinter-; **3.** zurück, wieder; **in the back** hinten *(im Auto)*
bacon ['beɪkn] (Schinken-)Speck
bad [bæd] schlecht; schlimm; **a bad cold** ein starker Schnupfen; **bad at** schlecht in; **do badly** schlecht sein *(in einem Fach)*
bag [bæg] Tasche, Beutel, Tüte; **lunch bag** Tüte mit dem eingepackten Mittagessen; **mixed bag** bunte Mischung
baggage ['bægɪdʒ] Gepäck
baker ['beɪkə] Bäcker/in
balcony ['bælkənɪ] Balkon
ball [bɔ:l] Ball
banana [bə'nɑ:nə] Banane
band [bænd] Band, (Musik-)Gruppe
bank [bæŋk] Bank, Sparkasse
barbarian [bɑ:'beərɪən] Barbar/in
barbecue ['bɑ:bɪkju:] Grillparty
bark [bɑ:k] bellen
baron ['bærən] Baron
barrel ['bærəl] Fass
baseball ['beɪsbɔ:l] Baseball
based [beɪst]**: be based on** basieren auf
basic ['beɪsɪk] **1.** Grund-; Haupt-; **2.** grundlegend; **basically** im Grunde; im Wesentlichen
basket ['bɑ:skɪt] Korb
basketball ['bɑ:skɪtbɔ:l] Basketball
bath [bɑ:θ] Bad; **have a bath** baden, ein Bad nehmen; **bathroom** ['bɑ:θrʊm] Bad(ezimmer)
battle ['bætl] Schlacht, Kampf
Bavaria [bə'veərɪə] Bayern
BC [ˌbi:'si:] v. Chr.
be [bi:] sein; stehen *(auf einem Schild usw.)*; **be about** handeln von; **be afraid** Angst haben; **be born** geboren sein/werden; **be descended from** abstammen von; **be early** zu früh kommen; **be frightened** Angst haben, sich fürchten; **be fun** Spaß machen; **be hungry** Hunger haben; **be late** zu spät kommen; **be lucky** Glück haben; **be missing** fehlen; **be pleased (with)** sich freuen (über), zufrieden sein (mit); **be right** Recht haben; **be smelly** stinken; **be thirsty** Durst haben; **be wrong** Unrecht haben
beach [bi:tʃ] Strand; **on the beach** am Strand
bean [bi:n] Bohne
bear [beə] Bär
beat [bi:t] schlagen, besiegen
beautiful ['bju:tɪfəl] (wunder)schön; **beauty** ['bju:tɪ] Schönheit
because [bɪ'kɒz] weil; **because of** wegen
become [bɪ'kʌm] werden
bed [bed] Bett; **bed and breakfast** Übernachtung mit Frühstück; **go to bed** ins Bett gehen; **bedroom** Schlafzimmer
beef [bi:f] Rindfleisch; **roast beef** Rinderbraten, Roastbeef
before [bɪ'fɔ:] **1.** vor; **2.** bevor, ehe; **3.** vorher, schon einmal; **before that** davor, vorher
beggar ['begə] Bettler/in
begin [bɪ'gɪn] beginnen, anfangen; **beginning** Anfang, Beginn
behave [bɪ'heɪv] sich verhalten, sich benehmen; **behaviour** Verhalten, Benehmen
behind [bɪ'haɪnd] hinter
belief (in) [bɪ'li:f] Glaube (an), (religiöse) Überzeugung; **believe (in)** [bɪ'li:v] glauben (an)
bell [bel] Klingel; Glocke
belong to [bɪ'lɒŋ] gehören
below [bɪ'ləʊ] unten; unter(halb von)
bend [bend] Kurve, Biegung
best [best] bester, beste, bestes; (das) Beste; **best wishes** mit den besten Wünschen; **like best** am liebsten mögen
better ['betə] besser; **like better** lieber mögen
between [bɪ'twi:n] zwischen
Bible ['baɪbl] Bibel
bicycle ['baɪsɪkl] Fahrrad
big [bɪg] groß
bike [baɪk] Fahrrad, Rad; **by bike** mit dem Fahrrad
bill [bɪl] (AE) Geldschein
biotechnology [ˌbaɪəʊtek'nɒlədʒɪ] Biotechnik
bird [bɜ:d] Vogel
biro ['baɪrəʊ] (BE) Kugelschreiber, Kul
birthday ['bɜ:θdeɪ] Geburtstag; **for sb.'s birthday** zum Geburtstag; **Happy birthday (to you)!** Herzlichen Glückwunsch zum Geburtstag! **on your birthday** an deinem Geburtstag; **When's your birthday?** Wann hast du Geburtstag?
biscuit ['bɪskɪt] (BE) Keks
bit [bɪt]**: a bit** ein bisschen, etwas
bitter ['bɪtə] bitter; verbittert; **bitterness** ['bɪtənɪs] Bitterkeit
black [blæk] **1.** schwarz; **2.** Schwarze(r)

block [blɒk]**: block of flats** [ˌblɒk‿əv ˈflæts] (BE) Mietshaus, Wohnblock
blouse [blaʊz] Bluse
blow [bləʊ] wehen, blasen; **blow up** sprengen, in die Luft jagen; explodieren
blue [bluː] blau
board [bɔːd] (Wand-)Tafel; Brett
boarding school [ˈbɔːdɪŋ skuːl] Internat
boat [bəʊt] Boot; Schiff; **by boat** mit dem Schiff
body [ˈbɒdɪ] Körper
boiled [bɔɪld] gekocht
bonfire [ˈbɒnfaɪə] Feuer im Freien
book [bʊk] **1.** Buch; **2.** buchen, reservieren
boot [buːt] Stiefel; BE *auch:* Kofferraum
border [ˈbɔːdə] Grenze, Grenzland
bored [bɔːd] gelangweilt; **boring** langweilig
born [bɔːn]**: be born** geboren sein/werden
borough [ˈbʌrə] Stadtbezirk, Stadtteil
borrow [ˈbɒrəʊ] sich (aus)leihen, entleihen
boss [bɒs] Chef/in, Boss
both [bəʊθ] beide, beides; **both … and** sowohl … als auch
bottle [ˈbɒtl] Flasche
box [bɒks] Kiste, Schachtel, Kästchen
Boxing Day [ˈbɒksɪŋ deɪ] (BE) der zweite Weihnachtsfeiertag
boy [bɔɪ] Junge; **boyfriend** [ˈbɔɪfrend] Freund *(eines Mädchens)*
bracket [ˈbrækɪt] Klammer
brake [breɪk] **1.** Bremse; **2.** bremsen
brave [breɪv] tapfer, mutig
bread [bred] Brot
break [breɪk] **1.** Pause; Bruch; **2.** (zer)brechen; kaputtmachen, kaputtgehen; **break away (from)** brechen (mit), sich trennen (von); **break into** einbrechen; **break off** abbrechen
breakfast [ˈbrekfəst] Frühstück; **at breakfast** zur Frühstückszeit, beim Frühstück; **for breakfast** zum Frühstück; **have breakfast** frühstücken
bridge [brɪdʒ] Brücke
bright [braɪt] hell, leuchtend; heiter
brilliant [ˈbrɪljənt] toll, erstklassig
bring [brɪŋ] (mit-, her)bringen
(Great) Britain [ˈbrɪtn] Großbritannien; **British** britisch; Brite, Britin; **Briton** Britannier
brochure [ˈbrəʊʃə] Broschüre, Prospekt
broken [ˈbrəʊkən] kaputt; zerbrochen, gebrochen
brother [ˈbrʌðə] Bruder
brown [braʊn] braun
brush [brʌʃ] **1.** Bürste; Pinsel; **2.** bürsten
budgie [ˈbʌdʒɪ] (BE) Wellensittich
build [bɪld] (er)bauen; **builder** Baumeister; **building** Gebäude
bull [bʊl] Bulle, Stier
bungalow [ˈbʌngələʊ] Bungalow
burn [bɜːn] (ver)brennen
bus [bʌs] Bus; **bus stop** Bushaltestelle; **by bus** mit dem Bus
business [ˈbɪznɪs] Geschäft(e), Unternehmen
busy [ˈbɪzɪ] **1.** beschäftigt; **2.** belebt, mit starkem Verkehr, hektisch
but [bʌt] aber, sondern; **not only … but also** nicht nur …, sondern auch
butcher [ˈbʊtʃə] Fleischer/in, Metzger/in
butter [ˈbʌtə] Butter
buy [baɪ] kaufen
by [baɪ] **1.** von; durch; **2.** (spätestens) bis, bis (zu); **3.** indem **by airmail** mit/per Luftpost; **by the way** übrigens, nebenbei (bemerkt); **go by** vergehen, vorübergehen; **go by bike** mit dem Rad fahren; **two by two** zu zweit, paarweise
Bye. [baɪ] Wiedersehen! Tschüs!

C

c. = circa [ˈsɜːkə] ca. = circa
cab [kæb] Taxi
café [ˈkæfeɪ] Café; kleines Restaurant; **cafeteria** [ˌkæfəˈtɪərɪə] Restaurant mit Selbstbedienung, Cafeteria
cage [keɪdʒ] Käfig
cake [keɪk] Kuchen
calculator [ˈkælkjʊleɪtə] Taschenrechner
calendar [ˈkælɪndə] Kalender
call [kɔːl] **1.** (An-)Ruf, Telefongespräch; **2.** nennen; **What do you call …?** Wie nennt man …? **be called** heißen; **3.** (an)rufen
calm: calm down [kɑːm ˈdaʊn] (sich) beruhigen
camel [ˈkæml] Kamel
camera [ˈkæmrə] Fotoapparat, Kamera
camp [kæmp] **1.** (Zelt-)Lager; **2.** zelten, campen; **camp site** Campingplatz, Zeltplatz; **camper** Camper; **camping** Camping, Zelten; Zelt-
can [kæn] Dose
can [kæn, kən] kann, darf; **can't** [kɑːnt] = **cannot** [ˈkænɒt] kann nicht
Canada [ˈkænədə] Kanada
canal [kəˈnæl] Kanal
canister [ˈkænɪstə] Kanister, Blechdose
canoe [kəˈnuː] **1.** Paddelboot; Kanu; **2.** Kanu fahren, paddeln;
capital [ˈkæpɪtl] Hauptstadt; **capital (letter)** Großbuchstabe
captain [ˈkæptɪn] Kapitän; Mannschaftskapitän
capture [ˈkæptʃə] erobern, erbeuten; gefangen nehmen
car [kɑː] Auto, Wagen; **by car** mit dem Auto; **car park** (BE) (großer) Parkplatz; Parkhaus; **car pool** (*meist* AE) Fahrgemeinschaft
caravan [ˈkærəvæn] (BE) Wohnwagen
card [kɑːd] (Spiel-, Post-, Kartei-)Karte
care [keə] **1.** Sorgfalt; Pflege **2. care (about)** sich kümmern (um), wichtig nehmen; **careful** vorsichtig; sorgfältig; **careless** sorglos, nachlässig, unbekümmert
Caribbean [kærɪˈbiːən] die Staaten in der Karibik
carol [ˈkærəl]**: (Christmas) carol** Weihnachtslied
carpenter [ˈkɑːpɪntə] Tischler/in, Schreiner/in
carpet [ˈkɑːpɪt] Teppich
carrot [ˈkærət] Karotte, Möhre
carry [ˈkærɪ] tragen; befördern; **carry on** weitermachen, fortfahren
case [keɪs] Fall
cassette [kəˈset] Cassette; **cassette-recorder** [kəˈset rɪˌkɔːdə] Cassettenrecorder
castle [ˈkɑːsl] Burg, Schloss
cat [kæt] Katze
catalogue [ˈkætəlɒg] Katalog
catch [kætʃ] fangen, erwischen; **catch a bus** einen Bus erreichen, nehmen
cathedral [kəˈθiːdrəl] Kathedrale, Dom
Catholic [ˈkæθlɪk] **1.** katholisch; **2.** Katholik/in
cattle *(pl.)* [ˈkætl] (Rind-)Vieh
cause [kɔːz] **1.** Ursache; **2.** verursachen
cave [keɪv] Höhle
ceiling [ˈsiːlɪŋ] Zimmerdecke
celebrate [ˈselɪbreɪt] feiern
Celsius [ˈselsɪəs] Celsius
Celtic [ˈkeltɪk] **1.** keltisch; **2.** das Keltische; **the Celts** [kelts] die Kelten
cent [sent] Cent *(US-Währung)*
centimetre [ˈsentɪˌmiːtə] Zentimeter
central [ˈsentrəl] Zentral-, Mittel-
centre [ˈsentə] Zentrum, *(Stadt-)*Mitte; **Information Centre** Auskunft, Verkehrsbüro
century [ˈsentʃərɪ] Jahrhundert; **a sixteenth-century house** ein Haus aus dem 16. Jahrhundert
ceremony [ˈserɪmənɪ] Zeremonie; Feier(lichkeit)
certain [ˈsɜːtn] sicher, gewiss, bestimmt
chain [tʃeɪn] Kette
chair [tʃeə] Stuhl
chance [tʃɑːns] Gelegenheit, Chance; **take a chance** ein Risiko eingehen; es darauf ankommen lassen
change [tʃeɪndʒ] **1.** (Ver-)Änderung, Wechsel, Umstellung; **(small) change** Wechselgeld; Kleingeld; **2.** (sich) verändern, umwandeln; (aus-)wechseln; **3.** umsteigen
channel [ˈtʃænl] Kanal, Programm; **(English) Channel** Ärmelkanal
character [ˈkærəktə] Charakter; Figur (in einem Roman usw.)
charter flight [ˈtʃɑːtə flaɪt] Charterflug
chase [tʃeɪs] jagen, verfolgen
cheap [tʃiːp] billig
check [tʃek] (über)prüfen, kontrollieren
cheer [tʃɪə] anfeuern, Beifall spenden
cheese [tʃiːz] Käse
chemist [ˈkemɪst] (BE) Apotheker/in;
cheque [tʃek] (Bank-)Scheck

chess [tʃes] Schach
chewing gum ['tʃu:ɪŋ gʌm] Kaugummi
chicken ['tʃɪkɪn] Huhn; (Brat-) Hähnchen
chief [tʃi:f] Oberhaupt; Häuptling
child, *pl.* **children** [tʃaɪld, 'tʃɪldrən] Kind
chimp [tʃɪmp] Schimpanse
Chinese [tʃaɪ'ni:z] **1.** Chinesisch; **2.** Chinese, Chinesin; **3.** chinesisch
chips [tʃɪps] (BE) Pommes frites
chocolate ['tʃɒklət] Schokolade
choice (of) [tʃɔɪs] (Aus-)Wahl (an)
choir ['kwaɪə] Chor
choose [tʃu:z] (aus)wählen, aussuchen; **choose to do sth.** es vorziehen, etwas zu tun; beschließen etwas zu tun
Christ [kraɪst] Christus; **Christian** ['krɪstʃən] **1.** Christ/in; **2.** christlich
Christmas ['krɪsməs] Weihnachten, das Weihnachtsfest; **Christmas Day** der erste Weihnachtsfeiertag; **Christmas Eve** Heiligabend
church [tʃɜ:tʃ] Kirche; **go to church** in die Kirche gehen
cinema ['sɪnəmə] (BE) Kino
circle ['sɜ:kl] Kreis
city ['sɪtɪ] Stadt, Großstadt
civil rights [,sɪvl 'raɪts] Bürgerrechte
class [klɑ:s] Klasse; Unterricht(sstunde)
clean [kli:n] **1.** sauber; **2.** putzen, reinigen
clear [klɪə] klar, deutlich
clerk [klɑ:k] Schalterbeamte(r)/-in
clever ['klevə] klug, schlau; geschickt; **cleverness** ['klevənəs] Klugheit
climate ['klaɪmɪt] Klima
climb [klaɪm] klettern, steigen; **climber** ['klaɪmə] Bergsteiger/in
clock [klɒk] *(Wand-, Stand-, Turm-)*Uhr; **o'clock** [ə'klɒk] ... Uhr
close [kləʊz] **1.** schließen, zumachen; **close down** *(eine Fabrik usw.)* zumachen, schließen; **closed** geschlossen, zu; **2. close** [kləʊs] nahebei
clothes *(pl.)* [kləʊðz] Kleidung(sstücke)
cloud [klaʊd] Wolke; **cloudy** ['klaʊdɪ] bewölkt, wolkig
club [klʌb] Verein, Klub
coach [kəʊtʃ] **1.** Trainer/in; **2.** (BE) Reisebus; **by coach** (BE) mit dem Reisebus
coal [kəʊl] Kohle
coast [kəʊst] Küste; **on the coast** an der Küste
coat [kəʊt] Mantel, Jacke
cocoa ['kəʊkəʊ] Kakao
coffee ['kɒfɪ] Kaffee
coin [kɔɪn] Münze
coke [kəʊk] Cola
cold [kəʊld] **1.** kalt; **2.** Kälte; Unterkühlung; **3.** Schnupfen; **a bad cold** ein starker Schnupfen; **have a cold** Schnupfen haben, erkältet sein
collect [kə'lekt] **1.** (ein-, ver)sammeln; **2.** abholen; **collection** [kə'lekʃn] Sammlung
college ['kɒlɪdʒ] Hochschule; College
colon ['kəʊlən] Doppelpunkt
colonist ['kɒlənɪst] Kolonist/in, Siedler/in; **colony** ['kɒlənɪ] Kolonie
colour ['kʌlə] Farbe; **What colour is/are ... ?** Welche Farbe hat/haben ... ? **coloured** ['kʌləd] farbig; bunt
column ['kɒləm] **1.** Spalte *(auf Buchseite);* **2.** Säule
comb [kəʊm] **1.** Kamm; **2.** kämmen
combination exercise [,kɒmbɪ'neɪʃn] Kombinationsübung, Zuordnungsübung; **combine (with)** [kəm'baɪn] (sich) verbinden (mit), kombinieren (mit)
come [kʌm] kommen, mitkommen; **come and see** besuchen kommen; **come from** von ... (her)stammen; **Come on.** Na, komm! Los, komm! **come out** herauskommen, hinauskommen; **come true** in Erfüllung gehen, wahr werden
comfortable ['kʌmftəbl] bequem, gemütlich
comic ['kɒmɪk] Comicheft
comma ['kɒmə] Komma
common ['kɒmən] üblich; normal
communicate (with) [kə'mju:nɪkeɪt] kommunizieren (mit), sich verständigen (mit); **communications** *(pl.)* [kə,mju:nɪ'keɪʃnz] Nachrichtentechnik, Telekommunikation
commuter [kə'mju:tə] Pendler/in
company ['kʌmpənɪ] Gesellschaft; Firma; Begleitung
compare [kəm'peə] vergleichen; **comparison** [kəm'pærɪsn] Vergleich; **make comparisons** Vergleiche machen, vergleichen
competition [,kɒmpə'tɪʃn] **1.** Wettbewerb, Wettkampf; **2.** Konkurrenz
complain [kəm'pleɪn] sich beschweren, sich beklagen
complete [kəm'pli:t] **1.** vervollständigen; ergänzen **2.** vollständig, völlig
comprehensive school [,kɒmprɪ'hensɪv sku:l] (BE) Gesamtschule
computer [kəm'pju:tə] Computer; **computer science** [kəm,pju:tə 'saɪəns] Informatik
concert ['kɒnsət] Konzert
conditions [kən'dɪʃnz] Verhältnisse, Umstände; Bedingungen
confident ['kɒnfɪdənt] (selbst)sicher, selbstbewusst, zuversichtlich
conflict ['kɒnflɪkt] Konflikt, Auseinandersetzung
conform [kən'fɔ:m] (sich) anpassen; (sich) einfügen
confusing [kən'fju:zɪŋ] verwirrend
connection [kə'nekʃn] Verbindung, Zusammenhang; Anschluss
conquer ['kɒŋkə] erobern, besiegen; **conqueror** ['kɒŋkərə] Eroberer/in, Bezwinger/in
consider sth./doing sth. [kən'sɪdə] über etwas nachdenken, etwas in Betracht ziehen
consist of [kən'sɪst] bestehen aus
consonant ['kɒnsənənt] Konsonant, Mitlaut
constitution [kɒnstɪ'tju:ʃn] Verfassung
construction [kən'strʌkʃn] Konstruktion; (Auf-)Bau, Bauweise; Bau-
consumer [kən'sju:mə] Verbraucher/in; Konsument/in
context ['kɒntekst] Zusammenhang, Kontext
continent ['kɒntɪnənt] Kontinent, Erdteil; **the Continent** das europäische Festland
continue [kən'tɪnju:] fortsetzen, fortfahren (mit), weiter(hin) (tun); andauern
contrast ['kɒntrɑ:st] Gegensatz, Kontrast
control [kən'trəʊl] beherrschen; die Kontrolle haben über; steuern
conversation [,kɒnvə'seɪʃn] Gespräch, Unterhaltung
convince [kən'vɪns] überzeugen
cook [kʊk] **1.** Koch, Köchin; **2.** kochen, zubereiten; **cooker** (BE) Herd
cool [ku:l] kühl
copy ['kɒpɪ] abschreiben; kopieren
corner ['kɔ:nə] Ecke
cornflakes ['kɔ:nfleɪks] Cornflakes
Cornish ['kɔ:nɪʃ] **1.** kornisch, aus Cornwall; **2.** die kornische Sprache; **Cornishman/Cornishwoman** Einwohner/in von Cornwall
correct [kə'rekt] **1.** richtig, korrekt; **2.** berichtigen, verbessern, korrigieren
correspond (to) [,kɒrɪ'spɒnd] entsprechen
cost [kɒst] kosten
cottage ['kɒtɪdʒ] (kleines) Landhaus, Häuschen
cough [kɒf] Husten
could [kʊd] konnte(n); könnte(n)
count [kaʊnt] zählen; **countable** ['kaʊntəbl] zählbar
country ['kʌntrɪ] Land, Staat; **in the country** auf dem Land; **countryside** (ländliche) Gegend, Landschaft
couple: a couple of (infml.) ein paar, einige
courier ['kʊrɪə] Kurier
course [kɔ:s] Kurs, Lehrgang; **of course** natürlich
cousin ['kʌzn] Vetter, Cousine
cover ['kʌvə] bedecken, zudecken
cow [kaʊ] Kuh; **cowboy** ['kaʊbɔɪ] Cowboy; **cowshed** ['kaʊʃed] Kuhstall
coward ['kaʊəd] Feigling
crane [kreɪn] Kran
crash [kræʃ] **1.** Zusammenstoß, Absturz; **2. crash (into)** [kræʃ] zusammenstoßen (mit), hineinfahren (in); verunglücken
crazy ['kreɪzɪ] verrückt, wahnsinnig; **be crazy about** ganz verrückt sein auf; **go crazy** verrückt werden

cream [kri:m] **1.** Creme; **2.** Sahne
create [kri:'eɪt] (er)schaffen
credit card ['kredɪt kɑ:d] Kreditkarte
cricket ['krɪkɪt] Kricket
crime [kraɪm] Verbrechen; Kriminalität; **criminal** ['krɪmɪnl] Verbrecher/in, Kriminelle(r)
crisps [krɪsps] (BE) Kartoffelchips
criticize (for) ['krɪtɪsaɪz] kritisieren (wegen)
cross [krɒs] **1.** Kreuz; **2.** überqueren, kreuzen; **crossing** Überfahrt, Übergang; **(a) crossroads** ['krɒsrəʊdz] (BE) eine Kreuzung; **pedestrian crossing** [pɪ,destrɪən 'krɒsɪŋ] Fußgängerüberweg
crossword ['krɒswɜ:d] Kreuzworträtsel
crowd [kraʊd] (Menschen-)Menge; **crowded** überfüllt, voll (gestopft)
crown [kraʊn] **1.** Krone; **2.** krönen
cruel ['kru:əl] grausam
cry [kraɪ] **1.** weinen; **2.** schreien
Cuba ['kju:bə] Kuba; **Cuban** **1.** Kubaner/in; **2.** kubanisch
culture ['kʌltʃə] Kultur; **cultural** ['kʌltʃrəl] kulturell
cup [kʌp] Tasse
cupboard ['kʌbəd] Schrank
curtain ['kɜ:tn] Vorhang, Gardine
custom ['kʌstəm] Brauch, Sitte, Gewohnheit
customer ['kʌstəmə] Kunde, Kundin
cut [kʌt] (ab)schneiden
cycle ['saɪkl] Rad fahren

D

dad [dæd] Vati, Papa, Papi
daily ['deɪlɪ] täglich
damage ['dæmɪdʒ] **1.** Schaden, Beschädigung; **do damage** Schaden anrichten; **2.** beschädigen
dance [dɑ:ns] **1.** Tanz, Ball; **2.** tanzen; **dancer** Tänzer/in
danger ['deɪndʒə] Gefahr; **dangerous** ['deɪndʒərəs] gefährlich
dark [dɑ:k] dunkel, finster; **after dark** nach Einbruch der Dunkelheit
dash [dæʃ] Gedankenstrich
date [deɪt] Datum; **What date is it (today)?** Der Wievielte ist heute?
daughter ['dɔ:tə] Tochter
day [deɪ] Tag; **the day after tomorrow** übermorgen; **the day before yesterday** vorgestern; **in those days** damals
dead [ded] tot
dear [dɪə] **1.** Liebling, Schatz; **2.** liebe, lieber, liebes; **Dear Sir/Madam/Sir or Madam,** Sehr geehrter Herr/Sehr geehrte Dame/Sehr geehrte Damen und Herren
death [deθ] Tod
debt [det] Schuld
December [dɪ'sembə] Dezember
decide [dɪ'saɪd] beschließen, (sich) entscheiden
decision [dɪ'sɪʒn] Entscheidung, Entschluss
make a decision eine Entscheidung treffen
deck [dek] Deck; **on deck** auf Deck, an Deck
declaration [,deklə'reɪʃn] Erklärung, Verkündung, Bekanntgabe
deep [di:p] tief
defeat [dɪ'fi:t] besiegen, schlagen
defend [dɪ'fend] verteidigen; **defender** Verteidiger/in, Schützer/in
definition [defɪ'nɪʃn] Definition
degree [dɪ'gri:] Grad
democracy [dɪ'mɒkrəsɪ] Demokratie
Denmark ['denmɑ:k] Dänemark
depend (on) [dɪ'pend] **1.** abhängig sein (von), abhängen (von); **2.** sich verlassen auf
descended: be descended from [dɪ'sendɪd] abstammen von
describe [dɪ'skraɪb] beschreiben
design [dɪ'zaɪn] entwerfen, konstruieren
desk [desk] Schreibtisch, Schülertisch; **information desk** [ɪnfə'meɪʃn desk] Auskunftsschalter, Informationsschalter
destroy [dɪ'strɔɪ] zerstören, vernichten
detached house [dɪ,tætʃt 'haʊs] frei stehendes Haus
detail ['di:teɪl] Detail; Einzelheit
detective [dɪ'tektɪv] Detektiv/in
develop [dɪ'veləp] (sich) entwickeln; **development** [dɪ'veləpmənt] Entwicklung; Erschließung; Verlauf
dial ['daɪəl] wählen *(am Telefon)*
dialect ['daɪəlekt] Dialekt, Mundart
dialogue ['daɪəlɒg] Dialog
diary ['daɪərɪ] Tagebuch; Taschenkalender, Notizbuch
dictate [dɪk'teɪt] **1.** diktieren; **2.** vorschreiben, bestimmen
dictionary ['dɪkʃənrɪ] Wörterbuch
die (of) [daɪ] sterben (an); **die out** aussterben
difference ['dɪfrəns] Unterschied; **different (from)** **1.** verschieden, unterschiedlich; **2.** anders (als)
difficult ['dɪfɪkəlt] schwierig, schwer
dig (up) [dɪg] (aus-, um)graben
dime [daɪm] (AE) 10¢-Münze
dining-room ['daɪnɪŋ rʊm] Esszimmer
dinner ['dɪnə] (Festtags-, Mittags-, Abend-)Essen
dinosaur ['daɪnəsɔ:] Dinosaurier
direct [dɪ'rekt, daɪ'rekt] direkt, unmittelbar
dirt [dɜ:t] Schmutz; **dirty** schmutzig, dreckig
disabled [dɪs'eɪbld] (körper)behindert
disadvantage [,dɪsəd'vɑ:ntɪdʒ] Nachteil
disagree (with) [,dɪsə'gri:] nicht übereinstimmen (mit), anderer Meinung sein (als)
disappoint [,dɪsə'pɔɪnt] enttäuschen; **disappointed** [,dɪsə'pɔɪntɪd] enttäuscht
disaster [dɪ'zɑ:stə] Katastrophe; Desaster, Fiasko
disco ['dɪskəʊ] Disko
discover [dɪ'skʌvə] entdecken; feststellen; **discovery** Entdeckung
discuss [dɪ'skʌs] besprechen, diskutieren über; **discussion** [dɪ'skʌʃn] Diskussion, Besprechung
dishes *(pl.)* ['dɪʃɪz] Geschirr
dislike [dɪs'laɪk] nicht mögen, nicht leiden können
distance ['dɪstəns] Entfernung; Ferne
district ['dɪstrɪkt] Gebiet, Bezirk
diver ['daɪvə] Taucher/in
divide (into) [dɪ'vaɪd] (auf)teilen (in)
divorce [dɪ'vɔ:s] Scheidung; **divorced** geschieden; **get divorced** sich scheiden lassen
do [du:] tun, machen; **do 50 metres** 50 Meter schaffen; **do a test/an exam** eine Arbeit schreiben/eine Prüfung machen; **do business (with)** Geschäfte machen (mit); **do damage** Schaden anrichten; **do one's homework** Hausaufgaben machen; **do magic** zaubern; **do sports** Sport treiben; **do the housework** die Haus(halts)arbeit machen; **do tricks** Kunststücke/Tricks vorführen; **do well/badly** gut/schlecht sein *(in einem Fach)*
docks [dɒks] Docks, Hafenanlagen
doctor ['dɒktə] Arzt, Ärztin
document ['dɒkjʊmənt] Dokument, Urkunde
dog [dɒg] Hund
dollar ['dɒlə] Dollar
door [dɔ:] Tür
dot [dɒt] Punkt, Pünktchen
double ['dʌbl] doppelt; Doppel-
down [daʊn] herunter, hinunter; herab, hinab; **down there** dort unten; **pull down** ab-, niederreißen; **sit down** sich setzen; **write down** aufschreiben; **downstairs** unten; nach unten; **downtown** (AE) in der/die Innenstadt, im/ins Zentrum
dozen ['dʌzn] Dutzend
Dr = Doctor ['dɒktə] Dr. = Doktor
dragon ['drægən] Drache
drama ['drɑ:mə] Drama, Schauspiel
draw [drɔ:] **1.** zeichnen; **2.** ziehen
dream [dri:m] **1.** Traum; **2.** träumen; **dreamer** Träumer/in
dress [dres] Kleid
drink [drɪŋk] **1.** Getränk; **2.** trinken; **drinkable** trinkbar; genießbar
drive [draɪv] **1.** (Auto) fahren; **2.** (an)treiben; **drive sb. crazy** (infml.) jn. wahnsinnig, verrückt machen; **driver** **1.** (Auto-)Fahrer/in; **2.** Lokführer/in; **driver's license** (AE) **driving licence** (BE) ['laɪsəns] Führerschein
drop [drɒp]**: drop out (of school)** (die Schule) abbrechen, vorzeitig verlassen

drown [draʊn] ertrinken, ertränken
drugs [drʌgz] Rauschgift
dry [draɪ] **1.** trocken; **2.** (ab)trocknen
during ['djʊərɪŋ] während
Dutch [dʌtʃ] **1.** holländisch, niederländisch; **2.** Holländisch, Niederländisch

E

each [i:tʃ] jeder, jede, jedes (einzelne ...); **each other** einander, sich (gegenseitig)
ear [ɪə] Ohr
early ['3:lɪ] früh, (früh)zeitig; **be early** zu früh kommen
earn [3:n] verdienen
earth [3:θ] Erde; **(earth)quake** ['3:θkweɪk] (Erd-)Beben
east (of) [i:st] **1.** östlich (von); **2.** Ost-; (nach) Osten; **eastern** östlich
Easter ['i:stə] Ostern, Oster-; **at Easter** zu Ostern
easy ['i:zɪ] leicht, einfach
eat [i:t] essen; **eat out** essen gehen; **eatable** essbar, genießbar
economic(ally) [ˌi:kə'nɒmɪklɪ] (volks)wirtschaftlich; Wirtschafts-; **economy** [ɪ'kɒnəmɪ] Wirtschaft
edge [edʒ] Rand, Kante
educate ['edjʊkeɪt, 'edʒʊkeɪt] erziehen; (aus)bilden
effect (on) [ɪ'fekt] Auswirkung (auf), Wirkung (auf)
e. g. [ˌi:'dʒi:] z. B. (= zum Beispiel)
egg [eg] Ei
Egypt ['i:dʒɪpt] Ägypten
either ... or ['aɪðə, 'i:ðə] entweder ... oder;
(not ...) either auch nicht, auch kein
election [ɪ'lekʃn] (politische) Wahl
electronics [ɪˌlek'trɒnɪks] Elektronik
elephant ['elɪfənt] Elefant
else [els] sonst (noch); anders; **Anything else?** Sonst noch etwas?
emigrate ['emɪgreɪt] auswandern, emigrieren
emperor ['empərə] Kaiser
empire ['empaɪə] Reich
employee [ɪm'plɔɪi:, ˌemplɔɪ'i:] Arbeitnehmer/in, Angestellte(r); **employer** [ɪm'plɔɪə] Arbeitgeber/in
empty ['emptɪ] leer
encourage [ɪn'kʌrɪdʒ] ermutigen, ermuntern; fördern
end [end] **1.** Ende, Schluss; **at the end** am Ende, am Schluss **2. end (in)** enden (auf, mit); beenden; **ending** Ende, (Ab-)Schluss; Endung; **endless** ['endləs] endlos
enemy ['enəmɪ] Feind
energy ['enədʒɪ] Energie
engine ['endʒɪn] Motor, Maschine
engineer [ˌendʒɪ'nɪə] Ingenieur/in, Techniker/in
England ['ɪŋglənd] England; **English** **1.** englisch; **2.** Englisch; **3.** Engländer/in; **in English** auf Englisch; **Englishman, Englishwoman** Engländer, Engländerin
enjoy [ɪn'dʒɔɪ] genießen, Spaß haben an, gern haben/tun; **enjoy oneself** viel Spaß haben, sich amüsieren; **enjoyable** [ɪn'dʒɔɪəbl] nett; unterhaltsam
enough [ɪ'nʌf] genug
enter ['entə] betreten, einreisen in
enthusiastic [ɪnˌθju:zɪ'æstɪk] begeistert, enthusiastisch
entry ['entrɪ] **1.** Einsendung; **2.** Eintrag *(in Wörter-, Tagebuch)*
envelope ['envələʊp] Briefumschlag
environment [ɪn'vaɪrənmənt] Umwelt, Umgebung; **environmental** [ɪnˌvaɪrən'mentl] Umwelt-
equal ['i:kwəl] gleich
equivalent [ɪ'kwɪvələnt] Entsprechung
escape [ɪ'skeɪp] **1.** Flucht; Entkommen; **2.** entkommen, entgehen; fliehen
Eskimo ['eskɪməʊ] **1.** Eskimo; **2.** Eskimo-
especially [ɪ'speʃlɪ] besonders; insbes.
essay ['eseɪ] Aufsatz, Essay
etc. [ɪt'setrə] usw. (und so weiter)
ethnic ['eθnɪk] Volks-, ethnisch
Europe ['jʊərəp] Europa; **European** [ˌjʊərəpi:ən] **1.** europäisch; **2.** Europäer/in
eve [i:v] Vorabend, Vortag; **New Year's Eve** Silvester(abend)
even ['i:vn] sogar, selbst; **even if** selbst wenn; **even worse** (sogar) noch schlimmer; **not even** nicht einmal
evening ['i:vnɪŋ] Abend; **in the evening(s)** abends; **on a cold evening** an einem kalten Abend; **this evening** heute Abend
event [ɪ'vent] Ereignis
ever ['evə] je(mals), schon mal; **for ever** für immer, ewig; **not ever** nie
every ['evrɪ] jeder, jede, jedes; **everybody/everyone** jeder(mann), alle; **everything** alles; **everywhere** überall, überallhin
evidence (of) *(sing.)* ['evɪdəns] Beweis(e) (für), Beleg(e) (für)
exact [ɪg'zækt] genau
exam(ination) [ɪgˌzæmɪ'neɪʃn] Prüfung, Examen
example [ɪg'zɑ:mpl] Beispiel; **for example** zum Beispiel
excellent ['eksələnt] ausgezeichnet, hervorragend
except [ɪk'sept] außer, bis auf
exchange [ɪks'tʃeɪndʒ] **1.** (Aus-, Um-)Tausch; (Geld-) Wechsel; **2.** austauschen, umtauschen; (Geld) wechseln
excited (about) [ɪk'saɪtɪd] aufregend, freudig erregt (wegen, über); **exciting** aufregend, spannend
exclamation mark [ˌekskləˈmeɪʃn mɑ:k] Ausrufezeichen
excuse: Excuse me [ɪk'skju:z ˌmi:] Entschuldigen Sie
execution [ˌeksɪ'kju:ʃn] Hinrichtung, Exekution
exercise ['eksəsaɪz] Übung(saufgabe); **exercise book** Heft, Schulheft
exhibition [ˌeksɪ'bɪʃn] Ausstellung
exist [ɪg'zɪst] existieren, vorhanden sein
exit ['eksɪt] Ausgang; (Autobahn-) Ausfahrt
expect [ɪk'spekt] erwarten; annehmen, vermuten
expedition [ˌekspɪ'dɪʃn] Expedition
expensive [ɪk'spensɪv] teuer
experiment [ɪk'sperɪmənt] Experiment, Versuch (mit)
expert (at/in) ['eksp3:t] **1.** Fachmann/-frau, Experte, Expertin (für); **2.** erfahren, geschickt
explain [ɪk'spleɪn] erklären, erläutern
explore [ɪk'splɔ:] erforschen; **explorer** Forscher/in
export 1. ['ekspɔ:t] Ausfuhr, Export; **2.** [ɪk'spɔ:t] exportieren
express [ɪk'spres] äußern, ausdrücken; **expression** [ɪk'spreʃn] Ausdruck, Äußerung
expressway (AE) Schnellstraße, Autobahn
extract (from) ['ekstrækt] Auszug (aus)
eye [aɪ] Auge; **keep an eye on** ein (wachsames) Auge haben auf

F

face [feɪs] Gesicht
fact [fækt] **1.** Tatsache, Information; **2.** Wirklichkeit; **in fact** eigentlich, genau gesagt, tatsächlich
factory ['fæktərɪ] Fabrik
fail [feɪl]**: fail (an exam)** (bei einer Prüfung) durchfallen, nicht bestehen
fair [feə] fair, gerecht
faith [feɪθ] Glaube(n)
faithfully ['feɪθfəlɪ]**: Yours faithfully** Mit freundlichen Grüßen; Hochachtungsvoll
fall [fɔ:l] **1.** (AE) Herbst; **2.** fallen; **fall in love (with)** sich verlieben (in); **fall off** herunterfallen; **fall over** hinfallen, umfallen
falls [fɔ:lz] (Wasser-)Fälle
false [fɔ:ls] falsch, unecht
family ['fæmɪlɪ] Familie; **start a family** eine Familie gründen
famous ['feɪməs] berühmt
fan [fæn] Fan
fantastic [fæn'tæstɪk] fantastisch, toll
far [fɑ:] weit (entfernt); **so far** bis jetzt, bisher
fare [feə] Fahrpreis, Fahrgeld
farm [fɑ:m] Bauernhof, Farm; **farmer** Bauer, Bäuerin; Farmer/in; **farmhouse** Bauernhaus; **farming** Landwirtschaft, Ackerbau
farther ['fɑ:ðə] weiter (entfernt); **farthest** ['fɑ:ðɪst] am weitesten (entfernt)

fast [fɑ:st] schnell
fat [fæt] dick
father [ˈfɑ:ðə] Vater; **Father Christmas** [ˌfɑ:ðə ˈkrɪsməs] (BE) der Weihnachtsmann
fault [fɔ:lt] Schuld, Fehler
favour [ˈfeɪvə] Gefallen; **do sb. a favour** jm. einen Gefallen tun
favourite [ˈfeɪvrɪt] Lieblings-
feature [ˈfi:tʃə] Merkmal, Eigenschaft
February [ˈfebrʊərɪ] Februar
fed: be fed up (with) [ˌfed‿ˈʌp] satt haben, die Nase voll haben (von)
federal [ˈfedrəl] Bundes-
feeble [ˈfi:bl] schwach
feed [fi:d] füttern; **feeding-time** Fütterungszeit
feel [fi:l] (sich) fühlen; **feel sorry (for)** bedauern, bereuen; **feeling** Gefühl
felt-tip [ˈfelt tɪp] Filzstift
fence [fens] Zaun
ferry (boat) [ˈferɪ] Fähre
festival [ˈfestəvl] Festspiele, Festival; Fest(-tag)
fetch [fetʃ] **1.** holen; **2.** abholen
few [fju:] wenige; **a few** ein paar, einige (wenige)
fiction [ˈfɪkʃn] Dichtung; Prosaliteratur; Fiktion
field [fi:ld] **1.** Feld, Wiese, Weide; **2.** (Sport-)Platz; **3.** Gebiet; **in the field(s)** auf dem Feld
fifth [fɪfθ] Fünftel
fight [faɪt] **1.** Kampf; **2.** (be)kämpfen
figure [ˈfɪgə] Figur, Gestalt
fill [fɪl] füllen, voll machen; **fill in** einsetzen
film [fɪlm] Film; **film star** Filmstar
finally [ˈfaɪnəlɪ] schließlich, endlich
financial [faɪˈnænʃl] finanziell
find [faɪnd] finden; **find out** herausfinden, erfahren
fine [faɪn] gut, fein, schön
finger [ˈfɪŋgə] Finger
finish [ˈfɪnɪʃ] (be)enden, aufhören (mit), fertig machen; ins Ziel kommen **I've finished.** Ich bin fertig. **finish line** Ziellinie
fire [ˈfaɪə] Feuer, Brand; **fireworks** *(pl.)* [ˈfaɪəwɜ:ks] Feuerwerk(skörper)
firm [fɜ:m] Firma
first [fɜ:st] (zu)erst, zunächst; **at first** zuerst, anfangs; **be first** der Erste sein, als Erster (an)kommen
fish [fɪʃ] Fisch, Fische; **fishing** **1.** Fischen, Fischerei; **2.** Fischer-; **go fishing** fischen, angeln (gehen)
fit [fɪt] **1.** fit, gut in Form; **2.** passen; **fitness** [ˈfɪtnəs] Fitness, Kondition
fix [fɪks] **1.** bestimmen, festlegen; **2.** befestigen, festmachen
flag [flæg] Fahne, Flagge
flat [flæt] **1.** (BE) Wohnung; **2.** flach, eben
flight [flaɪt] Flug
floor [flɔ:] **1.** Fußboden; **2.** Stockwerk; **first floor** (BE) erster Stock; (AE) Erdgeschoss; **ground floor** (BE) Erdgeschoss
flower [ˈflaʊə] Blume, Blüte
flu [flu:] Grippe
fly [flaɪ] fliegen; **flying time** Flugzeit
focus [ˈfəʊkəs] Blick-, Brennpunkt
fog [fɒg] (dicker) Nebel; **foggy** neblig
folk song [ˈfəʊk sɒŋ] Volkslied, Folksong
follow [ˈfɒləʊ] **1.** folgen; **2.** verfolgen, nachfolgen; **following** folgend
food [fu:d] Essen, Lebensmittel, Nahrung; Futter
fool [fu:l] Dummkopf, Narr; **make a fool of sb.** jn. lächerlich machen
foot, *pl.* **feet** [fʊt, fi:t] **1.** Fuß; **2.** *Längenmaß (= 30,5 cm)*; **football** [ˈfʊtbɔ:l] Fußball
for [fɔ:, fə] **1.** für; **2.** seit; **for about an hour** etwa eine Stunde lang; **for a long time** lange Zeit; **for breakfast, etc.** zum Frühstück usw.; **for ever** für immer, ewig; **for example** zum Beispiel; **for hours** stundenlang; **for sb.'s birthday** zum Geburtstag; **for seven miles** sieben Meilen weit; **for the first time** zum ersten Mal; **good for** gut gegen
force [fɔ:s] zwingen
forecast [ˈfɔ:kɑ:st] Vorhersage
foreign [ˈfɒrən] ausländisch, fremd; **foreign language** Fremdsprache
forest [ˈfɒrɪst] Wald, Forst
forget [fəˈget] vergessen
fork [fɔ:k] Gabel
form [fɔ:m] **1.** Form; **2.** (BE) Klasse, Jahrgangsstufe; **sixth form** Oberstufe, Sekundarstufe II
formal [ˈfɔ:ml] formal; formell
fortunately [ˈfɔ:tʃnətlɪ] glücklicherweise
found [faʊnd] gründen, errichten
fountain [ˈfaʊntɪn] Springbrunnen
France [frɑ:ns] Frankreich
free [fri:] **1.** frei; **2.** kostenlos; **free time** Freizeit; **freedom** Freiheit
freeze [fri:z] (ge)frieren; erstarren
French [frentʃ] **1.** französisch; **2.** Franzose, Französin; **3.** Französisch
fresh [freʃ] frisch
Friday [ˈfraɪdɪ] Freitag
fridge [frɪdʒ] Kühlschrank
friend [frend] Freund/in; **friendliness** [ˈfrendlɪnəs] Freundlichkeit; **friendly** freundlich; **friendship** Freundschaft
frightened [ˈfraɪtnd] erschrocken, verängstigt; **be frightened (of)** Angst haben (vor), sich fürchten (vor)
from [frɒm, frəm] aus; von; **from now on** von jetzt an, ab jetzt; **come from** (her)stammen von; **I'm from ...** Ich bin/komme aus ...; **Where are you from?** Wo kommst du her?
front [frʌnt] Vorderseite; **front door** Haustür; **at the front** vorn, an der Vorderseite (vorn); **in front of** vor; **to the front** nach vorn, zur Vorderseite (vorn)
fruit [fru:t] Obst, Früchte
full (of) [fʊl] voll (mit/von); **full stop** (BE) Punkt *(am Satzende)*
fun [fʌn] Spaß; **be fun** Spaß machen; **funny** [ˈfʌnɪ] lustig, komisch; seltsam
furniture *(sing.)* [ˈfɜ:nɪtʃə] Möbel
further [ˈfɜ:ðə] **1.** weiter; **2.** weitere(r, s), zusätzlich, noch
future [ˈfju:tʃə] **1.** Zukunft; **2.** (zu)künftig; **in future** künftig, ab jetzt

G

game [geɪm] Spiel
gang [gæŋ] Bande, Gang
garage [ˈgærɑ:dʒ] Garage
garden [ˈgɑ:dn] Garten
gas [gæs] Gas; AE *auch:* Benzin; **gas station** [ˈgæs ˌsteɪʃn] (AE) Tankstelle
gate [geɪt] Tor
GCSE [ˌdʒi: si:‿es‿ˈi:] = **General Certificate of Secondary Education** [ˌdʒenrəl səˈtɪfɪkət] (BE) *eine Art Hauptschulabschluss oder mittlere Reife*
general [ˈdʒenərəl] allgemein, generell
geography [dʒɪˈɒgrəfɪ] Geographie, Erdkunde
German [ˈdʒɜ:mən] **1.** deutsch; **2.** Deutsche, Deutscher; **3.** Deutsch; **Germany** Deutschland
get [get] **1.** bekommen, kriegen; **2.** werden; **3.** holen, besorgen; **4.** gelangen, (hin-)kommen; **get along** zurechtkommen, sich zurechtfinden; **get divorced** sich scheiden lassen; **get in (the train)** (in den Zug) einsteigen; **get into trouble** in Schwierigkeiten geraten; **get lost** sich verlaufen; **get married** (sich ver)heiraten (mit); **get off** aussteigen (aus), absteigen (von); **get on** einsteigen (in), aufsteigen (auf); **get on sb.'s nerves** jm. auf die Nerven gehen; **get out (of the train)** (aus dem Zug) aussteigen; **get ready** sich fertig machen, bereitmachen; **get up** aufstehen
ghost [gəʊst] Geist, Gespenst
giant [ˈdʒaɪənt] **1.** Riese, Riesin; **2.** riesig
giraffe [dʒɪˈrɑ:f] Giraffe
girl [gɜ:l] Mädchen; **girlfriend** [ˈgɜ:lfrend] Freundin *(eines Jungen)*; **Girl Scout** [ˌgɜ:l ˈskaʊt] (AE) Pfadfinderin
give [gɪv] **1.** geben; **2.** schenken; **give up** aufgeben
glad [glæd]: **be glad** froh sein, sich freuen
glass [glɑ:s] Glas
glove [glʌv] Handschuh
go [gəʊ] **1.** gehen; **2.** fahren; **Go!** Los! **go away** verreisen; **go back to** zurückgehen auf, zurückreichen bis; **go back to sleep** wieder einschlafen; **go by** vergehen, vorübergehen; **go fishing, etc.** fischen usw. gehen; **go for a ride** herumfahren, eine Spritztour

machen; **go for a swim** schwimmen gehen; **go for a walk** spazieren gehen; **go home** nach Hause gehen; **go in** hineingehen; **go on** weitermachen, weitergehen; **go on a bus tour** eine Bus(rund)fahrt machen; **go on a guided tour** eine Führung (mit)machen; **go on a trip** eine Reise/Fahrt machen; **go out (with)** ausgehen (mit); **go to bed** ins Bett gehen; **go to school** zur Schule gehen; **go wrong** schief gehen; **I'm going to ...** Ich werde/will ..., Ich habe vor/habe die Absicht zu ...
God, god [gɒd] Gott
gold [gəʊld] **1.** Gold; **gold rush** ['gəʊld rʌʃ] Goldrausch, Goldfieber; **2.** gold(en)
gone [gɒn] weg
good [gʊd] gut; **good at** gut in, geschickt in; **good for** gut gegen; **Good afternoon.** Guten Tag! **Good morning.** Guten Morgen!/Tag! **Goodbye.** [gʊd'baɪ] Auf Wiedersehen!
goods [gʊdz] Waren, Güter
gorilla [gə'rɪlə] Gorilla
gotten ['gɒtn] (AE) *Partizip Perfekt von „to get"*
government ['gʌvnmənt] Regierung
grade [greɪd] (Zeugnis-)Note, Zensur; AE *auch:* Klasse, Jahrgangsstufe
graffiti [grə'fi:ti:] Graffiti; Wandkritzeleien
gram [græm] Gramm
grammar ['græmə] Grammatik; **grammar school** (BE) Gymnasium
grandfather ['græn,fɑ:ðə] Großvater; **grandmother** ['græn,mʌðə] Großmutter; **grandpa** ['grænpɑ:] Opa, Großvater; **grandparents** Großeltern
grass [grɑ:s] Gras
grave [greɪv] Grab
great [greɪt] **1.** großartig, prima, toll; **2.** groß, beträchtlich; **3.** bedeutend, berühmt; **greatly** sehr, außerordentlich, höchst
Greece [gri:s] Griechenland; **Greek** [gri:k] **1.** griechisch; **2.** Grieche, Griechin; **3.** Griechisch
greedy ['gri:dɪ] (hab)gierig
green [gri:n] grün
Greenback ['gri:nbæk] Greenback *(US-Währung)*
grey [greɪ] grau
ground [graʊnd] (Erd-)Boden; **ground floor** (BE) Erdgeschoss
group [gru:p] Gruppe
grow [grəʊ] **1.** wachsen; **grow up** aufwachsen, groß werden; **2.** anbauen, anpflanzen
guess [ges] (er)raten
guest [gest] Gast; **guest house** Pension, Gästehaus
guidance counselor ['gaɪdns ,kaʊnsələ] (AE) *Beratungslehrer/in an einer amerik. High School, berät Schüler/innen über Schullaufbahn und Beruf*
guide [gaɪd] **1.** (Fremden-)Führer/in; **2.** führen, lenken, leiten; **go on a guided tour** eine Führung (mit-)machen
guitar [gɪ'tɑ:] Gitarre; **play the guitar** Gitarre spielen
gun [gʌn] (Schuss-)Waffe
guru ['gʊru:] Guru
guy [gaɪ] (infml.) Kerl, Junge, Mann
gym [dʒɪm] Turnhalle, Sporthalle; **gymnastics** [dʒɪm'næstɪks] Turnen, Gymnastik

H

hair [heə] Haar, Haare; **hairdresser** ['heə,dresə] Friseur, Friseuse; **hairstyle** ['heəstaɪl] Frisur
half [hɑ:f] Hälfte; halb; **half a mile** eine halbe Meile; **half past ten** halb elf (= 10.30); **half-sister** Halbschwester
hall [hɔ:l] Flur, Diele; Halle, Saal
Hallo. [hə'ləʊ] = **Hello.**
ham [hæm] Schinken; **ham salad** Schinken mit Salat
hamburger ['hæmbɜ:gə] Hamburger
hammer ['hæmə] Hammer
hamster ['hæmstə] Hamster
hand [hænd] Hand; **on the one hand/on the other hand** einerseits/andererseits; **handball** ['hændbɔ:l] Handball; **handbook** ['hændbʊk] Handbuch; **handbrake** ['hændbreɪk] Handbremse
hang [hæŋ] **1.** hängen, aufhängen; **2.** erhängen
happen (to) ['hæpən] passieren, geschehen (mit)
happiness ['hæpɪnəs] Glück
happy ['hæpɪ] glücklich, froh; **Happy birthday (to you)!** Herzlichen Glückwunsch zum Geburtstag!
harbour ['hɑ:bə] Hafen
hard [hɑ:d] **1.** schwer; hart; **2.** heftig, mit aller Kraft
hardly ['hɑ:dlɪ] kaum
harvest ['hɑ:vɪst] Ernte
hat [hæt] Hut
hate [heɪt] **1.** Hass; **2.** hassen, gar nicht mögen
have [hæv] **1.** haben; **2.** essen, trinken; **have a bath** baden, ein Bad nehmen; **Have a good time!** Viel Spaß! Viel Vergnügen! **have a nice time** eine schöne Zeit/viel Spaß haben; **have a picnic** ein Picknick machen; **have a race** ein Rennen veranstalten; **have a shower** (sich) duschen; **have a wash** sich waschen; **have breakfast** frühstücken; **have lunch** (zu) Mittag essen; **have tea** Abendbrot essen, zu Abend essen; **have got** haben, besitzen; **have to** (tun) müssen
he [hi:] er
head [hed] **1.** Kopf; **2.** Oberhaupt; **head teacher** Schulleiter/in; **headache** ['hedeɪk] Kopfschmerzen, Kopfweh
headword ['hedwɜ:d] Stichwort
health [helθ] Gesundheit; **healthy** gesund
hear [hɪə] hören; **hear of** hören von
heart [hɑ:t] Herz
heating ['hi:tɪŋ] Heizung
heavy ['hevɪ] schwer; heftig
hectic ['hektɪk] hektisch
hedge [hedʒ] Hecke
helicopter ['helɪkɒptə] Hubschrauber
Hello. [hə'ləʊ] Hallo! (Guten) Tag! **say hello (to)** grüßen
helmet ['helmɪt] Helm
help [help] **1.** Hilfe; **2.** helfen; **help oneself** zugreifen, sich bedienen; **helpful** hilfreich, nützlich; **helpless** hilflos
her [hɜ:] **1.** ihr, ihre; **2.** ihr, sie
here [hɪə] hier; **Come here.** Komm(t) her! **Here you are.** Hier bitte. Bitte sehr. **here and there** hie und da
hero, *pl.* **heroes** ['hɪərəʊ] Held; **heroine** ['herəʊɪn] Heldin
hers [hɜ:z] ihre(r, s); **herself** [hɜ:'self] sich (selbst)
Hi. [haɪ] (infml.) Hallo!
hide [haɪd] (sich) verstecken
high [haɪ] hoch; **high school** ['haɪ sku:l] (AE) Oberschule *(in den USA)*
hill [hɪl] Hügel, (kleiner) Berg
him [hɪm] ihm, ihn; **himself** [hɪm'self] sich (selbst)
hippo ['hɪpəʊ] Flusspferd, Nilpferd
hire ['haɪə] *(Boot, Auto, Saal)* mieten, leihen
his [hɪz] sein, seine(r, s)
Hispanic [hɪ'spænɪk] *(Nachkomme der Einwanderer aus Lateinamerika)*
historian [hɪ'stɔ:rɪən] Historiker/in; **historical** [hɪ'stɒrɪkl] historisch, alt; **history** ['hɪstrɪ] Geschichte
hit [hɪt] schlagen, treffen
hobby ['hɒbɪ] Hobby
hockey ['hɒkɪ] Hockey
hold [həʊld] **1.** halten; **2.** veranstalten, abhalten
hole [həʊl] Loch
holiday(s) ['hɒlɪdeɪ] **1.** Feiertag, freier Tag; **2.** (BE) Ferien, Urlaub; **go/be on holiday** (BE) in Urlaub fahren/sein, Ferien machen/haben
holy ['həʊlɪ] heilig
home [həʊm] Heim, Zuhause; **at home** zu Hause, daheim; **go home** nach Hause gehen; **homeless** obdachlos; **(do one's) homework** (seine) Hausaufgabe(n) (machen)
hooligan ['hu:lɪgən] Rowdy, Schläger
hope [həʊp] **1.** Hoffnung; **2.** hoffen; **hopeful** hoffnungsvoll, voller Hoffnung; **hopeless** hoffungslos
horse [hɔ:s] Pferd

hospital ['hɒspɪtl] Krankenhaus, Klinik; **in/to hospital** (BE) im/ins Krankenhaus
hostel ['hɒstl]**: youth hostel** Jugendherberge
hot [hɒt] heiß, warm
hot dog [hɒt 'dɒg] Hot Dog
hotel [həʊ'tel] Hotel
hour ['aʊə] Stunde; **for an hour** eine Stunde lang
house [haʊs] Haus; **at Dave's/my house** bei Dave/mir zu Hause; **housework** Haus(halts)arbeit; **do the housework** die Haus(halts)arbeit machen
hovercraft ['hɒvəkrɑ:ft] Luftkissenfahrzeug(e)
how [haʊ] wie; **How are you?** Wie geht es dir? **How many?** Wie viele? **How much?** Wie viel? **How much is ...?** Was kostet ...? **this is how you do it** so, auf diese Weise macht man es; **however** [haʊ'evə] **1.** jedoch, aber; **2.** wie (auch) immer
huge [hju:dʒ] sehr groß, riesig
human ['hju:mən] menschlich
hunger ['hʌŋgə] Hunger; **hungry** ['hʌŋgrɪ] hungrig; **be hungry** Hunger haben
hunt [hʌnt] jagen
hurrah! [hʊ'rɑ:] hurra!
hurry ['hʌrɪ]**: be in a hurry** in Eile sein, es eilig haben; **hurry up** sich beeilen
hurt [hɜ:t] wehtun, verletzen
husband ['hʌzbənd] (Ehe-)Mann
hut [hʌt] Hütte
hyphen ['haɪfn] Bindestrich

I

I [aɪ] ich
ice [aɪs] Eis; **ice-cream** [ˌaɪs'kri:m] (Speise-)Eis; **ice-cream parlor** ['pɑ:lə] (AE) Eisdiele; **ice-skating** ['aɪsˌskeɪtɪŋ] Schlittschuhlaufen; **icy** eisig
idea [aɪ'dɪə] **1.** Idee, Einfall; **2.** Begriff, Vorstellung; Meinung; **No idea.** Keine Ahnung.
i.e. d.h. (das heißt)
if [ɪf] **1.** wenn, falls; **2.** ob; **if I were you** (ich) an deiner Stelle; **if so** wenn ja
ill [ɪl] krank; **illness** ['ɪlnəs] Krankheit
illustration [ˌɪlə'streɪʃn] Illustration, Bild, Abbildung
imagine [ɪ'mædʒɪn] sich vorstellen; sich einbilden; **Just imagine.** Denk dir nur! Stell dir mal vor!
immigrant ['ɪmɪgrənt] Einwanderer/-in
immigration [ˌɪmɪ'greɪʃn] Einwanderung, Immigration
impatient [ɪm'peɪʃənt] ungeduldig
impolite [ˌɪmpə'laɪt] unhöflich; **impoliteness** [ˌɪmpə'laɪtnəs] Unhöflichkeit
import 1. ['ɪmpɔ:t] Einfuhr, Import; **2.** [ɪm'pɔ:t] einführen, importieren
importance [ɪm'pɔ:təns] Wichtigkeit; **important** wichtig, bedeutend
impossible [ɪm'pɒsəbl] unmöglich
impression [ɪm'preʃn] Eindruck
improve [ɪm'pru:v] (sich) (ver)bessern; besser machen/werden
in [ɪn] in; hinein; **go in** hineingehen; **in a hurry** in Eile; **in a minute** gleich, sofort; **in bed** im Bett; **in detail** im Detail; **in English** auf Englisch; **in front of** vor; **in future** künftig, ab jetzt; **in hospital** (BE) im Krankenhaus; **in January** im Januar; **in memory of** in Erinnerung an; **in my opinion** meiner Meinung nach; **in 1980** (im Jahre) 1980; **in ruins** zerstört; **in school** (*meist* AE) in der Schule; **in spite of** trotz; **in the back** hinten (im Auto); **in the country** auf dem Land; **in the field(s)** auf dem Feld; **in the morning(s)** am Morgen, morgens; **in the picture/photo** auf dem Bild/Foto; **in (the) spring** im Frühling/Frühjahr; **in the street** auf der Straße; **in those days** damals; **in town** in der (Innen-)Stadt; **interested in** interessiert an
including [ɪn'klu:dɪŋ] einschließlich
independence (from) [ˌɪndɪ'pendəns] Unabhängigkeit (von); **independent (of)** [ˌɪndɪ'pendənt] unabhängig (von)
India ['ɪndɪə] Indien; **Indian** ['ɪndɪən] **1.** Indianer/in; indianisch; **2.** Inder/in; indisch
indoors [ˌɪn'dɔ:z] (nach) drinnen, im Haus
industrial [ɪn'dʌstrɪəl] Industrie-; industriell; **industry** ['ɪndəstrɪ] Industrie(zweig)
inedible [ɪn'edɪbl] nicht essbar, ungenießbar
influence ['ɪnflʊəns] **1.** Einfluss; **2.** beeinflussen
informal [ɪn'fɔ:ml] informell, nicht förmlich
information [ˌɪnfə'meɪʃn] Information(en), Auskunft; **Information Centre** Auskunft, Verkehrsbüro; **information desk** Auskunftsschalter, Informationsschalter
injured ['ɪndʒəd] verletzt
inner city [ˌɪnə'sɪtɪ] problematisches Wohngebiet im Stadtkern
inside [ɪn'saɪd] innen/drinnen; nach drinnen
instead [ɪn'sted] stattdessen, dafür; **instead of** (an)statt, anstelle von
instinct ['ɪnstɪŋkt] Instinkt; Gefühl, Ahnung
instructor [ɪn'strʌktə] Betreuer/in, Lehrer/in
instrument ['ɪnstrəmənt] Instrument
intelligent [ɪn'telɪdʒənt] klug, intelligent
intend [ɪn'tend] beabsichtigen, vorhaben
intercultural [ˌɪntə'kʌltʃərəl] interkulturell
interested (in) ['ɪntrɪstɪd] interessiert (an); **interesting** interessant
international [ˌɪntə'næʃnl] international
intersection ['ɪntəˌsekʃn] (AE) (Straßen-)Kreuzung
Interstate ['ɪntəsteɪt] (AE) (staatenübergreifende Bundes-)Autobahn
interview ['ɪntəvju:] **1.** Interview; **2.** befragen, interviewen; **interviewer** ['ɪntəvju:ə] Interviewer/in
into ['ɪntʊ, 'ɪntə] in ... (hinein)
intolerance [ˌɪn'tɒlərəns] Intoleranz
introduce (to) [ˌɪntrə'dju:s] **1.** vorstellen, bekannt machen (mit); **2.** einführen; **introduction** [ˌɪntrə'dʌkʃn] Einführung
invade [ɪn'veɪd] einmarschieren, einfallen in; **invader** Invasor/in, Eindringling
invent [ɪn'vent] erfinden; **invention** [ɪn'venʃn] Erfindung; **inventor** [ɪn'ventə] Erfinder/in
invitation [ˌɪnvɪ'teɪʃn] Einladung; **invite** [ɪn'vaɪt] einladen
Ireland ['aɪələnd] Irland; **Northern Ireland** Nordirland; **Irish 1.** Ire(n), Irin(nen); **2.** irisch
irregular [ɪ'regjʊlə] unregelmäßig
is [ɪz] ist
island ['aɪlənd] Insel; **isle** [aɪl]**: the British Isles** die britischen Inseln
it [ɪt] es (er, sie; ihn, sie)
Italian [ɪ'tæljən] **1.** italienisch; **2.** Italienisch; **3.** Italiener/in; **Italy** ['ɪtəlɪ] Italien
item ['aɪtəm]**: vocabulary item** Vokabel
its [ɪts] sein, seine; ihr, ihre; **itself** [ɪt'self] sich (selbst)

J

jacket ['dʒækɪt] Jacke, Jackett
jam [dʒæm] Marmelade
January ['dʒænjʊərɪ] Januar
Japanese [dʒæpə'ni:z] **1.** japanisch; **2.** Japanisch; **3.** Japaner/in
jealous ['dʒeləs] eifersüchtig
jeans *(pl.)* [dʒi:nz] Jeans
Jew [dʒu:] Jude, Jüdin; **Jewish** ['dʒu:ɪʃ] jüdisch
jewel(s) ['dʒu:əl(z)] Juwel(en)
jigsaw ['dʒɪgsɔ:] Puzzle
job [dʒɒb] Beruf, Arbeit, Job; Aufgabe
jog [dʒɒg] joggen
join [dʒɔɪn] sich anschließen; mitmachen; eintreten *(in einem Klub usw.)*
joke [dʒəʊk] Scherz, Spaß; Witz
journey ['dʒɜ:nɪ] Reise, Fahrt
judo ['dʒu:dəʊ] Judo
juice [dʒu:s] Saft; **juicy** saftig
July [dʒu:'laɪ] Juli
jump [dʒʌmp] springen
June [dʒu:n] Juni
jungle ['dʒʌŋgl] Dschungel
junior ['dʒu:nɪə] Junioren-, Jugend-
just [dʒʌst] **1.** nur, bloß (mal); **2.** gerade (eben); **just (like, as)** genau (wie)
Jutes [dʒu:ts] Jüten

K

kangaroo [ˌkæŋgəˈruː] Känguru
karate [kəˈrɑːtɪ] Karate
keep [kiːp] behalten; aufbewahren; halten; *(Gesetz, Vorschrift)* einhalten, befolgen; **keep alive** am Leben erhalten; **keep a promise** ein Versprechen halten **keep cattle** (sich) Rinder halten; **keep an eye on sb./sth.** ein (wachsames) Auge auf jn./etw. haben; **keep ... ing** etwas weiter tun, weiter-; **keep (out)** (draußen) halten; **keep to** sich halten an; **keep up (with)** (sich) auf dem neuesten Stand/auf dem Laufenden halten (über); **keeper** Wärter/in, Wächter/in
key [kiː] Schlüssel
kid [kɪd] (infml.) Kind; Jugendliche(r)
kill [kɪl] töten, umbringen
kilo [ˈkiːləʊ] Kilo
kilometre [ˈkɪləˌmiːtə] Kilometer
kilt [kɪlt] Schottenrock
kind (of) [kaɪnd] Art; **kind (of you)** nett, freundlich (von dir)
king [kɪŋ] König; **kingdom** [ˈkɪŋdəm] Königreich
kit [kɪt]**: repair kit** Flickzeug
kitchen [ˈkɪtʃɪn] Küche
knee [niː] Knie
knife, *pl.* **knives** [naɪf, naɪvz] Messer
knight [naɪt] Ritter
knock [nɒk] **1.** (an)klopfen; **2.** schlagen, stoßen
know [nəʊ] **1.** kennen; **2.** wissen; **you know** weißt du, nämlich; **known** bekannt; **well-known** (wohl) bekannt
knowledge [ˈnɒlɪdʒ] Wissen; Kenntnis(se)
koala (bear) [kəʊˈɑːlə] Koala(bär)

L

ladder [ˈlædə] Leiter
lake [leɪk] (ein) See
lamp [læmp] Lampe
land [lænd] **1.** (festes) Land, Boden; **landowner** [ˈlændˌəʊnə] Grundbesitzer **2.** landen *(Flugzeug)*; **3.** anlegen *(Schiff)*
lane [leɪn] (Fahr-)Spur
language [ˈlæŋgwɪdʒ] Sprache; **foreign language** Fremdsprache; **official language** Amtssprache
large [lɑːdʒ] groß, umfangreich
last [lɑːst] **1.** letzte(r, s); **last night** gestern Abend; letzte Nacht; **last Saturday** (am) letzten Samstag; **at last** endlich, schließlich; **be last** der Letzte sein, als Letzter (an)kommen; **2.** (an-, fort)dauern; **3.** ausreichen
late [leɪt] spät; **be late** zu spät kommen; **latest** [ˈleɪtɪst] neueste(r, s)
Latin [ˈlætɪn] Latein, lateinisch
laugh [lɑːf] lachen; **laugh at** lachen über; auslachen
launching pad [ˈlɔːntʃɪŋ pæd] Abschussrampe
law [lɔː] Gesetz
laziness [ˈleɪzɪnəs] Faulheit; **lazy** faul, träge
lead [liːd] führen, leiten; **leader** [ˈliːdə] (An-)Führer/in
leaf, *pl.* **leaves** [liːf, liːvz] Blatt *(einer Pflanze)*
learn [lɜːn] lernen; herausfinden, erfahren; **learner** [ˈlɜːnə] Lernende(r), Anfänger/in
least [liːst] (der/die/das) wenigste, am wenigsten; **at least** mindestens; wenigstens, zumindest
leather [ˈleðə] Leder
leave [liːv] **1.** (ver-, zurück)lassen; **2.** stehen/liegen lassen; **3.** weggehen, abfahren; **leave alone** in Ruhe lassen; **leave school** von der Schule abgehen
left [left] **1.** linke(r, s), nach links; **on the left** links, auf der linken Seite; **2. be left** übrig sein
leg [leg] Bein
legacy [ˈlegəsɪ] Vermächtnis, Erbe
legend [ˈledʒənd] Legende, Sage
lemonade [ˌleməˈneɪd] Limonade
lend [lend] (ver)leihen
less [les] weniger
lesson [ˈlesn] Unterrichtsstunde
let [let] (zu)lassen; **Let me see.** Warte mal! Lass mich mal überlegen! **let's = let us** lass(t) uns; **Let's see.** Wollen mal sehen.
letter [ˈletə] **1.** Brief; **2.** Buchstabe; **letter box** [ˈletə bɒks] (*meist* BE) Briefkasten
lettuce [ˈletɪs] Salat, Kopfsalat
liberty [ˈlɪbətɪ] Freiheit
library [ˈlaɪbrərɪ] Bibliothek, Bücherei
lie [laɪ] liegen
life, *pl.* **lives** [laɪf, laɪvz] Leben; **lifeboat** [ˈlaɪfbəʊt] Rettungsboot; **lifeline** [ˈlaɪflaɪn] Rettungsleine
lift [lɪft] heben, hochheben
light [laɪt] Licht, Lampe; **traffic lights** *(pl.)* [ˈtræfɪk laɪts] (Verkehrs-)Ampel
like [laɪk] **1.** wie; **like this** so, auf diese Weise; folgendermaßen; **like that** so; **things like that** so etwas, solche Sachen; **What's it like?** Wie ist es? Wie sieht es aus? **2.** mögen, gern haben/tun; **How do you like ...?** Wie gefällt dir ...? Wie findest du ...? **I'd like** ich möchte; **like better/best** lieber/am liebsten mögen
limit [ˈlɪmɪt] begrenzen, einschränken (auf)
line [laɪn] **1.** Zeile; Linie; **2.** (*meist* AE) Schlange *(wartender Menschen)*, Reihe
lion [ˈlaɪən] Löwe
list [lɪst] Liste
listen (to) [ˈlɪsn] zu-, anhören; **listener** Zuhörer/in; **listening comprehension** [ˈlɪsnɪŋ kɒmprɪˌhenʃn] Hörverstehen
litre [ˈliːtə] Liter
litter [ˈlɪtə] Abfall, herumliegendes Papier
little [ˈlɪtl] **1.** klein, jung; **2.** wenig; **a little** ein wenig, ein bisschen
live [lɪv] wohnen, leben; **living-room** Wohnzimmer; **liveliness** Lebendigkeit; **lively** lebhaft
load [ləʊd] (auf)laden, (be)laden
local [ˈləʊkl] Orts-, Lokal-, örtlich
lock [lɒk] ab-, zuschließen
loneliness [ˈləʊnlɪnəs] Einsamkeit; **lonely** einsam, verlassen
long [lɒŋ] lang; **no longer** nicht mehr, nicht länger; **not long ago** vor kurzem
look [lʊk] **1.** sehen, schauen; **2.** aussehen; **look after** sich kümmern um, aufpassen auf; **look at** anschauen; **look for** suchen; **look forward to (doing) sth.** sich auf etwas freuen; sich darauf freuen, etwas zu tun; **look up** *(ein Wort usw.)* nachschlagen
lord [lɔːd] Herr, Adliger; Lord
lorry [ˈlɒrɪ] (BE) Lastwagen
lose [luːz] verlieren; **loser** [ˈluːzə] Verlierer/in
lost [lɒst]**: be lost** sich verlaufen haben; **get lost** sich verlaufen
lots [lɒts]**/a lot (of)** viele, viel, eine Menge
loud [laʊd] laut
lounge: arrivals lounge [əˈraɪvlz laʊndʒ] Ankunftshalle
love [lʌv] **1.** Liebe; **fall in love (with)** sich verlieben (in); **Love** Viele liebe Grüße von; **2.** lieben, sehr mögen, sehr gern haben/tun; **I'd love** ich hätte (liebend) gern; **I'd love to** ich würde sehr gern; **lovely** schön, herrlich, hübsch
low [ləʊ] niedrig, tief
lucky [ˈlʌkɪ]**: be lucky** Glück haben
lunch [lʌntʃ] Mittagessen; **lunch bag** Tüte mit dem eingepackten Mittagessen; **at lunch time** zur Mittagszeit, mittags; **for lunch** zum Mittagessen; **have lunch** (zu) Mittag essen; **What's for lunch?** Was gibt's zum Mitagessen?

M

machine [məˈʃiːn] Maschine; **machinery** *(sing.)* [məˈʃiːnərɪ] Maschinerie, Maschinen
madam [ˈmædəm]**: Dear Madam** Sehr geehrte Dame; **Dear Sir or Madam,** Sehr geehrte Damen und Herren,
made of (paper) [ˈmeɪd‿əv] aus (Papier)
magazine [ˌmægəˈziːn] Zeitschrift, Illustrierte
magic [ˈmædʒɪk] Zauberkunst, Magie; **do magic** zaubern; **magician** [məˈdʒɪʃn] Zauberer, Zauberin
mail [meɪl] (*meist* AE) Post(sendungen); **airmail** Luftpost

main [meɪn] Haupt-, wichtigste(r/s); **mainly** hauptsächlich
major ['meɪdʒə] gewichtig, bedeutsam
majority [mə'dʒɒrətɪ] Mehrheit
make [meɪk] machen, bauen; **make a fool of sb.** jn. lächerlich machen; **make a phone call** ein Telefongespräch führen; **make sb. sth.** jn. zu etwas machen; **make sure** sich vergewissern; darauf achten, dafür sorgen (, dass); **make tea** Tee kochen; **make up** sich ausdenken; erfinden
man, *pl.* **men** [mæn, men] Mann, Männer
manager ['mænɪdʒə] **1.** Geschäftsführer/in, Filialleiter/in; **2.** Führungskraft
many ['menɪ] viele
map [mæp] Landkarte, Stadtplan
marathon ['mærəθən] Marathon
march [mɑ:tʃ] marschieren
March [mɑ:tʃ] März
mark [mɑ:k] **1.** (BE) Note, Zensur; **2.** kennzeichnen, bezeichnen
market ['mɑ:kɪt] Markt
marry ['mærɪ] heiraten; **get married** (sich ver)heiraten
Mass [mæs] (kath.) Gottesdienst, Messe
match [mætʃ] **1.** Spiel, Wettkampf; **2.** passend zusammenfügen; zusammenpassen
material [mə'tɪərɪəl] Material, Stoff
math (AE)/**maths** (BE) [mæθ, mæθs] Mathe(matik)
matter ['mætə]: **no matter (how/what/...)** egal, (wie/was/...)
may [meɪ] darf, kann; (kann) vielleicht
May [meɪ] Mai
maybe ['meɪbi:] vielleicht
mayor [meə] Bürgermeister/in
me [mi:] mir, mich; **(It wasn't) me.** Ich (war's nicht). **older than me** älter als ich
meal [mi:l] Mahlzeit, Essen
mean [mi:n] **1.** bedeuten; **meaning** Bedeutung; **2.** meinen; **mean to do sth.** etwas absichtlich tun, etwas tun wollen
mechanic [mɪ'kænɪk] Mechaniker/in
media ['mi:dɪə] Medien
medical ['medɪkl] medizinisch, Medizin-; ärztlich; **medicine** ['medsn] Medizin, Arznei
medieval [ˌmedɪ'i:vl] mittelalterlich
meet [mi:t] **1.** (sich) treffen, kennen lernen; **2.** abholen; **meeting** ['mi:tɪŋ] Treffen, Versammlung; Veranstaltung
member (of) ['membə] Mitglied (in, von); **membership card** Mitgliedsausweis
memory ['memərɪ] Gedächtnis; **in memory of** in Erinnerung an
mention ['menʃn] erwähnen
menu ['menju:] Speisekarte
merry ['merɪ] froh, fröhlich
message ['mesɪdʒ] Nachricht, Botschaft; **(bike) messenger** ['mesɪndʒə] (Fahrrad) Bote/-in
metal ['metl] Metall
method ['meθəd] Methode, Verfahren
metre ['mi:tə] Meter
Mexican ['meksɪkən] **1.** Mexikaner/in; **2.** mexikanisch
micro-electronics [ˌmaɪkrəʊ‿ɪlek'trɒnɪks] Mikroelektronik
mid- [mɪd] mittlere(r/s), Mittel-
middle ['mɪdl] Mitte; **Middle Ages** [ˌmɪdl‿'eɪdʒɪz] Mittelalter; **the Middle East** [ˌmɪdl 'i:st] der Nahe Osten
midnight ['mɪdnaɪt] Mitternacht
might [maɪt] könnte(n) vielleicht
mild [maɪld] mild
mile [maɪl] Meile; **miles per hour = mph** [ˌmaɪlz pər‿'aʊə] Meilen pro Stunde
milk [mɪlk] **1.** Milch; **2.** melken
million ['mɪljən] Million
mind [maɪnd] etwas (einzuwenden) haben gegen; **Never mind.** Das macht doch nichts.
mine [maɪn] meine(r, s)
mine [maɪn] Bergwerk; **miner** Bergarbeiter, Bergmann
minerals ['mɪnərəlz] Mineralien, Bodenschätze
minister ['mɪnɪstə] Minister/in
minority [maɪ'nɒrətɪ] Minderheit
minus ['maɪnəs] minus
minute ['mɪnɪt] Minute; **in a minute** gleich, sofort; **Wait a minute.** Einen Augenblick! Moment mal!
mirror ['mɪrə] Spiegel
Miss [mɪs] Fräulein/Frau; **miss** *häufige Anrede für eine Lehrerin in Großbritannien*
miss [mɪs] verpassen, verfehlen; vermissen; **missing** fehlend; **be missing** fehlen
mistake [mɪ'steɪk] Fehler, Irrtum
mix [mɪks]: **mixed** ge-, vermischt; **mixed bag** bunte Mischung; **mixture** ['mɪkstʃə] Mischung
moccassin ['mɒkəsɪn] Mokassin
model ['mɒdl] Modell, Modell-
modern ['mɒdn] modern
mom [mɒm] (AE) Mutti, Mama, Mami
moment ['məʊmənt] Moment, Augenblick; **at the moment** im Moment, im Augenblick; zurzeit
monarch ['mɒnək] Monarch/in
monastery ['mɒnəstrɪ] Kloster
Monday ['mʌndɪ] Montag; **on Monday(s)** montags, am Montag
money ['mʌnɪ] Geld
monkey ['mʌŋkɪ] Affe
monster ['mɒnstə] Ungeheuer
month [mʌnθ] Monat
monument ['mɒnjʊmənt] Denkmal
moon [mu:n] Mond
more [mɔ:] mehr; **more and more** immer (mehr); **more exciting** aufregender; **no more** kein(e, n) mehr; **some more** noch einige/etwas
morning ['mɔ:nɪŋ] Morgen, Vormittag; **Good morning.** Guten Morgen!/Tag! **in the morning(s)** am Morgen, morgens; **on Monday morning(s)** am Montagmorgen; **this morning** heute Morgen; **tomorrow morning** morgen früh
most [məʊst] **1.** (der/die/das) meiste; **2.** am meisten; **3.** höchst; **most of all** am allermeisten; **(the) most exciting** (der/die/das) aufregendste; am aufregendsten; **mostly** meistens, hauptsächlich
mother ['mʌðə] Mutter
motorbike ['məʊtəbaɪk] BE: Motorrad, AE: Moped, Mofa; **motorcycle** ['məʊtəsaɪkl] AE: Motorrad; **motorhome** (AE) Wohnmobil, Campingbus; **motorway** (BE) Autobahn
mountain(s) ['maʊntən] Berg; Gebirge
mouse, *pl.* **mice** [maʊs, maɪs] Maus
mouth [maʊθ] Mund
move [mu:v] **1.** (um)ziehen; **2.** (sich) bewegen; **Keep moving.** Mach(t) immer weiter!
movie ['mu:vɪ] (*meist* AE) Film; **go to the movies** (AE) ins Kino gehen; **movie theater** (AE) Kino(gebäude)
MP = Member of Parliament Mitglied des brit. Unterhauses
mph = miles per hour [ˌmaɪlz pər‿'aʊə] Meilen pro Stunde
Mr ['mɪstə] Herr; **Mrs** ['mɪsɪz] Frau; **Ms** [mɪz] Frau *(familienstandneutrale Anrede)*
much [mʌtʃ] viel; **(like) very much** sehr (gern mögen); **Thank you very much.** Vielen Dank.
mud [mʌd] Schlamm, Matsch
mum [mʌm] (BE) Mutti, Mama, Mami
Munich ['mju:nɪk] München
museum [mju:'zɪəm] Museum; **Museum of Natural History** Naturkundemuseum
music ['mju:zɪk] Musik; **musical** ['mju:zɪkl] Musical; **musician** [mju:'zɪʃn] Musiker/in
Muslim ['mʊzlɪm, 'mʌzlɪm] Moslem; moslemisch
must [mʌst, məst] muss; **mustn't** ['mʌsnt] darf nicht
my [maɪ] mein, meine; **myself** [maɪ'self] mir/mich (selbst)
mystery person ['mɪstərɪ ˌpɜ:sn] Rätselfigur
myth [mɪθ] Mythos, Märchen

N

nail [neɪl] Nagel
name [neɪm] **1.** Name; **2.** (be-, er-) nennen, taufen; **What's your name?** Wie ist dein Name? Wie heißt du?
narrow ['nærəʊ] eng, schmal
nation ['neɪʃn] Nation, Volk; Stamm; **national** ['næʃnəl] national, National-; **nationality** [ˌnæʃə'nælətɪ] Staatsangehörigkeit, Nationalität
Native American ['neɪtɪv] Indianer/in, amerikanische(r) Ureinwohner/in

natural history [ˌnætʃrəl ˈhɪstrɪ] Naturkunde
navy [ˈneɪvɪ] Marine
near [nɪə] in der Nähe von, nahe; **nearly** [ˈnɪəlɪ] fast, beinahe
necessary [ˈnesəsərɪ] notwendig, nötig
neck [nek] Hals
need [niːd] brauchen, benötigen; **needn't** [ˈniːdnt] braucht nicht, muss nicht
neighbour [ˈneɪbə] Nachbar/in; **neighbourhood** [ˈneɪbəhʊd] Nachbarschaft; (Wohn-)Gegend
neither [ˈnaɪðə, ˈniːðə]**: neither do/will/am/... I** ich auch nicht
nerves [nɜːvz]**: get on sb.'s nerves** jm. auf die Nerven gehen; **nervous** [ˈnɜːvəs] ängstlich, aufgeregt, nervös; **nervousness** [ˈnɜːvəsnəs] Nervosität
net [net] Netz
network [ˈnetwɜːk] Netz(werk); Vernetzung
never [ˈnevə] nie, niemals
new [njuː] neu; **news** [njuːz] Nachricht(en), Neuigkeit(en); **newspaper** Zeitung
New Zealand [ˌnjuː ˈziːlənd] Neuseeland
next [nekst] nächste(r, s); **next Monday** (am) nächsten Morgen; **the next house** das Haus nebenan; **next to** direkt neben
nice [naɪs] nett, schön, hübsch; **nice of you** nett von Ihnen
nickel [ˈnɪkl] (AE) 5¢-Münze
night [naɪt] Nacht, (später) Abend; **at night** nachts, bei Nacht; **last night** gestern Abend; letzte Nacht; **on the first night** in der ersten Nacht
no [nəʊ] **1.** nein; **2.** kein, keine; **no longer** nicht mehr, nicht länger; **no matter (how/what/...)** egal (wie/was/...); **no more** kein(e, n) mehr; **nobody/no one** niemand
no = number [ˈnʌmbə] Nr. = Nummer
Noah's ark [ˌnəʊəz‿ˈɑːk] die Arche Noah
nod [nɒd] **1.** Kopfnicken; **2.** nicken (mit)
noise [nɔɪz] Lärm, Geräusch; **noisy** [ˈnɔɪzɪ] laut, lärmend
non- [nɒn] nicht-; Nicht-; **non-fiction** [ˌnɒnˈfɪkʃn] **1.** nicht fiktional; **2.** Sachbücher, -texte
nor [nɔː]**: nor do/will/am/... I** auch nicht
normal [ˈnɔːml] normal; **normally** normalerweise
Norman [ˈnɔːmən] **1.** normannisch; **2.** Normanne
north (of) [nɔːθ] **1.** nördlich (von); **2.** Nord-; (nach) Norden; **northern** [ˈnɔːðən] Nord-, nördlich
nose [nəʊz] Nase
not [nɒt] nicht; **not ... any** (gar) kein, keine; keins; **not ... anybody** niemand; **not ... anything** nichts; **not ... anywhere** nirgends, nirgendwohin; **not at all** überhaupt nicht, ganz und gar nicht; **not (...) either** auch nicht, auch kein; **not ever** nie; **not till** erst um, nicht vor; **not yet** noch nicht
note [nəʊt] **1.** (BE) (Geld-)Schein; **2.** Notiz
nothing [ˈnʌθɪŋ] nichts
notice [ˈnəʊtɪs] **1.** Anschlag; Mitteilung, Hinweis(schild); **2.** (be)merken, beachten
novel [ˈnɒvl] Roman
November [nəʊˈvembə] November
now [naʊ] jetzt, nun; **nowadays** [ˈnaʊədeɪz] heutzutage
number [ˈnʌmbə] **1.** Zahl, Nummer; **2.** Anzahl
nun [nʌn] Nonne; **nunnery** [ˈnʌnərɪ] Nonnenkloster
nurse [nɜːs] Krankenschwester, Krankenpfleger

O

O [əʊ] Null
obligation [ˌɒblɪˈgeɪʃn] Verpflichtung, Pflicht
obvious [ˈɒbvɪəs] offensichtlich
ocean [ˈəʊʃn] Ozean
o'clock [əˈklɒk] ... Uhr
October [ɒkˈtəʊbə] Oktober
Odd man out! [ˌɒd mæn‿ˈaʊt] Welches Wort passt hier nicht?
of [ɒv, əv] von; **of his own** sein eigene(r/s); **bottle of lemonade** Flasche Limonade; **both of them** sie beide, alle beide; **nice of you** nett von dir; **of course** [əv ˈkɔːs] natürlich; **the name of the street** der Name (von) der Straße; **the city/island of ...** die Stadt/Insel ...
off [ɒf] von ... herunter
offer [ˈɒfə] **1.** Angebot; **2.** anbieten
office [ˈɒfɪs] Büro; **official** [əˈfɪʃl] offiziell, amtlich; **official language** Amtssprache
often [ˈɒfn, ˈɒftən] oft
oil [ɔɪl] Öl
OK = okay [əʊˈkeɪ] gut, in Ordnung; **I'm OK.** Mir geht's gut.
old [əʊld] alt
Olympic [əˈlɪmpɪk] olympisch
omelette [ˈɒmlɪt] Omelett
on [ɒn] **1.** auf; an; **2.** weiter; **be on** an sein, laufen; **from now on** von jetzt an, ab jetzt; **on a bike** mit dem Fahrrad; **on a visit to ...** bei einem Besuch in ...; **on holiday** (BE) auf Urlaub, in den Ferien; **on Monday(s)** montags, am Montag; **on Monday morning(s)** am Montagmorgen; **on my way to** auf dem Weg/unterwegs nach; **on October 12th** am 12. Oktober; **on the first night** in der ersten Nacht; **on the left/right** links/rechts; **on the one hand ... on the other hand** einerseits ... andererseits; **on the phone** am Telefon; **on the radio/on TV** im Radio/Fernseher; **on the River Thames** an der Themse; **on the train/bus/plane** im Zug/Bus/Flugzeug; **on your birthday** an deinem Geburtstag
once [wʌns] **1.** einmal; **2.** (früher) einmal, einst; **at once** sofort, (so)gleich
one/one's [wʌn, wʌnz] man/sein; **the blue one, the blue ones** der/die/das blaue, die blauen; **oneself** [wʌnˈself] sich (selbst)
onion [ˈʌnjən] Zwiebel
only [ˈəʊnlɪ] nur; **not only ... but also** nicht nur ..., sondern auch; **only one week old** erst eine Woche alt; **the only** der/die/das einzige, die einzige
onto [ˈɒntʊ, ˈɒntə] auf ... (hinauf)
open [ˈəʊpən] **1.** offen, geöffnet, auf **2.** öffnen, aufmachen; **opening times** Öffnungszeiten
opera [ˈɒprə] Oper
opinion [əˈpɪnjən] Meinung; **in my opinion** meiner Meinung nach
opposite [ˈɒpəzɪt] **1.** Gegenteil; **2.** gegen überliegend; **3.** entgegengesetzt; gegenüber (von)
or [ɔː] oder
orange [ˈɒrɪndʒ] **1.** orange(farben); **2.** Apfelsine, Orange
order [ˈɔːdə] **1.** Reihenfolge, (An-)Ordnung; **2.** bestellen; befehlen, beauftragen; **in order to** um ... zu
ordinary [ˈɔːdənrɪ] einfach, gewöhnlich, normal
organization [ˌɔːgənaɪˈzeɪʃn] Organisation; **organize** [ˈɔːgənaɪz] organisieren, veranstalten
origin [ˈɒrɪdʒɪn] Ursprung; Entstehung; Herkunft; **original** [əˈrɪdʒənl] ursprünglich; Original-
orphan [ˈɔːfn] Waise, Waisenkind
other [ˈʌðə] andere(r, s)
ought to [ˈɔːtə] sollte eigentlich, müsste eigentlich
our [ˈaʊə] unser(e); **ours** [ˈaʊəz] unsere(r, s); **ourselves** [ˌaʊəˈselvz] uns (selbst)
out [aʊt] **1.** hinaus, heraus; **2.** draußen; **come out** herauskommen, hinauskommen; **die out** aussterben; **find out** herausfinden, erfahren; **get out (of the train)** (aus dem Zug) aussteigen; **go out (with)** ausgehen (mit); **read out** vorlesen; **out of** aus (... heraus/hinaus); von; **out of work** arbeitslos
outdoor [ˈaʊtdɔː] im Freien; **outdoors** [ˌaʊtˈdɔːz] (nach) draußen, im Freien
outlaw [ˈaʊtlɔː] Geächtete(r)
outside [aʊtˈsaɪd] draußen; nach draußen
over [ˈəʊvə] über; vorüber; **be over** vorüber sein, zu Ende sein; **over there** dort drüben, da drüben
overtake [ˌəʊvəˈteɪk] überholen
owe [əʊ] schulden
own [əʊn] **1.** eigene(r, s); **I pay for my own clothes.** Ich bezahle meine

Kleidung selbst. **of my own** mein eigene(r/s); **2.** besitzen; **owner** Besitzer/in
Oxfam ['ɒksfæm] *brit. Hilfsorganisation zur Bekämpfung der Hungersnot*

P

p [pi:] = **pence** Pence
Pacific [pə'sɪfɪk] Pazifik; pazifisch
pack [pæk] (ein)packen
packet ['pækɪt] Paket, Päckchen; Packung
page [peɪdʒ] Seite *(im Buch)*
pain [peɪn] Schmerz
paint [peɪnt] **1.** Farbe *(zum Malen)*; **2.** streichen, anstreichen; **3.** malen; **painter** Maler/in, Anstreicher/in
pair [peə] Paar
Pakistan [,pɑ:kɪ'stɑ:n] Pakistan; **Pakistani** [,pɑ:kɪ'stɑ:nɪ] **1.** Pakistaner/in; **2.** pakistanisch
palace ['pælɪs] Palast, Schloss
panic ['pænɪk] in Panik geraten
paper ['peɪpə] Papier; **paper = newspaper** Zeitung; **to have a paper route** (AE) Zeitungen austragen
parade [pə'reɪd] Umzug, Parade
parenthesis, *pl.* **parentheses** [pə'renθɪsɪs, pə'renθɪsi:z] Klammer
parents ['peərənts] Eltern
park [pɑ:k] **1.** Park; **2.** parken; **parking lot** (AE) großer Parkplatz; Parkhaus **parking space** ['pɑ:kɪŋ speɪs] Parklücke, Parkplatz
parliament ['pɑ:ləmənt] Parlament
parrot ['pærət] Papagei
part [pɑ:t] **1.** Teil; **2.** Gegend; **3.** Rolle (eines Schauspielers); **part-time** Teilzeit-, halbtags; **take part (in)** teilnehmen (an), mitmachen (bei); **partly** zum Teil, teilweise
partner ['pɑ:tnə] Partner/in
party ['pɑ:tɪ] **1.** Party, Fest, Fete; **2.** Partei
pass [pɑ:s] **1.** vergehen, vorübergehen *(Zeit)*; **2.** *(eine Prüfung)* bestehen; **3.** (herüber)reichen; *(Ball)* abgeben, abspielen
passage ['pæsɪdʒ] Gang
passenger ['pæsɪndʒə] Fahrgast, Passagier
passport ['pɑ:spɔ:t] (Reise-)Pass
past [pɑ:st] **1.** Vergangenheit; **2.** vorbei, vorüber (an); **half past ten** halb elf (= 10.30)
path [pɑ:θ] Pfad, Fußweg
patient ['peɪʃnt] geduldig
pavement ['peɪvmənt] (BE) Gehweg
pay (for) [peɪ] (be)zahlen
peace [pi:s] Friede(n); **peaceful** ['pi:sfəl] friedlich, friedfertig
pedestrian [pɪ'destrɪən] Fußgänger/in; **pedestrian crossing** [pɪ,destrɪən 'krɒsɪŋ] Fußgängerüberweg; **pedestrian precinct** [pɪ,destrɪən 'pri:sɪŋkt] (BE) Fußgängerzone
pen [pen] Füller; Stift; **pen-friend** Brieffreund/in; **sheep pen** Schafhürde
pence [pens] Pence
pencil ['pensl] Bleistift; **pencil-case** ['penslkeɪs] Federtasche, Federmäppchen
penguin ['peŋgwɪn] Pinguin
penisula [pə'nɪnsjʊlə] Halbinsel
penny ['penɪ] **1.** *kleinste britische Münze;* **2.** (AE) 1¢-Münze
pension ['penʃn] Altersrente, Pension
people ['pi:pl] **1.** Leute, Menschen; **2.** Volk
per cent [pə'sent] Prozent
perhaps [pə'hæps] vielleicht
period ['pɪərɪəd] **1.** Unterrichtsstunde; **2.** Zeitspanne, Zeitraum, Epoche; **3.** (AE) Punkt *(am Satzende)*
permanent ['pɜ:mənənt] dauerhaft, (be)ständig
permission [pə'mɪʃn] Erlaubnis, Genehmigung
persecute ['pɜ:sɪkju:t] verfolgen *(aus politischen oder religiösen Gründen)*; **persecution** [pɜ:sɪ'kju:ʃn] Verfolgung
person ['pɜ:sn] Person, Mensch; **personal** ['pɜ:snl] persönlich, Personal-
pet [pet] Haustier, Tier; **pet shop** Tierhandlung
petrol ['petrəl] (BE) Benzin; **petrol station** ['petrəl ,steɪʃn] (BE) Tankstelle
phone = telephone [fəʊn] **1.** Telefon; **2.** anrufen
phonetic [fə'netɪk] phonetisch
photo ['fəʊtəʊ] Foto, Bild; **in the photo** auf dem Foto; **take photos** fotografieren
phrase [freɪz] **1.** Redewendung; **2.** Wortgruppe
piano [pɪ'ænəʊ] Klavier
pick [pɪk] pflücken; **pick up** aufheben
picnic ['pɪknɪk] Picknick; **have a picnic** ein Picknick machen
picture ['pɪktʃə] Bild; Aufnahme, Foto; **in the picture** auf dem Bild; **take pictures** fotografieren, Fotos/Bilder machen
piece [pi:s] Stück
pig [pɪg] Schwein
pigeon ['pɪdʒən] Taube
pile [paɪl] Haufen
pilgrim ['pɪlgrɪm] Pilger/in
pilot ['paɪlət] Pilot/in
pink [pɪŋk] pink, rosa
pioneer [paɪə'nɪə] Pionier, Vorkämpfer/in
pirate ['paɪrət] Pirat, Seeräuber
pity ['pɪtɪ]: **It's a pity.** Das ist schade.
pizza ['pi:tsə] Pizza
place [pleɪs] Ort, Platz, Stelle
plain [pleɪn] einfach, klar
plan [plæn] **1.** Plan, Vorhaben; **2.** planen; **planner** Planer/in
plane [pleɪn] Flugzeug; **by plane** mit dem Flugzeug
plant [plɑ:nt] **1.** Pflanze; **2.** (ein)pflanzen, setzen
plate [pleɪt] Teller
platform ['plætfɔ:m] **1.** Bahnsteig; **2.** Plattform
play [pleɪ] spielen; **play a trick (on)** einen Streich spielen; **player** Spieler/in
please [pli:z] bitte; **be pleased (with)** sich freuen (über); zufrieden sein (mit)
pliers ['plaɪəz] (eine) (Kombi-)Zange
plunder ['plʌndə] (aus)plündern, (aus)rauben
pm [,pi:‿'em] Uhr nachmittags/abends
pocket ['pɒkɪt] Tasche; **pocket-money** Taschengeld
poetry ['pəʊɪtrɪ] Dichtung, Dichtkunst
point [pɔɪnt] Punkt; Komma
poison ['pɔɪzn] Gift
polar bear ['pəʊlə beə] Eisbär
police [pə'li:s] Polizei; **police officer** Polizist/in; **police station** Polizeiwache, Polizeirevier
policy ['pɒləsɪ] Politik
polio ['pəʊlɪəʊ] Kinderlähmung, Polio
polite [pə'laɪt] höflich; **politeness** [pə'laɪtnəs] Höflichkeit
political [pə'lɪtɪkl] politisch; **politician** [,pɒlə'tɪʃn] Politiker/in; **politics** *(sing.)* ['pɒlɪtɪks] Politik
pollute [pə'lu:t] verschmutzen; **pollution** [pə'lu:ʃn] (Umwelt-)Verschmutzung
pony ['pəʊnɪ] Pony; **pony-trekking** ['pəʊnɪ ,trekɪŋ] Ponyreiten
poor [pʊə, pɔ:] arm
popcorn ['pɒpkɔ:n] Popcorn
Pope [pəʊp] Papst
pop music ['pɒp ,mju:zɪk] Popmusik; **pop song** Popsong
popular (with) ['pɒpjʊlə] beliebt (bei)
population [,pɒpjʊ'leɪʃn] Bevölkerung, Einwohner(zahl)
port [pɔ:t] Hafen; Hafenstadt
Portugal ['pɔ:tʃʊgl] Portugal
position [pə'zɪʃn] Lage; Position
possibility [,pɒsə'bɪlətɪ] Möglichkeit; **possible** ['pɒsəbl] möglich; **possibly** möglicherweise, vielleicht
post [pəʊst] (BE) Post(sendungen); **post office** Post(amt); **postcard** Postkarte; **postcode** ['pəʊstkəʊd] *britische Postleitzahl*
poster ['pəʊstə] Poster, Plakat
potato [pə'teɪtəʊ], *pl.* **potatoes** Kartoffel
pound [paʊnd] **1.** Pfund *(britische Währung)*; **2.** *engl./amerik.* Pfund (= 454 g)
poverty ['pɒvətɪ] Armut
power ['paʊə] **1.** Macht, Kraft, Gewalt; **2.** Befugnis; **powerful** ['paʊəfəl] mächtig, stark; **powerless** ['paʊələs] machtlos, kraftlos
practice ['præktɪs] **1.** Übung; Praxis; **2.** (AE) üben, trainieren
practise ['præktɪs] (BE) üben, trainieren; ausüben
precinct: pedestrian precinct [pɪ,destrɪən 'pri:sɪŋkt] (BE) Fußgängerzone

prefer (to) [prɪ'fɜː] vorziehen, lieber haben (als)
prefix ['priːfɪks] Vorsilbe, Präfix
prejudice ['predʒʊdɪs] Vorurteil, Voreingenommenheit; **prejudiced** voreingenommen
preparation [prepə'reɪʃn] Vorbereitung; **prepare** [prɪ'peə] vor-, zubereiten
present ['preznt] Geschenk; **present-day** heutig, gegenwärtig
president ['prezɪdənt] Präsident/in
prestige [pre'stiːʒ] Ansehen, Prestige
pretend [prɪ'tend] so tun, als ob; vortäuschen
price [praɪs] (Kauf-)Preis
priest [priːst] Priester
primary school ['praɪmərɪ skuːl] (BE) Grundschule
prime minister [ˌpraɪm 'mɪnɪstə] Premierminister/in, Ministerpräsident/in
prince [prɪns] Prinz, Fürst; **princess** [prɪn'ses] Prinzessin, Fürstin
principal ['prɪnsəpl] (AE) Schulleiter/in, Direktor/in
prison ['prɪzn] Gefängnis; **prisoner** ['prɪznə] Gefangene(r)
private ['praɪvɪt] **1.** privat, Privat-; **2.** persönlich
prize [praɪz] Preis, Gewinn
probably ['prɒbəblɪ] wahrscheinlich
problem ['prɒbləm] Problem
produce [prə'djuːs] produzieren, herstellen, erzeugen; **product** ['prɒdʌkt] Produkt, Erzeugnis
professional [prə'feʃnl] Berufs-, professionell, Fach-; Berufssportler/in, Profi
professor [prə'fesə] Professor/in
programme ['prəʊgræm] (BE) Sendung, Programm
progress ['prəʊgres]: **in progress** im Gange
project ['prɒdʒekt] Projekt; Aufgabe
promise ['prɒmɪs] **1.** Versprechen; **2.** versprechen
pronounce [prə'naʊns] aussprechen; **pronunciation** [prəˌnʌnsɪ'eɪʃn] Aussprache
proper ['prɒpə] richtig, passend, geeignet
protect [prə'tekt] (be)schützen; **protection** Schutz
Protestant ['prɒtɪstənt] **1.** Protestant/in; **2.** protestantisch, evangelisch
proud (of) [praʊd] stolz (auf)
province ['prɒvɪns] Provinz
public ['pʌblɪk] öffentlich; **public school** (BE) (teure) Privatschule *(meist mit Internat)*; **public transportation** (AE) öffentliche Verkehrsmittel
pull [pʊl] ziehen; **pull down** abreißen, niederreißen
pullover ['pʊlˌəʊvə] Pullover
punctuation mark [ˌpʌŋktʃʊ'eɪʃn mɑːk] Satzzeichen
puncture ['pʌŋktʃə] (BE) Reifenpanne
punish ['pʌnɪʃ] bestrafen
pupil ['pjuːpl] Schüler/in
purpose ['pɜːpəs] Zweck
push [pʊʃ] stoßen, schieben; drängeln
put [pʊt] stellen, legen, setzen, *(an einen Platz)* tun; **put in** einsetzen; **put on** *(Kleidung)* anziehen; **put up** **1.** aufbauen, aufstellen; **2.** aufhängen, anbringen
puzzle ['pʌzl] Rätsel
pyjamas *(pl.)* [pə'dʒɑːməz] Schlafanzug, Pyjama

Q

quarter ['kwɔːtə] **1.** Viertel; **2.** viertel; **quarter past/to ten** Viertel nach/vor zehn; **3.** (AE) 25¢-Münze
queen [kwiːn] Königin
question ['kwestʃən] Frage; **ask a question** eine Frage stellen; **question mark** Fragezeichen
queue [kjuː] (BE) Schlange *(wartender Menschen)*, Reihe
quick [kwɪk] schnell
quiet ['kwaɪət] still, ruhig, leise
quit [kwɪt] aufhören; *(eine Stelle) aufgeben*
quite [kwaɪt] **1.** ziemlich; **2.** ganz; **quite a** ein(e) ziemlich(er, e, es)
quiz [kwɪz] Quiz
quotation mark Anführungszeichen

R

rabbit ['ræbɪt] Kaninchen
race [reɪs] **1.** Rennen, (Wett-)Lauf; **have a race** ein Rennen veranstalten; **racing driver** Rennfahrer/in; **2.** Rasse
radio ['reɪdɪəʊ] Radio, Rundfunk; **on the radio** im Radio
railway ['reɪlweɪ] Eisenbahn(strecke)
rain [reɪn] **1.** Regen; **2.** regnen; **raincoat** Regenmantel; **rainy** regnerisch, verregnet
raise [reɪz] (hoch)heben; erhöhen
rape [reɪp] vergewaltigen
raw [rɔː] roh; Roh-
reach (for) [riːtʃ] erreichen; greifen (nach)
react (to) [riː'ækt] reagieren auf; **reaction** Reaktion
read [riːd] (vor)lesen; **read out** vorlesen; **readable** ['riːdəbl] lesbar; **reader** Leser/in
ready ['redɪ] bereit, fertig; **Ready, steady, go!** Auf die Plätze, fertig, los!
real [rɪəl] echt, wirklich; **really** wirklich, tatsächlich, eigentlich
realize ['rɪəlaɪz] erkennen; sich klarmachen; einsehen; merken
reason ['riːzn] Grund, Begründung; **reasonable** ['riːznəbl] vernünftig
recently ['riːsntlɪ] neulich, vor kurzem
recognize ['rekəgnaɪz] **1.** erkennen; **2.** anerkennen
record **1.** ['rekɔːd] Rekord; **2.** Schallplatte; **record-player** Plattenspieler; **3.** schriftliche Überlieferung; **4.** [rɪ'kɔːd] aufzeichnen, aufnehmen *(auf Band)*
rectangular [rek'tæŋgʊlə] rechteckig
red [red] rot
redevelop [ˌriːdɪ'veləp] sanieren
refuse [rɪ'fjuːz] sich weigern; verweigern, ablehnen
region ['riːdʒn] Gegend, Gebiet, Region
regular ['regjʊlə] regelmäßig
reign [reɪn] Regierung(szeit)
reject [rɪ'dʒekt] ablehnen, zurückweisen
related [rɪ'leɪtɪd]: **be related (to)** verwandt sein (mit); sich beziehen (auf)
relations [rɪ'leɪʃnz] Beziehungen
relative ['relətɪv] Verwandte(r)
relax [rɪ'læks] (sich) entspannen, sich ausruhen
religion [rɪ'lɪdʒn] Religion; **religious** [rɪ'lɪdʒəs] religiös
remain [rɪ'meɪn] bleiben, übrig bleiben; **remains** (Über-)Reste
remember [rɪ'membə] **1.** sich erinnern (an); daran denken; **2.** sich merken
remind (of) [rɪ'maɪnd] erinnern (an)
repair [rɪ'peə] **1.** Reparatur; **2.** reparieren; **repair kit** [rɪ'peə kɪt] Flickzeug; **repair shop** Reparaturwerkstatt für Fahrräder
repeat [rɪ'piːt] wiederholen
reply (to) [rɪ'plaɪ] Antwort, Erwiderung (auf)
report [rɪ'pɔːt] **1.** Bericht; **2.** berichten, melden; *(bei der Polizei)* anzeigen; **reporter** Reporter/in
republic [rɪ'pʌblɪk] Republik
request [rɪ'kwest] Bitte
resort [rɪ'zɔːt] Ferienort, Urlaubsort
respect [rɪ'spekt] Achtung, Respekt
rest [rest] Rest
restaurant ['restrɒnt] Restaurant, Gaststätte
restore [rɪ'stɔː] wiederherstellen; restaurieren; neu aufbauen
result [rɪ'zʌlt] Ergebnis, Resultat
return [rɪ'tɜːn] zurückkommen, -gehen; **return fare** Fahrpreis hin und zurück; **return flight** Rückflug
revise [rɪ'vaɪz] (BE) *(Lernstoff)* wiederholen
rewrite [ˌrɪ'raɪt] neu schreiben, noch mal schreiben
rhyme [raɪm] Reim, Vers
rich (in) [rɪtʃ] reich (an)
ride [raɪd] **1.** *(auf einem Pferd)* reiten; **2.** (Rad) fahren; **a one-minute ride by bus/car** eine Minute mit dem Bus/Auto; **go for a ride** herumfahren, eine Spritztour machen; **rider** ['raɪdə] (Rad-)Fahrer/in; Reiter/in
right [raɪt] **1.** richtig; **all right** gut, in Ordnung; **be right** Recht haben; **My watch is right** Meine Uhr geht richtig. **That's right.** Richtig! Stimmt! **2.** rechte(r, s), nach rechts; **on the right** rechts, auf der rechten Seite;

to the right nach rechts;
3. direkt, genau; **4. rights** *(pl.)* Rechte
ring [rɪŋ] **1.** Ring; **2.** klingeln, läuten; **3.** anrufen
risk [rɪsk] **1.** Risiko; **2.** riskieren, wagen
rival ['raɪvl] Rivale/-in, Konkurrent/in
river ['rɪvə] Fluss; **on the (River) Thames** an der Themse
road [rəʊd] (Land-)Straße; **road sign** Verkehrszeichen
roast beef [,rəʊst 'bi:f] Rinderbraten, Roastbeef
rob [rɒb] be-, ausrauben
robot ['rəʊbɒt] Roboter
rock [rɒk] Fels(en); **rock-climbing** ['rɒk ,klaɪmɪŋ] Klettern (im Fels); **rocky** felsig
rocket ['rɒkɪt] Rakete
role [rəʊl] Rolle; **role-play** ['rəʊl pleɪ] Rollenspiel
roll [rəʊl] **1.** Brötchen, Semmel; **2.** rollen
Roman ['rəʊmən] römisch, Römer/in
roof [ru:f] Dach
room [ru:m, rʊm] Zimmer, Raum
rough [rʌf] rau, stürmisch; grob, gewalttätig, hart
round [raʊnd] **1.** um (... herum); **2.** rund; **3.** Kanon
route [ru:t] Route, Strecke
row [rəʊ] rudern
royal ['rɔɪəl] königlich
rub [rʌb] (ein)reiben
rubber ['rʌbə] **1.** (BE) Radiergummi; **2.** Gummi
rude [ru:d] unhöflich, grob; unanständig
ruin ['ru:ɪn] Ruine; **in ruins** zerstört
rule [ru:l] **1.** Regel, Vorschrift; **2.** Herrschaft; **3.** (be)herrschen, regieren
ruler ['ru:lə] Lineal
run [rʌn] **1.** rennen, laufen; **runner** Läufer/in; **2.** verkehren, fahren *(Zug, Bus)*

S

sad [sæd] traurig; **sadness** ['sædnəs] Traurigkeit
safari park [sə'fɑ:rɪ pɑ:k] Safaripark
safe [seɪf] sicher, gefahrlos
sail [seɪl] **1.** Segel; **2.** segeln, fahren; **sailor** Seemann, Matrose
saint [seɪnt] Heilige(r)
salad ['sæləd] (angemachter) Salat; **ham salad** Schinken mit Salat
salt [sɔ:lt] Salz; **salty** salzig; versalzen
same [seɪm]: **the same** der-, die-, dasselbe
sand [sænd] Sand; **sandy** sandig
sandwich ['sænwɪdʒ] belegtes Butterbrot
Santa Claus ['sæntə klɔ:z] Weihnachtsmann
sapphire ['sæfaɪə] Saphir
Saturday ['sætədɪ] Samstag, Sonnabend
sauce [sɔ:s] Soße
saucer ['sɔ:sə] Untertasse
sausage ['sɒsɪdʒ] Wurst, Würstchen
save [seɪv] **1.** sparen; **2.** retten
saw [sɔ:] Säge
Saxon ['sæksn] Sachse, Sächsin
say [seɪ] sagen; **say hello (to)** grüßen; **The sign says ...** Auf dem Schild steht/heißt es ... ;
school [sku:l] Schule; **at school, in school** *(meist* AE) in der Schule; **go to school** zur Schule gehen; **leave school** von der Schule abgehen; **start school** eingeschult werden; **schoolchildren** Schüler und Schülerinnen, Schulkinder
science ['saɪəns] (Natur-)Wissenschaft; **scientist** ['saɪəntɪst] (Natur-)Wissenschaftler/in
score [skɔ:] **1.** Spielstand; Ergebnis; **2.** *(einen Punkt/Treffer)* erzielen, *(ein Tor)* schießen
Scot [skɒt] Schotte, Schottin; **Scotland** Schottland; **Scotsman/Scotswoman** Schotte/Schottin; **Scottish** schottisch
scout [skaʊt]: **Girl Scout** (AE) Pfadfinderin
scream [skri:m] **1.** Schrei; Aufschrei; **2.** schreien, kreischen
screw [skru:] Schraube; **screwdriver** ['skru:,draɪvə] Schraubenzieher
sea [si:] Meer; **sea lion** ['si: ,laɪən] Seelöwe; **seasick** ['si:sɪk] seekrank; **seaside** ['si:saɪd] See-, Küsten-; Küste
season ['si:zn] Jahreszeit; Saison
seat [si:t] Sitzplatz; **seatbelt** ['si:tbelt] Sicherheitsgurt
second ['sekənd] Sekunde
secondary modern school [,sekəndrɪ 'mɒdn sku:l] (BE) *Mischung aus Haupt- und Realschule;* **secondary school** Oberschule
secret ['si:krət] **1.** Geheimnis; **2.** geheim
see [si:] sehen; **I see.** Ich verstehe. Ach so! **Let me see, ...** Warte mal! Lass mich mal überlegen! **Let's see.** Wollen mal sehen. **See you soon.** Tschüs. Bis bald.
seem [si:m] scheinen
sell [sel] verkaufen
semi-colon [,semɪ'kəʊlən] Semikolon
semi-detached house [,semɪ dɪ,tætʃt 'haʊs] (BE) Doppelhaushälfte
send [send] schicken, senden; **send for** kommen lassen, holen; schicken nach
sentence ['sentəns] Satz
separate 1. ['seprət] getrennt, selbstständig; **2.** ['sepəreɪt] trennen
September [sep'tembə] September
serious ['sɪərɪəs] **1.** ernst(haft); **2.** schlimm
serve [sɜ:v] (be)dienen, servieren; **servant** Diener/in, Dienstmädchen; **service** ['sɜ:vɪs] *(Zug-, Bus- usw.)* Verbindung; Dienst(leistung)
set [set] Satz
set off [set 'ɒf] aufbrechen
settle ['setl] sich niederlassen, ansiedeln; besiedeln; **settlement** Siedlung; **settler** Siedler/in
several ['sevrəl] mehrere; verschiedene
sex [seks] Geschlecht; Sex
shabby ['ʃæbɪ] schäbig
(milk) shake (Milch-)Shake, Mixgetränk
Shall I/we ... ? [ʃæl, ʃəl] Soll ich/Sollen wir ... ? **I shall (= I will)** ich werde/will
shampoo [ʃæm'pu:] Shampoo, Haarwaschmittel
shan't [ʃɑ:nt]: **I shan't = I shall not**
shape [ʃeɪp] Gestalt, Form
share (with) [ʃeə] (sich) teilen (mit), gemeinsam benutzen
she [ʃi:] sie
sheep [ʃi:p] Schaf(e)
shelf, *pl.* **shelves** [ʃelf, ʃelvz] Bord, Brett; Regal
shell [ʃel] Muschel(schale)
shine [ʃaɪn] **1.** scheinen *(Sonne)*; **2.** glänzen
ship [ʃɪp] Schiff
shirt [ʃɜ:t] (Ober-)Hemd
shoe [ʃu:] Schuh
shoot [ʃu:t] (er)schießen
shop [ʃɒp] Laden, Geschäft; **pet shop** Tierhandlung; **repair shop** Reparaturwerkstatt; **shop assistant** ['ʃɒp‿ə,sɪstənt] (BE) Verkäufer/in; **shopping** Einkauf(en); BE *auch:* eingekaufte Sachen; **do the shopping** einkaufen, Einkäufe machen/erledigen; **go shopping** einkaufen gehen
short [ʃɔ:t] kurz; **shorts** *(pl.)* Shorts, kurze Hose(n)
should [ʃʊd, ʃəd] sollte(n), müsste(n)
shout [ʃaʊt] (laut) rufen, schreien
show [ʃəʊ] **1.** Schau; Show; **2.** zeigen
shower ['ʃaʊə] Dusche, Brause; (Regen-) Schauer; **have a shower** (sich) duschen
shut [ʃʌt] schließen, zumachen
shy [ʃaɪ] scheu, zurückhaltend
sick [sɪk]: **be sick** (BE) sich übergeben (müssen); **feel sick** sich schlecht/übel fühlen; **sickness** ['sɪknəs] Krankheit
side [saɪd] Seite; Straßenrand
sidewalk ['saɪdwɔ:k] (AE) Gehweg
sigh (with) [saɪ] seufzen (vor)
sight [saɪt] Sehenswürdigkeit; Anblick; **see the sights** sich die Sehenswürdigkeiten ansehen; **sightseeing tour** Besichtigungstour, Rundfahrt
sign [saɪn] **1.** Zeichen; (Hinweis-) Schild; **road sign** Verkehrszeichen; **2.** unterschreiben
silly ['sɪlɪ] albern, dumm, doof, blöd; **silliness** ['sɪlɪnəs] Dummheit
silver ['sɪlvə] silbern; Silber
similar ['sɪmɪlə] ähnlich
simple ['sɪmpl] einfach; einfältig, naiv; **simplify** vereinfachen

since [sɪns] seit; seitdem
sincerely [sɪn'sɪəlɪ]: **Sincerely (yours)** (AE) Mit freundlichen/herzlichen Grüßen; **Yours sincerely** (BE) Mit freundlichen/herzlichen Grüßen
sing [sɪŋ] singen; **singer** ['sɪŋə] Sänger/in
single ['sɪŋgl] einzig, einzeln; Einzel-; ledig, unverheiratet; **single fare** (BE) einfacher Fahrpreis
sink [sɪŋk] **1.** sinken, untergehen; **2.** versenken
sir [sɜː] *höfliche Anrede für einen Mann;* **Dear Sir or Madam** Sehr geehrte Damen und Herren
sister ['sɪstə] Schwester
sit [sɪt] sitzen; **sit down** sich setzen; **sit still** still sitzen
site [saɪt]: **camp site** Campingplatz, Zeltplatz
situation [ˌsɪtjʊ'eɪʃn] Situation
sixth form ['sɪksθ fɔːm] (BE) Oberstufe, Sekundarstufe II
size [saɪz] Größe; **What size do you take?** Welche Größe hast du/haben Sie?
skateboard ['skeɪtbɔːd] Skateboard
ski [skiː] **1.** Ski; **2.** Ski laufen, fahren
skirt [skɜːt] Rock
sky [skaɪ] Himmel; **skyscraper** ['skaɪˌskreɪpə] Wolkenkratzer
slave [sleɪv] Sklave/-in; **slavery** ['sleɪvərɪ] Sklaverei
sleep [sliːp] **1.** Schlaf; **go back to sleep** wieder einschlafen; **2.** schlafen; **sleep on** weiterschlafen; **sleepless** ['sliːpləs] schlaflos
slow [sləʊ] langsam
small [smɔːl] klein
smell [smel] **1.** Geruch; **2.** riechen; **smelly** stinkend; **They're smelly.** Sie stinken.
smile (at) [smaɪl] (an)lächeln
smoke [sməʊk] **1.** Rauch, Dampf, Dunst; **2.** rauchen
smuggler ['smʌglə] Schmuggler/in
snow [snəʊ] Schnee; **snowy** verschneit
so [səʊ] **1.** darum, deshalb; **2.** also; **3.** so; **I don't think so.** Das glaube/finde ich nicht. **if so** wenn ja; **I think so.** Ich glaube (ja). **so-called** so genannte(r, s); **so do/will/am/... I** ich auch; **so far** bis jetzt, bisher; **so that** damit, sodass; **So what?** Na und?
soap [səʊp] Seife
social ['səʊʃl] gesellschaftlich; sozial; Sozial-; gesellig; **society** [sə'saɪətɪ] Gesellschaft; Verein, Arbeitsgemeinschaft
sock [sɒk] Socke, Strumpf
soda ['səʊdə] Limonade, Cola; Soda(wasser)
sofa ['səʊfə] Sofa
soldier ['səʊldʒə] Soldat/in
solve [sɒlv] *(Aufgabe, Problem)* lösen
some [sʌm, səm] **1.** einige, ein paar; **2.** etwas; **3.** irgendein(e); **some more** noch einige/etwas; **somebody/someone** jemand; **something** etwas; **sometimes** manchmal; **somewhere** irgendwo(hin)
son [sʌn] Sohn
song [sɒŋ] Lied
soon [suːn] bald
sore [sɔː] wund, rau, entzündet; **sore throat** Halsschmerzen, Halsweh
sorry ['sɒrɪ]: **(I'm) sorry.** Entschuldigung! Tut mir Leid! **Sorry?** Wie bitte? **Sorry I'm late.** Entschuldigen Sie, dass ich zu spät komme. **feel sorry (for)** bedauern; bereuen
sound [saʊnd] **1.** Laut, Ton; Klang; **2.** klingen, sich anhören
soup [suːp] Suppe
south (of) [saʊθ] **1.** südlich (von); **2.** Süd-; (nach) Süden; **southern** ['sʌðən] südlich, Süd-; **southernmost** ['sʌðənməʊst] südlichste(r, s)
souvenir [ˌsuːvə'nɪə] (Reise-)Andenken, Souvenir
space [speɪs] **1.** (Welt-)Raum; **2.** Platz
spaghetti [spə'getɪ] Spaghetti
Spain [speɪn] Spanien; **Spanish** **1.** spanisch; **2.** Spanisch
spanner ['spænə] Schraubenschlüssel
speak (to) [spiːk] sprechen (mit); **speaker** Sprecher/in; **Amy Connor speaking.** (Hier) Amy Connor. *(am Telefon)*
special ['speʃl] **1.** besondere(r, s); **2.** Sonder-
speed [spiːd] Geschwindigkeit
spell [spel] buchstabieren, schreiben; **spelling** Rechtschreibung, Orthographie
spend [spend] **1.** *(Geld)* ausgeben; **2.** *(Zeit)* verbringen
spider ['spaɪdə] Spinne
spite: in spite of [ɪn 'spaɪt‿əv] trotz
sponsored activity ['spɒnsəd æk'tɪvətɪ] *Aktivität um Geld für Wohltätigkeitszwecke zu sammeln*
spoon [spuːn] Löffel
sport [spɔːt] Sport, Sportart; **do sport(s)** Sport treiben; **sporting grounds** (AE)/**sports ground** (BE) Sportplatz
spray can ['spreɪ kæn] Sprühdose
spring [sprɪŋ] Frühling, Frühjahr; **in (the) spring** im Frühling/Frühjahr
square [skweə] **1.** Platz *(in einer Stadt)*; **2.** Quadrat; **3.** quadratisch, viereckig
squash [skwɒʃ] Squash
St. = Saint [snt] Sankt ...
stadium ['steɪdɪəm] Stadion
stairs *(pl.)* [steəz] Treppe(nstufen)
stamp [stæmp] (Brief-)Marke
stand [stænd] stehen; **stand up** **1.** aufstehen; **2.** aufrecht stehen; **stand still** stillstehen
star [stɑː] **1.** Stern; **2.** Star
start [stɑːt] **1.** Anfang, Beginn, Start; **2.** anfangen, beginnen (mit); **3.** starten; **4.** gründen; **start school** eingeschult werden; **starter** ['stɑːtə] Starter/in
state [steɪt] Staat
statement ['steɪtmənt] Aussage, Feststellung; Erklärung
station ['steɪʃn] Bahnhof; **police station** Polizeiwache, Polizeirevier; **(TV/radio) station** Sendestation, (Fernseh-/Rundfunk-)Sender
statistics *(pl.)* [stə'tɪstɪks] Statistik
statue ['stætʃuː] Statue
status ['steɪtəs] Status
stay [steɪ] **1.** bleiben; **2.** übernachten, wohnen
steak [steɪk] Steak
steal [stiːl] stehlen
steel [stiːl] Stahl
steering wheel ['stɪərɪŋ wiːl] Steuer(rad), Lenkrad
stereo ['sterɪəʊ] Stereo, Stereo-
stick [stɪk] Stock; (trockener, abgebrochener) Zweig
still [stɪl] **1.** (immer) noch; **2.** trotzdem, dennoch; **sit/stand still** still sitzen/stillstehen
stomach ['stʌmək] Magen, Bauch; **stomach ache** ['stʌmək‿eɪk] Magenschmerzen, Bauchschmerzen
stone [stəʊn] Stein
stop [stɒp] **1.** Bushaltestelle; **2.** aufhören; anhalten, stoppen
store [stɔː] (AE) Geschäft
storm [stɔːm] Sturm; Gewitter; **stormy** ['stɔːmɪ] stürmisch
story ['stɔːrɪ] Geschichte, Erzählung; **storyteller** ['stɔːrɪˌtelə] (Geschichten-)Erzähler/in
straight [streɪt] gerade(wegs), direkt
strange [streɪndʒ] seltsam, sonderbar; fremd; **stranger** ['streɪndʒə] Fremde(r
street [striːt] Straße; **in Sandfield Street** in der Sandfieldstraße; **in the street** auf der Straße
stress [stres] **1.** Stress; **2.** Betonung
strict [strɪkt] streng
strong [strɒŋ] **1.** stark; **2.** kräftig
student ['stjuːdənt] Student/in; AE *auch:* Schüler/in
studio ['stjuːdɪəʊ] Studio, Senderaum
study (for an exam) ['stʌdɪ] (für eine Prüfung) lernen, sich vorbereiten; studieren
stupid ['stjuːpɪd] dumm, blöd
style [staɪl] **1.** Stil, Mode; **2.** Art, Weise
subject ['sʌbdʒɪkt] (Schul-)Fach
submarine [ˌsʌbmə'riːn] Unterseeboot
suburb ['sʌbɜːb] Vorstadt, Vorort, Randbezirk
subway ['sʌbweɪ] (AE) U-Bahn
succeed (in) [sək'siːd] Erfolg haben (in, bei)
success [sək'ses] Erfolg; **successful** [sək'sesfəl] erfolgreich
such [sʌtʃ] solch, so (ein/e), so
suddenly ['sʌdnlɪ] plötzlich
suffer (from) ['sʌfə] ertragen; leiden
sugar ['ʃʊgə] Zucker
suggest [sə'dʒest] vorschlagen; **suggestion** [sə'dʒestʃn] Vorschlag, Anregung

suit [su:t] *(jm.)* stehen
suitable ['su:təbl] passend, geeignet
suitcase ['su:tkeɪs] Koffer
summarize ['sʌməraɪz] zusammenfassen; **summary** ['sʌmərɪ] Zusammenfassung
summer ['sʌmə] Sommer; **in (the) summer** im Sommer
sun [sʌn] Sonne; **sunshine** Sonne(nschein); **sunny** sonnig
Sunday ['sʌndɪ] Sonntag
super ['su:pə] fantastisch, toll; Super-; **supermarket** ['su:pə,mɑ:kɪt] Supermarkt
supper ['sʌpə] Abendessen
supply [sə'plaɪ] **1.** Versorgung; Vorrat; Lieferung; **2.** (be)liefern, versorgen
support [sə'pɔ:t] unterstützen; befürworten
suppose [sə'pəʊz] annehmen, vermuten
sure [ʃʊə, ʃɔ:] sicher, gewiss; **be sure of oneself** selbstsicher sein; **make sure** sich vergewissern; darauf achten, daür sorgen (dass); **Sure!** Sicher! Klar! Natürlich!
surprised [sə'praɪzd] überrascht; **surprising** erstaunlich, überraschend
surround [sə'raʊnd] umgeben
survey ['sɜ:veɪ] Umfrage, Untersuchung
survive [sə'vaɪv] überleben
sweets [swi:ts] (BE) Süßigkeiten, Bonbons
swim [swɪm] schwimmen; **go for a swim** schwimmen gehen; **swimming-pool** ['swɪmɪŋ pu:l] Schwimmbad; Schwimmbecken
switch [swɪtʃ] **1.** Schalter; **2.** (um)schalten; **switch on/off** ein-/ausschalten
sword [sɔ:d] Schwert
symbol ['sɪmbl] Symbol, Zeichen; **symbolize** ['sɪmbəlaɪz] symbolisieren
synonym ['sɪnənɪm] Synonym, bedeutungsähnliches Wort
system ['sɪstəm] System; Plan, Ordnung

T

table ['teɪbl] Tisch; **table-tennis** Tischtennis
tablet ['tæblɪt] Tablette
take [teɪk] **1.** (mit)nehmen; (hin)bringen; **2.** dauern; **it takes** es dauert; man braucht; **it takes me (an hour)** ich brauche (eine Stunde); **take a chance** ein Risiko eingehen, es darauf ankommen lassen; **take an exam** eine Prüfung ablegen, machen; **take off** *(Kleidung)* ausziehen; **take part (in)** teilnehmen (an), mitmachen (bei); **take photos/pictures** fotografieren, Fotos/Bilder machen; **take place** stattfinden; **take the dog for a walk** mit dem Hund rausgehen; **What size do you take?** Welche Größe hast du/haben Sie?
talk [tɔ:k] sprechen, reden; sich unterhalten
tall [tɔ:l] groß; hoch
tape [teɪp] (Ton-, Magnet-)Band; (Klebe-) Band
taste (of) [teɪst] kosten; schmecken (nach)
tax [tæks] Steuer
taxi ['tæksɪ] Taxi
tea [ti:] Tee; **have tea** (BE) Abendbrot essen, zu Abend essen; **make tea** Tee kochen
teach [ti:tʃ] unterrichten, lehren, beibringen; **teacher** ['ti:tʃə] Lehrer/in
team [ti:m] Team, Mannschaft, Gruppe
technology [tek'nɒlədʒɪ] Technologie, Technik
teenager ['ti:neɪdʒə] Teenager, Jugendliche(r)
(tele)phone ['telɪfəʊn] **1.** Telefon; **2.** anrufen; **answer the telephone** ans Telefon gehen; **be on the telephone** am Telefon sein, gerade telefonieren; **make a telephone call** einen Anruf machen, ein Telefongespräch führen
television ['telɪ,vɪʒn, ,telɪ'vɪʒn] Fernsehen, Fernseher; **on television** im Fernsehen; **watch television** fernsehen
tell [tel] **1.** sagen, nennen; **2.** erzählen, berichten; **tell the way** den Weg beschreiben
temperature ['temprətʃə] Temperatur; Fieber
temple ['templ] Tempel
temporary ['tempərərɪ] vorläufig, vorübergehend, (zeitlich) begrenzt
tennis ['tenɪs] Tennis
tense [tens] (an)gespannt, nervös
tent [tent] Zelt
terraced house [,terəst 'haʊs] (BE) Reihenhaus
terrible ['terəbl] schrecklich, furchtbar
test [test] Test, Prüfung, Klassenarbeit; **do a test** eine Arbeit schreiben, eine Prüfung machen
text [tekst] Text
than [ðæn, ðən] als *(nach Komparativ)*
thank [θæŋk] danken, sich bedanken (bei); **Thank you.** Danke (schön). **Thank you very much.** Vielen Dank. **Thanks.** Danke (schön).
Thanksgiving Day [,θæŋks'gɪvɪŋ] (AE) *Erntedankfeier/Familienfest im November*
that [ðæt, ðət] **1.** der/die/das (da), jene(r, s) (dort); **2.** dass; **3.** der/die/das *(Relativpronomen);* **(not) that bad** (nicht) so schlimm; **so that** damit, sodass; **that is (i.e.)** das heißt (d. h.)
the [ðə, ðɪ] der, die, das; die *(Plural);* **the ..., the ...** je ..., umso/desto ...
theatre ['θɪətə] Theater
their [ðeə] ihr, ihre; **theirs** [ðeəz] ihre(r, s)
them [ðem, ðəm] ihnen, sie; **themselves** [ðəm'selvz] sich (selbst)
then [ðen] **1.** dann, danach; **2.** zu der Zeit, damals
there [ðeə] **1.** da, dort; **2.** dahin, dorthin; **here and there** hie und da; **over there** dort drüben, da drüben; **there is/are** da ist/sind, es gibt
these [ði:z] diese, die (hier)
they [ðeɪ] **1.** sie; **2.** man
thick [θɪk] **1.** dick; **2.** dicht
thief, *pl.* **thieves** [θi:f, θi:vz] Dieb/in
thin [θɪn] dünn
thing [θɪŋ] Ding, Sache
think [θɪŋk] meinen, finden, glauben, denken; **I don't think so.** Das finde/glaube ich nicht. **I think so.** ich glaube (ja). **think of** denken an; halten von; **think up** (sich) ausdenken; **What do you think about ...?** Was hältst du von ...? Wie findest du ...?
third [θɜ:d] Drittel
thirst [θɜ:st] Durst; **thirsty** ['θɜ:stɪ] durstig; **be thirsty** Durst haben
this [ðɪs] diese(r, s), der/die/das (hier); **This is how you do it.** So/Auf diese Weise macht man es. **this morning** heute Morgen
those [ðəʊz] die/diese (da), jene (dort)
though [ðəʊ] obwohl
thought [θɔ:t] Gedanke; Einfall
threaten ['θretn] (be)drohen
throat [θrəʊt] Hals, Kehle; **a sore throat** Halsschmerzen, Halsweh
through [θru:] durch, hindurch
throw [θrəʊ] werfen; **throw away** wegwerfen
thumb [θʌm] Daumen
thunder ['θʌndə] Donner
Thursday ['θɜ:zdɪ] Donnerstag
ticket ['tɪkɪt] Eintrittskarte; Fahrkarte, Fahrschein; **ticket inspector** [ɪn'spektə] Kontrolleur/in
tidy ['taɪdɪ] ordentlich, aufgeräumt; **tidy up** aufräumen
tie [taɪ] Krawatte, Schlips
tiger ['taɪgə] Tiger
tight [taɪt] eng (anliegend), stramm
tilde ['tɪldə] Tilde
till [tɪl] bis; **not till six** erst um sechs, nicht vor sechs
time [taɪm] **1.** Zeit; **have a nice time** eine schöne Zeit/viel Spaß haben; **Have a good time.** Viel Spaß! Viel Vergnügen! **What time is it?** Wie spät ist es? **timeless** ['taɪmləs] zeitlos **timetable** (BE) Fahrplan; Stundenplan; **2. time(s)** Mal; -mal; **for the first time** zum ersten Mal
tin [tɪn] (BE) Dose, Büchse
tin mine ['tɪn maɪn] Zinnmine, Zinnbergwerk
tired ['taɪəd] müde
title ['taɪtl] Titel
to [tu:, tʊ, tə] **1.** zu, nach, in; **2.** um zu; **give to sb.** jm. geben; **happen to** passieren, geschehen mit; **I've been to ...** Ich bin in ... gewesen. **listen to**

(sich) anhören; **next to** neben; **quarter to ten** Viertel vor zehn; **speak to** sprechen mit; **talk to** sprechen mit; **Try to come.** Versuche zu kommen. **write to** schreiben an
toast [təʊst] Toast
tobacco [tə'bækəʊ] Tabak
today [tə'deɪ] heute; **today's paper** die heutige Zeitung, die Zeitung von heute
together [tə'geðə] zusammen
toilet ['tɔɪlɪt] Toilette
tolerant (towards) ['tɒlərənt] tolerant (gegenüber); **tolerance** ['tɒlərəns] Toleranz
tomato, *pl.* **tomatoes** [tə'mɑːtəʊ] Tomate
tomorrow [tə'mɒrəʊ] morgen; **tomorrow morning** morgen früh; **tomorrow's paper** die morgige Zeitung, die Zeitung von morgen; **the day after tomorrow** übermorgen
tonight [tə'naɪt] heute Abend/Nacht
tonne [tʌn] Tonne *(Gewicht)*
too [tuː] auch; **too small** zu klein
tool [tuːl] Werkzeug
tooth, *pl.* **teeth** [tuːθ, tiːθ] Zahn; **toothbrush** ['tuːθbrʌʃ] Zahnbürste; **toothpaste** ['tuːθpeɪst] Zahnpasta, Zahncreme
top [tɒp] **1.** Spitze; **2.** Kopfende, oberes Ende; **on top (of)** oben, zuoberst (auf); **top speed** [ˌtɒp 'spiːd] Höchstgeschwindigkeit
total ['təʊtl] gesamt; völlig, total
touch [tʌtʃ] berühren, anfassen
tough [tʌf] zäh; stark; robust
tour [tʊə] (Rund-)Reise, (Rund-)Fahrt, Tour; **go on a bus tour** eine Bus(rund)fahrt machen; **go on a guided tour** eine Führung (mit)machen; **tourism** ['tʊərɪzm] Tourismus, Fremdenverkehr; **tourist** ['tʊərɪst] Tourist/in
toward (AE), **towards** (BE) [tə'wɔːdz] auf ... zu, in Richtung auf
towel ['taʊəl] Handtuch
tower ['taʊə] Turm
town [taʊn] Stadt; **in town** in der (Innen-)Stadt
toy [tɔɪ] Spielzeug
track [træk] (Renn-)Bahn, Rennstrecke, Piste
trade [treɪd] **1.** Handel; **2. trade (with)** Geschäfte machen, handeln (mit); **trader** Händler/in
tradition [trə'dɪʃn] Tradition
traffic ['træfɪk] Verkehr; **traffic jam** ['træfɪk dʒæm] (Verkehrs-)Stau; **traffic lights** *(pl.)* (Verkehrs-)Ampel
trail [treɪl] Pfad; Weg; Wanderweg
train [treɪn] (Eisenbahn-)Zug; **by train** mit dem Zug; **on the train** im Zug
train [treɪn] trainieren, ausbilden; **training** Ausbildung, Schulung; Training
tram [træm] Straßenbahn
transcription [træn'skrɪpʃn] (phonetische) Umschrift
translate [trænz'leɪt] übersetzen; **translation** [trænz'leɪʃn] Übersetzung
transport ['trænspɔːt] (BE) Transport, Verkehrsmittel; **(public) transportation** [ˌpʌblɪk ˌtrænspɔː'teɪʃn] (AE) (öffentliche) Verkehrsmittel
travel ['trævl] **1.** (das) Reisen; **2.** reisen, fahren; **travel agency** ['trævl ˌeɪdʒənsɪ] Reisebüro; **space travel** ['speɪs ˌtrævl] Raumfahrt; **traveller** Reisende(r)
treasure ['treʒə] Schatz, Kostbarkeit
treat [triːt] behandeln
tree [triː] Baum
tribe [traɪb] (Volks-)Stamm
trick [trɪk] **1.** Kunststück; **2.** Trick; **play a trick** einen Streich spielen
trip [trɪp] Reise, Ausflug; **go on a trip; take a trip** (AE) eine Reise/Fahrt/einen Ausflug machen
trouble ['trʌbl] Schwierigkeiten; **get into trouble** in Schwierigkeiten geraten; Probleme bekommen; **give trouble** Schwierigkeiten machen, Probleme bereiten
trousers *(pl.)* ['traʊzəz] (lange) Hose(n)
truck [trʌk] LKW
true [truː] wahr; **come true** wahr werden
trunk [trʌŋk] (Baum-)Stamm
truth [truːθ] Wahrheit
try [traɪ] versuchen probieren; **try and do sth.** versuchen etwas zu tun; **try on** anprobieren
T-shirt ['tiːʃɜːt] T-Shirt
tube [tjuːb] (BE) *(Londoner)* U-Bahn
Tuesday ['tjuːzdɪ] Dienstag
tunnel ['tʌnl] **1.** Tunnel; **2.** Bergwerksstollen
turkey ['tɜːkɪ] Truthahn
Turkey ['tɜːkɪ] Türkei
turn [tɜːn] **1.** abbiegen, einbiegen; **2.** werden; **It's your turn.** Du bist an der Reihe. **turn round** (sich) (um)drehen; **turn to** sich wenden an, sich zuwenden
TV [ˌtiː'viː] = **television** Fernsehen, Fernseher; **on TV** im Fernsehen; **watch TV** fernsehen
twice [twaɪs] zweimal
type [taɪp] tippen, mit der Maschine schreiben; **typewriter** Schreibmaschine
typical (of) ['tɪpɪkl] typisch (für)

U

ugliness ['ʌglɪnəs] Hässlichkeit; **ugly** ['ʌglɪ] hässlich
unable [ʌn'eɪbl] unfähig, untalentiert
unacceptable [ˌʌnək'septəbl] inakzeptabel
unanswerable [ʌn'ɑːnsərəbl] unbeantwortbar
unavoidable [ˌʌnə'vɔɪdəbl] unvermeidbar
unbelievable [ˌʌnbɪ'liːvəbl] unglaublich
unbreakable [ʌn'breɪkəbl] unzerbrechlich
uncle ['ʌŋkl] Onkel
under ['ʌndə] unter; **Underground** ['ʌndəgraʊnd] (BE) Untergrundbahn, U-Bahn; **by Underground** (BE) mit der U-Bahn
underline [ˌʌndə'laɪn] unterstreichen
underprivileged [ˌʌndə'prɪvɪlɪdʒd] schlechter gestellt
understand [ˌʌndə'stænd] verstehen, begreifen; **understandable** [ˌʌndə'stændəbl] verständlich
underwater [ˌʌndə'wɔːtə] **1.** Unterwasser-**2.** unter Wasser
undrinkable [ˌʌn'drɪŋkəbl] nicht trinkbar, ungenießbar
uneatable [ˌʌn'iːtəbl] nicht essbar, ungenießbar
unemployed [ˌʌnɪm'plɔɪd] arbeitslos; **unemployment** Arbeitslosigkeit
unexplainable [ˌʌnɪk'spleɪnəbl] unerklärlich, unerklärbar
unfair [ˌʌn'feə] unfair, ungerecht; **unfairness** [ʌn'feənəs] Ungerechtigkeit
unforgettable [ˌʌnfə'getəbl] unvergesslich
unfriendliness [ʌn'frendlɪnəs] Unfreundlichkeit; **unfriendly** unfreundlich
unhappy [ʌn'hæpɪ] unglücklich, traurig
uniform ['juːnɪfɔːm] Uniform
unimaginable [ˌʌnɪ'mædʒɪnəbl] unvorstellbar
unit ['juːnɪt] **1.** Lektion; **2.** Einheit
united [juː'naɪtɪd] vereinigt; **United Kingdom** [juːˌnaɪtɪd 'kɪŋdəm] Vereinigtes Königreich; **the United Nations** [juːˌnaɪtɪd 'neɪʃnz] die Vereinten Nationen (UNO); **United States of America** Vereinigte Staaten von Amerika
universe ['juːnɪvɜːs] Universum
university [ˌjuːnɪ'vɜːsətɪ] Universität, Hochschule
unload [ʌn'ləʊd] ausladen, abladen
unlucky day [ʌn'lʌkɪ] Unglückstag
unpronounceable [ˌʌnprə'naʊnsəbl] nicht aussprechbar
unsingable [ʌn'sɪŋəbl] unsingbar, nicht singbar
unsinkable [ʌn'sɪŋkəbl] unsinkbar
unthinkable [ʌn'θɪŋkəbl] undenkbar
untidy [ʌn'taɪdɪ] unordentlich, unaufgeräumt
until [ʌn'tɪl, ən'tɪl] bis; **not until (six)** erst um (sechs), nicht vor (sechs)
unusual [ʌn'juːʒʊəl] un-, außergewöhnlich
up [ʌp] herauf, hinauf; **get up** aufstehen; **put up** aufbauen, aufstellen; aufhängen, anbringen; **stand up** aufstehen; aufrecht stehen **up there** dort oben; **up to** bis (zu)
upset (about) [ʌp'set] **1.** durcheinander, aufgeregt, betrübt (wegen) **2. upset** aus der Fassung bringen, ärgern, beunruhigen

upside down [ˌʌpsaɪd ˈdaʊn] verkehrt (herum), mit dem Kopf nach unten
upstairs [ˌʌpˈsteəz] oben; nach oben
us [ʌs] uns
use 1. [juːs] Benutzung, Gebrauch; **2.** [juːz] benutzen, verwenden; **useful** [ˈjuːsfəl] nützlich, brauchbar; **useless** [ˈjuːsləs] nutzlos, unnütz
usual [ˈjuːʒʊəl] üblich, gewöhnlich; **usually** [ˈjuːʒʊəlɪ] normalerweise, gewöhnlich

V

vacation [vəˈkeɪʃn] (AE) Ferien, Urlaub
valley [ˈvælɪ] Tal
vegetables [ˈvedʒtəblz] Gemüse
vehicle [ˈviːɪkl] Fahrzeug
very [ˈverɪ] sehr; **(like) very much** sehr (gern mögen)
via [ˈvaɪə] über, per, via
video [ˈvɪdɪəʊ] Video
Vietnam [vɪetˈnæm] Vietnam; **Vietnamese** [vjetnəˈmiːz] **1.** Vietnamese/in; **2.** vietnamesisch
view [vjuː] **1.** Aussicht, Blick **2.** Ansicht
Viking [ˈvaɪkɪŋ] Wikinger/in
village [ˈvɪlɪdʒ] Dorf
violent [ˈvaɪələnt] gewaltsam, gewalttätig; heftig
virus [ˈvaɪərəs] Virus, Krankheitserreger
visit [ˈvɪzɪt] **1.** Besuch; **on a visit** bei einem Besuch; **2.** besuchen, besichtigen; **visitor** [ˈvɪzɪtə] Besucher/in, Gast
vocabulary item [vəˈkæbjʊlərɪ ˌaɪtəm] Vokabel
voice [vɔɪs] Stimme
volleyball [ˈvɒlɪbɔːl] Volleyball
vote for [vəʊt] (ab)stimmen für, wählen
vowel [ˈvaʊəl] Vokal, Selbstlaut

W

wages *(pl.)* [ˈweɪdʒɪz] (Arbeits-)Lohn
waggon [ˈwægən] Pferdewagen, Planwagen
wait (for) [weɪt] warten (auf); **Wait a minute.** Einen Augenblick! Moment mal!
waiter [ˈweɪtə] Kellner, Ober
wake (up) [weɪk] **1.** aufwachen; **2.** (auf-) wecken
Wales [weɪlz] Wales
walk [wɔːk] **1.** Spaziergang; (Spazier-, Wander-)Weg; **go for a walk** spazieren gehen, einen Spaziergang machen; **take the dog for a walk** mit dem Hund rausgehen, mit dem Hund spazieren gehen; **2.** (zu Fuß) gehen, laufen; **go walking** wandern; **walk on** weitergehen
wall [wɔːl] Wand; Mauer
want (to) [wɒnt] wollen, mögen
war [wɔː] Krieg
warden [ˈwɔːdn] (BE) Herbergsvater/ -mutter
wardrobe [ˈwɔːdrəʊb] Kleiderschrank
warm [wɔːm] warm
warn [wɔːn] warnen, ermahnen
wash [wɒʃ] (sich) waschen; **have a wash** sich waschen; **wash the dishes** (das Geschirr) spülen, abwaschen; **washable** [ˈwɒʃəbl] waschbar; **washing machine** [ˈwɒʃɪŋ məˌʃiːn] Waschmaschine; **washroom** Waschraum
waste (of) [weɪst] **1.** Verschwendung (von); **2. waste** verschwenden
watch [wɒtʃ] **1.** (Armband-)Uhr; **2.** ansehen, beobachten; **3.** zuschauen; **My watch is wrong.** Meine Uhr geht falsch. **watchmaker** [ˈwɒtʃˌmeɪkə] Uhrmacher/in; **watch TV** fernsehen
water [ˈwɔːtə] **1.** Wasser; **2.** bewässern, gießen; tränken; **waterfall** Wasserfall
way [weɪ] **1.** Weg; **2.** Art und Weise; **a long way** ein weiter Weg; weit (entfernt); **by the way** übrigens, nebenbei (bemerkt); **in different ways** auf verschiedene Weise(n); **in the way** im Weg; **on my way (to)** unterwegs (nach); **tell the way** den Weg beschreiben; **the other way round** andersherum; **This is the way you do it.** So/Auf diese Weise macht man es. **way of life** [ˌweɪ‿əv ˈlaɪf] Lebensart, Lebensweise
we [wiː] wir
weak [wiːk] schwach; **weakness** Schwäche
weapon [ˈwepən] Waffe
wear [weə] tragen, anhaben
weather [ˈweðə] Wetter; **weather forecast** Wettervorhersage
wedding [ˈwedɪŋ] Hochzeit
Wednesday [ˈwenzdɪ] Mittwoch
week [wiːk] Woche; **Weekday** [ˈwiːkdeɪ] Wochentag, Werktag; **weekend** [ˌwiːkˈend, ˈwiːkend] Wochenende; **at the weekend** am Wochenende
weigh [weɪ] wiegen; **weightlifting** Gewichtheben
welcome (to) [ˈwelkəm] willkommen (in); **You're welcome.** Bitte (sehr). Nicht zu danken.
well [wel] **1.** gut; **2.** wohlauf, gesund; **3.** nun; also; **Well!** Na so was! Du meine Güte! Wirklich? **do well** gut sein *(in einem Fach)*; **well-known** (wohl) bekannt
Welsh [welʃ] **1.** Waliser/in; **2.** walisisch; **3.** Walisisch
west (of) [west] **1.** westlich (von); **2.** West-; (nach) Westen; **western** [ˈwestən] westlich, West-
West Indian [ˌwest ˈɪndɪən] **1.** Westinder/in; **2.** westindisch
wet [wet] nass; feucht
whale [weɪl] Wal
what [wɒt] was; was für ein(e); welche(r, s); **What a question!** Was für eine Frage! **What about ...?** Wie steht's/wär's mit ...? **What colour is ...?** Welche Farbe hat ...? **What date is it (today)?** Der Wievielte ist heute? **What do you call ...?** Wie nennt man ...? **What is it?** Was ist denn (los)? **What's it like?** Wie ist es? Wie sieht es aus? **What's wrong with Kevin?** Was fehlt/hat Kevin? **What time is it?** Wie spät ist es? **whatever** [wɒtˈevə] was (auch) immer; **So what?** Na und?
wheat [wiːt] Weizen
wheel [wiːl] Rad; **steering wheel** Steuer(-rad), Lenkrad; **wheelchair** Rollstuhl
when [wen] **1.** wann; **2.** wenn; **3.** als; **whenever** [wenˈevə] immer wenn, wann (auch) immer
where [weə] wo, wohin; **Where are you from?** Wo kommst du her? **wherever** [ˌweərˈevə] wo(hin) (auch) immer
whether [ˈweðə] ob
which [wɪtʃ] **1.** welche(r, s); **Which of you?** Wer von euch? **2.** der, die, das *(Relativpronomen)*; **whichever** [wɪtʃˈevə] welche(r, s) (auch) immer
while [waɪl] während
whisky, whiskey [ˈwɪskɪ] Whisky
white [waɪt] weiß
who [huː] **1.** wer; wem, wen; **2.** der, die; dem, den *(Relativpronomen)*; **whoever** [huːˈevə] wer/wen (auch) immer
whole [həʊl] ganz, gesamt; **the whole of** ganz
whose [huːz] **1.** wessen; **Whose is it?** Wem gehört es? **2.** dessen, deren *(Relativpronomen)*
why [waɪ] warum, weshalb; **Why not ...?** Warum nicht ...? Könnten wir nicht ...?
wide [waɪd] breit
wife, *pl.* **wives** [waɪf, waɪvz] (Ehe-)Frau
wild [waɪld] wild; ausgelassen; stürmisch
will [wɪl] wird (tun)
willingly [ˈwɪlɪŋlɪ] bereit(willig)
win [wɪn] gewinnen
wind [wɪnd] Wind; **windsurfing** [ˈwɪndˌsɜːfɪŋ] Windsurfen; **windy** windig
window [ˈwɪndəʊ] Fenster, Schaufenster
wine [waɪn] Wein
winter [ˈwɪntə] Winter; **in (the) winter** im Winter
wise [waɪz] weise, klug
witch [wɪtʃ] Hexe
with [wɪð] **1.** mit; **2.** bei; **within** [wɪˈðɪn] innerhalb, in; **without** [wɪˈðaʊt] ohne
wolf, *pl.* **wolves** [wʊlf, wʊlvz] Wolf
woman, *pl.* **women** [ˈwʊmən, ˈwɪmɪn] Frau

wonder ['wʌndə] **1.** Wunder, Verwunderung; **2.** sich fragen, gern wissen wollen; **wonderful** ['wʌndəfəl] wunderbar
won't [wəʊnt] = **will not** wird/will nicht
wood [wʊd] **1.** Holz; **2.** Wald
word [wɜ:d] Wort
work [wɜ:k] **1.** Arbeit; **2.** arbeiten; in Betrieb sein, funktionieren; **at work** bei der Arbeit; **go to work** zur Arbeit gehen; **out of work** arbeitslos; **workshop** Werkstatt
world [wɜ:ld] Welt; **in the world** auf der Welt
worry ['wʌrɪ] sich Sorgen machen; **Don't worry.** Mach dir keine Sorgen! Ist schon gut! **worried (about)** besorgt (um), beunruhigt (wegen)
worse (than) [wɜ:s] schlechter (als); schlimmer als; **(the) worst** [wɜ:st] **1.** (der/die/das) schlechteste, schlimmste; **2.** am schlechtesten, schlimmsten
worship ['wɜ:ʃɪp] (an)beten; seine Andacht verrichten
worth [wɜ:θ] wert; **worthless** wertlos
would [wʊd, wəd] würde(n) (tun); **I'd like = I would like** ich möchte; **I'd love (to)** ich hätte (liebend) gern; ich würde sehr gern
wreck [rek] Wrack; **wrecker** ['rekə] Strandräuber
wrench [rentʃ] (AE) Schraubenschlüssel
write (to) [raɪt] schreiben (an); **write down** aufschreiben; **writer** Schriftsteller/in, Verfasser/in
wrong [rɒŋ] falsch; **be wrong** Unrecht haben; **go wrong** schief gehen; **My watch is wrong.** Meine Uhr geht falsch. **What's wrong with Kevin?** Was fehlt Kevin? Was hat Kevin?

Y

yard [jɑ:d] Hof; (AE *auch:*) Garten
year [jɪə] Jahr
yellow ['jeləʊ] gelb
yes [jes] ja
yesterday ['jestədɪ] gestern; **the day before yesterday** vorgestern; **yesterday's lesson** die gestrige Stunde, die Stunde gestern
yet [jet] schon; **not ... yet** noch nicht
yoghurt ['jɒgət] Joghurt
you [ju:, jʊ, jə] **1.** du, ihr, Sie; **2.** man; **you know** weißt du, nämlich
young [jʌŋ] jung
your [jɔ:] dein(e); Ihr(e); euer, eure; **yours** [jɔ:z] deine(r, s); Ihre(r, s); eure(r, s); **Yours** dein(e); Ihr(e); euer/eure *(am Briefende);* **yourself** [jɔ:'self] dir/dich (selbst); **yourselves** [jɔ:'selvz] euch (selbst)
youth [ju:θ] **1.** Jugend; **2.** Jugendliche(r); **youth club** ['ju:θ klʌb] Jugendklub, Jugendzentrum; **youth hostel** ['ju:θ ˌhɒstl] Jugendherberge

Z

zebra ['zebrə] Zebra
zero ['zɪərəʊ] null
zoo [zu:] Zoo

Names

Family names

Alviar [ˌælvɪ'ɑː]
Chi [tʃiː]
Donovan ['dɒnəvən]
Evans ['evənz]
Hitchcock ['hɪtʃkɒk]
Lawrence ['lɒrəns]
McCormack [mə'kɔːmæk]
Minetti [mɪ'netɪ]
Mitchell ['mɪtʃl]
Nolan ['nəʊlən]
Potlowsky [pət'laʊskɪ]
Roberts ['rɒbəts]
Stephens ['stiːvnz]
Swytzer ['swaɪtsə]
Texiera [teksɪ'ɪərə]
Thomas ['tɒməs]
Warburton ['wɔːbətn]
Wells [welz]

Girls/women

Annabel ['ænəbel]
Cathy ['kæθɪ]
Cindy ['sɪndɪ]
Debbie ['debɪ]
Eleanor ['elənə]
Jody ['dʒəʊdɪ]
Kay [keɪ]
Lan [læn]
Margie ['mɑːdʒɪ]
Maureen ['mɔːriːn, mɒ'riːn]
Megan ['megən]
Melanie ['melənɪ]
Melissa [mə'lɪsə]
Miranda [mɪ'rændə]
Patsy ['pætsɪ]
Rita ['riːtə]
Rosamund ['rɒzəmənd]
Sue [suː]
Tara ['tɑːrə]
Wanda ['wɑndə]

Boys/men

Alfred ['ælfrɪd]
Aulus ['ɔːləs]
Billy ['bɪlɪ]
Binh [bɪn]
Bruce [bruːs]
Christopher ['krɪstəfə]
Dino ['diːnəʊ]
Ed/Eddie [ed/'edɪ]
Elliot ['elɪət]
Gwyn [gwɪn]
Harold ['hærəld]
Harris ['hærɪs]
Huw [hjuː]
Jamie ['dʒeɪmɪ]
Jerry ['dʒerɪ]
Kenny ['kenɪ]
Marvin ['mɑːvɪn]
Matthew ['mæθjʊ]
Moses ['məʊzɪz]
Nicholas ['nɪkələs]
Nico ['niːkəʊ]
Patrick ['pætrɪk]
Piso ['piːsəʊ]
Ray [reɪ]
Sid [sɪd]
Troy [trɔɪ]

*Place names**

Aberystwyth [ˌæbə'rɪstwɪθ]
Abilene ['æbəliːn]
Alabama [ˌælə'bæmə]
Alaska [ə'læskə]
Arizona [ˌærɪ'zəʊnə]
Arkansas ['ɑːkənsɔː]
Atlanta [ət'læntə]
Austin ['ɒstɪn]
Baltimore ['bɔːltɪmɔː]
Bayeux [bɑɪ'jɜː]
Bedford ['bedfəd]
Birmingham ['bɜːmɪŋəm]
Blenheim ['blenəm]
Boston ['bɒstn]
Brecon Beacons [ˌbrekn 'biːkənz]
California [ˌkælɪ'fɔːnɪə]
Cambridge ['keɪmbrɪdʒ]
Cape Cod [ˌkeɪp 'kɒd]
Carolina [ˌkærə'laɪnə]
Chester ['tʃestə]
Chicago [ʃɪ'kɑːgəʊ]
Cincinnati [ˌsɪnsɪ'nætɪ]
Cleveland ['kliːvlənd]
Colchester ['kɒltʃestə]
Colorado [ˌkɒlə'rɑːdəʊ]
Columbia [kə'lʌmbɪə]
Connecticut [kə'netɪkət]
Coventry ['kɒvəntrɪ]
Dakota [də'kəʊtə]
Dallas ['dæləs]
Delaware ['deləweə]
Detroit [dɪ'trɔɪt]
Dodge City [ˌdɒdʒ 'sɪtɪ]
Exeter ['eksɪtə]
Florida ['flɒrɪdə]
Georgia ['dʒɔːdʒə]
Glamorgan [glə'mɔːgən]
Gower ['gaʊə]
Hampton Court [ˌhæmptən 'kɔːt]
Hartford ['hɑːtfəd]
Hastings ['heɪstɪŋz]
Hawaii [hə'waiiː]
Heybridge ['heɪbrɪdʒ]
Houston ['hjuːstn]
Hudson River [ˌhʌdsn 'rɪvə]
Iceland ['aɪslənd]
Idaho ['aɪdəhəʊ]
Illinois [ˌɪlɪ'nɔɪ]
Indiana [ˌɪndɪ'ænə]
Indianapolis [ˌɪndɪə'næpəlɪs]
Iowa ['aɪəʊə]
Jamestown ['dʒeɪmztaʊn]
Kansas ['kænzəs]
Kentucky [ken'tʌkɪ]
Lake Erie [ˌleɪk‿'ɪərɪ]
Lake Huron [ˌleɪk 'hjʊərən]
Lake Superior [ˌleɪk suː'pɪərɪə]
Lancaster ['lænkæstə]
Leeds [liːdz]
Leicester ['lestə]
Llangollen [læn'gɒθlən]
Longleat ['lɒŋliːt]
Los Angeles [lɒs‿'ændʒəliːz]
Louisiana [luːˌiːzɪ'ænə]
Maine ['meɪn]
Manhattan [mæn'hætn]
Mars [mɑːz]
Maryland ['meərɪlænd]
Massachusetts [ˌmæsə'tʃuːsɪts]
Memphis ['memfɪs]

* Siehe auch S.133 (New York boroughs) und S.134/135 (Manhattan).

Miami [maɪ'æmɪ]
Michigan ['mɪʃɪgən]
Milford Haven
[ˌmɪlfəd 'heɪvən]
Milwaukee [mɪl'wɔ:ki:]
Minneapolis [ˌmɪnɪ'æpəlɪs]
Minnesota [ˌmɪnɪ'səʊtə]
Mississippi [ˌmɪsɪ'sɪpɪ]
Missouri [mɪ'zʊərɪ]
Montana [mɒn'tænə]
Mount Rainier
[ˌmaʊnt 'reɪnɪə]
Nantucket [næn'tʌkɪt]
Nebraska [nɪ'bræskə]
Nevada [ne'vɑ:də]
Newark ['nju:ək]
New Hampshire
[ˌnju: 'hæmpʃə]
New Jersey [ˌnju: 'dʒɜ:zɪ]
New Mexico
[ˌnju: 'meksɪkəʊ]
New Orleans [ˌnju:‿ɔ:'liə:nz]
New York [ˌnju: 'jɔ:k]
Normandy ['nɔ:məndɪ]
Nottingham ['nɒtɪŋəm]
Nova Scotia
[ˌnəʊvə 'skəʊʃə]
Ohio [əʊ'haɪəʊ]
Oklahoma [ˌəʊklə'həʊmə]
Ontario [ɒn'teərɪəʊ]
Opeka [ɒ'pi:kə]
Oregon ['ɒrɪgən]
Pembrokeshire
['pembrəkʃɪə]
Pennsylvania
[ˌpensɪl'veɪnɪə]
Pentre Ifan [ˌpentrə ɪ'van]
Philadelphia [ˌfɪlə'delfɪə]
Phoenix ['fi:nɪks]
Pittsburgh ['pɪtsbɜ:g]
Plymouth ['plɪməθ]
Portland ['pɔ:tlənd]
Providence ['prɒvɪdəns]
Rhode Island [ˌrəʊd‿'aɪlənd]
Rocky Mountains
[ˌrɒkɪ 'maʊntɪnz]
Salisbury ['sɔ:lzbərɪ]
San Antonio
[ˌsæn‿æn'təʊnɪəʊ]
Santa Barbara
[ˌsæntə 'bɑ:brə]
San Diego [ˌsæn dɪ'eɪgəʊ]
San Francisco
[ˌsæn frən'sɪskəʊ]
San Jose [ˌsæn həʊ'zeɪ]
San Salvador [ˌsæn 'sælvədɔ:]
Scarborough ['skɑ:bərə]
Seattle [si:'ætl]
Siberia [saɪ'bɪərɪə]
Sierra Nevada
[sɪˌerə nɪ'vɑ:də]
Snowdon ['snəʊdən]
Snowdonia [snəʊ'dəʊnɪə]
St Louis [ˌsnt 'lu:ɪs]
Stonehenge [ˌstəʊn'hendʒ]
Stratford-upon-Avon
[ˌstrætfəd əpɒn 'eɪvən]
Swansea ['swɒnzɪ]
Talyllyn [tælɪ'lɪn]
Teheran [teə'rɑ:n]
Tel Aviv [ˌtel‿ə'vi:v]
Tenby ['tenbɪ]
Tennessee [ˌtenə'si:]
Texas ['teksəs]
Tonganoxie [ˌtɒŋgə'nɒksɪ]
Toronto [tə'rɒntəʊ]
Tungria ['tʌŋgrɪə]
Utah ['ju:tɑ:]
Venice ['venɪs]
Vermont [və'mɒnt]
Vinland ['vɪnlənd]
Virginia [və'dʒɪnɪə]
Washington, D.C.
[ˌwɒʃɪŋtən ˌdi: 'si:]
Wichita ['wɪtʃɪtɔ:]
Williamsburg ['wɪljəmzbɜ:g]
Wisconsin [wɪs'kɒnsɪn]
Wyoming [waɪ'əʊmɪŋ]

Other names

Alistair Cooke [ˌælɪstə 'kʊk]
Amerigo Vespucci
[ˌæmə'ri:gəʊ ves'pu:tʃi:]
Amphibalus [æm'fɪbələs]
Barbara McClintock
[ˌbɑ:brə mə'klɪntɒk]
Battery Park [ˌbætərɪ 'pɑ:k]
Benjamin Franklin
[ˌbendʒəmɪn 'fræŋklɪn]
Boudicca [bəʊ'dɪkə]
Caligula [kə'lɪgjʊlə]
Chicago Tribune
[ʃɪˌkɑ:gəʊ 'trɪbju:n]
Chieftains ['tʃi:ftənz]
Christopher Columbus
[ˌkrɪstəfə kə'lʌmbəs]
Claudius ['klɔ:dɪəs]
Cosher Bailey [ˌkɒʃə 'beɪlɪ]
Cwm Rhondda [kʊm 'rɒndə]
David Dinkins
[ˌdeɪvɪd 'dɪŋkɪnz]
Diana Spencer
[daɪˌænə 'spensə]
Elizabeth Warren
[ɪˌlɪzəbəθ 'wɒrən]
Elvis Presley [ˌelvɪs 'prezlɪ]
Erasmus Hall
[ɪˌræzməs 'hɔ:l]
George Bernard Shaw
[ˌdʒɔ:dʒ ˌbɜ:nəd 'ʃɔ:]
Guy Fawkes [ˌgaɪ 'fɔ:ks]
Hadrian ['heɪdrɪən]
Iceni [aɪ'si:naɪ]
Inuit ['ɪnʊɪt]
Irving Berlin [ˌɜ:vɪŋ bɜ:'lɪn]
Isaac Allerton [ˌaɪzək 'ælətən]
Israel Baline [ˌɪzreɪl bə'laɪn]
Jehovah [dʒə'həʊvə]
Jerome K. Jerome
[dʒə'rəʊm keɪ dʒə'rəʊm]
Jerome Kern [dʒəˌrəʊm 'kɜ:n]
Jesus ['dʒi:zəs]
Joseph Pulitzer
[ˌdʒəʊzɪf 'pʊlɪtsə]
Julius Caesar [ˌdʒu:lɪəs 'si:zə]
Leif Ericson [ˌli:f 'erɪksn]
Martin Luther King
[ˌmɑ:tɪn ˌlu:θə 'kɪŋ]
Myles Standish
[ˌmaɪlz 'stændɪʃ]
Noah Webster [ˌnəʊə 'webstə]
Robin Hood [ˌrɒbɪn 'hʊd]
Santa Maria [ˌsæntə mə'rɪə]
St Albans [snt 'ɑ:lbənz]
Tacitus ['tæsɪtəs]
The Guardian [ðə 'gɑ:dɪən]
Thomas Cranmer
[ˌtɒməs 'krænmə]
Thomas More [ˌtɒməs 'mɔ:]
Thomas Wolsey
[ˌtɒməs 'wʊlzɪ]
Titanic [taɪ'tænɪk]
Tudor ['tju:də]
Waylon Jennings
[ˌweɪlən 'dʒenɪŋz]
Weston ['westn]
William Penn [ˌwɪljəm 'pen]
William Shakespeare
[ˌwɪljəm 'ʃeɪkspɪə]
Willie Nelson [ˌwɪlɪ 'nelsən]

Country/Continent	Person	People	Adjective
Africa ['æfrɪkə] Afrika	an African ['æfrɪkən]	the Africans	African
America [ə'merɪkə] Amerika	an American [ə'merɪkən]	the Americans	American
Asia ['eɪʃə, 'eɪʒə] Asien	an Asian ['eɪʃn, 'eɪʒn]	the Asians	Asian
Australia [ɒ'streɪlɪə] Australien	an Australian [ɒ'streɪlɪən]	the Australians	Australian
Austria ['ɒstrɪə] Österreich	an Austrian ['ɒstrɪən]	the Austrians	Austrian
(Great) Britain ['brɪtn] Großbritannien	a Briton ['brɪtn]	the British	British
Canada ['kænədə] Kanada	a Canadian [kə'neɪdɪən]	the Canadians	Canadian
China ['tʃaɪnə] China	a Chinese [tʃaɪ'ni:z]	the Chinese	Chinese
Cuba ['kju:bə] Kuba	a Cuban ['kju:bən]	the Cubans	Cuban
Denmark ['denmɑ:k] Dänemark	a Dane [deɪn]	the Danes	Danish
Egypt ['i:dʒɪpt] Ägypten	an Egyptian [ɪ'dʒɪpʃn]	the Egyptians	Egyptian
England ['ɪŋglənd] England	an Englishman/Englishwoman	the English	English ['ɪŋglɪʃ]
Europe ['jʊərəp] Europa	a European [ˌjʊərə'pi:ən]	the Europeans	European
France [frɑ:ns] Frankreich	a Frenchman/Frenchwoman	the French	French
Germany ['dʒɜ:mənɪ] Deutschland	a German ['dʒɜ:mən]	the Germans	German
Greece [gri:s] Griechenland	a Greek [gri:k]	the Greek	Greek
Holland ['hɒlənd] Holland	a Dutchman/Dutchwoman	the Dutch	Dutch [dʌtʃ]
India ['ɪndɪə] Indien	an Indian ['ɪndɪən]	the Indians	Indian
Ireland ['aɪələnd] Irland	an Irishman/Irishwoman	the Irish	Irish ['aɪrɪʃ]
Italy ['ɪtəlɪ] Italien	an Italian [ɪ'tælɪən]	the Italians	Italian
Japan [dʒə'pæn] Japan	a Japanese [ˌdʒæpə'ni:z]	the Japanese	Japanese
Korea [kə'rɪə] Korea	a Korean [kə'rɪən]	the Koreans	Korean
Mexico ['meksɪkəʊ] Mexiko	a Mexican ['meksɪkən]	the Mexicans	Mexican
New Zealand [ˌnju: 'zi:lənd] Neuseeland	a New Zealander [ˌnju: 'zi:ləndə]	the New Zealanders	New Zealand
Nicaragua [ˌnɪkə'rægjʊə] Nicaragua	a Nicaraguan [ˌnɪkə'rægjʊən]	the Nicaraguans	Nicaraguan
Pakistan [ˌpɑ:kɪ'stɑ:n] Pakistan	a Pakistani [ˌpɑ:kɪ'stɑ:nɪ]	the Pakistanis	Pakistani
the **Philippines** ['fɪləpi:nz] die Philippinen	a Filipino [fɪlə'pi:nəʊ]	the Filipinos	Philippine Filipino
Portugal ['pɔ:tʃʊgl] Portugal	a Portuguese [ˌpɔ:tʃu'gi:z]	the Portuguese	Portuguese
Scotland ['skɒtlənd] Schottland	a Scotsman/Scotswoman a Scot [skɒt]	the Scots	Scottish ['skɒtɪʃ]
Spain [speɪn] Spanien	a Spaniard ['spænjəd]	the Spanish	Spanish ['spænɪʃ]
Turkey ['tɜ:kɪ] (die) Türkei	a Turk [tɜ:k]	the Turks	Turkish
the **United Kingdom** = the **UK** das Vereinigte Königreich	a Briton ['brɪtn]	the British	British
the **United States of America** = the **USA** = die Vereinigten Staaten von Amerika = die USA	an American [ə'merɪkən]	the Americans	American
Vietnam [ˌvjet'næm] Vietnam	a Vietnamese [ˌvjetnə'mi:z]	the Vietnamese	Vietnamese
Wales [weɪlz] Wales	a Welshman/Welshwoman	the Welsh	Welsh [welʃ]

Irregular verbs

Infinitive	Simple past	Past participle	
(to) be	(I) was, (you) were	(I've/she has) been	sein
beat	beat	beaten	schlagen, besiegen
become	became	become	werden
begin	began	begun	beginnen, anfangen
blow	blew [uː]	blown [əʊ]	blasen, wehen
break [eɪ]	broke [əʊ]	broken [əʊ]	(zer)brechen; kaputtmachen
bring	brought [ɔː]	brought [ɔː]	(mit)bringen, (her)bringen
build	built	built	(er)bauen
burn	burned, burnt	burned, burnt	(ver)brennen
buy	bought [ɔː]	bought [ɔː]	kaufen
catch	caught [ɔː]	caught [ɔː]	fangen, erwischen; erreichen
choose [uː]	chose [əʊ]	chosen [əʊ]	(aus)wählen, aussuchen
come	came	come	kommen
cost [ɒ]	cost [ɒ]	cost [ɒ]	kosten
cut	cut	cut	schneiden
dig	dug	dug	(aus-, um)graben
do	did	done [ʌ]	tun, machen
draw	drew	drawn	zeichnen; ziehen
dream	dreamed [iː], dreamt [e]	dreamed [iː], dreamt [e]	träumen
drink	drank	drunk	trinken
drive	drove	driven [ɪ]	(Auto) fahren; (an)treiben
eat	ate [eɪ, BE *also:* e]	eaten	essen
fall	fell	fallen	fallen
feed	fed	fed	füttern
feel	felt	felt	(sich) fühlen
fight	fought [ɔː]	fought [ɔː]	(be)kämpfen
find	found [aʊ]	found [aʊ]	finden
fly	flew [uː]	flown [əʊ]	fliegen
forget	forgot	forgotten	vergessen
freeze	froze	frozen	(ge)frieren; erstarren
get	got	BE: got, AE: gotten	bekommen; gelangen, (hin)kommen; holen, besorgen; werden
give	gave	given	geben; schenken
go	went	gone [ɒ]	gehen; fahren
grow	grew [uː]	grown [əʊ]	wachsen; anbauen, anpflanzen
hang	hung	hung	(auf)hängen;
	hanged	hanged	(er)hängen
have (got)	had	had	haben
hear [ɪə]	heard [ɜː]	heard [ɜː]	hören
hide [aɪ]	hid [ɪ]	hidden [ɪ]	(sich) verstecken
hit	hit	hit	schlagen, treffen
hold	held	held	halten
hurt [ɜː]	hurt	hurt	verletzen, wehtun
keep	kept	kept	(be)halten, aufbewahren; einhalten
know [əʊ]	knew [juː]	known [əʊ]	kennen; wissen
lead [iː]	led [e]	led [e]	führen, leiten
learn [ɜː]	learned, learnt	learned, learnt	lernen

Infinitive	**Simple past**	**Past participle**	
leave	left	left	weggehen, verlassen; (zurück)lassen
lend	lent	lent	(ver-, aus)leihen
let	let	let	(zu)lassen
lie	lay [eɪ]	lain [eɪ]	liegen
lose [uː]	lost [ɒ]	lost [ɒ]	verlieren
make	made	made	machen; (veran)lassen
mean [iː]	meant [e]	meant [e]	bedeuten; meinen
meet	met	met	(sich) treffen, kennen lernen
overtake	overtook [ʊ]	overtaken	überholen
pay [eɪ]	paid [eɪ]	paid [eɪ]	(be)zahlen
put [ʊ]	put [ʊ]	put [ʊ]	stellen, legen, setzen
quit	quit	quit	aufhören, aufgeben
read [iː]	read [e]	read [e]	(vor)lesen
ride [aɪ]	rode	ridden [ɪ]	reiten; (Rad) fahren
ring	rang	rung	klingeln, läuten; anrufen
run	ran	run	rennen, laufen; fahren *(Zug, Bus)*
say	said [e]	said [e]	sagen
see	saw	seen	sehen
sell	sold	sold	verkaufen
send	sent	sent	schicken, senden
set off	set off	set off	aufbrechen
shine	shone [BE: ɒ, AE: əʊ]	shone [BE: ɒ, AE: əʊ]	scheinen *(Sonne)*
shoot [uː]	shot [ɒ]	shot [ɒ]	(er)schießen
show [əʊ]	showed [əʊ]	shown [əʊ]	zeigen
shut [ʌ]	shut [ʌ]	shut [ʌ]	schließen, zumachen
sing	sang	sung	singen
sink	sank	sunk	sinken; versenken
sit	sat	sat	sitzen
sleep	slept [e]	slept [e]	schlafen
smell	smelt, smelled	smelt, smelled	riechen
speak	spoke	spoken	sprechen
spell	spelt, spelled	spelt, spelled	buchstabieren, schreiben
spend	spent	spent	*(Geld)* ausgeben; *(Zeit)* verbringen
stand	stood [ʊ]	stood [ʊ]	stehen
steal	stole	stolen	stehlen
swim	swam	swum	schwimmen
take	took [ʊ]	taken	(mit)nehmen; (hin-, weg)bringen
teach	taught [ɔː]	taught [ɔː]	unterrichten, lehren
tell	told	told	sagen, nennen; erzählen, berichten
think	thought [ɔː]	thought [ɔː]	meinen, denken
throw [əʊ]	threw [uː]	thrown [əʊ]	werfen
understand	understood [ʊ]	understood [ʊ]	verstehen, begreifen
upset	upset	upset	verärgern
wake up	woke up	woken up	aufwachen; (auf)wecken
wear [eə]	wore [ɔː]	worn [ɔː]	*(Kleidung)* tragen, anhaben
win	won [ʌ]	won [ʌ]	gewinnen
write	wrote	written	schreiben

Bildquellen

Anthony Verlag, Starnberg (S. 39 oben links); Archiv für Kunst und Geschichte, Berlin (S. 5 unten links, S. 10, S. 33 oben links, S. 34, S. 35, S. 46, S. 71 oben, S. 74 unten, S. 76 oben, S. 77 oben, S. 99 oben links, oben rechts); Bavaria Bildagentur, Gauting (S. 8 Mitte rechts, S 9 oben rechts, unten links, S. 11, S. 18 Mitte, S. 21, S. 37 oben, S. 42 unten, S. 102, S. 108); Steve Benbow, London (S. 89 Mitte); British Tourist Authority, London (S. 89 unten); F. Barber/Bygott Photos, Oxford (S. 70 oben); D. W. Bygott/Bygott Photos, Oxford (S. 70 unten rechts, S. 71 Mitte, unten links, unten Mitte, unten rechts; S. 74 oben, S. 75 oben, unten rechts, S. 76 Mitte, S. 77 Mitte, unten links, S. 90, S. 92, S. 94, S. 96); Terence Spencer/Camera Press, Hamburg (S. 93); J. Allan Cash, London (S. 5 oben links, S. 36 Mitte rechts, Mitte links, S. 55 unten, S. 73, S. 88, S. 118); Celtic Picture Agency, St. Asaph (S. 89 oben); Cornelsen Archiv, Berlin (S. 9 Mitte rechts, S. 30, S. 42 links, S.99 unten rechts); Crown Copyright. Historic Royal Palaces, East Molesey (S.80); Walt Disney Productions, Frankfurt a. M. (S. 5 unten rechts); David Dore, Guildford (S. 9 oben links, S. 85, S. 99 Mitte oben); dpa, Frankfurt a. M. (S. 22); Express Newspapers PLC, London (S. 76 unten); Angelika Fischer, Berlin (S. 42 rechts); Dennis Stark/Magnum/Focus, Hamburg (S. 5 unten rechts); David Hissey, Oklahoma (S. 8 unten links, unten rechts, S. 38, S. 39 oben Mitte, oben rechts, unten, S. 51, S. 99 unten 2. von links); Bildarchiv Huber, Garmisch-Partenkirchen (S.17); Hulton Deutsch, London (S. 55 Mitte rechts, S. 119); Todd James, New York (S. 50); Keystone, Hamburg (S. 20); HG The Duke of Marlborough (S. 81); Mirror Syndication International (S. 61, S. 70 unten links, S.72, S. 75 unten links, S. 77 unten rechts); David Graham/Picturefile, London (S. 54 oben, S. 55 oben, Mitte, S. 58, S. 112); Bildarchiv Preußischer Kulturbesitz (S. 79 Mitte); Punch Publications Ltd., London (S. 14, S. 92 oben, S. 103, S. 117); Lonnie Schlein, New York (S. 8 oben links, oben rechts, Mitte links, S. 18 unten, S. 27, S. 29, S. 31, S. 32, S. 54 Mitte, unten, S. 67, S. 68, S. 99 unten links, unten 2. von rechts); The Spectator, London (S. 62, S. 64, S. 79 unten); Evin Thayer, Houston (S. 36 Mitte oben, Mitte unten); Transglobe Agency, Hamburg (S. 55 Mitte links); Ullstein Bilderdienst, Berlin (S. 5 Mitte links); Virginia State Travel Service (S. 33 unten rechts); Wales Tourist Board, Cardiff (S. 84, S. 86); ZEFA, Düsseldorf (S. 37 unten, S. 120).

Textquellen

The dictionary pages on pp. 100/101 are reprinted from *Langenscheidts Schulwörterbuch Englisch*, © 1997 Langenscheidt Verlag, Berlin und München; *Poem* from *The Dream Keeper and Other Poems* by Langston Hughes, © 1932 by Alfred A. Knopf, Inc. and renewed 1960 by Langston Hughes. Reprinted by permission of the publisher; *Friends* by Elizabeth Jennings from *The Secret Brother* (Macmillan) © Elizabeth Jennings; *Mother to Son* by Langston Hughes, © 1926 by Alfred A. Knopf, Inc. and renewed 1954 by Langston Hughes. Reprinted from *Selected Poems of Langston Hughes* by permission of Alfred A. Knopf, Inc.; an adaptation of *The Fun They Had* from *Earth Is Room Enough* by Isaac Asimov © 1957 by Isaac Asimov. Used by permission of Double Day, a division of Bantam Doubleday Dell Publishing Group, Inc.; *Roman Wall Blues* reprinted by permission of Faber & Faber from *Collected Shorter Poems 1927-1957* by W. H. Auden.

Liedquellen

New York, New York (Text und Musik: John Kander/Fred Ebb) © CPP/Belwin Europe; *Small Town* (Text und Musik: John Cougar Mellencamp) © 1985 by FULL KEEL MUSIC CO. für Deutschland, Österreich, Schweiz, ehem. Ostblockländer ex. Litauen, Lettland, Estland: HEINZ FUNKE MUSIKVERLAG GMBH; *Scarborough Fair* (Trad. / Arr. by Paul Simon & Art Garfunkel) © 1966 by Paul Simon Music. Für Deutschland, Österreich und Schweiz FANFARE MUSIKVERLAG, München.

Useful classroom phrases

What you can say ...

... when you're talking about tests.

Will this be in the next test?	Wird das in der nächsten Arbeit vorkommen?
We're doing a maths test tomorrow.	Wir schreiben morgen eine Mathe-Arbeit.
Can we use dictionaries for the translation?	Können wir Wörterbücher für die Übersetzung benutzen?
How much time have we got for the grammar/text production section?	Wie lange haben wir für den Grammatikteil/die Aufgaben zum Text Zeit?

... when you're talking about homework.

Can you give us less homework today, please?	Können Sie uns heute bitte nicht weniger aufgeben?
I'm afraid I couldn't do the homework you gave us yesterday.	Leider konnte ich die Hausaufgaben, die Sie uns gestern gegeben haben, nicht machen.
It was too difficult./I didn't understand .../ I forgot how to ...	Es war zu schwer./Ich habe ... nicht verstanden/ Ich habe vergessen, wie man ...
Could we go through the homework together, please?	Könnten wir bitte die Hausaufgabe zusammen besprechen?

... when you're working with cassettes.

Can you turn the volume up, please?	Können Sie den Ton bitte lauter stellen?
Can you turn it down, please?	Können Sie es bitte leiser stellen?
Can you play ... again, please?	Können Sie ... bitte noch mal vorspielen?
Could you please rewind the cassette to the part where ... ?	Könnten Sie bitte die Cassette zurückspulen zu der Stelle, wo ... ?

... when you're working with transparencies.

Can I set the projector up?	Darf ich den Projektor aufstellen?
Can I write the answers/sentences on the transparency?	Darf ich die Antworten/Sätze auf die Folie schreiben?
Can we pull the blinds down, please? It's too light in here.	Können wir bitte die Rolläden runterlassen? Es ist zu hell hier.

Talking about texts

I find the story/text interesting/boring/funny/ stupid/exciting/lovely/well written.	Ich finde die Geschichte/den Text interessant/ langweilig/lustig/blöd/spannend/schön/gut geschrieben.
I found the part where ... the best/the most interesting, etc./sad/weak.	Ich fand den Teil, wo ... am besten/interessantesten usw./traurig/schwach.
I didn't quite understand why ...	Ich habe nicht ganz verstanden, warum ...
I prefer stories about ...	Ich habe Geschichten über ... lieber.
The ending was very unusual/unexpected.	Das Ende war sehr ungewöhnlich/unerwartet.
The main characters are ...	Die Hauptpersonen sind ...
Their typical characteristics are ...	Ihre typischen Merkmale sind ...
The development of the action is typical of a western/love story because ...	Der Handlungsverlauf ist typisch für einen Western/eine Liebesgeschichte, weil ...
The climax of the story is when ...	Der Höhepunkt der Geschichte ist, wenn ...
There are several reasons why ...	Es gibt mehrere Gründe, warum ...
In line(s) ... on page ... the text says ...	In Zeile ... auf Seite ... steht: ...
The text says ... and I think that means ...	Im Text steht ... und ich glaube, das bedeutet ...
The text doesn't say so directly, but ...	Es steht nicht direkt im Text, aber ...
I think it's hard to say why/if/what ...	Ich glaube, es ist schwer zu sagen, warum/ob/ was ...
Firstly, ... ; secondly ...	Erstens ... ; zweitens ...